Malta Strikes Back

Malta Strikes Back

The Role of Malta in the Mediterranean Theatre 1940–1942

Ken Delve

Pen & Sword
AVIATION

First published in Great Britain in 2017 by
Pen & Sword Aviation
an imprint of
Pen & Sword Books Ltd
47 Church Street
Barnsley
South Yorkshire
S70 2AS

ISBN 978 1 47389 244 6

A CIP catalogue record for this book is available from the British Library

Typeset in Ehrhardt by
Mac Style Ltd, Bridlington, East Yorkshire
Printed and bound in the UK by CPI Group (UK) Ltd,
Croydon, CRO 4YY

Pen & Sword Books Ltd incorporates the imprints of Pen & Sword Archaeology, Atlas,
Aviation, Battleground, Discovery, Family History, History, Maritime, Military, Naval,
Politics, Railways, Select, Transport, True Crime, and Fiction, Frontline Books, Leo
Cooper, Praetorian Press, Seaforth Publishing and Wharncliffe.

For a complete list of Pen & Sword titles please contact
PEN & SWORD BOOKS LIMITED
47 Church Street, Barnsley, South Yorkshire, S70 2AS, England
E-mail: enquiries@pen-and-sword.co.uk
Website: www.pen-and-sword.co.uk

Contents

Chapter 1	Introduction	1
Chapter 2	The Italian Campaign: June 1940 to December 1940	4
Chapter 3	Luftwaffe Round One: January 1941 to May 1941	45
Chapter 4	Back on the Offensive: June 1941–November 1941	81
Chapter 5	Luftwaffe Round Two: December 1941 to May 1942	126
Chapter 6	Dominating the Sea Lanes: May 1942 to November 1942	183

Appendix A: Greece and Crete — 224
Appendix B: Chronology 1940–42 — 233
Appendix C: Battle Honours and Awards — 239
Appendix D: Order of Battle — 245
Appendix E: Anti Shipping Scores — 253
Appendix F: Convoys and Reinforcement Flights — 263

Chapter 1

Introduction

The Mediterranean was the key to success or failure in the land campaigns in countries around its borders, a fact that was as true in the Second World War as it had been for Ancient Rome and her enemies, for the medieval kingdoms (and the Crusades), and for Napoleon and his attempts to stifle Britain's commerce. Two of the greatest strategic mistakes by Hitler concerned his failure to take control of two key locations, Gibraltar and Malta; between them they were able to influence and, at times, dominate the western Mediterranean area and the surrounding land masses. Malta, with its strategic partner Alexandria (and Egypt), likewise dominated the eastern Mediterranean and surrounding land masses. Nowhere in the Mediterranean was more than 200 miles from land and so land-based aircraft could always be a deciding factor – for the side that controlled the land bases.

The Maltese group of islands are only 60 miles south of Sicily – but 1,000 miles from Gibraltar to the west and about the same from Alexandria to the east. The main island of Malta is only 98 square miles, being around 17 miles long and 9 miles wide. The rocky terrain provides very little soil, and very few flat areas for airfields, but that same rocky terrain (mainly limestone of various types) provided the essential building materials that made Fortress Malta, as did the fact the rock formation 'has one other invaluable quality in that underground chambers can be easily excavated to give excellent protection against aerial attack.' (AP 3236 Works).

Campaigns within the Middle East–Mediterranean theatre went well for the British while they were engaged against the Italians, even though these forces were invariably larger and better equipped; however, the arrival of combat-experienced German forces in 1941 was a turning point

Malta and, in the distance, Gozo. This post-war aerial shot clearly shows the main airfields, albeit in most cases with post-war additions to runway surfaces. The George Cross Island proved of critical importance in Mediterranean Theatre operations.

that almost brought disaster in the Desert War and Malta. The main battleground in the Desert War was a narrow strip adjacent to the coast that stretched for more than 1,000 miles; the distance from Alexandria (in the east in Egypt) to Tripoli (in the west and 100 miles or so from the border with Tunisia) was roughly the same as from Berlin to Moscow. More importantly, there were no natural military resources or supplies in the North Africa–Western Desert region and both sides were reliant on supplies being shipped in. The Mediterranean was thus the 'supply highway' for the Allied and Axis forces. If the highway were blocked or curtailed it had a direct and massive impact on land operations.

The Middle East had long been a strategic area for the British as a route, courtesy of the Suez Canal, to India and the Far East empire, but also with the increased importance of oil resources. Indeed, in the 1920s when the majority of RAF squadrons were based outside the UK, Middle East Area had control of three groups on a regional basis – Egypt, Palestine and Iraq. Each group was small and covered the full range of RAF 'colonial' tasks, primarily reconnaissance and support of the local ground forces. However, this changed somewhat following the 1921 Cairo Conference when it was decided that the RAF should be given full control of military operations in Mesopotamia – the introduction of the so-called 'Air Control Policy'. Expansion of the RAF organization overseas brought two new groups under the control of Middle East (ME) Area in the early 1920s, Indian Group and Mediterranean Group. Once again, these groups were quite small but the foundations of a chain of command suited for further expansion had been laid. RAF Middle East was formed on 1 April 1922 by renaming ME Area.

Empire on parade; a peaceful scene at Malta for an unknown ceremony. In the pre-war period the island was essentially a naval base, halfway along the Mediterranean from Gibraltar to Alexandria, the latter being the most important naval location for British strategy.

In the first book, *The Desert Air Force in World War II: Air Power in the Western Desert 1940–1942* (Ken Delve, Pen & Sword, 2017), we looked at the Desert Air Force or, more accurately, the Desert campaign, but made only fleeting reference to the part the Mediterranean campaign made in determining the winners and losers – all dictated by the logistical requirements of supplying modern armies with equipment … and fuel. That book took us from the initial Allied success against the Italians to the back and forth advances and retreats with Rommel. We left the campaign with Rommel poised on the borders of Egypt in late 1942 and seemingly only needing to win the cross-Mediterranean logistical battle to enable him to take Egypt and strike on eastwards.

In this book we look at the Mediterranean theatre in the Second World War in the period from 1940 to late 1942, with particular emphasis on Malta and its role in the Mediterranean and Western Desert campaigns, essentially the offensive aspect of Malta … 'Malta Strikes Back'.

Note on Sources

I have used a variety of sources in this book, both primary (official documents and personal accounts) and secondary (some of the very fine books published by historians, units or individuals and, increasingly, internet references, especially from squadron associations). Two of the main primary sources that you will see mentioned frequently are the operational record books (ORBs) of the squadrons; these are sometimes a mine of information and sometimes a struggle, where they say very little or allude to something really important – and then say nothing about it! There is also frequent reference to the Air Ministry Bulletin (AMB); the ones I have referenced here include signals, memos and notes between the various commanders, and those that detail the medals (gallantry awards) – the same data that would subsequently be published in the *London Gazette*. The Air Historical Branch also translated key German and Italian documents in the immediate post-war period, and some of these have been referenced where they provide insights into the 'mind' of the Axis commanders.

This book is not intended as a 'blow by blow' account of every attack on Malta and the defenders' response, or of Malta in isolation from the wider Mediterranean Theatre operations. By far the best 'day by day' accounts are those in the pair of volumes by Christopher Shores, Brian Cull and Nicola Malizia, published by Grub Street: *Malta: the Hurricane Years* and *Malta: The Spitfire Years*. These also provide excellent input from the Italian side. For detailed coverage of two of the main fighter squadrons the best reading is *249 at War* by Brian Cull and *185 The Malta Squadron* by Anthony Rogers; for anti-shipping operations, *The Winger Bomb, a History of 39 Squadron*, by Ken Delve, provides details for one of the main squadrons.

Ken Delve, 2017

Chapter 2

The Italian Campaign: June 1940 to December 1940

The defence of Malta is only important in that without the defence there could have been no offence and Malta played a key role in the anti-shipping war, which itself played a key role in the success of the overall North Africa campaign. Aircraft from both locations (Malta and North Africa) also flew convoy support, which again was crucial to the overall success of the campaign, and the defence of Malta itself. The Mediterranean could, especially from the anti-submarine war perspective, be divided into eastern Mediterranean and western Mediterranean, the west end (Gibraltar) having a direct connection with the submarine war in the Atlantic, whereas the east end (Alexandria, Egypt) was more concerned with operations in Greece, the Middle East and North Africa. Malta's primary strategic value was for the central Mediterranean, sitting astride the shortest supply routes between Italy and North Africa.

Prior to the entry of Italy into the war in June 1940, the area of most concern was the western Mediterranean – with Gibraltar as a major naval base but with, as yet, limited airfield facilities. The roles of the 'Rock' and the island of Malta were critical to Allied strategy (and survival) in this theatre. Maritime units based at Gibraltar were retained usually under the operational control of HQ Coastal Command in the UK, a slightly unusual procedure but one that reflected the part these units played in the Atlantic War.

While we will focus on the offensive role of Malta (and Gibraltar and Alexandria) in respect to aviation's role in the Mediterranean conflict, it must be pointed out that all three locations were also highly significant from a naval point of view. This is particularly true of submarine operations from Malta and fleet operations from Alexandria. However, the hub – or central pivot as a land campaign would see it – was the island of Malta, which was thus a critical strategic base for Britain and, as such, its defence assumed a high priority.

Two Sunderlands of 228 Squadron left Pembroke Dock for Malta on 29 April 1939. The original plan was soon modified as on 3 May a Warning Order was received from 16 Group that the squadron would deploy to Alexandria, as part of 86 Wing, to augment RAF Near East. With the ground party boarding HMT *Dumana* on 9 May, the move went ahead, the intention being that this ship, along with the refueller SS *Pass of Balmaha*, would be stationed at Alexandria as the squadron's base. During the early part of the summer the squadron visited a number of potential areas to check their suitability for either servicing or operations: Flying Officer Burnett took N6133 to the Sea of Galilee in July to ascertain the possibility of compass swinging by manhandling the aircraft in the shallow water, while N9070 flew to Lake Tiberias, this being one of the freshwater locations used for washing down the Sunderlands.

The strategic concept of offensive (bomber) air power controlling naval operations in the Med was well known; Air Commodore Slessor, Director of Plans at the Air Ministry, had recommended sending a force of six bomber squadrons to the Middle East by August 1939, even though Bomber Command was already short of squadrons; he saw this as one of the few hopes of really useful offensive action in the Mediterranean area. The general feeling expressed in naval reports in the late 1930s was that 'the Navy was fairly certain that Malta would be untenable as a Fleet Base in a

RN warships in Grand Harbour, 1940. The general feeling in the late 1930s was that 'the Navy was fairly certain that Malta would be untenable as a Fleet Base in a war with Italy'. The naval presence was to be an 'on-off' affair depending on the intensity of Axis attacks.

war with Italy' and that evacuation of the fleet, and any air assets, would likely be necessary. Indeed, in 1934 Air Vice-Marshal Ludlow-Hewitt had stated that: 'It is not a feasible operation, without effective support from other air bases, to defend the small island area within effective range of the main Metropolitan air force of a great Power.' (*RAF in the Maritime War Vol 6*, AHB). One of the main weaknesses in Malta air defence, it was stated, was a lack of 'depth' with which to provide adequate warning of an enemy attack – Sicily was simply too close.

A joint RAF–Navy conference in April 1939 highlighted the differences of opinion. 'Strong naval arguments were advanced for air reconnaissance in support of their plan for striking at Italy by operating light forces against communication with Libya.' In essence, air was seen only as being the eyes of the surface vessels, which would be responsible for doing the actual damage. The eyes of the fleet were indeed to be a key part of overall strategy, but the Navy still had to learn the threat from, and use of, air striking forces in the Med. Air Vice-Marshal Peirse, Deputy Chief of the Air Staff (DCAS), stated the Air Staff view that the Italians could cripple Malta if they wished, as it was not big enough for sustained fighter defence. The C-in-C Mediterranean Fleet, Admiral Sir Andrew B. Cunningham, disagreed, arguing that 'military targets were too small to bomb accurately and that experience in the Spanish Civil War showed the Italians lacked courage.' The debate continued and the best the RAF would commit to was the basing of Sunderlands for reconnaissance, it being considered that moorings would make them less vulnerable.

Gibraltar had also been ignored in the 1930s, in part because of the focus on naval strategy and needs, and a lack of appreciation of the increasing role of air power. As early as 1935 the Chief of the Air Staff (CAS) had stated that: 'Gibraltar is the key to the route [air reinforcement to Middle East], and therefore to the whole strategic conception of Imperial air defence. On the provision of an adequate intermediate air base at that port depends our ability to bridge the gap in our air communication for many years to come. An air base is also essential at Gibraltar for the operation of landplanes and seaplanes engaged on trade protection and air defence.' *(The RAF in Maritime War, ibid)*.

As we will see throughout this account, the role of Gibraltar was indeed crucial for Malta and the Mediterranean theatre. However, Admiral Cunningham's main concern was the Eastern Basin (which later became defined as the eastern Mediterranean and central Mediterranean), and for an RAF General Reconnaissance (GR) force to provide a system of patrols and continuous coverage of:

- Malta to Cephalonia line (350 miles) from Malta
- Eastern entrance of Aegean from Egypt
- Western entrance to Aegean from Malta or Egypt
- Protection of advanced surface forces
- Offensive anti–submarine patrols
- Occasional sightings (recce) of enemy ports
- Long-range reconnaissance for the fleet
- Shadowing sighted enemy forces and investigation of reports.

To achieve this, the Navy suggested it needed thirty-six GR aircraft at Malta and ten at Alexandria, in addition to its own Fleet Air Arm (FAA) aircraft. At the time, the RAF had no such aircraft in the Med. When pressed, it stated the Malta–Cephalonia line was the highest priority. A late 1939 recommendation by the Chiefs of Staff proposed eight GR squadrons to co-operate with the Navy in the Med 'as soon as resources will permit'. It also stated that the FAA should have two carriers, each with three squadrons. Carrier-based aircraft were also to prove essential in the Mediterranean War. A February 1940 conference listed the eight squadrons as:

- Malta: 2 GR flying boat and one TB/GR squadrons
- Gibraltar: one GR flying boat squadron
- Egypt: two GR landplane squadrons
- Gozo (Malta) or Tunisia: one GR landplane squadron – this is interesting as there was no discussion of building an airfield on Gozo
- Morocco: one GR landplane squadron.

As with most plans in the early part of the war, this one came to nothing! Indeed, when war broke out with Germany, GR assets were moved out of the Med, with the exception of Gibraltar, which looked to the Atlantic as well as the Mediterranean.

The RAF thus provided squadrons assigned for naval co-operation, and under HQ RAF Middle East this meant 200 (GR) Group at Gibraltar and 201 Group at Alexandria. Operating from Alexandria, 101 Wing had the Sunderlands of 230 Squadron, while the Gibraltar command comprised Saro Londons of 202 Squadron, plus a detachment of 3 Anti-Aircraft Co-operation Unit (AACU), and also responsibility for the main part of the Swordfish-equipped 3 AACU at Hal Far, Malta. A singularly unimpressive order of battle.

July 1939 had seen a promise to increase Malta's defence capability to 112 heavy and sixty light anti-aircraft guns, supported by twenty-four searchlights, as well as four fighter squadrons. The primary reason was for the defence of Malta as a Mediterranean Fleet base (and HQ), the Navy being the strategic element of British power in this theatre. However, promising and delivering are two different things, especially when balancing priorities and resources. When Germany declared war in September 1939 the only potential threat to the Mediterranean was from Italy, should she choose to join in with her German ally, something Hitler was actually keen to avoid. Furthermore, although Italy had strong naval forces, including modern warships and some 100 submarines, this was more than balanced by the very strong naval elements of France, alongside those of the Royal Navy, so the Mediterranean looked pretty secure for now. The air element at Malta was limited to the seaplane base and engineering workshops at Kalafrana, and two small grass airfields – Hal Far, used primarily by the FAA, and Ta Kali, the civil airport that was used mainly by Italian operators and sometimes referred to as Takali. Work commenced in October 1939 at Luqa on what was to be

Underground power station at Tel Handak. The ability to 'dig in' to Malta's rock, and to build aircraft pens from that same rock, were key elements in the defensive strategy.

the RAF's main airfield. The initial work was completed in May 1940 and provided four runways of 800 × 50 yards. Underground bomb stores at Luqa had not been completed by summer 1940 and neither had the underground bulk petrol chambers at Wied Dalam. Other underground work on power stations and other support facilities was either completed or under way, although some were not finished until June 1941. However, this early decision to 'dig in' was one of the factors that led to Malta's survival – and ability to fight back. It was only in July 1939 that work began on the seaplane station at Marsaxlokk (also referred to as Marsa Scirocco).

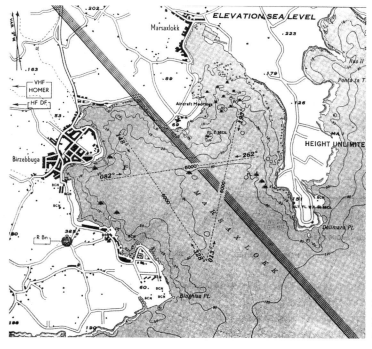

Marsaxlokk Bay was the main flying boat operating location; the plan shows directions and lengths of the main runs.

Post-war aerial of
Marsaxlokk Bay (right
with slipways visible)
and Fort St Lucien
(left). During the war,
Fort St Lucien was a
munitions depot.

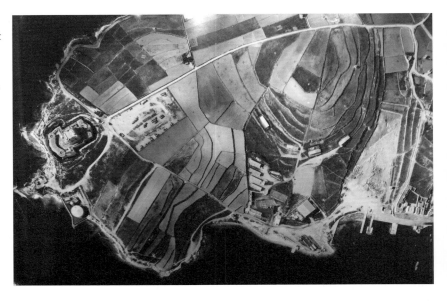

The outbreak of war saw five aircraft of 230 Squadron at Alexandria and three at Malta – all the Sunderlands serviceable and fully bombed up. Having spent a year becoming familiar with the needs of the Mediterranean theatre, the squadron had mixed feelings when it was ordered back to the UK, four more aircraft moving to Malta on 9 September. The following day, four Sunderlands flew back to Pembroke Dock via Marignane.

The European Phoney War of 1939 into 1940 came to end in May when Germany invaded France, but in the Mediterranean theatre the only change was the move of the Navy and its HQ to Alexandria on 30 April – the threat now being considered too great and the defences having made no real progress. Some guns had arrived, and there was an Air Ministry Experimental Station (AMES) (radar station) operating at Dingli, but without fighters to direct or sufficient guns to warn there was little they could contribute. The new Air Officer Commanding (AOC) had arrived in January, Air Commodore Forster H.M. Maynard RNZAF. He had originally joined the RNAS in 1915 and in the inter-war period had undertaken two tours in the Middle East. He was AOC for sixteen months during perhaps the most trying period of Malta's defence – starting with having to convince some that it was worth defending and could be defended. Promoted to air vice-marshal in February 1941, he was also created CB (Companion of the Order of the Bath) in recognition of his defence of Malta (AMB 4017, May 1941).

Shortly after the outbreak of war, 202 Squadron had moved to Gibraltar. The squadron had been a long-term resident at Malta, having been based at Kalafrana from January 1929. It moved its London flying boats to Gibraltar in September 1939 and was to remain the primary Gibraltar flying boat unit until late 1944. Kalafrana was the oldest base on Malta, having been used in the First World War, and now had good workshops and storage facilities, as well as moorings for flying boats at Cala Mistra and a landing ground at Hal Far. The squadron flew its first operational patrol on 11 September, two London flying boats flying reconnaissance and ASP (anti-submarine patrols). This was the first 'combat operation' (uneventful) in the Mediterranean theatre and the start of thousands of hours of such patrols by the GR aircraft. From that point on, the squadron flew regular ASP and convoy patrols, as did the Swordfish detachment of 3 AACU. The majority of patrols saw nothing but occasional attacks were made on 'suspicious patches of oil', which revealed that a large number of the anti-submarine bombs failed to explode; indeed, tests showed that about 50 per cent of bombs failed to detonate. Additionally, there were no proper maintenance facilities at Gibraltar and the Londons had to fly to Malta for overhaul.

With the Italians not yet in the war, the Mediterranean was very quiet, with the French responsible for the Western Basin, a Royal Navy destroyer force at Gibraltar, and the Mediterranean Fleet moving back to the UK, while the C-in-C 'raised his flag in Malta'. The fleet returned in March 1940 as by then it was clear that conflict with Italy was inevitable. To reinforce GR capability, 230 Squadron arrived at Alexandria in early May 1940 from the Far East, the CO, Wing Commander Bryer, flying to Cairo on 13 May for a conference with HQ Middle East and 201 Group (which Bryer, on promotion to group captain, took over in June). There it was confirmed that the squadron's main task would be the 'anti-submarine protection of the Allied Mediterranean Fleet whilst at sea'. Mersa Matruh lagoon was one of a number of locations examined for use as advanced landing bases.

An October 1942 report by the Italian Air Staff on the 'Air and Naval Bases on Malta June 1940 to October 1942' provides insight into the Italian perspective of the role of Malta. It divides its review into six periods, the first of which covers the period from June 1940 to 10 January 1941. It starts with an assessment of why Malta was important. 'The strategical and geographical position of Malta and its underground installations made it very powerful both defensively and offensively. At the beginning of hostilities between Germany and England (Sept. 1939), Malta was an efficient air and naval base which had been created as a key position between the Eastern and Western Mediterranean. By virtue of the naval installations, the airfields and formidable defences all over the Island, the British were in a position to make the Island a supporting base for the fleet; use it as a port of call for merchant shipping; hamper the traffic between Italy and Italian N. Africa; and dominate the air bases in Sicily and S. Italy from the air.' True – if the resources to develop that capability, especially the air capability, had been assigned, which at this stage they were not.

This part of the report continued: 'It can be assumed that England had foreseen an eventual Italian invasion of Tunisia a few days after the beginning of hostilities between Italy and France. As a result, she had foreseen the possible loss of Bizerta as a naval base and the Tunisian airfields which were used as landing stages for the air transports between England, Gibraltar and Egypt.' It is an interesting thought, and one that does not appear to have been considered in British strategic planning, partly no doubt because the expectation was that the French forces would have been able to resist any Italian incursion. In the event, of course, it was the rapid collapse of France that threw up the problem of the loss of these staging points, and changed the entire strategic position in the western Mediterranean. The day 26 April saw the formation of a new flying unit in Malta – 3 AACU, with an establishment, on paper, of seven Fairey Swordfish. The role of the unit was to provide targets on which the land and naval guns could practice anti-aircraft gun-laying, although they also performed a variety of other tasks. The Swordfish were also equipped with floats and used for air-sea rescue. Within weeks some of the pilots would also be called upon to become fighter pilots!

'In May 1940, C-in-C Mediterranean, at the request of the Air Officer Commanding, Mediterranean, agreed to the loan of four Sea Gladiators which were in store at Kalafrana, for the purpose of forming a local fighter defence unit. A fighter flight comprising these aircraft with six pilots drawn from local RAF resources was formed at Hal Far on 4th June, 1940, after a month's training of pilots, none of whom had had previous experience of fighter aircraft or methods of operation. On the outbreak of war, a continuous stand-by of two Gladiator aircraft was maintained during daylight hours. This small improvised Unit in the face of greatly superior numbers, met with considerable success against Italian bombers.' (Appendix to Intelligence Summary (Int Sum) 11 June–11 October 1940).

In the period April to June the Gladiators were flown by six pilots: Squadron Leader A.C. Martin, Flight Lieutenant G. Burgess, Flight Lieutenant P.G. Keeble, Flying Officer W.J. Woods, Pilot Officer J.L. Waters, and Pilot Officer P.B. Alexander. George Burgess later recalled: 'From time to time people refer to the story of Faith, Hope and Charity. Reference to Admiralty records proves that there were quite a few other Gladiators on the island when hostilities with Italy started. We were certainly given four aircraft to set up the Hal Far Flight, and there were certainly some others at Kalafrana in crates and from time to time aircraft with other 'rudder numbers' appeared to replace casualties. Whether these other aircraft had been completed in their crates I do not know. An enormous amount of improvisation had to go on to keep aircraft operational and a 'new' fuselage would have 'second-hand' wings or engine. As the 'rudder number' was on the fuselage this would seem to be yet another new aircraft.

Malta Fighter Flight pilots including Flying Officer John Waters, Flying Officer Peter Hartley and Pilot Officer Peter Alexander.

'Thus it was only during our training period, before the war started for us, and for only about the first week or ten days of the war period that the population ever saw three Gladiators in the air together – from then on it was two and sometimes only one. During this period none of us ever heard the aircraft referred to as Faith, Hope and Charity and I

Gladiator N5520 'Faith', one of the trio that became a legend in the early part of Malta's defence.

do not know who first used the description. Nevertheless, the sentiment was appropriate because the civil population certainly prayed for us and displayed such photographs as they could get hold of. There is no doubt that the Gladiators did not "wreak death and destruction" to many of the enemy, but equally they had a very profound effect on the morale of everybody in the island, and most likely stopped the Italians just using the island as a practice bombing range whenever they felt like it.'

Wing Commander G.A.V. Collins later recalled the time when, as Flying Officer Collins and in charge of the Aircraft Repair Section (ARS) at Kalafrana, he was called on to get these four aircraft built: 'Collins, there are four cased Naval Gladiators; unpack, erect, and get to Hal Far as fast as you can go. We will have a Fighter Flight if the pilots can get trained in time, so get going.' So to his staff he said: 'Muster four unpacking and erecting teams; towing party stand by for Hal Far [there was a mile stretch of road connecting the ARS at Kalafrana to Hal Far]. Start immediately and stop when last Gladiator at Hal Far.' And so it was done … but a few days later his phone rang again: 'Oh Collins. Seems the Admiralty have allocated the Gladiators to Alexandria and a ship is calling to collect them, so get them back from Hal Far, and into their cases again as quickly as you can. Ring me when you finish the packing.' And so to Warrant Officer Rayner, who was managing the erecting and

'Faith' was eventually rescued from the scrapheap and presented to the people of Malta by AVM Park on 3 September 1943. The aircraft is now with the National War Museum in Fort St Elmo.

moving, he said: 'Repack the Gladiators, carefully. Some poor devils may have to erect them, under war conditions.' Collins recalls that: 'It was just lunch time the following day and the weary packing party were securing the doors of the fourth Gladiator case … and the CO rang again … "How goes the packing?" "Just finished Sir and I was about to ring you." Yes, you guessed it – the military mind had changed yet again: "It's like this Collins, the AOC has obtained permission to keep the fighters, so, after lunch, get them back to Hal Far as quickly as possible. They look like being needed any time now. I'll come along and say a few words to the men."' As Collins recalls, 'He came – said necessary – and after a snatched meal the cases were opened up once more – and the care with which the aircraft had been dismantled helped considerably with the speedy return to Hal Far and readiness for flight.' (Letter from Wing Commander Collins).

Malta expected to be attacked as soon as Italy declared war and, with Sicily only 60 miles away, the Regia Aeronautica had good airfields from which to mount attacks. It also had a well-equipped air force, whereas Malta was virtually defenceless in June 1940. Just prior to the first attacks, Malta also received a new acting governor, Lieutenant General William Dobbie. The post of governor was an important one in that he was the overall Commander-in-Chief of Malta – despite what various Navy and Air Force officers believed, and there was a high degree of politics between them in 1940 – and he was also the link with the civilian government. In radio broadcasts the governor assured the Maltese people all was well, the Maltese considered Mussolini and the Italians to be bumbling fools (a view shared by Hitler and his generals), and there were enough anti-aircraft guns and troops visible to make it look like all was indeed well. A few modern aircraft in the sky would have helped, but there was none around. And so the island of Malta was getting ready for another sun-drenched summer.

Not everyone was convinced Malta was worth the effort; an interesting minute on one file gave the opinion that: 'Malta with its puny garrison would probably not be able to hold out for any length of time and in any case can only be regarded as a target for the Italian aircraft. I personally think we ought to abandon Malta and leave booby traps mixed up with all the immovable equipment so that we not only denied its use to the Italians but might also blow up a good many of them with it.' The handwritten note below this stated: 'I don't think there is much use you and I discussing this matter as it is mainly a political one.' Fortunately for the war in the Mediterranean, this was not a widely held view!

June 1940: First Italian Attacks

On 10 June Italy declared war on Britain and operations commenced in the Mediterranean and Western Desert against this new enemy. At the start of June there were three airfields on Malta but in essence almost no aircraft, so obstructions were placed on the runways at Luqa and Ta Kali to prevent any possible air landing operation by the enemy. Meanwhile, at Hal Far 'the landing ground was partially obstructed, but flightways left so that Gladiator and Swordfish aircraft could operate.' (AP3236 Works). On 5 June, C-in-C Mediterranean sent a signal to the First Sea Lord at the Admiralty expressing his concerns over Malta: 'I much regret to add to your anxiety nor do I wish to be unduly alarmist but I am seriously concerned about security of Malta in event of war with Italy. Although it is not to be expected that early warning would be obtained as there are now no fast craft I consider the island could hold out against parachute attack until assistance was forthcoming from the fleet.

'I am however of the opinion that if Malta was heavily bombed and invaded from the air while Garrison was engaged in dealing with panic and disorder caused among civil population it might well fall without fleet being able to lift a finger to prevent it. I am only too well aware how difficult it would be to spare fighter aircraft for defence of islands but when (loss?) of supplies, harbour defences and material totals of this Naval Fortress fall into the hands of the enemy … it might well be considered wise to send even one fighter squadron to Malta at expense of some other commitment. It is further suggested that immediately war breaks out a warning should be issued to Italy that if civil population of Malta is bombed, retaliatory action will be taken at once against some towns in Northern Italy.' (Signal C-in-C Med to Admiralty, 5 June 1940).

The first attack was delivered on the morning of the 11th, the primary target being Grand Harbour and Hal Far, although in reality it was 'that general area'. Flying Officer Collins recalled the attack: 'Several sticks of bombs straddled Kalafrana and all the anti-aircraft machine guns blazed away and so did many rifles of the Royal Malta Regiment, the troops standing in the open firing from the shoulder – a complete waste of ammunition for the enemy aircraft were very high. When the raid was over, apart from craters no damage had been done to Kalafrana and the engineer officer [Flying Officer 'Nobby' Clarke] at Hal Far (also bombed) informed ARS he needed no assistance, so far.' (Wing Commander Collins, letter). The comment about no assistance needed related to the fact that maintenance and repair for the Gladiators was the responsibility of the ARS.

The Italian formation had been picked up by Malta's sole radar unit and a warning passed to the readiness flight, Red Section, of three Gladiators. George Burgess led two colleagues off from Hal Far and they climbed towards the enemy, who were already dropping their bombs. Both sides took shots at each other but with no particular effect, although Flying Officer Woods in his combat report claimed one probable: 'We sighted a formation of five S.79s approaching Valetta at a height of approx. 15000 feet, and Red Two delivered an attack from astern. The enemy had turned out to sea. I delivered an attack from astern, and got in a good burst at a range of approx. 200 yards. My fire was returned. I then broke away and returned over the island at approx. 11,000ft south of Grand Harbour.

'While still climbing to gain height, I observed another formation of five enemy aircraft approaching. They were about the same height as myself. I attacked from abeam at about 150 yards and got in one good burst. The enemy started firing at me long before I opened up. This formation broke slightly but left me well behind them when I tried to get in an attack from astern. Just after that, when again climbing to gain more height, I suddenly heard machine gun fire from behind me. I immediately went into a steep left-hand turn and saw a single-engined fighter diving and firing at me. For quite three minutes I circled as tightly as possible and got the enemy into my sight. I got in a good burst, full deflection shot, and he went down in a steep dive with black smoke pouring from his tail. I could not follow him down, but he appeared to go into the sea.'

Post-war oblique aerial of Kalafrana, slipways and hangars on the left. The basic site had not changed from the wartime period.

In fact, the fighter was not seriously damaged and returned to base. This point that the bombers simply left the Gladiator behind would be a recurring theme of reports – the performance difference between the fast(ish) Italian bombers and the manoeuvrable but slow Gladiators. Likewise, the seeming lack of effect of the attack, the lack of 'hitting power', of the under-armed Gladiators would also be a focus of comment. The second attacks of the day targeted Luqa and Ta Kali but with little effect, while the last main

Sunderland in 'hangar' at Kalafrana.

Aerial view of Ta Kali in late 1940, some bomb craters visible. As one of the main fighter airfields, Ta Kali was frequently on the receiving end of attacks, although with little significant impact – a fact that was to change when the Luftwaffe appeared in 1941.

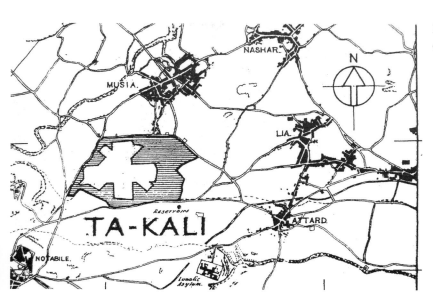

Plan and location map of Ta Kali.

attack of the day was against the docks. Bombing was inaccurate and the greatest damage was caused to the Cospicua area, killing twenty-two civilians. So ended day one of what would become the longest siege in British military history. It was a small beginning, with few aircraft involved and little military effectiveness on either side.

One of the dilemmas for Malta was that the primary targets of Grand Harbour and the dockyards were surrounded by housing, which meant that damage and casualties among the civilian population was inevitable. There was also really nowhere to go! Malta was a small island and so safe zones did not really exist, although some people moved to villages away from the docks area. For the next three years Malta and its people were effectively under siege, the weight of attack, death and destruction varied, as did the availability of even basic food. In the early part of the siege there was also the threat of invasion and occupation. That Malta and its people survived all of this and, whenever there was a pause or an opportunity, struck back rather than sat back, is without doubt one of the greatest stories of the Second World War. As we have alluded to already, the strategic position of Malta between the eastern Mediterranean (Egypt and Alexandria) and the western Mediterranean (Gibraltar), was only of value if Malta could play an offensive role within the overall Mediterranean and North Africa

Gladiator line-up in the hangar; the heroic fight by the small number of Gladiators may not have had any real military impact but it had great morale effect, and created the legend of 'Faith, Hope and Charity'.

(and later southern Europe) strategy. The ability to take the pounding, shake it off and fight back was the key. It needed determined leadership, external support dedicated to supplying the island and the resilience of all those on Malta.

12 June: 'Raids here yesterday show importance of fighter aircraft. The four Gladiators here though successful in bringing one plane down are too slow. There are five Hurricanes in Tunis en route to Egypt. AOC has asked Air Ministry to let them be directed here. Believe a few effective fighters would have a far reaching deterrent effect and produce very encouraging results.' (signal from Governor to War Office, 12 June).

The request was denied on the grounds that air defence of Alexandria was more important and, anyway, Malta had no spares and so aircraft would go unserviceable. The better news was that a fast convoy was planned and it would include twelve Hurricanes for Malta.

HQ Malta had signalled the Air Ministry on the 12th with a similar request, but also stating: 'have seven pilots here efficient on Gladiator and fighter drill and procedure. Consider these fully capable after short practice of operating Hurricanes.' This was perhaps a bit disingenuous as most of the pilots in the Fighter Flight had very little fighter experience! They got a similar response that the Hurricanes had to go to Egypt and 'with only 4 Gladiators your results are most encouraging and confirm our own experience here in Norway that Gladiators even though slower have proved a match for German bombers faster than the S.81.' In other words, just get on with it!

However, after the initial attack and a few reconnaissance flights, the Italians seemed to have lost interest in Malta. The warning that Italian cities would be bombed was never issued, but Bomber Command Whitleys attacked factories in Turin, northern Italy, on the night of 11th/12th, as a reminder that Italy was in range of the bombers from Britain. Throughout the period 1940–41 Bomber Command flew frequent raids, albeit primarily against targets in northern Italy. None of these was on a scale that would make a significant military impact, but they did lift morale and serve a political purpose. The main military effort, and even then limited, would come from bombers based in Malta or the Middle East. Other reasons for quiescence may be to do with Mussolini's desire to be involved with his German ally against France (and later Britain) so he could share the spoils, and perhaps his belief that effort should be focused on North Africa, taking British and French possessions. So the Italians had some reasons for leaving Malta alone, while some Allied commanders also believed it best not to provoke Italian interest in Malta by making the island an air threat.

Meanwhile however, the British were determined not to be quiet in the Mediterranean. In large part this was due to the basically aggressive nature of Admiral Cunningham, who has often been compared with Nelson as a naval leader and who believed that aggressive strategy and tactics was both in the tradition of the Royal Navy and the way to beat or cow opponents such as the Italians. His stance, ably supported by the commanders of his ships, played a major role in the Allied domination of the Mediterranean. Mussolini, like his ancient Roman forbears, may have called it *Mare Nostrum* (our sea) but Cunningham ensured this was far from true. In addition to his surface ships, and the limited numbers of submarines operating out of Alexandria and using Malta to refuel and rearm, naval operations were also supported from the air by the FAA, albeit never in large numbers but with remarkable success, and by the RAF. The RAF effort comprised reconnaissance, a critical element in having offensive forces in the right place at the right time; anti-submarine patrols, in which the Sunderlands out of Malta, Alexandria and Gibralar, were ever present and frequently effective; and, finally, anti-shipping operations. The latter started slow but, arguably, became the key factor in winning the war at sea and on land in this theatre.

Admiral Sir Andrew B. Cunningham, C-in-C Mediterranean Fleet

After an operational career that started in the First World War, during which he was awarded DSO and bar (DSO*), he received a second bar to this gallantry award for his actions in the Baltic in 1919. His inter-war staff career led to Flag rank in late 1932 and eventually to the post of C-in-C Mediterranean, hoisting his flag on the battleship Warspite on 6 June 1939. As we mention throughout this account, Cunningham was a 'fighting Admiral' in the finest traditions of the Royal Navy, and played a significant

role in the Mediterranean War. Also, as we mention, he was involved in a number of 'strong debates' over the provision of air cover for naval operations, but generally was able to work with senior air commanders. Leaving the Med for a special assignment in Washington, he was promoted to Admiral of the Fleet in January 1943, returning to his old post as C-in-C Mediterranean the following month.

The first operational sorties were flown by the Sunderlands out of Alexandria on 10 June – the strong Italian submarine force being seen as a high threat. Two aircraft carried out anti-submarine patrols (ASPs) ahead of an eight-destroyer force sweeping for submarines to the west of Alexandria. The patrol operated from dawn to shortly before dusk, the first pair of aircraft being relieved by a second pair at midday. This task continued the following day, with other aircraft tasked on recce sorties looking for minefields. If an air raid warning were received at Alexandria, the Sunderlands were 'dispersed' by being taxied around the bay, with all guns manned! The Sunderlands were based at Alexandria, using HMT *Dumana* as a base ship, with offices and stores at the nearby Imperial Airways depot. At this stage the Sunderlands were the only aircraft capable of long-rang/long duration patrols and as such were kept busy.

The debate over the Hurricanes and if Malta or the Middle East should have them had not stopped and the aircraft, having flown through France, arrived at Tunis (only five made it), North Africa, by which time it had been decided after all that Malta could have them 'temporarily'. By the 13th, three had arrived, led by Squadron Leader Ryley and escorted by Hudson. The other two Hurricanes arrived on the 21st. Malta was well placed as a staging post to the Middle East, which itself was also a staging post to the Far East, and prior to the fall of France, Hurricanes and bomber types such as Blenheims and Wellingtons would leave the UK, stage through France and Malta and then proceed to Egypt. This delivery flight was planned to pass Blenheims and Hurricanes through, with twelve of each type involved. The twenty-four aircraft were grouped into four flights, each with three Blenheims and three Hurricanes. Nothing went right; the Blenheim Delivery Flight lost seven Blenheim IVs, most due to bad weather over France, and while the Hurricanes fared better, they too were suffering mishaps. One Blenheim (L9334) was lost when the crew was unable to find Malta and eventually crashed into the sea off the Tunisian coast with the loss of the three crew. This highlights an important fact about Malta – it is small and not always easy to see, especially in hazy conditions.

Throughout the war a number of aircraft were lost when they failed to locate the island. Some landed at other airfields (Allied or Axis), some ditched in the sea, and of the latter a number of crews were lucky to be picked up by shipping or by the air-sea rescue (ASR) services. For those who missed Malta, the Italian islands of Lampedusa and Pantelleria were sometimes mistaken for Malta or were used as the nearest landfall when the aircraft was low on fuel, and a number of crews ended up as PoWs in this way.

Nevertheless, a number of Hurricanes had arrived safely; in fact, too many as far as HQ ME was concerned, and some were ordered on to Egypt. Since Hal Far was unsuitable for the operation of Hurricanes,

Blenheim N3589 in Italian markings. It landed in Pantelleria on a ferry flight on 13 September 40.

Luqa was opened up and the fighter flight was transferred there on 28 June. In an effort to improve the Gladiators they were fitted with armour plating to protect the pilots and, according to the technical report, 'other modifications are in progress to increase their speed, rate of climb and fire power, without exceeding the pre-war limitations to get the added performance.' (Int Summary)

The Hurricanes also needed some work, the same report stating: 'Prior to the receipt of constant speed units for the Hurricanes, the time to 20,000ft was improved from 15 minutes to 10 minutes, by alterations to the airscrews.' The author of this part of the summary also had a swipe at the pilots: 'The damage to aircraft and engines other than by enemy action, has nearly all been due to errors of judgement by the pilots, either by the mishandling of engine controls through inexperience, or mistakes made during the landing. Failures attributable to maintenance have been virtually non-existent.'

The French Armistice of 22 June gave the British in the Mediterranean another major challenge. Firstly, the speed of the collapse of France was unexpected, so no contingency plans had been made; secondly, what would happen to French military resources? And as far as the Mediterranean theatre was concerned, that meant naval capital ships and, to a lesser extent, land-based aircraft in the French North African colonies. If the French ships were added to the Axis forces, bolstering the Italian Navy, then Cunningham, already outnumbered and outgunned, would be in trouble. There was discussion of abandoning the Mediterranean, the fleet leaving Alexandria and being based at Gibraltar instead. This would have threatened the survival of Egypt and Malta, the dangers of the western Mediterranean becoming all too clear from the convoys that ran Gibraltar to Malta in 1941–42. In effect, two men prevented this. Churchill, recently taking over as Prime Minister and having a naval background (politically) and a cussed streak not to give ground to the enemy, and Cunningham, who believed that aggressive action would enable the British to maintain their naval dominance.

'The defection of the French, on whose Navy we had relied to hold the balance of sea power in the Western Mediterranean, transformed the strategic situation overnight. It placed Italy in a dominant position in the Central Basin. The best we could hope to achieve for some time was to keep the Axis foot from the Suez and Gibraltar gateways. Out fleet, heavily outnumbered, had to operate from

Alexandria – at least 800 miles from the route Italian supplies to Libya were likely to use. Malta became virtually isolated and at the mercy of air attack from Sicily.' (*The RAF in Maritime War*, ibid).

The loss of French capability and cover, including the North Africa base, also made Gibraltar more vulnerable and more important. The Royal Navy formed Force H at Gibraltar in late June, this capital ship force's main role being to deal with enemy raiders in the Atlantic, but it retained an Allied footing in the western Mediterranean as well. Indeed, it would become a key part of the supply and air reinforcement convoys to Malta and Egypt.

On 25 June the Air Ministry signalled that: 'Admiralty have agreed that Swordfish of 767 Squadron now at Malta are to come under your orders for attacks in Sicily against (a) oil targets, (b) air targets except when required by C-in-c Mediterranean for other operations.' (Signal Air Ministry to HQ Malta, 25 June).

The following day this was followed by: 'Appreciate your difficulties but consider most important that attacks on Sicily should be started as soon as possible even on small scale. Oil targets are much more profitable than others within range and morale effect of oil fires likely to be great.' It then went on to list oil installations at Messina, Palermo, Augusta and Catania as prime targets.

In these early months of RAF and Navy 'exchange of ideas', Malta signalled on the 28th: 'C-in-C Med has notified Admiralty he considers Swordfish 767 Squadron should not be employed against targets in Sicily but used for local reconnaissance anti-submarine patrols, and as torpedo strike force against surface forces which come within range of Malta. I have five RAF Swordfish [3 AACU] and crews organized to provide local reconnaissance anti-submarine patrols and bombing, but not torpedo striking force. Targets Sicily should undoubtedly be attacked if possible and plan for first raid already made 30/6 but must first know agreed Air Ministry and Admiralty policy for 767 Sqn.'

This was confirmed, and on 1 July the Admiralty also notified that 'the 12 Swordfish in Malta ex 767 Squadron are to constitute new first line squadron numbered 830.' No. 830 Squadron FAA went on to have an outstanding career, especially in anti-shipping operations. The Swordfish of 830 Squadron flew their first offensive mission on 30 June, bombing Augusta harbour.

Meanwhile, the Sunderlands from Alexandria were flying a variety of operations, including reconnaissance of Tobruk and searches for the Italian fleet. The first U-boat attack was carried out on 28 June, Wing Commander Nicholetts (L5806) of 228 Squadron dropping three bombs on a large submarine. The bombs overshot the target, although it appears from subsequent revelations that his attack damaged the *Anfitrite*, causing the Italian submarine to return to base for repairs. The following day he attacked a small submarine, dropping four bombs in his first attack, all of which failed to explode; two more bombs were dropped in a second attack, these falling 20 yards ahead of the submarine track but with no apparent effect. The squadron also deployed Sunderlands to Malta as required to give added protection to eastbound convoys. The first success for 230 Squadron came in late June, Flight Lieutenant Campbell, airborne from Aboukir in L5804, finding and sinking the *Argonauta*. The following day the same crew were successful again. The aircraft was on a recce to the west of Zante when it picked up a submarine; this vessel was sunk in the attack and the Sunderland then landed and picked up four survivors. An Italian report stated that two bombs had hit the stern and conning tower, causing the boat to sink very rapidly. The crew, out of bombs, machine-gunned another submarine found on the return journey. The following day this same pilot was involved in a dive-bomb attack on a destroyer in Augusta harbour, the elevator fabric of L5803 being damaged by the high-speed dive! Another bombing attack was made on 1 July when L5803 was en route to Egypt from Malta, the target being a destroyer near Tobruk. The four bombs missed but the aggressive intent of 230 Squadron and Flight Lieutenant Campbell was certainly evident. Taking on a destroyer with a Sunderland was a bold act!

HQ Med signalled on 1 July: 'In view of paucity information regarding possible suitable targets Sicily and desirability ascertaining results of bombing by Swordfish of Augusta oil depots, I despatched Hudson on high altitude photographic recco today. Reconnaissance of this kind is not only essential if Swordfish offensive operations are to be [successful? – words missing] but affords ready means of providing C-in-C Med with information when required concerning shipping Sicily otherwise only obtainable by Sunderland from Egypt.'

The request was also made for the Hudson to be kept, and to be joined by Hudson 7357 from Egypt. The important point here is the recognition of Malta as the eyes of the central Mediterranean, crucial for both offence and defence. In an interesting exchange of signals, Malta was told to return the Hudson to Coastal Command in the UK – which seems to have been ignored. The same series of signals continued to discuss who had use of the Navy Swordfish and for what purpose. On 9 July the governor weighed in with a signal to the War Office! 'With reference to offensive raids from Malta undertaken recently by Swordfish of Fleet Air Arm against objectives in Sicily, I have come to the conclusion that unless they form part of a combined operation with Fleet they should be discontinued.' He then gave various reasons, which he summed up as: 'Until our air defences in shape of fighters are considerably increased I am sure it is a false policy to provoke aircraft attacks on Malta, and fritter away our very slender resources on tasks which can produce only meagre results.' The Italians had actually recorded that one attack, on the night of 5–6 July on Catania airfield, had been effective, with aircraft destroyed and personnel killed and wounded.

Meanwhile, at the western end of the Med; 228 Squadron had detached two Sunderlands to join 202 Squadron at Gibraltar, one of their main tasks being reconnaissance of French naval bases such as Oran, Mers-el-Kébir and Algiers. The first reconnaissance of these bases was made on 1 July, two sorties confirming the presence of major French warships. On 4 July Flight Lieutenant Brooks in P9621 was on a recce of Oran and Algiers when attacked by three French Curtiss 75As; the Sunderland claimed to have shot down one fighter and damaged another, although in return it had been badly damaged and one crew member was injured. The aircraft had to return to Pembroke Dock for repairs. British warships, having failed to negotiate the surrender of the French warships at Oran, opened fire and destroyed or seriously damaged most of the major vessels, with heavy loss of life among the French sailors. This attack has caused controversy ever since, but it was seen at the time, by the Royal Navy, as essential in order to maintain naval dominance in the Mediterranean. A Sunderland reconnaissance sortie on 5 July confirmed the result of the bombardment.

The squadron also deployed aircraft to Malta; on 9 July Flight Lieutenant McKinley (L5807) took off from Malta on a search for the Italian fleet – and eventually located approximately forty ships, which it then shadowed for nine hours. A second 228 Squadron Sunderland (N9020, Squadron Leader Menzies) took over and flew a further nine-hour shadow, during which time the crew had an inconclusive engagement with an He 115. Three days later Squadron Leader Menzies was flying a Malta patrol when he came across a U-boat: 'In the first stick three 250lb A/S bombs were dropped and fell close to the stern. Two bombs were dropped in the second attack whilst the U-boat was submerging and these fell abaft the conning tower. A single bomb was then dropped ahead of the submarine. Excessive quantities of air were observed to come up a short distance from the last observed position and this was taken as a final indication of the U-boat's end.' (228 Squadron ORB, July 1940). It is likely that this was the 954-ton *Settimo*, this submarine reporting an air attack on July 13 in which it suffered light damage.

Sunderland of 230 Squadron with Latécoère 298B (ex Aeronavale Ex. 2HT, whose crew decided to join the Allies when France surrendered).

On 2 July, Wing Commander Moreton had sent a memo to his colleagues at Plans 3 on the greater use of Malta: 'It has survived a month of war with very few scars to show. With the prescribed 4 fighter squadrons instead of 4 Gladiators, we could go far to render Malta comparatively safe from Italian attacks.' He went on to describe Malta's use as an air reinforcement route to the Middle East, its use as a Wellington base to bomb Italy and as a key location for Naval light forces. He concluded: 'In any case Malta would be a running sore in the side of Italy and might lead to a large expenditure of their effort to attack it.'

Meanwhile, Malta was still on the receiving end of Italian attacks, and on 3 July the Hurricanes scored their first success, Flying Officer J. Water shooting down one of a pair of SM.79s. On approach to land, his Hurricane was attacked by a CR.42 and, although Waters put it down and walked away from it, the aircraft was damaged beyond repair. The 7th July was the first time George Burges was able to scramble in a Hurricane and take advantage of the additional performance and firepower. Two Hurricanes scrambled after an escorted recce aircraft, with Burges claiming the primary target and his colleague claiming one of the fighters. Burges was awarded a DFC in July, the citation reading: 'Although normally a flying-boat pilot, and only transferred to fighter duties since the commencement of war with Italy, Flight Lieutenant Burges has shot down three enemy aircraft and so damaged three more that they probably failed to reach their base. He has shown great tenacity and determination in seeking combat, usually in the face of superior numbers.'

The 7th of July was also the date of a signal from VA (Vice Admiral) Malta to the Admiralty in which he says the stark choice was to send adequate air defences or abandon the island. 'The future of Malta would seem to be:

• Evacuating it if the value to Fleet is considered insufficient to justify amount of defence required
• To defend it as long as possible with existing defences
• To provide it with defences on a scale to make successful defence possible.

He goes on to say that the first two are not sensible and so 'if Malta is to be held active measures in improving our A/A defences are imperative. If no action is taken our defences will be imperiled and we shall be courting disaster.'

The ARS was called on to keep the limited number of fighters serviceable, which could prove challenging, especially for the Gladiators. 'The damage received on some occasions had to be seen to be believed. On three occasions a tail was nearly shot off and once an aileron was almost cut in two, but in all cases the aircraft remained under control. Bullet holes were found around the cockpit and in the centre section of a mainplane above a pilot's head – and one through a dashboard. A spare tail portion was made up from bits and pieces and facilitated rapid repair on tails. The use of explosive bullets by the enemy caused extreme damage of a type repaired only by the replacement of a component. The structure of the Gladiator lent itself to rapid repair. Only once did things look like a hold up. In the tail of the fuselage there is a transverse member of quite a large diameter. Two thirds of this one had been shot away by explosive bullets and at first nothing could be found to suit for replacement. To turn from solid metal would have taken a long time. Then OC ARS spotted the gun flash tube in a damaged Hurricane. The outside diameter was exact, but the gauge of the metal much too thin, so, recalling the days of wooden aircraft and iron men, the tube was plugged with a hardwood ply, and another Gladiator was serviceable.' (Collins, *ibid*).

Most of July's reconnaissance effort by the Sunderland was spent keeping tabs on the Italian fleet, both squadrons flying similar patrols from Egypt and Malta. Flight Lieutenant Woodward of 230 Squadron claimed to have attacked and sunk an Italian submarine on 7 July, but there appears to be no confirmation of this. The Italian fleet was found on the 8th, having been spotted initially by a submarine but subsequently shadowed by aircraft of 228 and 230 Squadrons. Cunningham was steaming in the general direction aboard his flagship HMS *Warspite* and with the carrier *Eagle*, with Swordfish for attack and a small number of Sea Gladiators for defence, and in company with two other battleships, five cruisers and an assortment of destroyers, he was expecting to catch a number of major warships and a merchant convoy.

It was a bit of a surprise therefore when Italian bombers appeared – the British fleet position had been shadowed by recce aircraft and Italian torpedo-bombers soon appeared, with one hit being scored on the cruiser *Gloucester*. Undeterred, Cunningham changed course to place his ships between the Italians and their home base, a manoeuvre based on recent air reports. The following day the cruiser *Neptune* signalled that the enemy had been sighted. This opened the Battle of Calabria, in which long-range naval gunnery saw *Warspite* cause critical damage to the battleship *Giulio Cesare*. With ships manoeuvring, smoke screens being laid, and waterspouts being thrown up by the large-calibre shells, it was the first such action in the Mediterranean. Some, like Cunningham, revelled in this traditional action, but for the Italians it appears to have been too much. Italian bombers appeared once more, but despite the heavy concentration of bombs no significant damage was done, although it did cause concern among some commanders as to what could have happened and gave them an increased appreciation of the potential threat from aircraft.

One important result was the reinforcing of the Navy's opinion of its superiority over the Italians. It also reinforced Churchill's view that his decision to veto any plan to abandon Malta was the right one and that, instead, Malta needed to be made secure so that it could remain an operational base for the fleet, as an anchor in the overall naval strategy. In a note to Admiral Dudley Pound (First Sea Lord) on 15 July, which followed earlier exchanges in the month, Churchill made his position clear: 'We must take the offensive against Italy, and endeavour to make Malta once again a Fleet base for special occasions. *Illustrious*, with her armoured deck, would seem to be better placed in the Mediterranean.' He also called for strengthening of the air defences, guns and fighters.

On Malta, 10 July was the heaviest attack for some time, with twenty or so bombers involved, along with escorting CR.42s. The defending Hurricanes claimed two bombers for no loss, and many of the other bombers had been damaged, although most of that damage appears to have been shrapnel from anti-aircraft fire. The Malta AA barrage was already quite effective, and over the next few months was to develop into one of the most intense of any location, although, as we shall see, not without some challenges and shortages. The shrapnel was not only a threat to the raiders; many

Sunderland attack on an Italian submarine (not the one referred to above). Hunting submarines and shadowing surface shipping were the main roles of flying boats.

accounts speak of people on the ground having to be wary of the 'deluge of shrapnel', never mind the intense noise if you happened to be close to a gun site.

The Sunderlands continued to range far and wide on reconnaissance and anti-submarine patrols, and they encountered Italian fighters from time to time; Flight Lieutenant Garside encountering

Luqa under attack in mid-July; as the main airfield for operating larger aircraft, including bombers, this was a primary target for attack.

three Macchi 200s on 28 July, the crew claiming one shot down and one damaged in a fifteen-minute combat. The same day, another 230 Squadron crew (Squadron Leader Ryley, L5804) tangled with four Macchis, shooting down one in a fifty-seven-minute combat. The Sunderland was badly damaged and three gunners wounded. 'Much credit went to LAC Campbell, a fitter, who remained in the wing of the aircraft plugging holes in the tanks until rendered unconscious by petrol fumes. The aircraft landed at 1215 and was beached in a sinking condition.' (230 Squadron ORB). A number of such combats had been reported by Sunderlands of both squadrons during recce flights of Italian ports.

In early August, the AOC was unhappy at the lack of offensive aircraft: 'Land based GR aircraft if operated from Malta in sufficient numbers could achieve continuously and economically much of the sea reconnaissances now undertaken by Sunderlands, which owing to the limited maintenance facilities at Malta can operate away from Alexandria for brief periods only.'

The signal proposed a squadron of Hudsons, and if not Hudsons, then Beauforts. 'Suggest one complete TBGR [Torpedo Bomber General Reconnaissance] squadron of 15 aircraft would produce results here out of all proportion to the numbers of aircraft involved.' (Signal HQ Malta to Air Ministry, 2 August.)

The signal also praised the work of the one Hudson, which was used primarily for checking on shipping in Sicily. The counter-proposal the following day was to disband 3 AACU, give its Swordfish to 830 Squadron and hold its personnel ready to form a GR unit with four Blenheims that would be sent from the UK. The Air Ministry had approved the establishment of the Fighter Flight 'on a proper basis comprising 8 IE

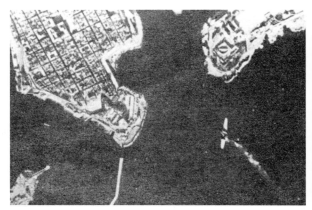
10 July 1940, SM.79s over Grand Harbour.

The SM.79 was the main Italian bomber type engaged over Malta and against naval targets, the torpedo units being among the elite of the Regia Aeronautica.

The carrier *Ark Royal* with near misses from Italian bombs. Carriers played a key role in resupply of aircraft to Malta and the Middle East, as well as providing air cover to convoys and offensive support for operations.

Swordfish off *Ark Royal* 1940. The *Ark* was eventually sunk by a German U-boat on 13 November 1941.

and 4 IR aircraft'. Under Operation Hurry, twelve Hurricanes escorted by two Skuas were flown off HMS *Argus* and arrived at Malta on 2 August. Among the convoy, *Ark Royal* was responsible for fleet air defence, and 803 Squadron's Skuas had some success in breaking up attacks and also claiming at least one SM.79. Skuas were also tasked to lead the Hurricanes to Malta, and they were also shadowed by two Sunderlands from Gibraltar. HQ Malta signalled: '12 Hurricanes, 2 Skuas and 2 Sunderlands arrived 0600 GMT. One Hurricane crashed on landing, write off, pilot injured. One Skua collided with aerodrome obstruction.' A following signal attributed both accidents to pilot error, the Hurricane 'following unmannerly low flying round over hangars'. The signal continued: 'Hurry pilots have no orders but most of them under impression they are to return to UK. Cannot agree to this and propose to retain them all.'

The new arrivals, combined with the remaining Fighter Flight, became Malta's first operational fighter squadron when 261 Squadron was formed on 2 August 1940, under the command of Squadron Leader Martin (although Squadron Leader Balden took over in the middle of the month). The

261 Squadron Badge

According to the RAF Heraldry Trust records (www.rafht.co.uk), the squadron badge was:

Awarded: *May 1946*

Blazon: *In front of a sword, erect point downwards, argent pommelled and hilted, or a mullet argent, the whole over a Maltese Cross, sable fimbriated Or*

Link: *The Maltese Cross edged with gold commemorates the squadron's part in the defence of Malta. The five-pointed star indicates the five subsequent campaigns in which it operated in the eastern theatres. The sword is indicative of the spirit of a fighter squadron*

Motto: *Latin:* Semper contendo – *I strive continually.*

squadron was formed but not operational; some servicing personnel and equipment had been brought in the Sunderlands, while more was delivered by submarine, but the Hurricanes had to be made combat ready.

'Recent reductions in scale of air attacks has brought dockyard back to almost normal conditions. Light forces can now use Grand Harbour as temporary base provided care is taken to conceal their movements. Reduction of attacks is probably temporary, but may be partly due to enemy believing severe damage has been done. Until the

Country.	Location.	Unit.	Aircraft.	Remarks.
Malta ..	Valetta ..	A.H.Q.	—	—
		Base Accounts Office ..	—	—
		Base Personnel Office ..	—	—
		Met. Station	—	—
	Kalafrana ..	S.H.Q.	—	—
		Inter-Command W/T Station	—	—
	Hal Far ..	S.H.Q.	—	—
		Station Flight	Various ..	—
	Luqa	No. 261 (F) Squadron ..	Hurricane ..	—
		No. 431 (G.R.) Flight ..	Glen Martin	—
	Ta Salvatur ..	D.F. Station	—	—
		No. 241 T.R.U.	—	—
		No. 242 T.R.U.	—	—

Extract of SD161 Location of Units; for August 1940, now showing two based flying units – 261 Squadron and 431 Flight.

defences and Air Force are further strengthened consider it desirable that this belief continues.' This bluff concept was one that was mentioned a number of times in subsequent months, including requesting press releases to be less 'upbeat'. 'I do not think outside publicity necessary to maintain civilian morale.' (signal to C-in-C Mediterranean).

The Malta Intelligence Summary included an appendix on the Italian tactics in the period June to August:

'1. For the first month of the war with Italy, S79 bombers carried out raids and reconnaissance unescorted by fighters. When successes against them by our fighters started the tactics changed and no bomb was dropped by day on Malta for a continuous period of five weeks. The period was occupied by the Italians in sending strong formations of up to twenty fighters carrying out offensive patrols in an evident attempt to neutralize our fighter effort. The attempt met with little success and our few fighters were instructed that unless bombers were included action against fighters was to be avoided and only stragglers were to be attacked.

2. The next phase commenced when day bombing was resumed by large formations of 10 to 15 bombers escorted by 10 to 25 fighters. This presented a difficult problem but our few fighters tackled it courageously and succeeded in obtaining an occasional success. The attacks however, were fortunately not sustained and were next followed by dive bombing attacks with Ju.87s also heavily escorted by fighters. On the third dive bombing attack two bombers and one fighter were shot down by Hurricanes and no further dive bombing attacks have taken place.

3. In view of night bombing which occurred during moonlight in the early weeks of the war a night fighter effort was worked up. The first occasion it was called into action a Hurricane carried out a determined attack on an SM.79 which was last flying very low and apparently in great difficulty. No further night attack took place for several weeks. The next attempted night attack did not materialize since the enemy aircraft when caught in searchlights turned back before the Island. After several further weeks an attempt was made by approximately four bombers working in pairs to raid by moonlight. A Hurricane shot one bomber down in flames and so seriously damaged a second that it probably never returned to its base. The remaining bombers approached the Island but returned before crossing the coast.'

The latter comment referred to the actions of the hastily formed night fighter section, the Hurricanes being considered suitable for this 'cats eye' style of operation, and a number of pilots volunteered or selected. The first success occurred on the night of 13 August, when Flying Officer R.H. Barber, one of the original Fighter Flight pilots, closed in on an SM.79 from below and claimed it as a probable. As expected, he had located the bomber because it had been picked up by searchlights, although his final attack was made by moonlight. The bomber failed to make it back to Sicily. That same night, 830 Squadron was out again attacking Augusta harbour, nine Swordfish taking part with a mix of bomber and torpedo aircraft. Only one of the three torpedo attackers made it back to Malta – and even then only to ditch offshore, although the crew (Hall and Brooks-Walford) were picked up by launch *ST280* on the 14th.

Malta's airfield infrastructure had stood up reasonably well to the summer bombing, but in September the increased use of dive-bombing caused heavier damage; 'Hal Far was attacked and barracks, hangars and airfield badly damaged. Emergency repairs were carried out immediately and the station continued to function. Luqa continued to be regularly attacked and such resources as the Departments [of Works] had in plant, materials and labour were concentrated in effecting emergency repairs of air raid damage.' (AP 3236).

Without this constant attention from the seldom recognized works teams, the airfields would have been unserviceable and no air defence (or attack) possible. The repair work also slowed down or prevented some of the planned development and expansion work.

The convoy route from Gibraltar to Malta was crucial and whenever a convoy sailed, details were soon passed to the Axis forces courtesy of spies in Spain, or picked up by submarines on port watch. Knowing a convoy had sailed and being able to interdict it were, of course, not the same thing. The Italians had three options if they wanted to engage convoys – air attack, submarine attack and surface fleet action. One of their main problems was the seemingly poor communication and co-operation between air and naval forces, both tending to operate independently. Convoys were the key for both sides and the war of the supply convoys effectively began with an Allied victory with the arrival in Malta on 2 September of an escorted convoy of three merchant ships from Alexandria and additional warships from Gibraltar. The Alexandria convoy was attacked from the air and one ship (*Cornwall*) damaged, but all made it to Malta and unloaded more than 40,000 tons of supplies, most of a military nature that boosted Malta's defensive capability.

One of the main advantages the Navy had over its opponents was the presence of aircraft carriers, a capability that improved with the arrival of HMS *Illustrious* at the start of September. The new 23,000-ton carrier was better in that it was faster (30kt) and had an armoured deck, so it stood more chance of surviving a bomber attack. The fleet air defence capability was still very limited as the FAA still lacked an effective fleet defence fighter, still relying on the Skua, and for attack the Swordfish remained the main type. However, carriers were also vulnerable assets that needed to be protected, so it was a bit of a double-edged sword. In 'blue water' operations this may have been fine, other than the submarine threat, but in the constrained waters of the Med, with the enemy dominating the land areas and able to operate land-based aircraft from airfields, the balance remained in favour of the enemy. 'Bomb Alley', the area south of Crete, was the worst area westbound, while the area between Sicily and Tunisia was worst for the eastbound shipping. Both meant that ships came within easy striking distance of land-based attack aircraft. The ebb and flow of the Desert War had a distinct influence on the balance, especially the area between Egypt and Tripoli; whoever controlled that area controlled key air bases for offence – attack enemy ships – and defence – defend own ships.

Gibraltar had always appeared somewhat vulnerable to air attack, but with Spain remaining neutral there was really no threat – until the French Vichy government authorized attacks. The first attempt was on 14 July but the bombs fell short; the second and more serious attack was on 24 and 25 September, notionally in response to the British attack on French ships at Dakar. On both days the French bombers bombed with impunity as there were no fighters at Gib, but caused little significant damage, although a number of aircraft were damaged. With the importance of Gibraltar in the Allied Mediterranean strategy, and its anti-submarine role into the Atlantic, it is one of the strategic failures of the Axis forces not to have taken more action against the Rock.

The other big change, and one that had been requested for some time, was the arrival of dedicated air reconnaissance aircraft with the capability to range far and wide. On 6 September three Martin Marylands arrived at Luqa; in most records they are referred to as Glenn Martin, the full name of the manufacturer, and not as Marylands, but we will use the name Maryland, as it is more appropriate. One of the crew on the ferry flight from the UK was Pilot Officer Adrian Warburton; 'Warby' was to become one of the legends of Malta and this theatre, but at this stage he was an unknown quantity. Although detached from 22 Squadron, this was little more than an administrative convenience and source of crews, and the Marylands officially became 431 Flight, under the command of Flight Lieutenant 'Titch' Whiteley. The flight absorbed the personnel of 3 AACU and that unit disbanded. The primary tasker of the unit was Cunningham as the main purpose at this stage was to keep an eye on the Italian naval bases and fleet operations, which meant that places such as Taranto were high up the list. In an article in the RAF Review of 1978, Group Captain Whiteley recalled that Pilot Officer Warburton was one of the three navigators on the outbound trip from the UK and, along with Pilot Officer Devine, had devised a direct routing that suited the Marylands' capabilities; on the flight over Sardinia the aircraft made first use of their F24 camera fit. He recalled the first operations: 'Our first sortie was PR of Tripoli on the 8th September, perfect pictures being taken by Pilot Officer Foxton (Warburton navigating). After Tripoli it was Taranto, Naples, Brindisi, Bari, Palermo, the airfields of Sicily, Pantelleria and Sardinia.'

He also recalled that: 'Shortly after our arrival in Malta the other two pilots (Foxton and Bibby) suffered temporary indispositions. I therefore decided to train two navigators (Warburton and Devine) as pilots. Both had flown Ansons, but Warby not recently. Warby's first solo almost ended in disaster. He eventually landed cross wind with the top strands of the fence around his tail – watched by an irate Wing Commander from HQ. I was firmly reprimanded.'

It could have been the end of Warburton's piloting career, but as pilots were in short supply, Whiteley stuck with him. Despite the arrival of the three Marylands and the great work they were already doing, and would continue to do, the AOC's signal to HQ ME of 17 September stated: 'Arrival of three Glen Martin in Malta has not materially changed scale of systematic long distance reconnaissance that can be carried out in the Central Mediterranean. Small experience of aircraft shows that high degree of unserviceability can be expected almost immediately unless comprehensive range of spares, of which there are none here, is made available. Glen Martins appear unsuitable for continuous and protracted periods of reconnaissance over the sea, as pilot has no relief [no second pilot] and no automatic pilot, while each member of crew is separated from others.'

He suggested that Sunderlands were best for Ionian Sea recce and 'to make reconnaissance watertight, necessary to maintain daily patrol of three aircraft'. He considered the Marylands ideal for the occasional recce of Italian ports and for the route Malta–Tunisia. With the limitation of the Swordfish to a 150-mile strike range, the major thrust of his message was the need for Beaufort-type aircraft.

Meanwhile, the Italians had acquired Ju 87 Stukas in August, as it was recognized that dive-bombers were the most effective type against ships, especially if used in a co-ordinated attack by torpedo-bombers. The Italian mindset, as was the British, was that aerial torpedoes were the way to go, and the Italians proved capable and resolute. The number of torpedoes required to score a damaging hit was considered to be six to eight, although this depended on a number of factors, not least of which was the capability of the attacker to meet the exacting launch parameters, and of the

Maryland of 431 Flight; the type is usually referred to as 'Glenn Martin' in the records.

defender to spot and avoid torpedo tracks. The Italian torpedo-bomber units were something of an elite, attracting the best crews and demonstrating an elan that was often missing in other parts of the Italian military. September saw the first success for the SM.79 in its torpedo-bomber role, with the cruiser *Kent* heavily damaged on the 17th. The cruiser had been bombarding Fort Capuzzo and after the attack was taken in tow by *Nubian* and returned to Alexandria for repairs, which took until late October. The Germans, and later the Japanese, favoured dive-bombers for anti-shipping, with Ju 87s and Ju 88s being the main exponents of the art in the Mediterranean. The first outing for the Italian Stukas was against the *Illustrious* and her escort on 2 September, causing no damage, but also losing no aircraft. It was certainly a shock for the Navy and a cause for concern that this proven type was active in theatre. It would get worse.

Airfields on Rhodes were to be frequent targets for Blenheims and Wellingtons operating out of the Middle East, but the Italian air elements at Rhodes never developed into a significant threat. With Turkey neutral, the islands of Crete and Rhodes were the two main land masses on which airfields could be sited, and as such played a role in the overall strategy, while at the eastern end of the Med, the land areas of Syria and Palestine also played a part, as did Cyprus. As part of the strategy to dominate the eastern Mediterranean, Cunningham looked at the Italian-controlled territory and determined that the airfield on Rhodes might pose a threat. The Italians built a major airfield in 1938, which in the early part of the war housed SM.81s and CR.32s. A major attack was launched on 4 August, using two carriers and supporting warships. A strike force from each carrier was launched against the two main airfields, 815 and 819 from *Illustrious* attacking Calato and 813 and 824 from *Eagle* going after Maritza.

The Swordfish made their attacks with some success, but the Maritza attack was intercepted and four aircraft shot down. Although eight of the aircrew became PoWs, the other four were killed. When the Italians went looking for the ships, they were intercepted by a stopper patrol of fighters, which destroyed a number and damaged others. The attack was, overall, considered a success, in part because it demonstrated Allied control of the eastern Mediterranean. The same day that the Ju 87s were engaging the Navy, they also made their first attack on Malta, five aircraft attacking targets around Valetta harbour. It was the start of what would become regular Stuka 'visits' to Malta, and the garrison and locals soon became used to the sight and sound of the gull-winged attackers, albeit not in significant numbers, or effect, until the arrival of the Luftwaffe. Raids took place throughout the rest of September, but it was all still fairly low scale and did not affect Malta's offensive capability.

With 431 Flight now consisting of Marylands and Hurricanes, Malta and C-in-C Mediterranean had another set of eyes. The first mission was flown by Pilot Officer Foxton on 8 September, over Tripoli, and it is interesting to note that it was to the south, to the North African coast rather than to Sicily. In this direction were targets and not threats. Tripoli was the main unloading port for the supply ships from Italy and throughout the campaign was one of the main targets for recce and bombing, much of the latter by Egypt-based bombers.

Vice Admiral Malta submitted his 'situation in Malta – naval appreciation' to C-in-C Mediterranean on 12 September. 'The scale of air attacks has for some reason lightened [a pencil note in the margin said 'and the fighter and ack boys' – suggesting this is why attacks had lessened] and it has been possible to use Malta to a limited extent as an advanced base for submarines, a refuelling base for ships of the Fleet and for the refit of destroyers. There are no ships capable of offensive operations based on Malta, except for the odd submarine or destroyer which may be spending a short time at Malta. Fairly frequent air reconnaissance of Augusta and other East Sicilian ports suggest that the Italians have ceased using these ports as permanent bases for their warships. They have probably been frightened out by the successes of our Fleet Air Arm aircraft against ships in harbour. Reconnaissance of the area to the westward of Malta has been even more irregular than to the eastward. Sustained reconnaissances of this route [Cape Bon to Trapani and down Tunisian coast] will be carried out as soon as aircraft are available.'

He discussed that one reason for the low intensity of bombing – little more than harassing raids – was that: 'The hearts of the Italians are not really in the war nor are they as yet fully prepared. If they start a serious air blitzkrieg they cannot help causing severe civilian damage and many civilian casualties. The Maltese are already fairly bitter against the Italians, but if the Italians think that Malta is going to be one of the spoils of war they will not wish to alienate the population by increasing this bitterness.'

It was an interesting line of reasoning, but one that soon vanished in 1941 as civilian casualties began to mount. His view on the course of action was open: 'It has already been decided that our policy is to be as follows:

1. To refrain from local offensive action until our defensive position has been improved
2. To carry out all necessary works and to build up supplies so as to have achieved a satisfactory internal position by the end of March 1941
3. From April 1941 to operate a striking force of cruisers, destroyers and other vessels from Malta when desired by C-in-C Mediterranean.

He also saw that the enemy had three options:

1. An attempt to capture the Island by a large combined operation
2. To carry out a continuous bombardment of the Dockyard area from the air and sea with the object of destroying all facilities
3. To carry out harassing attacks on a scale he thinks sufficient to prevent us from using Malta as base.

For the next few months, it was all still very low key.

During one Italian bombing raid on 17 September, a Wellington was hit and two airmen were subsequently awarded the BEM (British Empire Medal). Joint citation to Aircraftman First Class Thomas McCann and Corporal Joseph Davis. 'During September 1940, these airmen approached a burning aircraft and succeeded in detaching Vickers guns and magazines of ammunition and removing them to a place of safety. Both displayed conspicuous gallantry in disregarding imminent personal danger from exploding ammunition and the likelihood that the petrol tanks might explode.' (AMB 2792, dated 22 January 1941).

The 17th was also notable for the first night bombing of Benghazi port by FAA Swordfish, some tasked to dive-bomb and others to drop magnetic mines. This port was, with Tripoli, to become one of the most intensively bombed targets in theatre, with the exception of Malta on the other side.

Dock workers head to a rock shelter near the port area; the ability to work for as long as possible despite air raid warnings was crucial in offloading vital supplies before the ships were attacked in harbour.

On the 18th the Air Ministry signalled HQ Middle East for an extension of attacks on port facilities at Benghazi: 'Fully realize you have other important targets, but we feel the key to the defence of Egypt is ultimately the prevention of further reinforcements reaching Libya.' (*The RAF in Maritime War, ibid*).

Wellingtons from Egypt picked up this task, the first op being flown by 70 Squadron on the night of the 19th by four aircraft that used Fuka as a forward base, and dropped 32 × 250lb bombs. On 11 October the COS memo to HQ Middle East stated: 'If Benghazi could be made unusable, any plans for large-scale Axis advance against Egypt would be seriously delayed, if not entirely dislocated. It is realized that sustained attack on Benghazi would entail all available forces in Egypt. As we view the situation from here, the latest reports of enemy intentions clearly indicate that this is the best way in which our air forces can make effective and possibly decisive contribution towards neutralizing the probable enemy land and air threat to Egypt. Simultaneously, Tobruk should be kept under harassing attack by short range aircraft so far as your resources and other commitments permit.' (*The RAF in Maritime War, ibid*).

Blenheims and Bombays joined the offensive in October, and more Wellingtons were sent to Egypt, but the details are out of the scope of this book. The main point of note is that the receiving points were part of the overall supply disruption strategy, just as much as departure ports and convoys at sea. The AOC considered that the weight of attacks on Benghazi forced the Italians to make more use of Tripoli, with a consequent major lengthening of the land route from port to front line.

An Operational Intelligence Summary for Malta was issued in October covering the period 11 June (start of Italian war) to 11 October and shows the limited nature of operations in this period of what in many ways was Malta's version of the 'Phoney War'. The report was submitted by Air Commodore Maynard, as AOC RAF Mediterranean. The total number of 'flying hours by fighters on patrol' was a mere forty-three hours and fifty minutes over the four months, and the average daily availability of fighters was 6½ aircraft and ten pilots. There were 161 air alarms in the period, comprising thirty-six day bombing, thirteen night bombing, twenty-one recce, fifteen fighter patrols, and seventy-six 'not materialized' (i.e. no aircraft turned up over Malta). The fighters made seventy-two day intercepts and two night intercepts, with the following claims:

Type	Destroyed		Unconfirmed		Damaged	
	Fighters	AA	Fighters	AA	Fighters	AA
Ju 87	2	–	1	–	–	–
CR.42	7	–	2	1	2	–
MC.200	4	–	1	–	1	1
SM.79	9	3	5	3	5	2
Totals	22	3	9	4	8	3

From 08.00 hrs. 14.9.40. to 09.55 hrs. 28.9.40. By No. 69 Squadron Luqa. No. of pages used for day..............
MALTA (G.R.) FLIGHT

Aircraft Type & No.	Crew.	duty.	Time Up.	Time down.	Remarks.	References.
Maryland I. AR. 712. 14.9.40.	Pilot Officer Foxten. Flying Officer Warburton. Sergt. Gridley.	Recce.	08.00	12.15.	Reconnaisance of Tripoli, Sicily, Pantalleria. Naval Units Seen 1 Cruiser, 3 destroyers. Photographs taken. Moderate inaccurate A.A. Fire.	
Skua. L.2911. 14.9.40.	S.Lieut.Newell. Captain Ford.	Recce.	10.00.	12.50.	Reconnaisance on Messina, Augusta, Syracuse and Catania. A few Merchant Vessels and Warships seen in each harbour.	
Maryland I. AR. 707. 18.9.40.	Sergt. Bibby. Sergt. Bastard. Sergt. Moren.	Recce.	11.50.	16.55.	Reconnaisance to Zante. Nil report.	
Maryland I. AR. 712. 18.9.40.	P.O. Devine. P.O. Warburton. Cpl. Shephard.	Recce.	14.30.	18.20.	Reconnaisance to Strevathi. Nil Report.	
Skua. L.2911. 22.9.40.	S.Lieut.Newell. Captain Ford.	Recce.	12.00.	14.25.	Reconnaisance of East Coast of Sicily. Negative Report. Very little shipping movement. Five CR.42's Seen off Taormina. No Engagement.	
Skua. L.2911. 23.9.40.	S.Lieut.Newell. P.O. Pinkerton.	Recce.	16.00.	17.30.	Reconnaisance of East Coast of Sicily to Messina. Negative Report. Chased back to base by small formation of Macchi 200's.	
Maryland I. AR. 712. 22.9.40.	P.O. Warburton. Sergt. Bastard. Sergt. Moren.	Recce.	14.20.	15.20.	Patrol to Corfu. Patrol was abandoned owing hydraulic failure and aircraft crashed on landing.	
Maryland I. AR. 707. 28.9.40.	F.Lieut. Whiteley. P.O. Warburton. Sergt. Gridley.	Recce.	05.30.	09.55.	Patrol to Greece and reconnaisance of Taranto and Brindisi harbours. Photographs taken.	

From 09.55 hrs. 28.9.40. to 23.59 hrs. 30.9.40. By No. 69 Squadron Luqa. No. of pages used for day..............
MALTA (G.R.) FLIGHT

Aircraft Type & No.	Crew.	duty.	Time Up.	Time down.	Remarks.	References.
Maryland I. AR. 705. 28.9.40.	P.O. Devine. Captain Ford. L.A.C. Levy.	Recce.	13.40.	18.30.	Patrol to Corfu and Reconnaisance of Taranto harbour. Convoy sighted 77 miles from Taranto. Two battleships, Seven Cruisers, Thirty destroyers and fifty fleet planes seen in harbour.	
Maryland I. AR. 705. 29.9.40.	P.O. Foxten. P.O. Devine. L.A.C. Levy.	Recce.	05.20.	09.40.	Reconnaisance Corfu and Ionian Sea. Nil report.	
Maryland I. AR. 707. 29.9.40.	P.O. Warburton. Sgt. Bastard. Sgt. Moren.	Recce.	13.30.	17.30.	Patrol to Corfu, Good Visibility but nil report.	
Maryland I. AR. 707. 30.9.40.	Sgt. Bibby. Sgt. Bastard. Sgt. Moren.	Recce.	05.50.	10.10.	Patrol to Zante. Enemy fleet, consisting of Nine Cruisers, 18 destroyers sighted and reported by W-T.	
Maryland I. AR. 707. 30.9.40.	F.Lieut. Whiteley. Capt. Ford. Sgt. Gridley.	Recce.	13.20.	17.45.	Reconnaisance to Albania. Two battleships, Three Cruisers, sighted South of Cape Collonne. Shadowed for One hour fourty minutes.	

431 Flight operations September 1940. From the middle of the month the Flight was active most days with at least one sortie. The Skua was generally flown by Sub-Lieutenant Newell and based on this period he seems to have attracted more Italian fighter interest! The regular reporting of shipping in ports was crucial for naval planning and for air strikes.

431 Flight record parts 1–4 of 15 September 1940 showing a Maryland reconnaissance mission and a Skua reconnaissance mission.

431 Flight record parts 5–8 showing aircraft and personnel strength. Part 5 shows three Marylands (Glenn Martins), of which two were serviceable, and one Skua. The total strength of the unit was a mere twenty-one personnel!

'Own casualties' were recorded as two pilots killed and one severely wounded in action, three aircraft written off by enemy action (two Hurricanes and one Gladiator) in the air, and six aircraft written off on the ground. The dockyards were the most frequent target (sixteen attacks), followed by Luqa (thirteen) and Hal Far (twelve), with single-figure attacks on Kalafrana, Ta Kali, and ships around Malta. Offensive action was restricted to the Swordfish of 830 Squadron FAA, but there were only five such missions, and two of those were with no result:

- Augusta oil refinery and tanks, 5 Swordfish, small fire and brown smoke in vicinity of target
- Catania airfield, 9 Swordfish, 2 hangars hit and 4 fires started
- Enemy ships, 9 Swordfish, target not found
- Enemy ships, 8 Swordfish, target not found
- Augusta harbour shipping, 9 Swordfish, low bombing and torpedo, results not known.

These inconclusive attacks did cost three Swordfish and '2 Naval Officers and 2 Naval Airmen missing, believed PoWs.'

Luqa was the main bomber and offensive airfield for the RAF; location and layout plan.

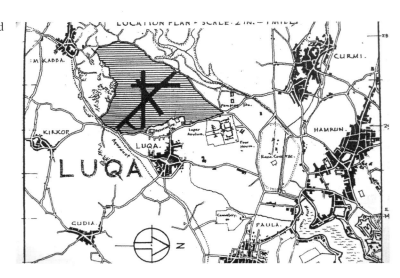

The major operations from Malta were reconnaissance, with more than 1,320 hours flown on local sorties (thirty-one anti-submarine and three search) and extended reconnaissance (104 visual for shipping, seven photographic, two search, two leaflet dropping, and one to deposit a French officer on the Tunisian coast … one wonders what the last one was all about!) The recce sorties were flown by Sunderlands (228 and 230 Squadrons), Swordfish (830 Sqn FAA and 3 AACU), and Marylands (431 Flight). Malta also received and passed on thirty Blenheims, eleven Wellingtons and three Hurricanes.

Despite the focus on reconnaissance, the Navy remained unhappy with the coverage, although some senior RAF officers saw this more as a 'turf war' about who controlled assets. The Chief of the Naval Staff (CONS) wrote: 'The Admiralty feel that there is a reasonable chance that we could so defend Malta as to make it usable as a Fleet base, and the advantages of getting the Fleet back there are so enormous that they consider an experiment must be tried … the first requirement is to get adequate air reconnaissance established so that we can establish the facts as to where Italian shipping is moving.' (Memo dated 8 Oct 1940).

The CONS also urged provision of 112 heavy and 100 light AA guns, as well as 6 fighter squadrons. On the 14th, CAS outlined proposals to increase the existing Hurricane flight to sixteen IE aircraft and the 'Glenn Martin unit' to seven IE plus five IR. The prime minister also weighed in and rated the reinforcement of Malta as the first urgency. This showed determination all round, and to some extent helps explain the efforts (and cost) to which the Navy went in supplying Malta. However, it was still, for now, a very weak establishment on the island.

The Italians launched a number of attacks, primarily by SM.79s. The bombers achieved no results, but some near misses, and suffered heavily at the hands of the patrolling Fulmars. There was concern that the Italian fleet might join in, and the Marylands were tasked to recce ports and likely approach vectors, but turned up nothing of interest. 'Enemy air activity over Malta during the latter half of October was confined to two fighter patrols, one of eight CR.42s, the other of 8 Macchi 200s. Our fighters, which shot down one Macchi and damaged another, were still under orders to attack only straggling enemy fighters as it was expected that bomber formations would follow up.' (Intelligence Summary).

The Navy was establishing a reputation for night action, something the Italians tried to avoid as they had no radar, and on the night of 11 October the cruiser *Ajax* came across a number of

Italian destroyers, which she engaged promptly. Two were sunk, one damaged, and two escaped. The following day a Sunderland spotted the damaged *Artigliere* in tow, reported the position and shadowed the ships. The cruiser *York* was duly homed in, by which time the towing destroyer had sped off. The cruiser dropped rafts for the Italian crew and sank the *Artigliere*. Sunderlands subsequently homed an Italian hospital ship to the position of the rafts. It was not all one-way traffic and in a moonlight attack on the 14th, Italian torpedo-bombers damaged the cruiser *Liverpool*, which turned out to be the first of two occasions on which the cruiser was hit by torpedoes from the air. On 12 October, Flight Lieutenant McCall (Sunderland L2164) having been diverted from his patrol to search for a Fairey Fulmar downed by a Cant, located the sinking aircraft and landed to pick up three survivors. The FAA crew was given a hot meal and a change of clothes, the Sunderland completed its patrol and then landed at Kalafrana Bay.

If it seemed as if the war in the Mediterranean had settled into something of a pattern that caused no real concern for the Allies, the situation changed at the end of October with Mussolini's decision to invade Greece. The ramifications of this, from Allied involvement and the arrival of German forces, and its relationship to the overall strategic situation would not be clear for some months, but without doubt it was a turning point. The Italians invaded Greece on 28 October but the operation went badly from the start and ended with their withdrawal in mid-November. The Greek escapade was not yet over and in 1941 would become a major strategic element in the Mediterranean war.

With Churchill still pressing for more action against the Italians, and with Cunningham ever eager to pursue such a strategy, the increased intelligence provided by the reconnaissance flights, and the increase in carrier-based aircraft capability, led to one of the most daring operations of the Second World War, the attack on the Italian Navy in Taranto harbour. Throughout late October, 431 Flight had been making regular runs over the harbour to build up an accurate picture of defences and shipping layouts. They were helped to some extent by the fact that the Italian Navy was fairly inactive at this period. One of the most famous missions, and one that helped define Warburton's reputation, was that of 30 October. The weather was poor but he was determined to obtain his pictures, and so went in at very low level. The oblique photos he took proved invaluable in determining details of the way the ships were moored and protected, something that was difficult to determine from the usual high-level images. He was also able to describe the type and accuracy of the anti-aircraft fire! On the return flight he came across an Italian seaplane and shot it down. However, Group Captain Whiteley's article pointed out that 'the ten or twelve aircrew of 431 Flight took their turn on operations – and most were involved in the PR watch on Taranto September/October; equally deserving of mention were Terry Foxton, John Gridley, Frank Bastard, Paddy Moren, and Paddy Devine.'

In early October the Air Ministry stated that strength of 431 Flight was being increased to '7 plus 5. Seven Glen Martins are now being prepared for delivery by air from the UK.' (signal dated 12 October). The same signal also stated that '12 Hurricanes will be flown off from carrier leaving UK about November 1 to bring 261 Squadron to 16 plus 8; stores spares and personnel will be shipped simultaneously.'

On 1 November, Flight Lieutenant Ware (Sunderland L5806) was attacked by two Italian fighters, two of his crew being wounded. 'Mattresses and clothing in the aircraft were set on fire, burning articles were thrown out of the rear door. Flame floats and practice bombs were set off by explosive bullets and caused the aircraft to fill with smoke. The rear turret was put partially out of action by having the starboard control handle shot away. The Sunderland was badly holed below the waterline and was taken up the slip immediately on return to Kalafrana.' (228 Squadron ORB).

Ware was awarded the DFC and one of his crew, Leading Aircraftman R. Barton, the DFM; neither had a specific citation. (AMB 2986 dated 12 February 1941). It is always surprising and, as a historian, disappointing when no citations are given for gallantry awards. It is surprising because it seems fairly arbitrary and you would have thought that the write-up for the award, to have it granted, would have included wording suitable for a citation. In some cases an individual may have finished up with two or three awards, none with a citation.

Pilots of 261 Squadron in relaxed mode – while they can.

The Wellington Flight was tasked to attack Naples on 3 November but two aircraft crashed on take-off, R1094 (Sergeant P. Forrester and crew) and T2743 (Sergeant Raymond Lewin and crew). There was only one survivor of the first crash, but for T2743, all except one survived, injured, and Sergeant Lewin was awarded the George Cross, the citation reading: 'In November 1940, Sergeant Lewin was the captain of an aircraft on a night bombing mission against Italy. Shortly after take-off the aircraft began to sink and crashed into a hillside where it burst into flames. Sergeant Lewin extricated himself and saw three of his crew of four climbing out of the escape hatch. He ordered them to run clear. He then ran round the blazing wing in which full petrol tanks were burning and crawled under it to rescue his injured second pilot. Despite his own injuries – a cracked kneecap and severe contusions on the face and legs – he dragged and carried the pilot some 40 yards from the aircraft to a hole in the ground, where he lay on him just as the bombs exploded. This superbly gallant deed was performed in the dark and under most difficult conditions and in the certain knowledge that the bombs and petrol tanks would explode.' (AMB 3226). During the first eleven days of the month, twenty Wellington sorties were flown from Malta, mainly to Italy.

Cunningham had set a date of 11 November for his planned attack on Taranto and while his strike force prepared and planned, the Marylands continued to provide intelligence. Warburton seemed to be specializing in taking pictures of Taranto, and in the ten days of the month flew a number of such sorties, often having to go in low because of weather, and on at least two occasions being pursued by fighters. His last sortie before the raid confirmed the presence of six battleships, fourteen cruisers and twenty-seven destroyers, a very attractive target indeed. Other than the reconnaissance by RAF aircraft, the Taranto raid was a Navy affair, albeit delivered from the air by the FAA. The raid has had many a published account in its own right, so we will only cover it briefly here, as it did play a significant role in the overall Mediterranean campaign.

Wellingtons transited through Malta en route to the Middle East but also became part of the based strike force, with the Wellington Flight and detachments from Bomber Command and the Middle East.

Cunningham was on board *Warspite* as his flagship, but the key ship was the carrier *Illustrious*. The plan was essentially quite simple, two waves of attackers, the first to bomb and dive-bomb the Mar Piccolo, the inner harbour where most of the cruisers and destroyers were, and the torpedo force to attack the battleships in the Mar Grande, the larger outer harbour. Launching from 170 miles away, the first attackers reached the target under moon conditions around 11 pm. The Swordfish crews performed superbly and the attack was a resounding success, with only two of the twenty-two attackers failing to return.

The results were reviewed the following day with a post-attack reconnaissance by a Maryland, this time flown by the CO and not Adrian Warburton. The initial assessment suggested three battleships sunk or severely damaged, and a cruiser and two destroyers damaged. Considering the scale of the attack this was an excellent result, and had only cost two of the attacking Swordfish. The loss of capital ships to the Italian fleet was high (50 per cent of the battleships present) but of more importance to the overall campaign was that the Italians withdrew the battle fleet from this vulnerable southern port to the perceived safety of Naples. Furthermore, it was yet another blow to their confidence and reinforced the Royal Navy's dominance. Cunningham wrote to Maynard: 'I hasten to write you a line to thank you for the most valuable reconnaissance work carried out by your squadrons, without which the successful attack on Taranto would have been impossible. I well know what long monotonous flying time they have had to put in, and I am very grateful to them.'

Malta PR shot of Taranto 10 November 1940.

Not long after, a surface attack added to the Navy's laurels by sinking three of four merchant ships in a convoy in the Straits of Otranto, heading to Brindisi. The Navy still marks Taranto Day with celebrations, and it was always worth (as an RAF officer) trying to get an invite to one of the Mess parties!

Wellingtons of 37 Squadron arrived overnight on the 12th, with four aircraft attacking Taranto the following night. More of the squadron's aircraft arrived in Malta, but it was only a temporary arrangement as they were destined

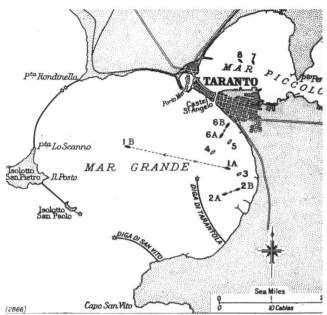

Taranto after the attack; plan shows ships assessed as damaged and air photo shows damaged ships 7 and 8 (from plan).

for Egypt. Wellington R3179 (Sergeant B.W. Green) of 37 Squadron was lost of the night of the 16th/17th, failing to return from a mission to Durazzo. This target, now in Albania, was attacked as part of the RAF's support of the Greece operation, and Malta-based aircraft flew a number of bombing missions to support this ill-fated campaign.

Malta had been anticipating an increase in attacks, in part in response to the greater threat it was now posing, and with the Italians under pressure from their German allies to take decisive action. 'At the beginning of November expectations proved correct when 9 Macchi 200s came over, followed after a short interval by a formation of' 9 S.79s, escorted by 9 C.R.42s which high level bombed the Dockyard and Luqa aerodrome. Our fighters shot down a Macchi 200, an S.79, and damaged two CR.42s, whereupon the enemy discontinued these tactics. In mid-November the enemy carried out low flying machine gun attacks with C.R.42s. On two consecutive days a single CR.42 dived out of' low clouds to machine gun Sunderlands moored in Marsaxlokk Bay. A few days later 2 CR.42s machine-gunned Swordfish on Hal Far aerodrome, damaging several. The most successful planned attack of 'this kind was on November 24th when 6 CR.42's came in at dusk and machine gunned, from a very low altitude, Wellingtons dispersed round Luqa aerodrome, destroying one and damaging several. This form of attack was disturbingly successful and the enemy were suffering no losses mainly because our Hurricanes were waiting high up to catch the bombers which usually came over at 15,000 feet or higher. Consequently, it was decided that when raiders were approaching, Hurricanes would go high for the bombers and Gladiators remain lower to deal with the low flying attackers.' (Intelligence Summary).

The attempted air reinforcement of mid-November was a failure when only four of the twelve Hurricanes flown off *Argus* reached Malta in Operation White. On 14 November, as part of the exchange of signals ahead of this reinforcement, the Air Ministry had signalled to AOC ME: 'Anticipate that 12 Hurricanes will be flown into Malta on or about November 16th. You have complete freedom to use these aircraft as you think best and to fly all or part to Middle East should you think the situation demands. HM Government are of the opinion that we must be prepared to take risks at Malta for the time being if this is necessary to ensure success of your intended operation.'

So it was clear that aircraft flown into Malta from these reinforcement routes were not automatically *for* Malta, and indeed in this case, with major land operations in the Western Desert scheduled, they might all move right on through, although the signal did state that the Hurricanes would not have long-range tanks, and only three such tanks were available in Malta.

The operation was hit by a combination of poor weather and other factors; the first flight hit problems and two aircraft ran out of fuel, their pilots having to bail out. The first to do it, Sergeant Spyer, was fortunate that the escorting Sunderland of 228 Squadron was able to land and pick him out of the sea; the second pilot, Sergeant Cunningham, was never found. The remaining four aircraft made it to Malta, along with their accompanying Skua, landing at 0825.

'Six Hurricanes and one Skua of second formation missing and must be presumed lost. Search by Sunderlands and other aircraft have so far failed to locate any survivors of second formation.' (signal 17 Nov). A signal the following day provided more information: 'Flying times for Hurricanes which arrived were between 3 hours 5 minutes and 3 hours 10 minutes and petrol left was 2, 3, 4 and 12 gallons for the 4 aircraft.'

So, in essence, all were about to run out of fuel, whereas the average left on the previous reinforcement flight had been 20 gallons 'which gave average margin of 35 minutes further flying at low altitude.' It was then suggested that the low-level flying by inexperienced pilots led to higher fuel consumptions, and the fact that aircraft were launched too far away led to the problem. Another

Wing Commander Adrian Warburton DSO* DFC**

Adrian Warburton was commissioned into the RAF in 1939 and on completion of pilot training joined Coastal Command, ending up with 22 Squadron at North Coates. He was selected by 'Titch' Whiteley to be one of the crews to take three new Marylands to Malta, albeit acting as an observer and not a pilot. However, he was soon back in the pilot's seat and, despite continued 'challenges' over his take-off style, his performance in the air soon marked him as exceptional.

Sergeant Paddy Moren was the usual wireless operator/air gunner flying with Adrian Warburton, and he later recalled: 'I flew over a hundred operations and participated in shooting down ten enemy aircraft with Adrian Warburton. When the siege of Malta was at its height and things were at their worst, Warburton's exploits made him, I think, a living legend. His enthusiasm for any task and his ability to complete the impossible were unparalleled. On one occasion we were asked to photograph the Tripoli–Benghazi road – or a section of it – and it was important that photographic overage of the entire road be made available. Warby was briefed to tackle it in a series of five different trips. It was typical of the man that we did the whole job on one operational trip, notwithstanding the fact that we were chased out to sea by enemy fighters on at least four occasions. His persistence and skill were backed by his sheer unorthodoxy ... a complete individualist with both courage and flair.'

By February 1943 he was a squadron leader and took over 683 Squadron; late in 1943 he was given command of a recce wing. By early 1944 he was a highly decorated wing commander and was assigned to the USAAF 7th PRG. Flying an F-5B (recce variant of the P-38 Lightning) on 12 April 1944, he failed to return from a mission over Germany.

DFC: 'This officer has carried out numerous long distance reconnaissance flights and has taken part in night air combats. In October, 1940, he destroyed an aircraft and again, in December, he shot down an enemy bomber in flames. Flying Officer Warburton has at all times displayed a fine sense of devotion to duty.' (AMB 2935 dated 5 Feb 1941)

DFC: 'This officer is a most determined and skilful pilot and has carried out 125 operational missions. Flying Officer Warburton has never failed to complete the missions be has undertaken, and in the actions fought he has destroyed at least three hostile aircraft in combat and another three on the ground.' (AMB 4933 dated 3Sep 1941)*

*DFC**: 'Since August, 1942, this officer has completed numerous operational photographic sorties, many of them at low altitudes and often in the face of opposition from enemy fighters. His work has been of the utmost value. In October. 1942, his gallantry was well illustrated when be directed an enemy destroyer to a dinghy in which were the crew of one of our aircraft. which had been shot down. Although he was fired upon by the destroyer and engaged by Italian aircraft, he remained over the area until he observed that the drifting crew were picked up by the destroyer.' (AMB 8416 dated 31Oct 1941)*

DSO: (AMB 6511 dated 20 Mar 1942)

DSO: (AMB 11066 dated 5 Aug 1943)*

Adrian Warburton was without doubt one of the 'characters' of Malta; his reconnaissance operations with 69 Squadron became legendary.

signal commented: 'To summarize this calamity it appears that margins of safety in distance to be flown or for navigational errors unreasonably small, reducing enterprise to most hazardous undertaking.'

Perhaps the most unfortunate loss in November (20th) was the 214 Squadron Wellington that was carrying the new Deputy AOC Middle East, Air Marshal O.T. Boyd, from Stradishall to Egypt, via Malta. The aircraft force-landed at Comiso and the crew and passengers were taken prisoner.

The British needed to run a fast convoy via the Mediterranean rather than round the Cape and through the Suez Canal, to provide the land commander in Egypt, General Wavell, with armour and equipment for his planned offensive. Operation Collar sailed in late November with three supply ships and a substantial naval escort from the west, with the convoy from Gibraltar and including the carrier *Ark Royal*, and from the east, battleships and cruisers from Alexandria. In addition to the land–based aircraft threat, the Italian Navy had also sailed in some numbers.

Up to the end of 1940 the Italians had flown around 7,410 sorties against Malta, dropping 550 tons of bombs and losing between 30 and 40 aircraft. They claimed to have destroyed 66 RAF aircraft, although the actual number was far less. However, the important point was that it was not working: Malta was getting stronger not weaker and was far from neutralized.

The Intelligence Summary for the period 11 October 1940 to 10 February 1941 spent some time discussing the RDF (radar) cover that Malta had in late 1940. 'Until December, the Island was protected solely by 241 and 242 AMES [Air Ministry Experimental Stations] working alternately and receiving some assistance from one GL [gun-laying] set which came on the air when tracks were picked up by the AMES. [In the SD161 Location of Units they are located at Ta Salvatur and are referred to as 241 and 242 TRU, with three AMES stations and a DF Station.] Although sited within 300 yards of each other they have slight but important differences in performance resulting in varying gaps in the RDF screen. Formations flying 20,000ft were normally detected at 65–75 miles. On 241 AMES the raids faded at 35–28 miles but this caused no serious operational drawback. On 242 AMES, however, the fading area was between 50–39 miles, a most inconvenient distance since it covered the period during which fighters had to be flown off if interceptions were to be made.'

Malta rural scene; during the early part of the siege with weak Italian attacks, life on Malta did not change a great deal.

At this period, therefore, Malta was not well served with radar coverage, although what was in place was crucial. Over the next few months there are various signals and reports that comment both on the lack of cover and the lack of expertise of the controllers acting on the information.

Attempts to fill in the radar gaps included the first COL (Chain Overseas Low) commencing operation on 28 December (and joined by another in January and another in February), although 'these stations are able to plot aircraft at their extreme range of 70 miles, the operational height of enemy aircraft has been such that they have provided only a little extra coverage over No. 241 and 242 AMES.' (Appendix D to Malta Operational Intelligence Summary Oct 1940–Feb 1941). The report also stated that the Italian tactics were poor in as much as they were easy to pick up and track on radar, a situation that changed the following month with the arrival of the Luftwaffe.

'This policy [when raiders were approaching, Hurricanes would go high for the bombers and Gladiators remain lower to deal with the low flying attackers] was justified when on 9 January twelve Macchi 200s came over, of which six machine gunned Luqa and six stayed above to protect them. The Macchis did not push home their attack as the CR.42s had done, and our fighters shot down four of them, A.A. claiming a fifth. Up to January there were four other day bombing raids by S.79s always escorted by strong fighter formations. Objectives were Dockyard, ships entering harbour, Luqa, and a weak attempt at Ta Kali. Very little damage resulted from any of these raids· which were always from a height of above 15,000 feet.

'As a general rule a large fighter patrol consisting of any number up to 15 CR.42s or Macchi 200s came over on days following an enemy day bombing raid. These patrols probably served the dual purpose of reconnaissance combined with an offensive patrol in an endeavour to weaken our fighter defence. Our fighters frequently scored successes and shot down a mixed bag of S.79s, C.R.42s, and Macchi 200s.

'Night raids up to mid-January consisted, on four occasions, of a maximum of four S.79s coming in singly on moonlight nights and dropping bombs from about 12,000 feet on various parts of the Island and sometimes in the sea with no fixed objective. On the night of December 19th an S.79 was shot down in flames by a Hurricane.' (Intelligence Summary).

On 4 December, AOC Malta sent a signal concerning bombing ops from Malta. 'Would be glad to have more settled policy for bombing operations from Malta. [I] requested some identity for the

Malta radar site (Il Qurtin in post-war period); whilst radar was not a 'battle winner' as it had been in the Battle of Britain, it did play a role in the air battle – once there were enough fighters to take advantage of the, albeit short, warning (Sicily is very close). This shot also demonstrates the rugged nature of Malta that would have presented major problems for a sea assault.

Wellington Unit now here. Necessity for this more apparent every day since personnel have feelings of considerable uncertainty as to their future. The Unit has now operated here for a month. It has no Commanding Officer and one of the Flight Commanders is a Squadron Leader belonging to 37 Squadron who should rejoin his unit when further Wellingtons arrive here to release that Squadron's remaining aircraft to Middle East. In spite of commendable efforts by individuals, Wellington Unit lacks cohesion and drive while lack of Squadron spirit is marked and in my view very detrimental to success of operations.'

According to some records, the 37 Squadron basing ended on 1 December, with the unit moving to Fayid, although it would continue to detach aircraft to Malta. The Wellington Unit duly became 148 Squadron in December 1940, under the command of Squadron Leader Foss, becoming the based unit until April 1941.

The second part of the AOC's signal concerned the Navy's concerns over air attacks, and the lack of fighters. 'He [C-in-C Med] is further opposed in principle to bombing attacks [of] local targets Sicily until retaliatory action which may be directed against dockyard can be better resisted. Additional guns now reaching Malta but main defence undoubtedly best provided by fighter aircraft. Owing unfortunate failure to reinforce 261 Squadron, fighter effort is meagre though so far more than held its own and morale is high. Position of 261 Squadron likely become difficult shortly. Squadron is incomplete, can never be released, operates by night as well as by day. Some pilots tiring after 6-months work and both rest and recreation difficult to arrange. Can compete for present but immediate future must be considered.' (signal AOC Malta to Air Ministry dated 4 Dec 1941).

An Italian report of May 1941 summarized what they classified as the First Period of operations against Malta – June 1940 to 10 January 1941. 'At the outbreak of hostilities with Italy, Malta was not given any clearly defined duties. The enemy was probably waiting for the development of operations in order to use the Island to the best advantage. It was difficult to ascertain the strength of the air force because of camouflage and concealment. From the outbreak of hostilities until the 10th Jan 1941, reconnaissance revealed that there were between 10 and 35 aircraft on Malta, with a daily average of 10 bombers, 12 fighters and 3 various types.' ('Air and Naval Bases on Malta Situation Report' May 1942 translated by AHB as VII/43); a copy of this report can be downloaded from the Aviation History Research Centre website.

'From chance remarks dropped by prisoners of war there are indications that a full scale attack employing German troops on Malta may be contemplated in the immediate future.' This signal of 3 January elicited an immediate response: 'Although full-scale attack on Malta may be contemplated, there is little likelihood that it is planned in the near future. There is no evidence to confirm this report and it is reasonable to assume that we shall obtain some weeks' warning before an attack of this nature. The necessary German troops are not available in Italy and it is not considered that they can be made available until early in March.' (signal C-in-C Mediterranean 4 January).

By early December General Wavell was ready to launch his offensive, and part of the RAF's task was to prevent supplies reaching the Italians. On 2 December, Operation X was put into effect, the intention being to intercept fast Italian convoys running from Italy to Benghazi. The role of 228 Squadron's Sunderlands was to locate these convoys 'with the aid of moonlight and ASV. On the captain's discretion the convoy could then be attacked, but a special force of FAA torpedo-bombers was held at readiness for such attacks. The Sunderland carried four SAP and four A/S bombs to drop in sticks of four – A/S, SAP, SAP, A/S.' (228 Squadron ORB, December 1940).

On 9 December, Wavell launched his offensive, Operation Compass, and the Italians were soon falling back. Sidi Barrani was captured on the 10th, providing the first of many new airfields for

Allied aircraft to support both the land offensive and the supply war at sea. By the 16th the Italians had been expelled from Egypt and Sollum had been taken. And so it continued it early 1941, with Tobruk falling on 22 January, Derna on the 30th, and Benghazi on 6 February. The upside of this was that airfields were denied the enemy and made available to the Allies, the downside was that Allied supply lines became longer and more vulnerable, while those of the Axis shortened, with Tripoli now the main offload point. The ME commanders' conference in late December recognized that: 'Air attack by RAF and FAA on merchant shipping and warships in enemy ports in Italy and Libya is producing good results but should be augmented by sinking ships in passage and at assembly ports. Reliable reconnaissance reports of movements of enemy warships would provide greater security for passage of our warships and convoys through the Mediterranean and at the same time provide the opportunity for attacking them by sea and air.'

The requests for a TBGR squadron had still not been met, but 1941 was to bring Blenheims of 2 Group to Malta as part of an intensified 'attack them at sea' strategy.

Chapter 3

Luftwaffe Round One: January 1941 to May 1941

A Fuhrer Directive of January 1941 addressed the need to provide assistance to the Italians: 'The situation in the Mediterranean area, where England is using superior forces against our Allies, renders German assistance necessary for strategical, political and psychological reasons.' Among the orders to support this: 'The X Flieger Korps will retain Sicily as an operational base. Its most important task is to attack English naval forces and sea routes between the Western and Eastern Mediterranean.' The result was the deployment of Fliegerkorps X to Sicily, taking up residence at Catania, Gerbini, Trapani, Comiso and Gela. Under the command of Hans Geisler, they were given four interrelated tasks:

- Mount an air offensive against Malta
- Provide air support for Italian land operations in North Africa
- Secure transport routes for German forces to Tripoli
- Attack allied reinforcement lines, including the Suez Canal.

'At the beginning of January, Intelligence showed the movement of German aircraft and crews into Italy and Sicily. On January 9th, nine Ju.87s escorted by nine C.R.42s dive bombed ships anchored in Marsaxlokk Bay. This attack was carried out with about the same determination as dive bombing already experienced by Malta in earlier months. For this reason, it may be supposed that these were not flown by Germans but by Italians who are known to have operated Ju.87s from Pantelleria.' (Intelligence Summary).

The Italians operated the Ju 87 Stuka – and a number ended up in RAF markings; operating one like this in mixed markings was very brave as a 'shoot first' policy would certainly have applied against this very distinctive bomber.

The first major interference by the Luftwaffe was against an inbound convoy on 10 January, with German dive-bombers once again proving effective. The fleet had sailed from Alexandria on the 7th to head close to Malta and pick up and escort a convoy (Excess) from Gibraltar. As was usual now, the carrier *Illustrious* was part of the fleet and she kept a number of Fulmar fighters over the fleet whenever there was a threat of air attack. In the early afternoon two Italian torpedo-bombers flew in low to attack, causing no damage but causing the Fulmars to dive down from their cover position. Shortly afterwards, and with the fighters now down low, the main attack formation arrived. The Navy was about to be introduced to effective dive-bombing. Not for the last time, a co-ordinated low and high attack had dragged covering fighters away – and the vulnerable Stukas would not have to face fighter attack. Operating out of

The Battle area; this map clearly shows how Malta was surrounded by enemy locations, especially when the Axis forces controlled North Africa to Tripoli and beyond. It also shows how well placed Malta was to strike at sea communication between Italy and North Africa.

Trapani, Sicily, some forty Stukas of II./StG 2 and I./StG 1 arrived over the convoy at 12,000ft and dived down to 2,000ft in their attacks, focusing on the carrier HMS *Illustrious.*

Desperate attempts to launch more fighters proved futile and, despite an intense AA barrage, the dive-bombers scored at least six hits on the carrier in as many minutes. The fact that the carrier deck was armoured, that the Stuka's bombs were relatively small, and that the fire-fighting and damage control on *Illustrious* was very efficient meant she was crippled but did not sink. The following day the Stukas were back, focusing on the elements of the convoy that had turned back

HSL107 was one of a number of rescue launches operating from Malta and had an excellent record of picking up downed aircrew. (*Allied and Axis*)

towards Gibraltar, with the cruiser *Southampton* being sunk. Further attacks were made before the carrier made it to Valetta harbour in Malta, having lost 126 of her crew killed. Despite being in harbour, *Illustrious* was to become the main target for renewed attacks on Malta itself. The defences responded as best they could and eventually the carrier was able to escape and make its way to Alexandria. However, the '*Illustrious* Blitz' was followed by an intense campaign against Malta's airfields and harbour facilities. One of the most important ships to dock safely was the *Essex*, as among the cargo were twelve crated Hurricanes.

On 10 January, 431 Flight was raised to squadron status, as 69 (GR) Squadron, under Squadron Leader Whiteley; this unit was to have a long association with wartime Malta, operating a variety of types up to its final departure in early 1944. One of the 'new' pilots to join 69 Squadron was George Burges, moving from 261 Squadron and his career as a fighter pilot.

Reconnaissance reports suggested there were more than 250 German aircraft on Sicilian airfields by 12 January; a tempting target for the bombers. On the 12/13 January mission to Catania, two Wellingtons of 148 Squadron were lost, one over the target (T2874, Pilot Officer G. Noble) and one (T2892, Flying Officer A. Osborn) damaged and having to ditch some 140 miles from Malta, close to the trawler *Jade;* the crew were picked up High Speed Launch (HSL) *107*. This was the second rescue recorded by *107*, of the Marine Craft Unit, the first having taken place on 18 November 1940. The records showed all five crew were picked up alive; however, two subsequently died of their injuries.

'The 16th January left us in no doubt about the arrival of Germans in Sicily. From 16th to 19th January, determined dive bombing attacks were made on the Dockyard, Luqa, and Hal Far aerodrome. In the Dockyard the already damaged 'Illustrious' received a direct hit, as also did the 'Essex'. At Luqa and Hal Far considerable damage was done to aircraft, hangars and Camp buildings. The raids were carried out by large formations of Ju.88s and Ju.87s escorted, but little protected, by CR.42s. Some of the dive bombers came down to 500 feet and showed complete recklessness, but attacks became progressively less determined as enemy losses grew. Our fighters and A.A., however, took their toll and in four days accounted for a total of 40 confirmed, 5 more unconfirmed, and a further 12 damaged, which consisted of mostly Ju.88s and Ju.87s, some CR.42s and one Cant Z.506 which was probably engaged in searching for missing aircraft between Malta and Sicily.' (Intelligence Summary).

Despite the raids since the carrier arrived, *Illustrious* was considered fit enough to sail on 23 January, and she arrived at Alexandria two days later. The *Illustrious* Blitz was over; it had caused heavy damage and loss of civilian lives in the areas around the harbour, but it had also shown the weight of firepower from the AA batteries and the fact that, with enough Hurricanes in play, the Ju 87s were as vulnerable as ever.

The pilots of 261 Squadron had been kept busy in January, and Flight Lieutenant J.A.F. MacLachlan was awarded a bar to the DFC he had won in 1940: 'During intensive operations one day in January, 1941, this officer destroyed four and possibly five enemy aircraft. Ten days previously he destroyed two enemy aircraft one of which he had pursued for many miles out to sea. Flight Lieutenant MacLachlan has set a fine example of courage, initiative and leadership.' (AMB 2935 dated 5 February 1941). The destruction of four in one day was on the 19th.

A report entitled 'Analysis of destruction of enemy aircraft in low flying attacks on Malta 16 Jan–31 Mar 1941' makes interesting reading as it 'is chiefly concerned with the effectiveness of anti-aircraft fire', a subject that is often glossed over in the defence of Malta. It states that 'the main attacks were made by concentrated dive-bombing against one objective at a time, for which purpose up to 100 aircraft were employed. The first attack took place on 16 January in a large-scale dive-bombing attack on the Dockyard, when HMS illustrious was the main target. A prepared geographical barrage at a height of 2,000/2,500 feet was put into operation by 38 Heavy AA guns and proved a decided success, this being the first opportunity for the employment of such a barrage since the commencement of operations against Malta.' The heavy AA guns and the lighter Bofors guns were positioned around all key targets and were used primarily for 'geographical barrages' or 'predicted barrages'. The report provides additional detail and statistics, which are covered later.

The effectiveness of the AA defences was also covered in the Operational Intelligence Summary: 'The advent of the German Air Force to Sicily has increased the difficulties of the Anti-Aircraft defences in Malta to a considerable degree. Air attacks have increased, both in number and intensity, while the changed tactics of the enemy have necessitated the introduction of various additional counter-measures.' This involved the use of geographical and predicted barrages, the latter being first used on the night of 16/17 'with successful results, the aircraft engaged retiring forthwith.' The geographic barrages were designed to combat dive-bombing and were co-ordinated with fighters to avoid errors. They were initially established over six target areas: the airfields at Luqa, Hal Far and Ta Kali, along with Grand Harbour and the dockyard, Kalafrana and Merse Scirocco. 'They have

261 Squadron Hurricanes at Ta Kali, early 1941.

Anti-aircraft battery overlooking Grand Harbour; the heavy and light AA installations were a key part of Malta's defences.

already proved their usefulness, that over Grand Harbour having been particularly effective during the dive-bombing attacks on 16th, 18th and 19th January.'

Meanwhile, as well as the attacks, the weather in January 1941 was also causing trouble for the Sunderlands of 228 Squadron operating out of Malta. The danger from big swells was such that a skeleton crew of one pilot, one rigger and one wireless operator slept on each aircraft. On 21 January, two aircraft were moved to the more sheltered waters of St Paul's Bay. Operations against Italian merchant ships and warships remained a top priority into 1941. In its record for 26 January the squadron noted: 'Modified C3 patrol [Flight Lieutenant Glover, L5807], sighted one small MV and seven self-propelled barges just east of Kerkennah [Gulf of Gabes, Tunisia]. Reported to base and shadowed for two hours. No striking force sent out and Sunderland was ordered to continue patrol, but nothing sighted. Until the position has been clarified by the Admiralty it was laid down that aircraft may not attack either unescorted merchant ships or unescorted merchant convoys as this infringes International Law. Any ship within 30 miles of any Italian territory in the Mediterranean may however be sunk on sight. During this patrol one Cant 501 was observed to be shadowing the Sunderland but when chased by the latter it made off towards Tripoli first jettisoning two or three bombs.'

Groundcrew of 261 Sqn pose with a Hurricane at Ta Kali, early 1941, wearing standard RAF uniform as it is still the winter!

The following day the Modified C3 patrol flown by Flying Officer Lamond (T9048) was more productive: 'Early in the patrol one Italian MV sighted and reported to base, ordered to continue patrol. Sighted aircraft, identified as Ju.52. Sighted one EV and two MV north-east of Kerkennah Bank on southerly course. Reported them to base and shadowed for three hours. ASF of seven Swordfish, escorted by two Fulmars, then arrived and carried out attack. One MV sunk and one hit. Followed ASF back to base. One Swordfish having petrol trouble asked for Sunderland to escort but Sunderland also had engine trouble and had to return to St Paul's Bay. Message from Admiralty: "The combined RAF and Naval Aircraft Operations which resulted in successful attack on the convoy at a distance of 160 miles from Malta was well planned and executed. Those concerned are to be congratulated. This provides an excellent illustration of the correct employment of air search and striking forces."'

This was one of the first successes for the recce-attack concept, the attack part comprising Swordfish of 806 and 830 Squadrons. The MV that was sunk was the German 3,950-ton *Inigo*. This basic tactical concept of recce to find targets and then calling in a strike force was the principle of most successful anti-shipping operations over the next two years. February also brought an extension of the 'sink at sight' policy to the central Mediterranean, which was also extended to the eastern Mediterranean in April. One of the main problems was that, while the Sunderlands were able to find targets, many of them were outside the range of the Swordfish.

'Once only since the Germans have operated from Sicily has an S.79 been seen over Malta. This was on February 1st, when one came over very high escorted by twelve CR.42s, two of which were shot down by our Hurricanes.' (Intelligence Summary). Three Hurricanes had intercepted the Italians; the SM.79 had been attacked and damaged, while one fighter was shot down. A second attack raid hit Malta at dusk, with Ju 88s escorted by fighters. Again they were intercepted and one Ju 88 was damaged. One of the pilots recorded the events of 3 February in his diary: 'Yesterday [3rd] poor old W. caught it. Some Ju.88s came over, escorted by 109s. The 109s got into a good position and attacked two of our sections out of the sun, as we were positioning to attack the 88s. W. was probably killed instantly for he went on to his back and dived straight into the sea. B. was hit badly. His machine was ripped to hell by cannon. Amazingly enough, however, he got it down and force-landed with his engine u/s. M. jumped and landed 7 miles out to sea. JB although being chased by a 109, saw M's falling parachute. He kept around until he could plot his position in the sea. This he did and informed the base by R/T. M. was picked up by a speedboat after being in the sea about an hour.' (Diary entry 4 February 1941 from AMB 6612). The diarist was Flying Officer (soon to be Flight Lieutenant) Whittingham.

'One more dive bombing attack by 20 Ju.88s at dusk on 4th February was much less determined though considerable damage was done to buildings at Hal Far and Luqa. On this occasion three were shot down and two damaged. Night attacks, which have been far more frequent since the German participation in Mediterranean activities, have consisted of varying numbers up to forty Ju.88s and He.111s coming over singly and dropping bombs from high and low levels anywhere on the Island or in the sea nearby. On moonlight nights Luqa and Hal Far have been located and repeatedly bombed and the enemy have succeeded

Atmospheric dispersal shot of Hurricane, truck and 'pilots. Various.'

in hitting runways and preventing our offensive aircraft taking off. There has been one case of a searchlight being machine gunned. They have not confined their efforts to moonlight nights and have frequently been in the vicinity without locating Malta.' (Intelligence Summary).

'Searchlights have had difficulties in picking up these German night raiders as, unlike the Italians, they take effective avoiding action, usually coming in on a long glide, dropping their bombs and getting way by desynchronizing their engines and changing throttle settings. On February 8th, however, one Hurricane at a time was up throughout an eight-hour night attack and accounted for 2 Ju.88s confirmed and damaged a third after the searchlights had illuminated.' (Intelligence Summary). This was one of MacLachlan's night victories and it was actually an He 111, although on a second sortie he did damage a Ju 88.

'The Ju.88 has been used extensively for reconnaissance over Malta in addition to dive bombing and on most days a single aircraft either comes over the Island at a great height or else does a reconnaissance in the vicinity for shipping. Seldom does the German raider come straight in over Malta from the North. There appears to be a definite attempt to evade our warning system and frequently a raider starts from Sicily, circumvents Malta, disappears from RDF range, and re-appears from a southerly or westerly direction to carry out the task.' (Intelligence Summary).

RAF personnel have always had a 'habit' of acquiring dogs, and Malta was no exception, with Whittingham noting: 'I have been given a dog – a mongrel pup called 'Lady'. He also recorded that: 'I have bought a wizard little pony and trap for £70 – a trim grey called 'Lucky'. He is one of the best ponies on the island. It's an excellent thing to have a hobby here. It's such a dangerous sort of life that one can't help thinking about it a bit. So it's a good thing to get one's mind off in one's spare time.' (Diary entry for 10 February).

The pony and trap was mentioned again a few days later: 'P. and I drove 'Lucky' to Valetta in the morning. An air raid took place when we got there. The people rushing to the shelters upset 'Lucky' a bit. We stopped with him. The AA guns did not worry him much, nor did a bit of shrapnel that whistled down near him.' He also jotted down his thoughts on survival: 'What with continual air raids (seven times a day) and the presence of 109s about the place, it is a logical conclusion that our chances for survival are not very high. But one simply must not think about this, at any rate, I am enjoying myself while it lasts. Now that the risk of death is so much more increased I've been doing a spot of philosophizing. My attitude is that somebody has to do the job and if I get bumped off, I have experienced much more that the average bloke.'

In many years of talking with veterans, especially aircrew, I have constantly admired the matter of fact and honest way that most of them viewed their role in the war – and their prospects. As a squadron historian in the 1980s I encouraged young aircrew members to sit and chat with those attending reunions, both to get a sense of the squadron's history and their part in that, but also to be humbled by the total lack of ego of their predecessors.

On 10 February, Malta supported Operation Colossus, the commando raid on an aqueduct at Trigano, near Naples. This was the first airborne operation by the new Special Air Service Battalion and the target had been suggested by the engineering firm (George Kent and Sons) that had built it, and by the 'target experts', who said that, as it supplied water to three major locations, its destruction would have a major impact on the war. Pictures of the target were provided by 69 Squadron (Warburton) on the 9th and used for the final detailed planning.

The attack was by thirty-five men, led by Major T.A.G. Pritchard, with six Whitleys to drop the paratroops and two others on diversionary attacks. Whitley T4617 of 78 Squadron was part of the diversionary attack on Italian targets, in this case, Foggia and its airfields. The aircraft had an engine failure and was unable to maintain height; the crew of five bailed out and became prisoners. Sergeant Frederic Southam was Second Pilot in this Whitley and his escape and evasion report states: 'I took off from Malta in a Whitley aircraft on 10 Feb 41 to bomb Foggia. Owing to engine trouble the captain gave the order to bail out when we were just south of Salerno.' His account had no details of his capture of the fate of the rest of the crew and picks up with: 'I was sent to Naples and after two weeks I was transferred to Camp 78 (Sulmona) where I arrived on 27 Feb 41.' In September 1942 he was sent to Camp 102 (Aquila), from where he escaped on 10 September 1943, following news of the Armistice with Italy. He escaped with Sergeant Raymond Appleyard, who had been shot down in a 211 Squadron Blenheim over Valona on 6 January 1941.

The attack on the aqueduct was a success in that the target was damaged by the explosive charges, although this was repaired within days. The main value was that it showed a capability to make such attacks, which heightened security concerns in Italy. It also was another, albeit infrequent, operational activity from Malta – special operations, of which a number were flown over the next few years.

The Operational Intelligence Summary for period 11 October 1940 to 10 February 1941 show how much the situation on Malta had changed since the preceding four months. The total number of 'flying hours by fighters on patrol' had increased from 43 hours to 492 hours, of which 440 were flown by Hurricanes and the remainder by Gladiators and Fulmars. Interestingly, the average daily availability of fighters had only increased from 6.5 aircraft to eleven aircraft, and pilots from ten to seventeen. There were actually fewer air alarms in the period (138 instead of 161) but the scale and effectiveness of attacks was improved (from an Axis point of view!). While Ta Kali suffered no damage and Kalafrana only sustained a few broken windows, Luqa and Hal Far were hit quite hard with damage to hangars and other buildings (at both stations the officers' mess buildings were completely destroyed), while water and electricity mains were damaged, and at Luqa the runway had numerous craters. The fighters made fewer intercepts during the period – fifty-seven day intercepts (instead of seventy-two) and five night intercepts, with the following claims:

Type	Destroyed		Unconfirmed		Damaged	
	Fighters	AA	Fighters	AA	Fighters	AA
Ju 87	13	11	2	–	6	–
Ju 88	12	7	2	1	5	3
CR.42	6	1	2	–	2	1
MC.200	6	1	2	–	2	–
SM.79	2	1	2	–	2	–
Z.506	2	–	–	–	–	–
Totals	40	21	10	1	17	4

'Own casualties' were recorded as four pilots killed, five aircraft written off by enemy action (three Hurricanes and two Fulmars) in the air, and two aircraft written off on the ground. Luqa was now the most frequent target (twelve attacks), followed by the dockyards (eight) and Hal Far (six), with single-figure attacks on Kalafrana, Ta Kali, and ships around Malta. The intelligence summary recorded that one of the aircraft written off was the only Gladiator 'fitted with six guns, but this, unfortunately, was destroyed on the ground by enemy action the day it was completed.'

Indicating the increasing importance of Malta as an offensive base, the number of offensive and reconnaissance sorties had increased significantly in number and capability, the big difference being the operations by the Wellingtons of 148 Squadron. The Wellingtons flew 217 sorties in 48 missions, dropping 446,930lb GP, 103,650lb SAP, and 57,370lb incendiary bombs. The top four targets were two aerodromes (Castel Benito with twenty-eight sorties and Catania with thirty-three sorties) and two ports (Tripoli with thirty-seven sorties and Naples with twenty-one sorties, with another nineteen sorties to other targets in the Naples area). This was in line with an early February exchange between CAS and DOO (Director of Overseas Operations) that discussed the best use of the Middle East Wellingtons, including those on Malta, and related to various debates since the Excess convoy. 'As a result of German dive bomber attacks made on the Mediterranean Fleet during the passage of the convoy Excess, C-in-C Mediterranean signalled the Admiralty to the effect that he considered that the Wellingtons at Malta should regard as their primary targets the aerodromes

Sunderlands made a number of attacks on submarines, scoring a number of successes.

and establishments at which the dive bombers were based. The Wellingtons have in fact confined their attacks to aerodromes in Sicily and recently to Castel Benito aerodrome at Tripoli.'

Also grouped in the report under bombing missions were the ops flown by 830 Squadron's Swordfish, with forty-one sorties in five attacks dropping 6 torpedoes, 14,840lb GP and 11,500lb SAP bombs. The stats lump both types together for losses, showing ten crew killed, nineteen crew missing and eleven crew

Wellington of 148 Squadron damaged in the air raid on 26 February 1941.

injured, with aircraft losses at six Wellingtons (two not due to enemy action) and five Swordfish (three not due to enemy action) lost in the air and eight others on the ground (three Wellingtons and five Swordfish).

Reconnaissance missions were once again extensive, with 1,449 hours and 25 minutes flown on 268 sorties, of which 170 were 'extended reconnaissances for ships, including Ionian Sea, Eastern Tunisian coast, and area between Sardinia, Sicily and Tunis'. There were also 77 photographic reconnaissances and 21 visual reconnaissances, the remainder being searches and local anti-submarine patrols. The effort was made up of:

- 228 Squadron Sunderlands: 562 hours 40 minutes
- 69 Squadron Marylands and Blenheims attached to 69 Squadron: 747 hours 40 minutes
- 830 Squadron Swordfish: 43 hours
- PRU Spitfire: 6 hours and 15 minutes
- FAA Skuas: 48 hours and 30 minutes
- French Latécoère seaplane: 41 hours 20 minutes.

For this effort, thirteen aircrew were missing and three aircraft were lost in the air (one each of Maryland, Spitfire and Sunderland). The PRU Spitfire had been acquired when it had force-landed, short of fuel, on Malta after a recce of Genoa (from the UK). In typical Malta fashion, it was 'retained' and used for a number of special missions, before being lost over Italy on 2 February.

Although the Luftwaffe had operated bombers and Bf 110s over Malta since the start of the year, it was only in February that the first single-seat fighters appeared, when 7./JG 26 arrived in Sicily with fourteen Bf 109Es. Jerry Scutts in his excellent *Bf 109 Aces of North Africa and the Mediterranean* summarizes this initial period very well: 'The JG 26 detachment began an unparalleled run of good fortune. Sweeping aside the weak RAF defences, the German pilots strafed Maltese airfields at will, shot down defending Hurricanes almost with impunity, and generally made life very unpleasant for the defenders, who were already having to put up with a constant pounding from Italian and German bombs. Although the RAF put up numerous interception sorties and succeeded in ensuring that the bombing was rarely achieved without some cost to the attackers, it was singly unable to counter the Bf 109s effectively.' The first such escort mission had been flown on 12 February and it was a shock to 261 Squadron's pilots when they were bounced by a trio of 109s, one of whose

pilots was to become known as the 'scourge of Malta', Oberleutnant Muncheberg. All three claimed a Hurricane, and indeed two were shot down, while the third was badly damaged and its pilot wounded. One of the pilots, Pilot Officer Thacker, was plucked from the sea by *HSL107*.

A few days later, HQ Malta sent an urgent signal to HQ RAF ME: 'Germans making systematic attempt to neutralize our small fighter effort which at present pressure may be unable to continue withstand incessant and increasing attacks by superior numbers. Consider one complete additional fighter squadron necessary to maintain air defence Malta. This squadron and in fact 262 Squadron should be equipped with Hurricane Mark 2 or Spitfire as we cannot fight Me.109 above rated height of Mark 1 Hurricane. If this provided will somehow contrive to house and operate from present bases. Anticipate one landing strip Safi ready for use within 3 weeks. 261 Squadron on duty day and night now has 30 effective pilots out of establishment of 43. 19 Hurricanes available plus 9 various stages of repair. Present bad patch with casualties without return will doubtless pass but

Luftwaffe recce shot of Luqa, aircraft in dispersals, bomb damage and smoke.

fighter defence in present circumstances is inadequate and consistently diminishing.' (signal dated 16 Feb 1941). Meanwhile, the Swordfish of 830 Squadron notched up another success on the 15th, sinking the Italian 4,920-ton *Juventus*.

On 19 February Cunningham signalled to the Admiralty: 'An aircraft carrier can no longer expect to enjoy the immunity experienced during the last few months with only the Italian Air Force to compete with. Apart from the increased risk of damage, it will now be necessary to embark a higher

Sunderland patrol over the Ionian Sea and Greek Islands.

Hurricane P3733 was one of those lost with 261 Squadron on 12 February. It is shown here aboard a carrier on the reinforcement convoy.

proportion of fighters at the expense of TSR [Swordfish] and the striking effect of the carrier will be proportionally reduced. Malta and Aegean convoys and supply ships to Libya ports are threatened, and some means of affording them fighter protection is an urgent requirement, for the aircraft carrier cannot be everywhere.'

He argued for an expansion of AS and fighter patrols from Malta, Crete, Cyrenaica, and the west coast of Epirus. In essence he was asking for a 'Coastal Command in the Med' under the AOC ME with 'operational control being a question of co-operation between us.' He was right in that Coastal Command was becoming an increasingly effective entity with its mix of aircraft capability and close co-ordination with the Navy. Sir Arthur Longmore, for the RAF's side, was not so convinced: 'Liaison and co-operation with Cunningham are as good as can be expected as long as C-in-C Mediterranean has no shore based HQ and so liable to go to sea at short notice and out of touch with us.' He stated that the need for aircraft and mixed capability was clear – especially torpedo-bombers and long-range fighters – but a separate Command structure would be ineffective.

The politics between the command levels of the Navy and RAF never went away, but at an operational level things generally went well. The exchange also included a request for more effort against ports such as Tripoli and Benghazi. The limited number of Wellingtons available were out and about to such targets as often as possible, and still suffering losses. Wellington T981 of 70 Squadron failed to return from one such mission from Luqa to Tripoli on the night of 24 February. Having failed to find Malta on the return leg, the crew flew on way to the north-west and bailed out when the aircraft ran out of fuel. They bailed out over Catanzanio, almost 240 miles north-west of Malta, both pilots were killed and the other four crew were taken prisoner.

25 February: Fighter sweep over Malta, claimed one Hurricane shot down in flames. (German situation report [sitrep]). Our diarist, however, recorded this as a Red Letter Day. He had been promoted to flight lieutenant two days before – 'this will please mother' – and given command of B Flight. The entry for the 25th states: 'The squadron sighted four enemy bombers "stooging" around. Everyone went hell for leather at them. I saw one straggling about half a mile behind the rest, so left the squadron and attacked it from the stern. I had given him a three-second burst when he opened up at me. He was a good shot. I broke away sharply to the right after about one and a half seconds of his fire. I do not see what happened to him, but the AA people reported having seen him burst into flames and go into the sea, so that is my second since coming here. H. [Pilot Officer Hamilton] got another, so did B. [Flying Officer Barber]. All the flight fired their guns. We celebrated this with a bottle of beer.'

Malta-based Wellingtons were an important part of the bombing strategy, but for periods of time the one suitable airfield, Luqa, was not available to them or was simply too dangerous for effective operations.

The following day was a disaster for both Wellington units, when Luqa was heavily hit in an air raid by Ju 87s and Ju 88s. Six difficult to replace Wellingtons were destroyed, one of 70 Squadron and five of 148 Squadron. The German sitrep for 26 February stated: '62 bombers and dive-bombers attacked Luqa airfield. Hits were observed near dispersed aircraft and on hangars, causing fires and explosions. Some bombs probably hit a fuel dump. Fighter sweep. No combat.'

The RAF were up and were in combat, and it was chaotic with dive-bombing by Ju 87s, bombing by Ju 88s, and 109s looking after both. The end result appears to have been three Ju 87s and five Hurricanes lost, with three pilots killed. *HSL107* was out again, this time picking up a Stuka crew.

February closed with a fighter sweep on the 27th and a mine-laying of Valetta harbour by six bombers on the 28th. The last week of February was quiet compared to what was to happen in March, when seventeen days of the month brought significant air activity over Malta. The German sitrep for 1 March recorded that the main attack of the day was by six bombers, escorted by fighters, on Valetta harbour. The results were recorded as: 'Some bombs fell on fortified parts of the town, east and south of Dockyard Creek. A pontoon with two guns, near the coast NW of Dragut, was sunk. Other bombs fell on AA sites north of Sliema Creek and on Manoel Island [the submarine base]. One 1,000 SAP fell SW of the floating dock and caused a tremendous explosion.' It is interesting that the Germans reference attacks on gun positions, as these are seldom referenced in the British reports.

On 4 March, Vice Admiral Malta sent a 'revised survey of the present situation at Malta' to C-in-C Mediterranean in which he stated that since his previous survey in September 1940 conditions had generally improved there and in the central Mediterranean. 'Malta has been partially re-armed, but the task is by no means yet complete. However, the strength of the garrison has been materially increased both in men and weapons … although the full 8 months' stocks approved by HM Government will not have been built up.' He then stated that: 'Our fighter defences are very weak and cannot possibly prevent a succession of heavy attacks if the enemy concentrates his Central Mediterranean air forces on the island.'

His view was that the enemy bombing attacks had not caused serious damage to the war effort 'except for certain dive bombing attacks on the aerodromes and the Dockyard' and that 'HM Dockyard has been able to play its part in maintaining the Mediterranean Fleet, though its production has been considerably lessened by the damage caused by enemy air raids and by the difficulty of maintaining the flow of supplies required.'

As to offensive action, he praised the work of the Malta submarines, the Wellington squadron and 830 Squadron FAA, which 'have met with considerable success and the enemy has not succeeded in seriously hampering our activities against their shipping.' He was not very complimentary about the Italians: 'The activities of the Italian Air Force have become more and more feeble and practically no Italian aircraft are now seen in the Central Mediterranean.' Ships that faced Italian torpedo-bombers may not have agreed with that!

He was, unsurprisingly, more concerned with the Luftwaffe: 'Heavy day attacks started again on 26th February and may be continued if it is obvious that we are using Malta for surface forces or when convoys are known to be unloading in harbour. It is considered probable that the bombers would prefer to carry out their attacks on shipping at sea rather than against defended harbours like Malta.'

He concluded that: 'Our [Royal Navy] main object is still to be able to use Malta regularly as an advanced base for the Mediterranean Fleet and as a refitting base for the vessels of the Fleet. It is considered that our Malta policy must continue to be mainly defensive, though not entirely so. That is the present position and we cannot become genuinely offensive in the naval sense until surface forces are based semi-permanently on Malta. This cannot be done until the air menace is mastered, a state of affairs not likely to happen for some considerable time. Our immediate problem is to keep the fortress supplied with consumable stores in the face of the air menace. The provision of additional weapons, other than fighter aircraft, is of secondary importance. The major items which are urgently required now are coal, aviation spirit, naval and dockyard equipment and stores; other major items of which stocks should be kept high are human foodstuffs, Benzine and kerosene, and anti-aircraft ammunition.'

His final sentence was: 'The whole problem can be summed up in three phrases, bluff, fighter aircraft, and the maintenance of supplies.' By bluff he meant not letting the enemy know how important Malta was – by concealing as much of its activities as possible.

The next significant attack was on the 5th against Hal Far by 'three waves of 76 bombers and Stukas. Hits were scored on hangars, barracks, amongst dispersed aircraft, and on the runway. Several explosions and fires observed.' (German sitrep). The sitrep for the following day included a recce report on Hal Far that 'showed the following damage – workshop hangar totally destroyed, one hangar half destroyed, one hangar damaged in the middle, one hut completely destroyed, and one hut damaged.' The main attack on the 6th was an evening raid by a small formation of nine Stukas against port installations, dropping nine 500kg and sixteen 50kg bombs and claiming some hits.

Flight Lieutenant Whittingham noted in his diary: 'A flap on about 5 o'clock. I was up and saw them being bombed below. I positioned myself to run down in a right hand dive in case of being chased by 109s. In doing so, I blacked out for a bit, but came out at about 1,200 feet.' It is an interesting observation and an example of a problem, one that no doubt claimed a number of RAF pilots – coming out at 1,200ft is not much time between surviving or ending up in the sea.

He continued: 'I soon recovered and attacked one of the many enemy aircraft in front of and below me. My first shot was at a Ju.87 and the next at a Ju.88. They both fired back at me. I then spiraled to ground level for safety and to get away from any 109s that might have been positioning themselves against me. Making for base I saw about five Ju.88s going out to sea. I hadn't much ammunition but decided to climb in their direction. This I did and pointed my nose at one and gave him a burst. I may have hit him a bit but he fairly let me have it from his underneath guns. I twisted and was making for land when I saw a machine burst into gigantic flames about 100 yards from me. It was an Me.110 which had been hit by ack-ack. It was a stroke of luck for myself, as I learned afterwards he was firing at me just previous to being hit. In the engagement the squadron got seven confirmed. Poor old M. [Sergeant McDougal] was killed. A 109 got him just after he bagged an '87.' (Diary entry 5 March).

One of the most useful aspects of Whittingham's diary is its honesty about basic situations – blacking out, being caught unawares by the 110, and so on. These were the reality of many pilots, and for some those situations would have ended in tragedy.

On 7 March, L2164 of 228 Squadron was attacked at its Kalafrana moorings by two Bf 109s; Sergeant Jones, acting as boatguard, managed to get his gun into action before being fatally hit. The Sunderland was badly damaged – it was in trouble again a few days later. Three days later (11th) two of the squadron's aircraft were attacked by 109s. 'T9046 was damaged and L2164 caught fire … a party boarded this aircraft and fought the fire which was apparently got under control, but after an interval blazed up again. The machine was taxied inshore and beached but had to be abandoned, and ultimately sank. T9046 was flown from St Paul's Bay to Kalafrana and taken up the slip for inspection.'

This loss took place when a fighter sweep of eleven aircraft appeared at midday; in addition to the Sunderland they claimed to have shot down one Hurricane and one Blenheim. The main assault was another Stuka attack on the port installations and surrounding area. Eleven Stukas dropped 6,500kg of bombs and claimed: 'Direct hit on a torpedo store, followed by heavy fire, and an explosion in the State Wharf in Cospicua.'

For the Malta reconnaissance aircraft, 'the hazards were increased when the Luftwaffe attacks developed, for part of the enemy tactics was to put a ring of fighters round the island to hem in reconnaissance aircraft. Evading the enemy cordon became part of the Marylands' [and Sunderlands'] routine.' (*The RAF in Maritime War, ibid*). On 7 March a Maryland on a recce of Taormina exchanged shots with a fighter; on the way back it damaged a Cant Z.506 but 'on reaching Malta was intercepted by Me.109s, which set it on fire and shot down a Hurricane which tried to give protection.' Only one of the Maryland's crew was able to bail out. Later the same day a Maryland flown by Adrian Warburton was 'chased from Taranto across the Adriatic by four Macchi 200s. The pursuers were shaken off, but on heading home the Maryland was intercepted off Cape St Maria di Leuca by two Macchi 200s. A chase continued for 100 miles during which shots were exchanged. When the Maryland finally escaped, it was short of petrol, but made a safe landing at Menidi, Greece, and returned the next day.' Warburton had more than his share of fighter encounters, and he and his crew were successful in shooting down a number of their tormenters.

Small number of Hurricanes continued to arrive in March, in this case spared by squadrons in North Africa, but it was now invariably too little and too late in the face of the German fighter threat. Indeed, by now it was considered too risky to keep the Wellingtons operating from Malta, and so on 9 March 148 Squadron moved to Egypt, taking up residence with 205 Group at Kabrit in the Canal Zone. The bombers were still very much engaged in attacking a range of targets connected with the air and sea war, and sent detachments to operate from Malta from April. According to the German sitreps, Valetta and Luqa were the targets on the 10th with twenty-three bombers involved. On 11 March six bombers attacked Valetta, and on 12 March one bomber attacked Valetta.

15 March: Stukas attacked Hal Far and Luqa, with some damage claimed and 'AA positions and searchlights attacked.' A fighter sweep intercepted a Wellington on delivery to Malta and shot it down. The aircraft was W5644 en route from Gibraltar with a crew from the 3 Group Training Flight; in addition to Sergeant R. Alington and his crew, Group Captain D. Humphreys was a passenger on the flight. They were intercepted north-west of Gozo and Oberleutnant Muncheberg claimed the victory; he also reported that at least some of the crew made it to their dinghy. However, no trace was found and all seven men were reported killed in action. The overall total of AA guns on

Malta had increased from seventy heavy and thirty-four light in January to ninety heavy and fifty-two light by March. By March the AA defence for the main airfields comprised:

- Hal Far: 4 Bofors and 20 light automatics
- Luqa: 6 Bofors and 31 light automatics
- Ta Kali: 5 Bofors and 27 light automatics
- Marsa Scivicco [sic] seaplane base: 10 Bofors and 29 light automatics.

However, it was agreed by all that only fighters could provide really effective defence. A communication of 17 March at Vice Chief of the Air Staff (VCAS) level once again addressed fighter strength on Malta: 'It has been obvious since the arrival of the GAF in the Central Mediterranean that if we are to retain Malta in a fit condition to permit its occasional use as an advanced base, and its eventual use as a base from which to stage a more forward offensive policy, we must improve our fighter defence there. One of the reasons why we have not been able to build up the number of fighter squadrons at Malta is that aerodrome accommodation there is limited. But two new aerodromes Safi and Krendi are nearing completion and when they are ready Malta will have five aerodromes.'

In the event, neither of these new strips played a significant role in Malta's operations in the period covered in this account. It went on to address the question of the aircraft: 'I understand fighter aircraft are expected to become available in large numbers and with the passing of the 'Lease and Lend' Bill and the possibility of using American ships we expect to receive more fighters in the Middle East.' To some extent this was still wishful thinking, at least until the build-up of P-40s with the Desert Air Force.

The final part of the communication suggested that the additional three squadrons requested should be positioned in the Middle East, so that they could be moved to Malta as soon as the decision was taken to increase the Malta force and thus avoid considerable delay. Hurricane reinforcements arrived on the 17th, with aircraft and pilots of 274 Squadron being detached from the parent unit at Amriya. The addition of more aircraft was welcome, as was the experience level of some of the pilots, although they were soon to find that Malta was different to anything they had experienced before.

The Mediterranean situation was discussed in the 18 March report by the German C-in-C Navy to Hitler, two of the key points being:

1. The war situation in the Mediterranean. Offensive use of Italian naval forces. Use of mines in the Mediterranean, with special reference to the need for closing the Straits of Sicily. Escorts for transports to Libya
2. Increase in the freedom of action of the Italian Navy through the occupation of Greece.

Adding detail, the report dealt with Malta: 'In order to enable the Navy to carry out its tasks in the Mediterranean, it is particularly important to take Malta. In British hands this base represents a strong threat to our troop transports to Africa and later for the supply transports. Besides, it is an undesirable supply base for the shipping plying between the western and eastern Mediterranean. In the opinion of the Air Force, it appears possible to capture Malta by airborne troops; the Navy is in favour of this as soon as possible.' (Fuhrer Conferences on Naval Affairs.)

An interesting note in the appendix referenced Gibraltar and suggested that IF the French could be encouraged to become active participants ('to win France over to full political action against Britain') then the 'Air Force based in Morocco could eliminate Gibraltar to a great extent, with all this implies for British supply lines and the strategic situation in the western Mediterranean. This would make it easier to restore the situation in Libya.'

Interesting and by no means impossible, although the Vichy Regime, which exercised a degree of control over the French colonial areas, or at least some of them, attempted to maintain a type of neutrality. French fighters in North Africa did shoot down a number of Allied planes that strayed over their territory, and interred aircrew they picked up, but there was never a concerted involvement.

Gibraltar was supremely vulnerable and if Spain had joined the Axis cause, as Hitler had expected of this fascist regime that he had helped put in place, and if the French from North Africa joined in, then Gibraltar would have been untenable. The loss of Gibraltar would, without a doubt, have had a major impact on the Mediterranean war.

Airfield construction work on the Rock; Gibraltar was an essential forming up and staging post for operations to Malta and the Middle East.

As this account continually references, all eastbound convoys gathered and prepared at Gibraltar before entering the Med on runs to Malta or the Middle East. Aircraft from Gibraltar supported convoys and swept the western Mediterranean and parts of the Atlantic for submarines. Without Gibraltar these convoys would have been impossible or unacceptably costly. Back in January,

Gibraltar putting up an impressive searchlight display.

Fortress HQ had looked at options for building a fighter strip on Europa Flats, but this would involve 'demolishing some buildings, filling in a small quarry and other levelling, to construct a strip 300 yards long and 40 yards wide which could be used by aircraft of the Grumman type with the aid of catapults and arrestor gear.' (*The RAF in Maritime War, ibid*). It was considered that hangars could be tunneled into the rock itself. However, this was seen as a long-term project and for now, while Spain remained neutral, the existing strip would suffice. The AS patrols were flying an average of 180 a month in patrolling the Straits.

The report on 'Analysis of destruction of enemy aircraft in low flying attacks on Malta 16 Jan–31 Mar 1941' referring to the period after the 16 January air assault on the dockyard, was primarily concerned with the overall analysis of effectiveness across the period of the January to March 'blitz'. While the statistics of confirmed and probables provide the hard evidence of the value of AA fire, what they do not highlight is the tactical effect, whereby pilots were unable to aim weapons as effectively, so the overall result of an attack would, invariably be poorer even if there were no actual losses of attacking aircraft.

'Geographical barrages were put into operation against dive-bombing attacks on Grand Harbour, Dockyard, Luqa and Hal Far on several occasions. These barrages naturally increased the expenditure of ammunition, but this was amply rewarded by the high destruction of aircraft obtained. Predicted fire was put into operation at night and although no actual destruction was recorded, it undoubtedly proved a deterrent to enemy attacks. Prediction was employed with Bofors guns to a limited extent only, owing mainly to the fact that sufficient trained personnel were not available. The opinion was formed that they could only be usefully employed when Bofors were sighted at some distance from the objective, in which case the rate of change [of angular velocity] would be less rapid.

'Ammunition expenditure for Heavy AA over the period was 21,176 rounds, the number of rounds expended for each aircraft destroyed being 605. Expenditure for Bofors and 2 Pounders Mk VIII was 18,600 rounds, the number of rounds per aircraft destroyed being 1,695.' The report also contained a note extracted from a German document (from an 8th Abteilung lecture). 'Dive-bombing and level attacks made from medium height, in which escorting aircraft also took part, achieved on the whole good results … our own losses were tolerable and were caused mainly by accurate flak and, to a lesser extent by Hurricanes.'

The day 22 March was busier, ahead of the arrival of convoy MW6. Thirteen bombers, with eighteen fighters as escort, attacked Valetta harbour, dropping 9 × 500kg and 132 × 50kg; it is interesting that the Luftwaffe was dropping so many smaller calibre bombs, a tactic that continued in subsequent days. Hurricanes went up to intercept and the German sitrep claimed seven destroyed and one probable. A second bombing mission saw eleven bombers attack Luqa and Valetta, dropping 160 × 50kg bombs. It had indeed been a bad day for the defenders, for the first time in some weeks they had been able to put up what seemed like a reasonable force of eight Hurricanes to go after a formation of Ju 88s escorted by 109s. The 109s had it all their own way, and only three of the Hurricanes made it back.

On 23 March convoy MW6 arrived at Malta. The convoy had been eagerly anticipated to boost some of the 'civil requirements' stocks. In his March assessment, the vice admiral had included an annex on the 'Food Supply Position', as it was when he wrote it and as it was expected to be when MW6 arrived. 'The safe arrival of the four ships in convoy MW6 will relieve the situation to a very large extent and the local position will not become difficult before August except for coffee, lard, milk and soap.' The key commodities listed were butter and margarine, cheese [with a note that there was none at present], coffee, lard, matches, tinned milk, edible oil, rice, soap, sugar, tea, wheat flour, and animal fodder. Soap was clearly very important as it was the only commodity that was carried

Hurricane scramble; all too often the fighters got up OK but were then hit by the 109s, who had the advantage of height.

in all four ships, the 8,000-plus cases being split between them. Interestingly the shipping list also showed sixty cases of Bovril. None of the manifests included tobacco or beer, but the survey stated 'although they cannot be classed as essentials still I am afraid that the troops cannot do without beer nor the population in general without tobacco.'

As usual the presence of shipping in the harbour brought intensified attacks. The German sitrep reported: '24 Stukas, escorted by fighters, attacked Valetta harbour. They dropped 5 × 1000kg, 19 × 500kg and 71 × 50kg bombs. Hits were observed on: One cruiser with one 500kg bomb on the forward part of the ship, one 500kg bomb between cruiser and quayside, and four 500kg bombs immediately beside the cruiser; one large passenger ship with one 1,000kg bomb forward and one 1,000kg bomb immediately at the side of the ship. There were other detonations in quay installations and in the neighbouring parts of the town.'

Despite the losses of the previous day, the defenders put up twelve Hurricanes. The Luftwaffe was back again in the afternoon when '18 Stukas, escorted by German and Italian fighters, attacked ships in Valetta harbour under heavy AA fire.' The attackers claimed hits on the same cruiser as the morning attack, plus four merchant ships, one being the same as had been attacked in the morning. In return, they admitted four fighters missing including 'one had a direct hit from AA fire over Malta.' The sitrep also said that 'in an air battle between German, Italian, and enemy Hurricane fighters, the Italians shot down four Hurricanes.'

Flight Lieutenant Whittingham's diary entry for the 23rd read: 'In the afternoon there was a big dive-bombing attack on Grand Harbour. L. [Squadron Leader Lambert] was leading the two flights. They were just in the right position at the time of the attack. The Hurricanes dived at the 87s and two were seen to burst into flames and fall into the sea. It transpired afterwards that we got seven confirmed, one probable and six damaged. Ack–ack got three. R. [Sergeant Robertson] who bagged two, got shot himself. His starboard tank caught fire and he bailed out, landing in a nearby village where the locals carried him on their shoulders and cheered him.'

It is generally considered that Squadron Leader Lambert was an excellent leader, and his tactical positioning was responsible for the successes. Whittingham had this to say: 'Squadron Leader L. should go down in history for the calm courage and complete lack of side that he displays. He is a complete inspiration to every member of the squadron. This despite the fact that he has neither the liking nor the inclination to be a fighter pilot.' The ships *City of Lincoln* and *Perthshire* were seriously damaged.

24 March: The Stukas were back again, although only seven this time, claiming 'one cruiser hit by two 500kg bombs; other hits were on sheds and on an oil tank. The two ships hit the previous

day, the oil tank, and the city quarter between French and Dockyard Creeks, were still showing strong signs of smoke.' (German sitrep). On 25 March a lone attack dropped two 250kg bombs on 'Venezia' airfield, and the fighter escort of a recce flight tangled with Hurricanes but with no result. The German sitreps refer to Venezia, which to the RAF was Ta Kali; where sitreps are quoted, I have left the name Venezia.

For the next three days the German sitrep reported: 28 March: strong fighter sweep by 36 aircraft but few combats; claimed one Hurricane. 29 March: Hal Far was the target for nine bombers in the main attack. 30 March: two fast-bomber attacks on Hal Far and Venezia airfields and 'bombs fell in front of a hangar, and flames and smoke were seen.'

It was also decided to move 228 Squadron's Sunderlands – very tempting targets for German strafing – out of Malta, and in the middle of March their Kalafrana detachment rejoined the squadron at Alexandria, 'a small maintenance party remaining at Kalafrana to complete work on Sunderland L5807 and to service Sunderland aircraft operating from Malta subsequent to the departure of the main party. An advance party, together with certain stores, were moved from Malta by air, the remaining personnel embarking at Valetta on HMS *Bonaventure*, *Calcutta* and *Greyhound* en route to Alexandria. On arrival at Alexandria the aircraft and crews and members of the advance party were accommodated at No. 201 Group but owing to the limited space available, personnel, other than aircrews, were transferred to Aboukir. There was little available accommodation at Aboukir and the Squadron offices were situated in a Beach Hut with workshops in Blenheim cases and outbuildings – the Squadron NCOs had to find a mess of their own.' (228 Squadron ORB).

This also meant that the 230 Squadron detachment in Greece was even busier, as C-in-C Med had, on 26 March, requested dawn to dusk patrols in patrol areas Q, R and S (see map) 'to within visibility distance of the west coast of Greece'; he suspected the Italians were about to attempt a

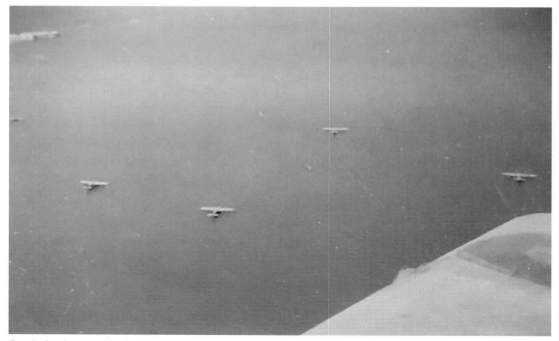

Sunderlands at anchor in Aboukir Bay.

major action against Allied convoys. This is also a good point to mention that the Allies relied heavily on the intercepts provided by Ultra, and that it was common for additional recce to be tasked to provide a plausible reason for Allied action that would persuade the enemy that the intelligence was from normal sources and not from code-breaking. Nevertheless, on 27 March, six hours into its patrol a Sunderland out of Scaramanga picked up an Italian cruiser force.

In the last week of March, Cunningham, using the intelligence and recce reports, was at last able to manoeuvre the Italian fleet to battle, although, in the best traditions of the Navy, it was a risky plan that relied on individual commanders to perform well but within his overall plan. With his cruiser force facing heavy odds while the battleships steamed to position, Cunningham launched two waves of torpedo-bombers from *Formidable*; the first wave scored no hits on the main target, the battleship *Vittorio Veneto*, but distracted it from its shelling of the British cruisers. The second strike was more effective, and one torpedo hit was scored, damaging a propeller and slowing the ship down, which was just what Cunningham needed to give himself time to catch up. Blenheims also joined in the attack, three squadrons in Greece mounting twenty-four sorties and dropping 23,750lb of bombs. The missions flown were:

1430: 3 Blenheims of 84 Sqn
1437: 6 Blenheims of 113 Sqn
1530: 6 Blenheims of 113 Sqn
1630: 5 Blenheims of 84 Sqn
1700: 4 Blenheims of 211 Sqn

The Blenheims claimed some hits, but no significant damage was caused; however, despite heavy AA fire, all aircraft returned safely. *Formidable* launched a third strike and the British main force continued to close. A torpedo from this attack caused damage to the cruiser *Pola* and she was left with an escort of cruisers and destroyers, thus splitting the Italian fleet and leaving this force in the path of the advancing Royal Navy ships. Cunningham decided to risk a night engagement as by the following morning the battle area would have moved within range of Axis land-based aircraft, and Cunningham had already seen what that could mean. The Battle of Cape Matapan saw the destruction of three Italian cruisers, *Pol*, *Zara* and *Fiume*, the latter two by devastating short-range naval gunfire, as well as the early damage to the battleship. While aircraft did not sink any of the ships, the carrier-launched torpedo-bombers had been decisive in causing the damage that left the cruiser force in place and ready to be destroyed.

Formation of 84 Squadron Blenheims.

The destruction of the Axis supply pipeline to North Africa was one of deciding factors in the eventual victory of the Allies in the Western Desert. Air and naval, including submarine, attacks from the Middle East and Malta were decisive, and in the periods when Malta's strike capability was reduced, the percentage of supplies reaching Rommel increased dramatically.

The arrival of Axis land-based aircraft the next day persuaded the Allies to move back towards Alexandria, although they had already done all the damage that was needed. As part of the overall war in the Mediterranean, this battle confirmed a number of things: firstly; naval air power (carrier-based) was an essential part of the force mix, and was something the Axis forces lacked, which meant holding land bases that could support naval operations became a key of strategy. Secondly, that keeping away from land-based aircraft by day was a good idea. Finally, that once again the vaunted Italian Navy with its modern and powerful capital ships was not up to the fight – when faced by commanders of the ilk of Cunningham. The bravery of Italian seamen was never in doubt, especially merchant seamen as the campaign progressed, but the ineptitude of senior commanders and the failure of air-sea co-ordination meant that the Allies were invariably able to seize and maintain the strategic initiative. March had also seen the arrival of German land forces in some strength into the Desert War with the arrival of General Rommel and the Afrika Korps (DAK). The importance of Malta to the Mediterranean was to increase greatly, as a key element in staving off defeat or ensuring victory in the Western Desert. Rommel launched his attack in Cyrenaica at the end of March and the Allies were soon tumbling backwards; Tobruk held out but the key port of Benghazi fell on 3 April.

On 3 April, Operation Winch saw another twelve Hurricanes flown off *Ark Royal*, led by two Skuas. Malta signalled to Air Ministry: 'Operation very satisfactory. No difficulty in take-off from carrier. All aircraft were airborne in approximately 10 minutes. Hurricane leader considers that 15 Hurricanes could have been flown off *Ark Royal*. Ample fuel margin most aircraft had 50 gallons. Speed 136 to 140 kts, height 1500 to 2000 feet, average RPM 1850. Weather conditions at rendezvous excellent but only one group of Hurricanes contacted escorting Sunderland and Glenn Martin. Hurricanes were inclined to straggle making it difficult for Sunderland to keep all aircraft under observation. No enemy except an ineffective attack by 2 S.79s on our high speed launch which was patrolling west of Malta.'

An HQ Med signal of 3 April started with 'Rejoice with me. 12 Hurricanes and 2 Skuas arrived.' An interesting turn of phrase! It went on to say that one Hurricane crashed on landing and ran into another Hurricane on the ground, with major damage to the former. The same day the Luftwaffe sent four escorted bombers to attack two ships East of Malta, but without result.

On 5 April HQ Malta sent a signal to Air Ministry that said: 'Experience air attack since intervention Luftwaffe last Jan. has resulted radical reconsideration of local policy in absence adequate fighter

Fleet Air Arm Skua takes off from HMS Formidable; the Skuas acted as fleet defence fighters but also escorted Hurricane reinforcement flights to Malta.

defence. Am now dispersing personnel and equipment off station target areas far as possible especially Kalafrana highly concentrated and vulnerable target although luckily little damaged so far. Have already dispersed 50 percent stores from Kalafrana elsewhere in island and have now requisitioned workshop accommodation for repair Hurricanes and Merlins in garages Gzira district. Dispersal aims at further 25 percent store. A hangar at Hal Far and majority Bellmans in Command already destroyed consider most inadvisable now proceed erection hangar Kalafrana scheme even if materials could be shipped here, same objection T type hangar Hal Far. Consider best policy duration war is (a) one increase technical and storage hangars and develop scheme for cutting small underground general engineering section in rock face as annex present workshops and to take more vital and irreplaceable machine tools, (b) complete road widening Kalafrana – Hal Far – Birsebbugia – Hal Far already well advanced, (c) erect large covered store pen Hal Far suitable for final erection of aircraft up to Wellington size instead of T type hangar. All above feasible on local materials.' Underground facilities and roads/taxiways joining facilities made Malta unique among RAF locations, and played a major role in keeping the island operational.

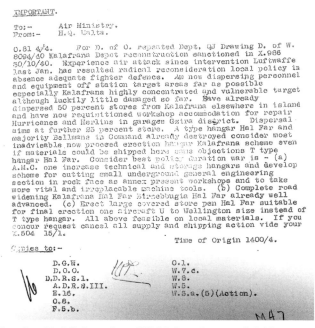

Signal to Air Ministry from HQ Malta reference airfields.

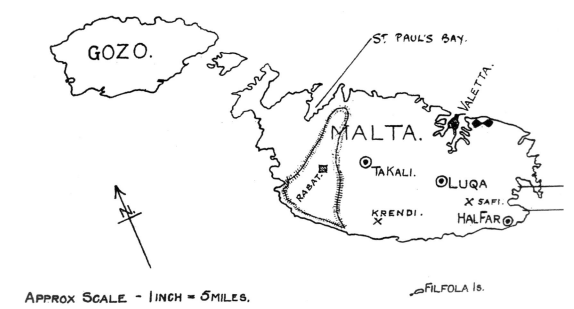

Sketch map dated 10 April 1941 of Malta airfield locations. The lines on the right point to Marsaxlokk and Kalafrana.

The main activity on the 11 April was combat between the fighters escorting a recce aircraft and the intercepting Hurricanes, with the Germans claiming three confirmed and one probable of the eight with which they tangled. Pilot Officer Kennett was one of two pilots killed, his body being recovered by *HSL107*. A small-scale Stuka attack on the 12th was followed by a busier day on the 13th, with various operations and a number of combats. A number of airfields were attacked, Luqa being the most frequent target during the day. Flying Officer Mason was shot down but was rescued by *HSL107* (note: the HSL records have this as 12 April). Luqa was the primary target again on the 14th, with the German sitrep claiming: 'Nine Stukas attacked Luqa airfield with 9 × 500kg bombs and 37 × 50kg bombs, scoring hits in front of the hangars on the north side of the field. Other hits were scored between aircraft bays, on the water-works, on an AA position, in the village of Luqa [not much of a hit as the village was some distance away] and on Valetta State Wharf. Venezia airfield was also attacked.'

After a lull of a couple of days a few bombers appeared over Malta on the 17th to bomb Valetta harbour and searchlight positions. The port area was again the main target on the 18th, with eighteen Stukas attacking shipping, claiming near misses for the

Luqa tower with its sandbag protection, April–May 1941.

loss of one aircraft. It was the same again on the 20th, with three small bombing attacks on the harbour. On the 22nd the German sitrep stated: '19 bombers attacked Valetta harbour, dropping 16 × 500kg bombs and 256 × 50kg bombs. The target could be easily seen, but no ships were seen. Most of the bombs fell on French Creek and the State Wharf. One aircraft is missing. Five Stukas attacked Valetta harbour and Luqa airfield. One fire was started.'

A further group of Hurricanes were scheduled to arrive in late April courtesy of Operation Dunlop. On 8 April, a signal to Senior Officer Force H reported: 'There will be approximately 20 Mark I and 6 Mark 2 Hurricanes all fitted with long range tanks and six guns. Transfer of aircraft to HMS *Ark Royal* will take place at Gibraltar. Aircraft will not be tropicalized. Presume that only half total number of Hurricanes will be on deck initially and the remainder being stowed in hangars with wings off. The latter would be rigged on deck after departure of first batch, and flown off 25 hours later.' The plan was later changed to have all aircraft erected and ready to go to avoid delay and rigging when carrier was in an area subject to air attack. A later signal also stated that 'calculations show that with 30 kt wind speed [over the deck] Hurricane 1 with all tanks full, 6 guns and 150 rounds per gun, should take off in 425 feet. To give necessary safety margin of 33 per cent the flying off distance from Malta should not exceed 420 sea miles in still air. Malta is to provide additional escort (Sunderland or Glenn Martin) for each formation from rendezvous.'

AHQ Malta subsequently reported that: 'Operation Dunlop proceeded according to plan without incident. Time of flights varied between 3 hours and 3 hours and a quarter. Rendezvous off Galita satisfactory contact with escort made by each formation. Average fuel remaining in Hurricanes was 85 gallons, except for one aircraft which flew in rich mixture all the way and arrived with 50 gallons only. Fulmars arrived with 36 to 40 gallons. Formation keeping by Hurricanes much better than previously but they should keep more abeam than astern so that escort can keep them in view. One formation flew so fast that escorting Sunderland was unable to take lead and Fulmar led them in.' (Signal AHQ Malta to HQ RAF ME).

Pilot Officer Rees of 228 Squadron was tasked to rendezvous with and escort eight Hurricanes and a Fulmar to Malta: 'The aircraft arrived 30 minutes late. The arrival at Malta coincided with an Air Raid and the Captain decided to make a landing as quickly as possible with the intention of getting the Boat into the hangar. However, this proved unsuccessful, for after mooring up in the Camber and adjusting one of the beaching legs, the mooring and maintenance party were compelled to leave the Boat owing to enemy aircraft being overhead. Whilst the party were making for the shore two Me 109s dived out of the sun above Kalamata, attacking from a westerly direction. Before any protection could be given they strafed the Boat and caused it to burst into flames immediately. The Boat was towed in a burning condition out of the Camber, but sank near the entrance when the starboard wing fell off.' (228 Squadron ORB,

One of the Luftwaffe Malta aces, Oberleutnant Muncheberg, receiving Oak Leaves on 7 May, by which time his total had risen to 116, including nineteen over Malta.

April 1941). The 109 pair from JG 26 were flown by Oberleutnants Muncheberg and Mietusch, both experienced fighter pilots – and the destruction of the Sunderland took only a single pass.

The strong Hurricane reinforcement was good news for the defenders and more than made up for recent losses in aircraft and crews; it was a much-needed morale boost after the recent losses, although the feeling that the old Hurricanes were outclassed by the 109s would only increase in the coming weeks. On 27 April a detachment of six Blenheims of 21 Squadron arrived from 2 Group. Equipped with Blenheim IVs, the squadron had been operating against naval and land targets in Europe from its base at Watton, Norfolk. As with all the Blenheim

Blenheim of 21 Squadron at its home base of Watton; this was one of the No. 2 Group Blenheim units to rotate anti-shipping detachments through Malta.

units, the squadron had established a reputation for determined attack, and like the other units it had a high attrition rate. With the desire to increase Malta's offensive capability, the Blenheim was, at the time, the only option. The Blenheims' primary role would be anti-shipping and they were considered more suitable for the under-attack Malta, as they required less support and less runway. On 28 April: '20 bombers and 16 Stukas attacked Valetta harbour. They dropped 6 × 1000kg bombs, 26 × 500kg bombs, 239 × 50kg bombs. Bombs fell near the ships, on the State Wharf, or quay installation in French Creek, on the oil dump and in the Florina quarter of the sea. At the same time, six bombers dropped bombs on Venezia airfield. Several small fires could be seen on the runway. A further 36 aircraft attacked ships in Valetta harbour; one 1000kg bomb hit a light cruiser of the Southampton Class amidships to the starboard, and another bomb hit the same ship. The other bombs fell along the quay installations. A fire was seen in the oil harbour.' (German sitrep)

The 29th saw the harbour and airfields still the focus. Of the six bombers in the first attack on Valetta, one was shot down by the AA defences. The escorting fighters tangled with Hurricanes and claimed two for no loss. A second attack on the harbour was made by twenty-two bombers and Stukas: 'On the outward flight a large fire could be seen in the north of Valetta; there were other large fires, and one was definitely in the oil-tank installation.' (German sitrep). There were also raids on Luqa and Venezia, both of which involved the dropping of land mines, the first time the weapon is referred to in the German sitrep, with eighteen dropped on Venezia and ten on Luqa.

For the RAF bombers, Tripoli and Benghazi remained the key targets for bombing and mine-laying, as it was the main receiving port for the supplies running from Italy to North Africa, the lifeline that fed Rommel's success. There were constant calls from all sides, including London, for increased efforts against the port. A naval bombardment in April had caused some damage, but as usual this was repaired quickly. The air effort was conducted from bases in Egypt, primarily by Wellingtons, and from Malta, by RAF bombers and the FAA, with 830 Squadron specializing in 'planting vegetables' (mine laying). In the period 21 April to 4 May, Wellingtons flew fifty-three sorties against Benghazi. In addition, Blenheims flew day patrols on 'search and destroy' for ships near the port, and on May two Blenheims of 45 Squadron made claims for two ships.

The role of mines, air-laid and sea-laid (often by submarine) both in port approaches and 'clear water', was another key part of the overall maritime war. Mines either had a direct effect with ships being damaged or sunk, or slowed down shipping because of the need to sweep or pass slowly. Mines also funnelled ships in order to avoid minefields and so presented them as targets to other forms of attack.

The Luftwaffe fighters flew sweeps on the 1st, in which they claimed five Hurricanes shot down, at least two of these falling to Muncheberg. On the evening of 3 May, thirty-three bombers and Stukas attacked Valetta

The Ju 87 had mixed fortunes over Malta.

harbour, while seven attacked Luqa. Valetta was hit again on the 4th, twenty-nine bombers and Stukas focusing on shipping, while some also bombed airfields. The German sitrep reported: 'One Ju87 is overdue.' On the 6th, the bombers were after Luqa, but failed to find the target and so attacked other targets, while the escort of twenty-nine fighters tangled with fifteen Hurricanes, claiming one. There were minor operations on the 7th, 9th and 11th, the latter being reported as: 'In the evening and during the night, bombers attacked the airfield at Luqa and the harbour at Valetta. Heavy explosions and large fires were seen in the hangars and further hits on the landing area and the runways. The Stukas which attacked Valetta reported hits on the Royal Dockyard and on the torpedo store.' (German sitrep).

The Blenheims of 21 Squadron flew their first anti-shipping op on 1 May, with six aircraft going after a 3,000-ton MV, with a destroyer escort, near the Kerkennah Islands. They claimed three hits on the destroyer and one on the MV, along with several near misses. They also tangled with three Cant Z.501s, claiming one as a probable. Two Blenheims had been hit by AA fire, but all returned to Malta, and it seemed like the concept of using the Blenheims for this type of attack was sound. They were experienced at the necessary mast-height attacks, weaving around escorts and dropping their delayed action (DA) bombs. On this occasion they claimed both ships sunk, but Italian records do not confirm this. They were out again the next day, with four Blenheims attacking a large convoy that had been spotted by a Maryland. They claimed hits on one destroyer, and three MVs (8,000-ton, 4,000-ton and 2,000-ton).

The plan for long-range escorts at last came to fruition as part of an air reinforcement plan connected with the May convoys; first Beaufighters to Malta, a detachment of 252 Squadron's Beaufighter ICs, under Squadron Leader Yaxley, arriving via Gibraltar on 2 May. The thirteen coastal-type Beaufighter ICs were to provide long-range convoy cover,

Maryland of 69 Squadron at Ta Kali.

while the Hurricanes would cover ships when they came within 40 miles of Malta, but they would, whenever possible, also escort the Blenheim anti-shipping sorties. In the first joint op between the Blenheims and Beaufighters on 7 May, five Blenheims with an escort of three Beaus went after a convoy that had been spotted off Lampedusa by a Maryland. It was a success in that no losses were incurred, the escort shot down an Italian transport, and Pilot Officer Dennis scored a hit on a 5,000-ton

The Malta Blenheims were also tasked against land targets, in this case attacking a factory at Locri.

MV, which was later reported to have sunk – the first Blenheim success in the Med.

The Blenheims of 21 Squadron were out again the following day, claiming hits on an MV and a destroyer, and more success followed a few days later. For these missions in May, Flying Officer David Dennis was awarded the DFC: 'This officer has displayed great skill and daring in attacks against enemy merchant ships and escorting vessels. In May, 1941, he attacked a merchant vessel of about 5,000 tons, obtaining hits which caused the ship to founder. The next day he attacked and secured hits on an enemy sloop. A few days later he executed an attack against a merchant ship in convoy and, as a result of his bombing, the ship took a list to starboard emitting much black smoke. On all these occasions, Pilot Officer Dennis showed the greatest determination.' (AMB 4080 dated 6 June 1941).

One of the other pilots, Sergeant W.M. Osborne, was awarded the DFM in the same list. No. 21 Squadron was not destined to stay long, departing back to the UK on 11 May, and the only recorded loss appears to be V5461 destroyed on the ground at Luqa, probably a lame duck left behind as its demise was recorded as 12 May.

Anti-shipping attacks at mast head height were highly dangerous; the 21 Squadron Blenheim in this shot is in its death throes having lost half its starboard wing. The squadrons perfected the technique in North Sea operations (as in this shot) and with the desperate need for anti-shipping capability from Malta the Blenheims were seen as the only option.

One reason why it had been so quiet on Malta was that the main Axis air effort was targeting the Operation Tiger convoy, which was mounted in response to the losses of equipment caused by the Greek campaign as almost none of the equipment from Greece or Crete was returned to the Middle East. Indeed, as Chapter 4 shows, it was a remarkable achievement to rescue the men never mind the equipment. However, men without equipment are not operational, and hence the decision to run a fast convoy from Gibraltar to Alexandria – and not to send any of the ships of that convoy to Malta. The convoy eventually comprised five merchant vessels (*Clan Campbell, Clan Chattan, Clan Lamont, Empire Song* and *New Zealand Star*) and a significant escort, including the carrier *Ark Royal*; it was also boosted by additional warships destined to join the Mediterranean Fleet, including the battleship *Queen Elizabeth*. The convoy suffered its first attack in the early afternoon of the 8th, Italian torpedo-bombers making a determined but ineffective attack. The Fulmars of 807 and 808 squadrons claimed one bomber but lost some of their number to the escorting CR.42s. An evening attack by Stukas escorted by Bf 110s was equally unsuccessful; it was notable from these engagements that, although the Fulmars were far better than the Skuas, they were still outclassed. A final torpedo attack also brought no result.

At the same time that these actions were taking place, two westbound convoys (M7A and MW7B) had left Alexandria for Malta. The strategic intent of running east and west convoys at the same time had the advantage of dividing the attacking assets and, more significantly, passing ships on between the east west escort forces. MW7A had four MVs (*Amerika, Settler, Thermopylae* and *Talabot*) escorted by three cruisers and four destroyers. MW7B consisted of two tankers (*Hoegh Hood* and *Svenor*), with two cruisers and five other escorts, including a minesweeper. They were all scheduled at Malta on 10 May, as Tiger passed Malta. The convoys also had a strategic cover provided by the main fighting component of the Mediterranean Fleet, with three battleships, the carrier *Formidable*, three cruisers, and twelve destroyers, and with the *Breconshire* along as well, and planned to make a dash for Malta at the appropriate time. Other than a brief engagement with Italian aircraft from Rhodes, which were dealt with by the Fulmars from *Formidable*, claiming at least six of the attackers, the westbound convoys were virtually trouble-free and ships started to arrive at Malta from midday on the 9th.

Some of the escorts had steamed ahead to join with Tiger to assist in the anti-aircraft coverage. The core of this reinforcement were five of the AA cruisers, which would increase appreciably the barrage that the defenders could put up. In the event it was an unseen enemy that caused damage, with two ships striking mines; *New Zealand Star* was only slightly damaged, but *Empire Song* suffered a critical blow and, after the crew had been evacuated, the old whaler exploded. There was little further of note to report, and the convoy arrived in Alexandria on the 12th and discharged its supplies, which included 238 tanks, 64 Hurricanes, and large quantities of other equipment and ammunition. Both convoys, under the overall umbrella of Mediterranean Fleet Operation MD4, had been a great success for the Allies; indeed, a critical success. Conversely, it was a massive failure and missed opportunity for the Axis – where was the determined air assault? Where were the submarines and surface fleet?

HMS *Formidable* played a role in a number of the convoy operations.

Malta's direct role in the operation had been to fly reconnaissance patrols, keeping an eye on enemy assets to see what action they might be preparing, and, once the convoys were in range, to provide fighter cover, initially by Beaufighters and then Hurricanes. The Beaufighters also undertook strafing sorties on airfields such as Comiso and Catania on 10 May: 'At Comiso, six Beaufighters destroyed several aircraft, including two Ju.52s, by machine gunning, which caused fires. Three Beaufighters caused damage to groups of He.111s and Ju.88s at Catania by machine gunning from a height of 50ft. Both attacks achieved complete surprise, and there was no flak until the Beaufighters were near the end of their attacks.' (*The RAF in Maritime War, ibid*).

This initial operation was considered by many to be an indication of what could be achieved. The CO of 252 Squadron proposed using the moon period to operate night intruder ops over the Sicilian airfields. In an expression of Malta's 'reach', Beaufighters of 252 Squadron detached at first light to Crete on the 16th; from here they flew strafing missions on the packed airfields in Greece that the Germans were using for the build-up for the assault on Crete; one of the eight aircraft failed to return. However, the lack of spares, space at Luqa, and other considerations led to them departing for the UK from 20 May. The type was certainly of value but it was also in great demand.

As part of a reorganization, and for inexplicable reasons, 261 Squadron was disbanded and became 185 Squadron on 12 May. The latter had been a Hampden squadron in the UK in 1940, disbanding in May of that year, so it was perhaps a strange number to choose for a fighter squadron in Malta! For 261 Squadron, disbandment was short-lived and the unit was reconstituted on 12 July at Habbaniya by renumbering 127 Squadron.

185 Squadron Badge

Awarded: February 1945 (BR177)

Blazon: In front of a Maltese Cross or a griffin sergeant per fess argent and gules armed and langued azure

Link: The badge was selected by the squadron during the severe enemy attacks on Malta. The reason for the griffin was that this animal – half eagle and half lion – was indicative of the co-operation between the air- and groundcrews in the defence of Malta and is shown in the country's national colours

Motto: Maltese: Ara fejn hu – Look where it is.

The first scramble for the 'new' squadron was on the 13th and it had a melee with 109s, with two Hurricanes being shot down and the loss of one pilot. Over the next few days it was more of the same; Hurricanes and pilots being lost to 109s. All too often they were bounced from high, and increasingly there was discontent at the poor performance of the Hurricane and the warning time they were given.

As part of a rotation plan, the Blenheims of 21 Squadron were replaced by 139 Squadron and 82 Squadron. The deployment started badly with two of the aircraft being lost on 11 May on the ferry route, the initial leg being St Eval to Gibraltar. One aircraft ditched when an engine failed on approach to Gib, the crew being picked up by a freighter, and the second was written off when it swung on landing. All crew from both incidents were safe, but an 82 Squadron crew was not so lucky on 21 May when they crashed into the Mediterranean off Algeria during the delivery flight.

1 8 5   SQUADRON.

30ᵗ. April. 1941.

The following is a list of pilots posted from 261 Squadron to Hal Far for the purpose of forming a new fighter squadron to be known as No. 185 Squadron. These were commanded by F/LT. P.W.O. Mould. D.FC., and were divided into Flights as follows.

X. Flight.
F/o   Eliot.
F/LT. Jeffries
P/o   Hamilton
P/o   Innes.
P/o   Hall
Sgt   Bamberger.
Sgt   Ottey
Sgt   Walmsley
Sgt   Wynne
Sgt   Burton

Y. Flight.
F/o   Westmacott.
F/LT. Hancock.
P/o   Bailey
P/o   Thomson.
P/o   DREDGE.
Sgt   Branson
Sgt   Hodson
Sgt   Jolly.
P/o   Gray

All aircraft in the Squadron are to be Mark II Hurricanes and during the afternoon they were all ferried over from Ta-Kali without incident. The Squadron goes on "readiness" for the first time at dawn tomorrow and much organization has been going on to prepare for this event.

At the moment we are known as "C" Flight 261 Squadron but we are all looking forward to the time when our new number is officially allotted to us. and we can become the rivals of our friends at Ta Kali.

The 185 Squadron ORB was initially handwritten; the entry for 30 April, before the actual formation date, lists the pilots in X and Y Flights, the CO being Flight Lieutenant P.W. Mould DFC.

These incidents highlight two things: firstly, the continued importance of Gibraltar as the western 'anchor' of the Mediterranean theatre, and secondly, the hazards of getting aircraft and crews to the Mediterranean theatre. As we shall continue to discuss, the failure of Axis strategy to break the Gibraltar–Malta–Alexandria connection was the primary cause of its ultimate defeat in the Mediterranean and surrounding areas. The antiquated London flying boats of 202 Squadron gave way to the far more modern and capable Catalina in late April, and the squadron extended the range of its ASPs.

The Italian Situation Report covering the period 10 January to 22 May 1941 stated that this phase of operations had two aims:

```
HAL FAR
HQ MED NR3
GR28                    TO:- HAL FAR
                        FROM:- HQ MED
OPS49 12/5/41. PERSONAL FROM A.O.C.  . PLEASE GIVE O.C. 185 SQDN
MY VERY BEST WISHES FOR A MOST SUCCESFUL RECORD FOR HIS SQUADRON
WHICH IS OFFICIALLY BORN TODAY =============== 0735 GMT
PEGG    VA    V    R 0802 GMT  ES  VA
```

```
HAL FAR
HQ MED  NR7   IMPORTANT
GR84                    TO:- KALAFRANA  HAL FAR  LUQA  TA/KALI
                        FROM :- HQ MED
0:142 12/5 . FURTHER PARA 3 THIS HEADQUARTERS INTERNAL CIRCULAR
MEMORANDA SERIAL NUMBER 30 DATED MAY 3RD . NUMBER 185 SQUADRON
FORMED AT R.A.F. STATION HAL FAR WITH EFFECT FROM MAY 12TH FROM
''C'' FLIGHT NUMBER 261  SQUADRON WHICH CEASED TO EXISTS WITH
EFFECT FROM SAME DATE . NUMBER 185 SQUADRON IS PLACED UNDER THE
ORDERS OF THE OFFICER COMMANDING R.A.F. STATION HAL FAR FOR
OPERATIONS AND ADMINISTRATIONS . F/ LT P.W.O. WOULD IS APPOINTE
TO THE COMMAND OF NUMBER 185 SQUADRON WITH EFFECT FROM DATE
OF FORMATION =========== 1230. G.M.T.
```

Signal approving formation of 185 Squadron.

1. To interrupt or at least to hamper the continuous supply of reinforcements to Egypt via the Mediterranean
2. To protect our shipping to Italian North Africa by neutralizing the defences and the air and naval forces.

'The passage through the Sicilian Narrows was heavily guarded against enemy shipping on which the following losses were inflicted by the Axis Air Force: Sunk: 3 naval ships and 12 merchant ships; Damaged: 29 naval ships and 57 merchant ships.

'In spite of this, 32 naval ships and 24 transports passed through the Sicilian Narrows during this period and at the end of the offensive the enemy forces on Malta were practically intact due to supplies of air and naval material to the Island. The pressure which Malta had brought to bear against our shipping had lessened right from the first days of the offensive, and this tendency became even more noticeable towards the end of it.' (Air and Naval Bases on Malta Situation Report, May 1942 translated by AHB as VII/43).

The 185 Squadron ORB was initially handwritten; the entry for 1 May ends with 'taken all round – not a brilliant start but we hope better may be accomplished' … as indeed it was!

139 Squadron pose in front of Blenheim IV; as with other detachments, the 139 crews were to suffer heavy losses when operating from Malta.

In the first half of the year the Works Department had been able to do little more than patch up damage, a crucial task, although it did extend the main runway at Luqa and build some large protective pens for Wellingtons. However, the respite that came from May to November 1941 provided the opportunity for major construction work, which, unknown at the time, would prove the difference during the 1942 blitz.

More work was required than availability of labour, plant and materials would permit. Strict priority had to be agreed and worked to in order to ensure the completion of the most vital works during the period of calm. The works commenced during this period included:

Luqa: NW–SE runway extended to 1,776 yards [this was the only really suitable runway for Wellingtons]; NE–SW runway extended to 1,400 yards (and later to 2,000 yards); temporary perimeter tracks and extensive dispersal areas and tracks laid; aircraft pens constructed; airfield lighting; underground power station and operations room

Safi: Connection of Luqa and Safi by 40ft wide access track with a continuous dispersal along it together with bomb store area

Hal Far: Hard runway extension in NW–SE direction; perimeter and dispersal tracks; connecting track with Safi; underground power station and operations room

Ta Kali: Perimeter and dispersal tracks and pens; underground power station and operations room

Valletta: Underground War HQ with two operations rooms

Qrendi: Work had been commenced in December 1940 on construction of a hard-paved airfield of two strips 1,200 yards in length. Owing to lack of resources and pre-occupation with air raid damage, the work was suspended until 1942.

Overnight on 18/19 May the Hurricanes of 249 Squadron were transferred from HMS *Furious* to HMS *Ark Royal* at Gibraltar. The squadron, having made a name for itself as a fighter squadron in the Battle of Britain and then moving to offensive sweeps over Europe, had been 'warned off' in April for a move to the Middle East, as had 213 and 229 Squadrons, two equally experienced units. The two carriers, with their escorts, set sail, the Hurricane ferry being coded as Operation Splice, which carried sixty-four Hurricane IIs. The convoy sailed on the 19th and two days later launched forty-six Hurricanes and five Fulmars to Malta, after which it returned to Gibraltar. On 21 May the Hurricanes of 213 Squadron were first away, losing one aircraft when it hit the sea; the pilot (Pilot Officer N. Downie) was picked up by the Italians. Six of 229's aircraft also made the trip, the remainder staying aboard, destined for Egypt. The flights had been led by FAA Fulmar guides, although in some case this caused problems due to the poor serviceability of the Fulmars. It was a similar tale for 249 Squadron, with the first section returning when the Fulmar went unserviceable. Flight Lieutenant Ginger Neil was leading the second section, but it too had problems with the Fulmar, which at one point pulled up and vanished; after some uncertainty, and with concerns over fuel, he led the section on to Malta ... after 5 hours and 35 minutes flying time, an amazing figure for a Hurricane even with its long-range tanks, and with excellent navigation: 'Malta, when it came, appeared with magical suddenness and in the form of cliffs adjacent to my left ear. They loomed white and brown out of the mist and sea and were almost within touching distance. Filfla Rock being just ahead, I made a token dart at it before turning north on order to climb over the cliffs that formed the island's southern boundary.' (Ginger Neil, in *249 at War*, Brian Cull, Grub Street.)

The Hurricanes landed at Luqa, which was under attack at the time, Hal Far and Ta Kali; all made it down safely and were guided to protective pens. Having expected to be on their way to the Middle East, 249 was 'not amused' to hear that it was staying in Malta – while the personal kit, and the groundcrew, continued on the Egypt. They were even more dismayed when told they would be taking over the battle-weary aircraft of 261 Squadron. The battle-weary aspect of the Hurricanes was in large measure due to the lack of spare parts, and it was actually a great tribute to the groundcrew that the aircraft were even kept flyable. It is certain that in Fighter Command many of the aircraft would have been cannibalized for spares as not being fit to fly! The aircraft situation soon became worse.

For 213 and 229 squadron it was a short stop, and in the afternoon they were off to Egypt, escorted by Beaufighters of 252 Squadron. On the 20th, the Stukas went after different targets: 'attacked a searchlight position in St Elmo and the district of Florina, and the fortifications at Picasoli. Fires were observed in St Elmo and Florina.' (German sitrep). Attacks were also made on Luqa and during combat with five Hurricanes one was claimed destroyed. On the same day an airborne force that could have been used to assault Malta was instead launched against Crete, and despite the

Malta's easy to work stone also proved ideal for constructing protective pens, although a variety of materials were used and Army 'labour' was co-opted for this crucial passive defence task.

fairly rapid success of the invasion, the airborne force was decimated and any thoughts of a second use against the even more difficult target of Malta were soon forgotten.

An Axis naval conference on 22 May stressed the importance of bases for the eastern Mediterranean strategy: 'Attention is called to the decisive importance of defending the main strategic points such as Salonika, Lemnos, Piraeus, Melos, and Crete. These points are of decisive importance as strategic bases for any further operations in the eastern Mediterranean. It is essential that they shall be adequately protected against all eventualities and be ready to offer determined resistance to any enemy action. This is a necessary condition for successful operations by the X Air Corps. This applies especially to Crete, which is essential to the X Air Corps.' (Fuhrer Conferences on Naval Affairs). Strangely it fails to mention Rhodes, where the Italians built a major airfield in 1938 that in the early part of the war housed SM.81s and CR.32s, and which was a frequent target for RAF bombers from Egypt.

The Blenheims of 139 Squadron had success on 22 May when they sank the Italian 4,857-ton *Perseo*, this victory being shared with the Navy. The previous day, 82 Squadron had arrived, and so now Malta had a reasonable attacking force. A Blenheim strike force from 82 Squadron and 139 Squadron sank the Italian 6,342-ton *Marco Foscarini* on the 26th. The target was a convoy heading to Tripoli and Sergeant E. Inman (V6460) was shot down by anti-aircraft fire, although one account suggests the aircraft suffered critical damage from its own bomb strike on a ship; only one of the crew survived, becoming a PoW. A second Blenheim was lost, the reason stated was blast damage from the bombs of V6460, all crew being lost. Less than a week later, two Blenheims of 139 Squadron were lost in similar fashion. Damage from the explosions from other attackers was not unusual, although co-ordinated attacks were planned to avoid both self-damage and damage to following aircraft, by either splitting aircraft over the target area by lateral distance or by time. However, weaving and jinking at mast-top height, and the massive explosion caused if the target was an ammunition ship, meant that the risk of such frag damage was always a factor. The month ended with a success, however, the Blenheims sinking the Italian 3,314-ton *Floida II* on the 30th. The Assessment Committee that looked at the results credited the May detachments with:

- Cat I (sunk or constructive loss): 2 ships totaling 6,315 tons
- Cat II (seriously damaged): 5 ships totaling 22,500 tons
- Cat III (damaged): 5 ships totaling 25,000 tons.

These results were achieved in thirty-four sorties and attacks against fifteen ships, and for the loss of two Blenheims. It was a good start.

Hurricanes of 249 Squadron ablaze after the 25 May attack; the lack of dispersal and protective pens is clear in this view – but such pens also restricted scrambles.

Installing a drop tank on a 109 of JG 26 at Gela.

A Blenheim mast height attack on MV off Tripol

No. 249 Squadron split into two Flights (A and B) with a half-day standby period for each of them, which meant maybe eight aircraft or so ready at any one time, with readiness being either at dispersal or in the cockpit. The first such standby was on 25 May, and when the alarm was sounded in the early afternoon the pilots were put on cockpit readiness but not scrambled. As they sat at the dispersal at Ta Kali they were hit by Bf 109s of JG 26, which resulted in two aircraft being destroyed and three damaged, with three pilots and a number of groundcrew wounded. One of those wounded was Flying Officer Wells: 'This was our first readiness in Malta and whilst sitting in the crew room were astonished to hear the air raid sirens howling – in the UK we had always been airborne before the sirens sounded. We rushed out to our aircraft and got ready for scramble which never came. The next thing I saw was people running and on looking round saw the 109s starting their dive on the airfield. I tried to start the engine but the airman on the starter battery trailer had fled, so I could not do a thing except huddle in the cockpit, waiting for the sensation of being hit. The aircraft was burning well and this, plus exploding ammunition, drove me out. Only when I got on the ground and tried to walk did I realize that I had a bullet through the top of my right ankle.' (Flying Officer Wells in *249 at War*, *ibid*).

It was the parting 'gesture' of Muncheberg's fighter unit, and one that rounded off a very successful period for his 109s, with claims of forty-two aerial victories over Malta's Hurricanes. Not a great start for 249 and something of a shock to the fighter pilots who in the UK had been used to having plenty of warning and being in a position to intercept raiders – rather than being stuck on the ground. As it turned out, the Luftwaffe was about to all but vanish from Malta (for a while) as it was called on to take part in Hitler's main war aim – the conquest of Russia, although some units moved to North Africa for Rommel's 'final push'. This enabled 249 to settle in, Malta to recover, some supplies to arrive – and pilot morale to improve by once more scoring well against the Italians.

The transfer of Luftwaffe assets to other campaigns meant that the task of destroying Malta reverted to the Italians, who proved no more capable of this in 1941 than they had in 1940, even though additional air assets were moved to Sicily and a new type, the BR.20, entered the conflict area. So Malta recovered and the offensive aircraft returned. Air Vice-Marshal Hugh Lloyd arrived to take command on 25 May, and Malta entered its next phase – as a base for attack.

Chapter 4

Back on the Offensive: June 1941–November 1941

O n 29 May, Tedder wrote to VCAS that: 'The air has come into its own with a vengeance in the Mediterranean. I need hardly say I have refrained from saying "I told you so".' He was referring to the now overwhelming evidence that land-based air power now dominated – following the doctrine 'protect your own and, more especially, destroy the enemy'. The Allies were back on the offensive, having weathered the Luftwaffe attacks.

While Malta was not 'off the hook' and there was hard fighting to come, the island played an increased role in the supply war, and in the period June to November Malta-based aircraft made 544 sorties against Tripoli, Benghazi and the smaller harbours on the Gulf of Sirte, with other sorties

Map showing Malta as a strike base, its ideal location – and why the Axis should have eliminated Malta as a threat.

against the Italian end of the chain. In addition, Malta was the main hub of reconnaissance sorties and at varying times in the period led, or contributed to, the anti-shipping strikes. The Middle East-based aircraft were even more heavily engaged in the bombing of ports such as Benghazi, with more than 1,000 sorties, as well as their contribution to the anti-shipping strikes. The Mediterranean was increasingly a dangerous place to be in an Axis ship. Vice Admiral Weichold was to state in August 1941: 'Apart from the possible mounting of an offensive in this theatre, which owing to the geographical situation would necessarily increase the demand on transport, the mere maintenance of the military forces overseas requires more tonnage than will be available in the future if the present rate of losses continues. An appreciable decrease in losses is no way to be reckoned with.' And later: 'It was no longer possible for all convoys to include ships loaded with heavy material. This caused a remarkable decline in the transport of heavy vehicles.' (*RAF in the Maritime War*, ibid).

So what happened in the second half of 1941? A new AOC arrived on 1 June, with Air Vice Marshal Hugh P. Lloyd taking over from Air Commodore Maynard. With the policy for Malta to be increasingly an offensive base for bombers to reach out in all directions and disrupt Axis supplies, the appointment of a 'bomber man' seemed most appropriate. Before he left the UK, he had been told by Sir Charles Portal that Malta's main task was to sink Axis shipping running from Europe to Africa. He certainly took this on board.

The Hurricanes of 249 Squadron scored their first success from Malta on 3 June, with Squadron Leader Barton downing an SM.79. He followed this success a few days later (8 June) when on a night patrol over the harbour area he shot down a BR.20, with a further bomber damaged by two other pilots.

The following day's mission flags up two frequently ignored aspects of operations; firstly, the role of the radar units on Malta in finding targets and, secondly, the much appreciated rescue service provided by the high speed launch. The radar picked up a formation of aircraft headed from Sicily to North Africa, passing some 50 miles from Malta. This serves to demonstrate that Malta's offensive role was not restricted to anti-shipping, but it also interdicted air routes. The targets this time were SM.79s of 193 Squadriglia en route to Castel Benito. The Hurricanes were vectored on to the target, shot down one and probably damaged the other three. On the return flight, Sergeant Rex (Z4087) had to bail out because of a glycol leak, possibly caused by return fire from one of the bombers. His general position was passed and a Malta HSL was sent out to pick him up. Flight Lieutenant Edward Hardie was commander of the rescue launch (*HSL107*) and he recorded: 'We had a very vague idea of where he was; we knew he was about 50 to 60 miles out. Visibility was poor and we went on and on – we did not see anything and I was about to give up in despair when I saw something on the horizon that looked like wreckage. It was the wreckage of an Italian troopship. It was only the fact that I altered my course like that I came across the fighter pilot swimming like mad and, when I got him on board, I said, where were you going? And he said: "I thought I would give you boys a helping hand in getting nearer Malta." I told him that he had been heading for Benghazi! He told me before he did ditch he had shot down one of the Italian bombers and he did not know if any of the crew were still alive … we looked around and came across one of the wings of the Italian bomber, on which was the very badly burned pilot. When we got him aboard, I had to restrain him because he wanted to shake the hands of the boys who had shot him down. I was nearer Benghazi than I was to Malta and when I was on my way back I saw something else in the water – a dinghy with two FAA officers. They had ditched after running out of fuel whilst on a submarine patrol. So I went out for one and came back with four.' The two FAA personnel were from a Swordfish (recorded as Jopling and wireless operator) and the Italian was the pilot of the SM.79, Luciano Fabbri, whose co-pilot was also subsequently rescued.

Hurricanes being prepared on HMS *Argus* for one of this carrier's trips on the air reinforcement route.

The Blenheims of 82 and 139 squadrons also had a good start to the month, sinking two ships on 3 June, the 6,117-ton *Montello* and the 6,132-ton *Beatrice C.* One of the five Blenheims flew into the sea, either while manoeuvring or shot down by a CR.42. Wing Commander Pepper took six of 139 Squadron's Blenheims on an offensive sweep the following day, locating an escorted convoy of five MVs that also had four Ju 88s in attendance. The first section attacked and scored hits on at least one ship; the second section ran in against the same large ship – which promptly blew up, causing fatal damage to the lead aircraft flown by Wing Commander N. Pepper. One of his crew survived to become a PoW. The first Blenheim (V5460) to bomb had been damaged but made it back to Malta, where it was assessed as DBR (damaged beyond repair). The Blenheims of 139 Squadron departed back to the UK on 5 June.

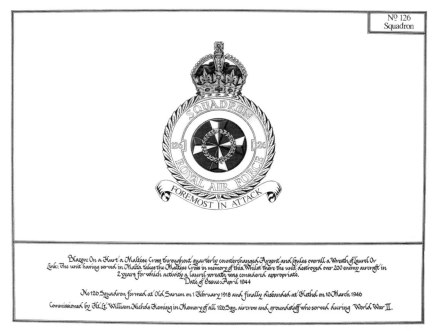

126 Squadron badge. (*source RAF Heraldry Trust, www.rafht.co.uk*)

More Hurricanes were destined for Malta, again as a formed squadron, 46 Squadron, as well as replacement aircraft, under Operation Rocket. HMS *Argus* loaded the twenty-nine cased Hurricanes on the Clyde and joined convoy WS8B to Gibraltar, arriving on 31 May, with another forty-eight Hurricanes arriving on *Furious* the following day. Some aircraft were off-loaded for erection in Gib, the rest were shared between *Furious* (twenty) and *Ark Royal* (twenty-four). The escorted convoy sailed on the 4th and launched all forty-four on the 6th, escorted by eight Blenheims from Gibraltar; one Hurricane had to return with a problem but the rest made it to Malta. Meanwhile, *Furious* headed back to the Clyde for more aircraft, in what was a seemingly unending, but vital, shuttle. The decision was taken that 46 Squadron would 'donate' aircraft and pilots to form a new squadron, 126 Squadron, which duly formed at Ta Kali on the 28th. According to RAF records, 46 Squadron's groundcrew, who ended up in the Middle East, effectively became a maintenance unit, firstly at Abu Sueir. They were reborn as an operational unit in May 1942, from an element of 89 Squadron, operating Beaufighters.

The periodic War Summary for Malta provided a summary of the damage caused in the period 11 February to 11 June. The Station Commander at Hal Far: 'A hangar and annexes severely damaged, barrack block damaged, barrack block C one end badly damaged, standby power house direct hit on tank room, D hangar direct hit, required demolishing, barrack hut no. 2 direct hit, completely demolished, barrack hit no. 3 severely damaged, not worth repair, aircraft store in front of NAAFI completely demolished, naval stores Bellman hangar severely damaged by direct hit.' Damage to aircraft was recorded as: 806 Squadron: 2 Fulmars seriously damaged and 1 slightly damaged; 830 Squadron: 2 Swordfish burnt out and 12 damaged; Station Flight: 1 Seal burnt out and 1 Swordfish damaged; Fulmar Flight: 3 Fulmars damaged.

The Station Commander at Kalafrana, which included St Paul's Bay, reported his stats by month and day:

March 5th: Slight superficial blast damage to a few buildings, one Sunderland and Loire at moorings damaged by shrapnel, one Sunderland at St Paul's Bay damaged by machine-gun attack.

March 10th: One Sunderland at St Paul's Bay set on fire and sunk and another slightly damaged during enemy machine-gun attack.

April 27th: One Sunderland set on fire and sunk at Kalafrana by machine-gun attack by ME.109s.

May 10th: One Sunderland set on fire and sunk at Marsa-Xlokk [sic] by enemy machine-gun attack.

June: nil.

Sunderland N9049 sunk at its moorings.

The SIO (Station Intelligence Officer) at Luqa also provided detail by raids:

February 26th: Six Wellingtons burnt out, seven badly damaged, three slightly damaged. Buildings damaged – airmen's cookhouse, NAAFI, three barrack blocks and a storehouse.

March 11th: Night raid. One Maryland damaged and a dope store destroyed.

March 14th: Night raid. No damage apart from overhead cables.

April 25th: Night raid. One Maryland and one Miles Magister written off, one barrack block destroyed.

May 4th: Night raid. Chance Light badly damaged.
May 6th: Daylight raid. One Beaufighter written off, eight other slightly damaged.

May 14th: Night raid. Three Marylands damaged, one motor truck destroyed, NAAFI kitchen damaged.

May 15th: Daylight raid. One Wellington burnt out, three Beaufighters damaged.

May 20th: Daylight raid. One Beaufighter burnt out, control tower damaged, one civilian employee killed.

May 21st: Daylight raid: One Wellington and one Blenheim written off, slight damage to a Beaufighter and a Maryland.

The SIO at Ta Kali sent his summary as: 'There have been 14 raids between 11th February 1941 and 31st May 1941. Aerodrome twice shot up; first time 0730 hours 9/3/41 one Hurricane written off, two Hurricanes put unserviceable, no casualties. Second time 1329 hours 25/5/41 two Hurricanes burnt out, three Hurricanes put unserviceable, four casualties. There have been 2 mines explode on aerodrome – about 16 bombs exploded and about 17 unexploded during the period. Other than the shoot ups, 11 Hurricanes have been damaged in air raids. Buildings and glass have been shattered by blast.'

The same summary also provided total flying times in hours for all aircraft operating from Malta for the period 11 February to 7 June:

Type	Hours	Casualties	Type	Hours	Casualties
Hurricane	1719.30	39	Hurricane II	69.10	
Beaufighters	410.50	4	Glenn Martins	1099.35	5
Blenheims	395.20	12	Wellingtons	422.50	18
Swordfish	541.00	9	Fulmars	28.35	2
Sunderlands	168.55				
Casualties: included killed, missing and injured					

The air alarm was sounded 388 times during the period, of which ninety-nine were for night bombing and thirty-eight for day bombing/dive-bombing. The claims made by the defenders were sixty-seven confirmed, thirty-four unconfirmed (probable) and twenty-seven damaged, as shown in the table below, for the loss of thirty-two aircraft and seventeen pilots, not including ground losses:

Type	Destroyed		Unconfirmed		Damaged	
	Fighters	AA	Fighters	AA	Fighters	AA
Ju 87	15	10	6	4	5	4
Ju 88	4	7	6	4	4	3
Bf 109	6	1	2	–	1	1
Bf 110	2	1	–	–	1	1
Do 215	4	–	3	–	–	2
CR.42	3	–	3	–	–	–
He 111	1	–	2	–	–	–
Z.506	1	–	1	–	–	–
BR.20	1	–	1	–	–	–
SM.79	1	–	1	–	–	–
SM.81	1	–	–	–	–	–
Unidentified	–	9	–	1	–	6
Total	39	28	25	9	11	16

On the offensive side, six squadrons flew sorties in this period, as summarized below:

Squadron	Target	Operations	Sorties	Results	Remarks
148 Sqn	Catania	3	8	22,850lb GP + 4,320 incendiary	Wellington
148 Sqn	Comiso	3	5	11,400lb GP + 2,640 incendiary	Wellington
148 Sqn	Tripoli	9	47	149,750lb GP + 7,750 incendiary	Wellington
148 Sqn	Gela	1	1	500lb GP	Wellington
830 Sqn	'Rat Hunts'	14	76	16 torpedoes; 3 MV of 5,000–7,000 tons sunk, 1 destroyer hit	Swordfish
830 Sqn	Tripoli	10	48	25 mines, 14,000lb GP	Swordfish
830 Sqn	Lampedusa	2	9	2 mines, 1 torpedo	Swordfish
830 Sqn	Shadowing	2	4		Swordfish
252 Sqn	Catania	1	3	Strafe Bf 109s and Ju 88s	Beaufighter
252 Sqn	Comiso	1	6	2 Ju 52 burnt out, strafe Bf 109s and Ju 88s	Beaufighter
21 Sqn	Shipping	4	11	1 MV 8,000 tons probable, 1 MV 4,000 tons sunk, 3 MV 3,000 tons sunk, 1 destroyer sunk, 1 MV and 1 destroyer badly hit	Blenheim
139 Sqn	Shipping	7	16	2 MV 4,000–5,000 tons sunk, 2 MV damaged, 1 MV 8,000 tons severe damage, 1 MV 8,000 tons sunk	Blenheim
82 Sqn	Shipping	7	17	1 MV 10,000 tons smoking, down at stern, 1 MV 5,000 tons damaged	Blenheim

Blenheims of 21
Squadron at low level
over the sea en route to
a target.

On 12 June, 249 Squadron claimed one fighter destroyed (Flight Lieutenant Neil) and one probable (Sergeant Livingstone), with 46 Squadron claiming two others. However, 249 lost two aircraft in return, one pilot being killed (Pilot Officer Munro) and one (Pilot Officer Saunders) bailing out and being picked up by rescue launch. A number of Italian fighters circled over the rescue but did not intervene, a situation that might have been different had the rescue been by air and not sea. Two Italian air-sea rescue Cants were shot down by Hurricanes during the day, an action that was given a mixed reception, some believing that aircraft on such missions should be left alone.

This had been the busiest day for some time, and also saw MC.200s appearing as escorts in larger numbers than before, as the Italians continued to struggle to replace the loss of the Luftwaffe air assets. Unfortunately for the Italians, Malta now had a more effective radar and control system, with six AMES stations in operation at Dingli (three), Magdalena, Rabat, and Ta Silich, albeit, as we shall see later, there were still problems. The island also had a reasonable number of Hurricanes and pilots, such that it was able to put up twelve to eighteen at a time, although some of the pilots lacked experience in theatre even though most were very experienced as far as Fighter Command was concerned.

In the middle of the month Malta received more Hurricanes courtesy of Operation Tracer. The forty-eight fighters were for 238 Squadron and 260 Squadron and were flown off HMS *Ark Royal* and HMS *Victorious*; this was the first use of the latter on this route. The Hurricanes were split into twenty-six on *Ark Royal* and twenty-two on *Victorious*. Air navigation was provided by Hudsons from Gibraltar to shepherd the fighters from the fly-off point to Malta. One Hurricane ditched, but the pilot (Sergeant Campbell) was spotted by an air search and was picked up by *HSL107*. Another pilot was killed when he crashed on landing. However,

Numerous signals were exchanged with high command trying to get cannon-armed Hurricanes to provide greater hitting power. This 3 Squadron IIC is not a Malta-based aircraft.

Tropicalized Hurricane IIA Z4533, with Beaufighter of 252 Squadron (minus outer part of wing) in the background.

both squadrons were only passing through on their way to the desert war. Some records show only forty-three Hurricanes arriving from this resupply.

A few days later the *Ark* and *Furious* were once more dispatching Hurricanes, although the planned forty-eight aircraft was curtailed following a take-off incident on *Furious*, the tenth aircraft to go hitting the carrier's island. Operation Railway saw twenty-one Hurricanes delivered in the first phase (Railway I) and thirty-five in the second (Railway II). Squadron Leader Barton received a number of IICs for 249 Squadron and commented: 'Towards the end of June we received

Iraq and Syria 1941

Iraq Revolt 1941

The German-inspired revolt in Iraq was led by Rashid Ali and started at the beginning of April 1941. Principal targets for the rebels included the oil pipeline to Palestine, and the RAF's major (training) airfield at Habbaniya. The rebels were provided a small degree of air support by the Italian 155 Squadron and the Luftwaffe Sonderkommando Junck. By the end of April Rashid's forces were besieging Habbaniya, home of 4 FTS. This became a spirited little action during which the training aircraft – Audaxs, Oxfords, Gladiators – of the FTS were modified for offensive action and in which capacity they flew 1,400 sorties! The revolt was over by 31 May as British forces regained control of the rebel areas.

Syria

Vichy French control of Lebanon and Syria provided problems with supply of British areas and also provided a potential line of attack for German forces, and the Axis air support to the Iraq rebellion had gone via Syria. The decision was taken to seize these areas and an offensive was launched on 8 June, the ground forces being supported by four and a half squadrons, these being primarily engaged on a counter-air campaign to negate the French air presence as well as providing ground support on the few occasions that the situation so demanded. A ceasefire was declared on 12 July.

The importance to our account is that enemy-held land bases in Syria would have an influence over sea operations in the eastern Mediterranean, and in addition there was a French naval force, with four destroyers and three submarines, based at Beirut. The Allies landed on 8 June, with air cover by Fulmars, although this was soon replaced by RAF units, such as the Tomahawks of 3 Squadron RAAF and the Hurricanes of 80 Squadron, and for offensive operations, the Blenheims of 45 Squadron. The Blenheims moved to Palestine (Ramleh and Aqir) on 19 June as part of the air support, although they were still rebuilding after the losses of April and May in the Western Desert and Greece/Crete. 'The first op was flown on the 23rd when three Blenheims attacked Fort Soueida, whilst a fourth aircraft flew a recce mission over Beirut. The latter was intercepted by four French fighters and damaged, which resulted in a ground loop (courtesy of a bullet through a tyre) and collapsed undercarriage but no injuries.' (45 Sqn history).

On 22 June Blenheims of 11 Squadron attacked French destroyers in Beirut harbour, with further attacks by RAF and FAA aircraft over subsequent days. Patrols were flown over all the harbours and attacks made whenever suitable targets were found, the intention being to negate any possible naval threat and to prevent any reinforcements arriving by sea. Operations were also supported by aircraft operating from Cyprus, and the Allies had air superiority within a few days.

some Hurricane IICs (four cannon), hence cannon firing practice. These aircraft were heavier but had hitting power if you could get the enemy in your sights.' The need for more hitting power, and thus cannon, had been clear – and requested – for some time.

In a co-operative sortie with the Royal Navy on 15 June, a Sunderland of 228 Squadron located and shadowed the French destroyer *Chevalier Paul*, passing reports until the attack force of 815 Squadron Swordfish arrived to sink the vessel. This was connected with operations in Iraq and Syria – see panel.

During July the Axis air forces made a number of attacks on Cyprus, targeting shipping in Famagusta harbour and the airfield at Nicosia. The latter attack caused some damage and was seen as evidence of the need to reinforce the defence of Cyprus. Up to this point detachments comprised three RAF squadrons (80 Squadron Hurricanes, 203 Squadron Blenheims

Trio of torpedo-equipped Albacores over Malta.

and 272 Squadron Beaufighters) and two FAA squadrons (815 Swordfish and 826 Albacore). During this period Churchill stated that the campaign in Syria and the safeguarding of Cyprus should take priority over the projected offensive in the Western Desert. It is certainly true that it would not be in the Allied interest to lose Cyprus so soon after losing Crete, as that would provide the Axis with a stronger network of air bases and enable domination of the eastern Mediterranean and an increased threat to Egypt. Along with the promise of one Army Division (50th Division), Tedder agreed to reinforce Cyprus with 259 Wing, which meant the provision of three Hurricane squadrons, although initially only 80 Squadron would be based in Cyprus and the other two in Palestine to deploy 'as needed', plus a GR flight. In addition to the defence of the island against air and air-sea assault,

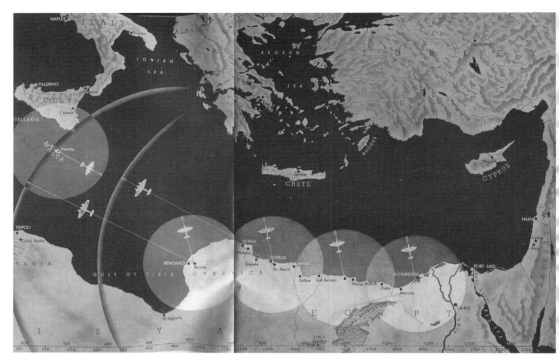

Map showing some aspects eastern Mediterranean air strike range, but with Malta limited to short-range ops for this map. The importance of controlling airfields on the North African coast is clear from this map.

the air elements, like those in Malta, were also given key roles in reconnaissance and co-operation with naval forces, including Fleet movements in the neighbourhood of Cyprus. Aircraft of No. 201 Group were tasked with reconnaissance of designated areas, and Cyprus was assigned Areas C, E, I and M (see map below). Each of these areas was to be covered by daily reconnaissance.

As the eastern Mediterranean remained fairly calm for shipping other than the submarine threat, the activities from Cyprus are not covered in this account. On 1 August, the changing nature of the strategic scene saw 228 Squadron depart the Mediterranean theatre en route to West Africa, leaving 230 Squadron at Aboukir as the sole Sunderland unit in the eastern Mediterranean. However, other units, 10 Squadron RAAF in particular, continued to mount detachments at Gibraltar. For the

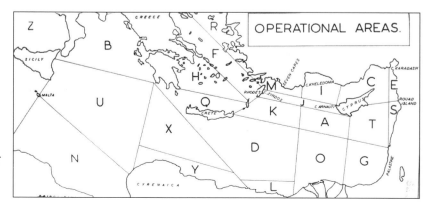

Map showing division of Eastern Mediterranean into operational areas.

82 Squadron detachment, June had proved a trying month, with a number of losses, with some successes at the start of the month (as detailed above) but then a series of losses:

- 11th: Z6526, Squadron Leader M. Watson and crew lost on anti-shipping strike
- 19th: T1888, Sergeant J Harrison and crew lost on shipping sweep
- 22nd: Z6422, Squadron Leader J. Harrison-Broadley and crew PoW on anti-shipping strike
- 29th: Z9545, Sergeant J. Cover and crew lost on attack on Tripoli.

Sergeant Stewart Thompson was the wireless operator/air gunner in Z6422 and his Escape and Evasion report provides an account of the loss and his subsequent captivity and escape: 'I was a member of the crew of a Blenheim aircraft which left Malta on 22 Jun 41 to attack a convoy sailing between Malta and Lampedusa. We sighted our target and went into the attack. We hit the engine room of a merchantman, but were then fired at by an Italian destroyer, and hit in our port engine. The aircraft caught fire and plunged into the sea about 2 kms from Lampedusa. I managed to launch the dinghy just before hitting the water and we all three climbed into it. The observer [Sergeant P L Felton] had been injured. We tried to paddle away, but were picked up by the destroyer, which had remained behind to tow the damaged merchantman. We were taken to Pantelleria, which we reached about 24 Jun 41. We were treated excellently in the destroyer, and given dry clothes and all possible comfort.

'At Pantelleria, Sergeant Felton went into hospital and S/Ldr Harrison-Broadly and myself were taken to a big house next to the aerodrome. Here we were visited by the Governor of Pantelleria. We were entertained by Italian Air Force officers and flown next day to Sicily. There were four carabinieri in the plane in addition to the aircraft crew. The Italians were apparently afraid we might try to get control of the aircraft.'

By the end of June, they were in Rome, and Sergeant Felton rejoined them. They were all sent to Campo 78, Sulmona, which held about 3,000 PoWs. The account has no details of the next two years as a prisoner, as it was only concerned with capture, escape and evasion, so it takes up the story again on 8 September 1943, with his escape.

June had also been a bad month for the OADU (Overseas Aircraft Delivery/Despatch Unit), and once again flags up the use of Gibraltar and Malta in the transit of aircraft to operational squadrons, and the hazards on the route. In what was a bad two weeks for the OADU, six Wellingtons were lost:

- 15th: N2803, Pilot Officer R. Campbell and five crew, departed Gibraltar, hit mountain in Algeria
- 16th: R3293, Sergeant E. Beattie and five crew, departed Gibraltar, crashed on approach to Luqa
- 20th: X3211, Sergeant P. Bold and five crew, departed UK for Gibraltar but bad weather led them to land in Portugal; crew interned but quickly released
- 20th: Flying Officer E. Bell and five crew, departed UK for Gibraltar but bad weather led them to ditch off Aguilas, Spain; crew interned and not released until March 1942
- 27th: P9277, Pilot Officer C. Butler and five crew, departed Luqa for Egypt but ditched; two of crew killed
- 2nd Jul: Z8730, Sergeant J. Hamborough and six crew, departed Luqa for Egypt but ditched.

The OADU had formed as the OAD Flight at Kemble in September 1940, with the responsibility to prepare aircraft for air dispatch (ferry) to the overseas theatres. According to John Manners, who flew Beaufighters with 39 Squadron, the crews on the ferry route from the UK to Gibraltar were briefed to land in Portugal if they had any problems, as it was likely that they would be released very quickly and thus able to rejoin their units.

Meanwhile, mid-June saw the latest Allied offensive in the desert, when General Wavell launched Operation Battleaxe, one of whose primary aims was to relieve the siege of Tobruk. The operation was short-lived and heavy losses were suffered in the crucial armoured formations. Much of the air effort in the weeks before, and in the following weeks, was spent on preparing for or covering the offensive, although it had little direct impact on Malta. Although Rommel won the contest, he too had suffered losses, and every time one side or the other attacked, the supply war became even more important. The question now was, who could replace the losses in material?

The last week of June had been a busy one for the defenders of Malta, with the Italians appearing on most days, usually as fighter-escorted recce missions. Some combats took place and the Hurricanes invariably came off best. On 23 June the Hurricanes also made an offensive sweep of their own, a strafing run over the seaplane base at Syracuse. While this was generally considered a success by its leader, Squadron Leader Rabagliati, it was not popular with some command elements, who were of the opinion it was not worth risking precious fighter aircraft and pilots in this way.

June had seen more than 140 Hurricanes arrive on Malta, and with losses light this meant the RAF had air superiority and had more than recovered from its battering during the Luftwaffe's brief intervention. The German invasion of Russia in late June seemed to confirm that the Luftwaffe would be fully occupied elsewhere for the foreseeable future. Supplies, however, were a concern, and also how Malta could handle shipping in the harbour. A signal exchange of late June between the governor and the War Office discussed the resupply plans. 'This would mean a convoy of 75,000 tons for civil and co-ordinated items only and excluding fodder. Vice Admiral Malta considers that the greatest tonnage the port can handle at one time is five ships with a total capacity of 50,000 tons. From the point of view of berthing and safety he considers the maximum number of ships in the port should not exceed seven.' This took into consideration that once a ship had been unloaded it had to wait in Malta until it could be passed out safely, and 'five ships of around 48,000 tons and two tankers each of 10,000 tons which formed the last convoy from Egypt are still lying here awaiting escort to Egypt or elsewhere.' Sitting in Malta empty they were nothing more than targets for air attack. The standard plan was for empty ships to be escorted away by the escort that brought the full ships.

The governor went on to explain that he only needed 40,000 tons, as long as it was the right stuff, and then he would have his eight months' stock, but 'it is essential that all services and Government should complete to the same reserve, for present organization of the fortress makes each entirely dependent on the other. Convoy will not achieve its object if it completes all military stores to eight months, and does not bring sufficient flour and/or wheat to complete whole population to eight months. He then went on to list the supplies required:

a. Wheat: 7,500 tons and flour 5,000 tons (flour must be fresh)
b. Coal: Welsh – 800 tons; domestic – 3,000 tons; Thornley Gas – 1,900 tons
c. Pick or Horse Beans – 4,000 tons; barley – 1,500 tons; oats – 500 tons. If beans not available, increase maize to 5,500 and barley to 2,500
d. Cement: 3,000 tons; previous 10,000 tons represents full requirement for all defence works. It could only be used if more benzine were available. 3,000 tons represents maximum which should be sent in a 40,000-ton convoy
e. White Oils: if tanker cannot be sent, essential send as much cased aviation spirit as possible in foreholds of ships up to maximum of 1,500 tons 100 Octane and 500 tons DTD 230.

PART III.   COMMERCIAL LIST.

A.   FIRST PRIORITY.

1.   200 tons Powdered Sulphur in bags (Smith's Star).
2.   6000 lbs. Anhydrous Ammonia.
3.   4 Diesel air compressors with 8 Siscol cutters.
4.   200 tons Ship or Army Biscuits.
5.   100 tons Nitrate of Soda.
6.   100 tons Sulphate of Ammonia.
7.   500 tons Anthracite, doubly-screened first class beans (suggest
      from Harris & Dixon, 81 Grace-church, E.C.3).
8.   200 tons Edible Oil.
9.   100 tons coffee.
10.   40 tons refined salt.
      20 tons domestic salt.
11.   200 tons leaf tobacco for manufacturing two hundred million
          cigarettes; also necessary quantity of cigarette
          paper, packets, etc.   Consult British-American
          Tobacco Co.)
12.   5 tons Smoking Tobacco.
13.   2 tons Desiccated Yeast.
14.   20 tons Cocoa.
15.   15,000 lbs. Meat extracts (in 2 oz. tins).
16.   500 gross Toilet paper.
17.   15 gross Feeding bottles, complete.
18.   120 gross Teats (assorted).
19.   25,000 lbs. Infant foods.
20.   2,000,000 yards Cotton tape (Nos. 4, 5,6 and 10).
21.   5,000 Knitting needles.
22.   150 lbs. Wicks 1".
23.   250 "   Wicks 68 mm.
24.   1,200 pieces Wicks for Valor Stoves No. 64.
25.   20,000,000 Sharps sewing needles (one quarter Nos. 1 to 3.
                                        one-half Nos. 4 to 6.
                                        Remainder: other numbers).
26.   Rayon elastic braid :-
          50,000 yards No. 8 (white).
          10,000   "   No. 14 (white).
          10,000   "   No. 24 (white and black).

B.   SECOND PRIORITY.

1.   120 tons Butter and Margarine.
2.   75 tons Cheese.
3.   200 tons Rice.
4.   1,500,000 Razor blades (bulk of the Nacet type).
5.   Cells for torches:
          U.2.   20,000
          U.11   10,000
          Flat   10,000

C.   THIRD PRIORITY.

1.   100 tons Malt (70 tons Lager type; 30 tons Munich type).
2.   40 bales Hops (consult Messrs. Simonds, Brewers of Reading
                                        on items 1 and 2).
3.   150 cases Shaving creams.
4.   1,000 cases Toilet soaps.
5.   15,000 Fasteners (haberdashery).
6.   Knitting wools: White 6,000 lbs.
                      Services colours 10,000 lbs.
                      Other colours 4,000 lbs.
7.   Blankets: Cotton 10,000
                Wool   2,000
8.   25,000 yards Khaki drill.
9.   10,000   "   Khaki shirting.
10.   3,000   "   Barathea khaki.
11.   1,000   "   Barathea Air Force.
12.   10,000   "   Navy wool flannel.
13.   5,000 dozen Ladies and Girls underwear (cheap lines of
                                        rayon and wool mixtures).
14.   2,000,000 Brass pins.
15.   2,000,000 Iron-plated pins.
16.   300,000 Safety pins.

Wars are won on the ability to keep supplies flowing – and not just 'war stores'. This list of commercial items
to be shipped to Malta makes interesting reading.

It also stated requirement for 'three-months essential items for 28,000 men, three-months standard naval rations for 3,000 men, and military equipment as listed in other telegrams.' One wonders why the naval rations were separate and if it included a rum ration!

Documents of this type are very useful in helping to put context and scale to Fortress Malta. Discussions on how many fighters were available would be pointless if there was no fuel for them. If the garrison and population starved, then their effectiveness would be reduced drastically. And, it was clearly not just 'send as many ships and as much as you can', there were considerations of capability to handle the ships and store the supplies. The detailed lists were arranged under Naval stores, RAF stores, Army stores, and then various other categories including commercial supplies. These latter were split into first, second and third priority. Among the first priority was '200-tons leaf tobacco for manufacturing 200 million cigarettes, also necessary quantity of cigarette paper, packets, etc. Consult British-American Tobacco.' Priority one also included 5,000 knitting needles – whereas the knitting wools were only priority three (6,000lb white, 10,000lb Services colours, and 4,000lb other colours). Interestingly, priority three also had '5,000 dozen ladies and girls' underwear – cheap lines of rayon and wool mixtures.' As a historian I find these 'little' details fascinating as part of the overall picture; the siege of Malta was not just about who shot who down!

July started well for the anti-shipping effort. It was the turn of the Wellingtons to score against Axis shipping early in the month, and also to justify the effort (and losses) in attacks on Tripoli. On the 1st the 148 Squadron Wellingtons put paid to the Italian 2,517-ton *Eritrea* in Tripoli harbour. On the 3rd, a combined Wellington and Swordfish attack claimed the 1,274-ton *Sparta*. While sinking ships in Tripoli often meant that supplies had already been unloaded, every ship sunk meant a problem for the Axis supply lines, as shipping was hard to replace. The Swordfish of 830 Squadron were still active in the anti-shipping role, and on the night of 16 July two bomber and one torpedo aircraft attacked Tripoli, with the torpedo attack claiming to have damaged the tanker *Panuco*.

On the night of the 6th/7th the new night fighter unit claimed its first success. The arrival of a number FAA Fulmars in late June had been part of a plan to form an NF unit, which was very quickly assigned as 800X Squadron. In the early hours of the 7th, Sub-Lieutenant Tritton with Lieutenant Manning shot down one of a number of BR.20s.

It was the turn of 110 Squadron to provide the Bomber Command detachment, with Blenheim IVs deploying from 4 to 28 July. The day 9 July was a bad one for 110 Squadron's Blenheims. The squadron had only recently arrived from Wattisham, Suffolk, to take its turn in the 2 Group rotation. The target was shipping in Tripoli harbour and of the seven aircraft that went out, four were lost: Z6449 (Squadron Leader D.H. Seale and crew all killed), Z9537 (Flight Lieutenant M.E.

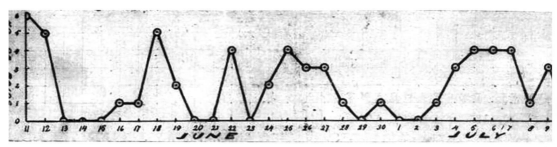

Graph showing scale of attacks against Malta from 11 June to 10 July 1941, the scale on the left being the number of raids.

Potier killed and his two crew PoW), Z9578 (Pilot Officer W.H. Lowe and crew all killed), and Z9533 (Sergeant W.H. Twist and crew all PoW). They claimed a number of hits, but no ships are recorded as heavily damaged or sunk. The CO, Wing Commander T.M. Hunt, was lost a few days later (18th) during an attack on the power station at Tripoli. One of six attackers, his Blenheim was picked up by an Italian fighter shortly after he had dropped his bombs, and he was shot down into the sea, all the crew being killed.

There were a number of 'operational days' over Malta in July, usually when the Italians were sending strong fighter escorts with the recce flights, anything from ten to thirty fighters, although this was also partly due the fact that Malta's radar would pick up the raid and the fighters would scramble, leading to air combats from which the Italians hoped to achieve air superiority. Most combats, however, tended to end with higher losses on the Italian side, although with a drain on the RAF as well. Sometimes, the recce aircraft was very much a priority target, such as on 25 July, the day after the arrival of a convoy from Gibraltar, with the Italians clearly keen to observe its status and the unloading. The morning recce flight was escorted by nearly fifty fighters and was intercepted by Hurricanes of 185 and 249 Squadrons, who had orders to prevent the reconnaissance at all costs.

Flight Lieutenant Don Stones, a recent arrival on Malta and flying with 249 Squadron, and a number of 185 machines, got through the escort to the Cant Z.1007 recce aircraft: 'As I went in to attack, something fell away from our target and nearly hit me. I assumed he was jettisoning a bomb. We set him on fire and down he went into the sea. Only later did we discover that the object which had flown past me was the rear gunner bailing out.' The rest of the crew were lost with the aircraft. Meanwhile, in the fighter combat, the RAF claimed three MC.200s.

Two more ships were sunk in July, both on the 22nd; the German 8,230-ton *Preussen* and the 6,996-ton tanker *Brarena*. The first attack was made by Blenheims of 110 Squadron and they scored hits on the *Preussen*, which promptly blew up, and hits and damage on the tanker. A follow-up attack by Swordfish of 830 Squadron put paid to the tanker courtesy of two torpedoes. Another Blenheim and crew was lost on the 23rd, when Z7409 was lost during an attack on Trapani harbour. The aircraft had hit the sea twice on its way to the target but had pressed on and dropped its bombs in a surprise attack that met no opposition. Pilot Officer N.A.C Cathles and crew were killed. The three Blenheims claimed to have made a number of hits on two MVs.

Meanwhile, Operation Substance was a major success, with six ships arriving in Malta with an impressive 60,000 tons of supplies. The operation comprised convoy GM1, to get supply ships to Malta, and MG2, to move empty ships out of Malta. The inbound comprised six merchant ships and one small 'personnel ship' (*Leinster*). Additional Beaufighters, 252 and 272 squadrons, had moved to Malta to provide long-range cover. There was also substantial air effort in terms of reconnaissance, especially by 69 Squadron Marylands, AS patrols by Sunderlands and Blenheims, and attacks on Italian ports and airfields by Wellingtons (148 Squadron) and Blenheims (110 Squadron) and Fulmars (FAA). The convoy passed the Strait in the early hours of the 21st, air cover being provided by *Ark Royal*, and the usual strong contingent of warships. As usual, Malta was keeping an eye on the Italian fleet, 69 Squadron flying regular missions over and around Naples.

By the 23rd the convoy had been located by the Italians and while, once again, the Italian Battle Fleet stayed put, aircraft were out as soon as the targets had been found. For the Axis, airfields on Sardinia were the first to come in range, and from then on the ships were in range of one or more Axis air bases. Until the Allied shipping came under the air umbrella of Malta, it relied on fleet air defence by the Fulmars, and the very considerable weight of AA fire. In the first attacks during mid-morning on the 23rd, the cruiser *Manchester* and the destroyer *Fearless* were hit by torpedoes; the

Combat report for the 'Boys from Syracuse' as 185 Squadron takes the war to the enemy in Sicily.

P. M.   The Boys From Syracuse

Comment is unnecessary, save that the snap shows them taking off, regarding the most successful and energetic beat-up of the sea-plane base at Syracuse.

Our industrious C.O and F/Lt. Jeffries went with the C/O and Sgt. Meekie of 46 Squadron.

¾.   from the C.O's official report. —.

₪/₁.

We approached the harbour from the East; entered the harbour through the entrance at about 50 feet and immediately did a steep right hand turn and slipped out into echelon port and opened fire at a cluster of three seaplanes. (Cant) I was then at about 5feet off the water.   I saw my shells going low to start with and after raising my aim one of the three seaplanes caught fire, the tail fell off another and I could see my shells going into the third machine.   I then turned slightly and saw the remainder of my shells go into the hangar, but no definite damage was seen.   I nearly hit one of the seaplanes and then the hangar and eventually nearly removed my starboard wing on some large building¶   There was quite a lot of A.A. but all bursting at about 250 feetthis started just before I started breaking away.

Col₪/₁²   from F/Lt. Jeffries official report.—.

I, F/Lt. Jeffries was following S/Ldr. Mould, we approached Syracuse harbour from the East, I saw several seaplanes on the water.   I opned fire on the nearest one I observed several strikes.   I then concentrated my fire on the slipway on which there were about five aircraft.   I saw one floatplane burst into flames as my shots entered it.   I sprayed the other a/c and then fired a long burst into the hangar.   Several men working there scattered. As I flew over the slipway I observed about 3 a/c on fire. A huge pall of smoke hung over the harbour as we flew out to sea.

+ 800 cannon shells were contributed to this, our latest war effort.

flight coastal batteries opened up on the 4 Hurricanes as they went out to sea, causing no damage but slight wing total.

latter had to be sunk and the former was sent back to Gibraltar. It has always been acknowledged that the Italian torpedo-bombers were among the most courageous and most successful of the often derided air units; this attack was no exception and, despite suffering losses to the patrolling Fulmars and to AA fire, they pressed their attacks. A third ship, *Firedrake*, was hit later in the day and also had to return to Gib. The final attacks were made by motor-torpedo boats, with *Sydney Star* being damaged. Now in range of Malta, the convoy was pleased to see Beaufighters providing cover, and early on the 24th three troop-carrying fast MVs went direct to Malta at speed, arriving around midday. The rest of the convoy arrived a few hours later in what had been a very successful venture, as no supply ships had been lost. It had been costly for the Fulmars, with twelve aircraft lost, six in combat, although most crew were rescued by the escort ships. DSOs went to Lieutenant

I was flying No. 2 to Yellow Section L. Leader, P/O Barnwell, when at 10,000 ft. I sighted two M.T.Bs travelling line abreast. I followed my leader down and did a diving beam attack on the rear M.T.B. which was turning round very slowly. I broke away and did an astern attack on the front M.T.B. without visible effect. I turned and came in on a front meter attack on the same boat, and broke away again. The first M.T.B. was stationary with a small boat behind it. Just before I again attacked the front M.T.I., which was still travelling fast and weaving, I saw an aircraft, which I took to be a Hurricane dived vertically into the sea. I did a beam attack on the front boat and saw a flame from the starboard.

I broke away and after circling, I followed two Hurricanes and used up all my ammunition, the boat STOPPING and catching fire.

above report.   S/N Lillywhite

Report below.   The P/offensw

I was flying Blue 1. The squadron patrolled at 10,000 ft. we went out tosea and saw 2 M.T.B's going W. E. very fast. The squadron attacked. I remained at 18,00 ft. for a few minutes and saw a Macchi 200 attacking a Hurricane. I dived on the Macchi and from astern and fired from 50-100 X I then broke away and attacked M.T.B. my incendiary causing fire in the rear of boat. I saw the Macchi again and fired again from astern causing smoke and pieces to fall off. The Macchi was seen to go into the sea by Sgt. Westcote. I fired the remainder of my ammo. into M.T.B. I saw one M.T.B. sinking and the other was seen by Sgt. Lillywhite to be on fire.

I was flying No.3 to Red 1. P/Lt. Brancook, and at 10,000 foot sighted 2 M.T.Bs. I followed Red 1 down and while we were diving the T.Bs. broke up. He took the rear one and I closed to 50 yards after Red 1 had attacked and saw the gun on the launch hanging vertically. ... first attack Hurricane (P/O Thompson) attack a Macchi. The tracers entered the cockpit of this machine and I saw a red glow from the cockpit. The Macchi turned over on its back and dived into the sea. I made another attack on the M.T.B. which had now stopped and seemed to be sinking slowly. I climbed up after this attack and had to return to my base, owing to high radiator temprature.

above report   Sgt. Wescott.

Commander Sholto Douglas and Lieutenant Cockburn, a DSC to Lieutenant Guthrie, and a DSM to Pilot Officer Curtis. Meanwhile, the outbound empty ships headed off in matched pairs, decided by speed, and while all sections were attacked by aircraft, only *Hoegh Hood* was damaged, by a torpedo, but still made it to Gibraltar.

The Italian recce sortie on the 25th – checking up on the convoy – was escorted by twenty-five or more fighters; the defenders put up an impressive response, with twenty-two Hurricanes of 185 and 249 Squadrons heading off. In what became a bit of a confused free-for-all, numerous pilots attacked and claimed the aircraft, which was indeed shot down. No doubt the crew wondered what had happened to its defending fighters, who appear to have done a terrible job of offering any protection. The fighters were engaged, losing two of their number, with one pilot (De Giorgi) being picked up by *HSL107*. The next day also saw the Italians launch a daring but flawed and disastrous attack on Grand Harbour using torpedo boats. The attack force was spotted and was engaged by searchlights and guns around the harbour. The following day the RAF went up looking to finish off any damaged attack craft. Pilot Officer Winton was shot down when he was bounced by a Macchi; bailing out he

Hurricanes of 185 Squadron were involved in an attack on an Italian torpedo boat, as recounted in these combat reports.

A line-up of 185 Squadron
Hurricanes.

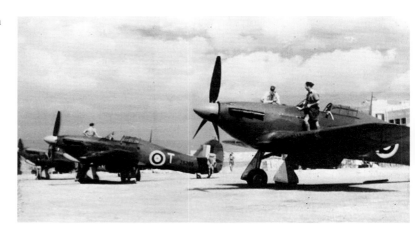

took to his dinghy but then moved on to what seemed like an abandoned motor boat (it turned out
to contain eight dead Italians) and he was concerned that his new 'home' might become a target.
However, he was soon rescued by a floatplane Swordfish, while two of the Italian boat crewmen
(Paratore and Zaniboni) became the latest live pick-ups for *HSL107*.

The Beaufighters were making fairly regular 'trips' to the airfields in Sicily, such as on the 28th
when they strafed Catania, but on 30 July six aircraft went all the way to Sardinia, strafing Elmas
airfield, with all pilots claiming various aircraft destroyed or damaged.

Up to this point, the squadrons had been taking it in turns to man night fighter standby but at the
end of July the Malta Night Fighter Unit (MNFU) was formed, equipped with eight Hurricanes
(four IIBs and four IICs) and with ten pilots assigned from squadrons. This was in part a reaction to
the fact that the Italians had now turned most of their attention to night attacks. The unit was based
at Ta Kali under the command of Squadron Leader George Powell-Sheddon; the tactical concept
was 'cats eye', with the fighters relying on searchlights or natural illumination to find, close and kill
their quarry.

The concept of the NFU and its establishment was to be the subject of some debate between the
AOC and HQ RAF Middle East. A signal from AOC Malta to AOC ME sought to regularize the
position of the NF unit: 'Experience shows that a separate fighter unit is vital for reasonable defence
by fighters at night. Request concurrence and Air Ministry asked to allot a squadron number to
establish identity and help morale (at present it is made up of detachments and pilots, maintenance
and aircraft from 3 fighter squadrons. Do not propose to ask for additional aircraft or pilots as we can
work with what we have. Proposed establishment of night fighter unit to be 11 pilots, 14 Hurricanes
with few airmen for maintenance, remainder being on station on servicing basis as for other fighter
units here.' (Signal AOC Malta to AOC ME, 20 August 1941).

Four days later the reply agreed with the concept of the unit but queried how it could be
established from existing resources. This was picked up again in September, see later. Interestingly,
there is confusion in the records around this, with some saying that the MNFU became 1435 Flight
on 23 July and was raised to squadron status as 1435 Squadron on 2 August. It was certainly unique
as a squadron designation as it sat well outside of the numbers assigned for use, the highest block
being 600 numbers. The unit, still recorded as the MNFU in some sources, scored its first success
on the night of 5 August, a BR.20 being shot down by Flying Officer Cassidy.

The Blenheims of 105 Squadron took over from 110 Squadron in late July, and operated a
detachment at Luqa to mid-October. The squadron sent four aircraft on the Portreath–Gib–Luqa

route in the middle of July; one Blenheim out of four on the 17 July leg from Portreath had to force land in Portugal, the crew being interned. The first operational loss occurred on 1 August, Flight Lieutenant A. Bradley being shot down by flak when attacking shipping in Lampedusa harbour, the pilot and wireless operator/air gunner survived, but the navigator (Pilot Officer A. Ramsay) was killed; Alistar Ramsey had been awarded the DFC a few weeks previously for an attack on Bremen. The highly successful and popular Beaufighters departed in the first week of the month, but Malta's attack potential was increased with the

A slight Italian exaggeration

'a slight Italian exaggeration' is how 185 Squadron recorded this Italian news broadcast of August 1941.

arrival of 38 Squadron Wellingtons, which flew their first mission on the night of the 8th, the target being Tripoli.

Night and poor weather was also the preferred 'medium' of the Swordfish, especially as they now had a number of aircraft with ASV (air to surface vessel) – radar. This was still rare in the Mediterranean theatre but over the next few months ASV-equipped aircraft would become a key element in the anti-shipping campaign. The favoured tactics of the Swordfish also included a flare dropper and an attack force of torpedo droppers. A number of attacks were made over the nights of 5 to 11 August and the main prize was the 12,768-ton Italian cargo liner *California* on the 11th, sunk off Syracuse.

In a very successful operation on 7 August, 105 Squadron claimed four ships hit. The Swordfish were out on the night of 6th/7th, with seven aircraft making torpedo attacks on a convoy of six MVs escorted by six destroyers. They claimed two sunk plus a destroyer damaged. The one confirmed victim appears to have been the 6,813-ton *Nita*, which was sunk 25 miles south of Lampedusa.

The next Blenheim loss occurred on the 11th, when Squadron Leader Goode (Z7503) was hit by flak while attacking a chemical works at Crotone. Hit in the engine, he was able to crash-land in a field and he and his crew became prisoners. The following day, the AOC was expressing concern to HQ 2 Group: 'Edwards very concerned about morale of his crews. He is most disappointed with results to date. He feels his position here keenly as he is not allowed to fly and that squadron is slipping from his grasp. He arrived here wanting leaders and this now aggravated by loss of Goode and crew [Squadron Leader G. Goode DFC; 11 August attack on Crotone] whom Rome reports are prisoners and undamaged. Can you send good material to help Edwards before arrival of main part of 107 Squadron? I have a number of important jobs but cannot do them, as Edwards has no confidence in leaders and if job is done badly surprise is sacrificed and I would rather wait to do job properly.' (Signal AOC Med to AOC 2 Group, 12 August 1941).

Another of the hazards of attacking ships was the risk of colliding with parts of the superstructure, especially masts. Pilots flew as low as they could to avoid flak, popping up to bomb release height, then dropping low and jinking over the ships, often between superstructure elements. This inevitably led to some losses; such as Flying Officer H. Roe of 105 Squadron on 15 August when attacking a convoy off the Libyan coast. According to other attackers, the aircraft struck a mast and span into the sea, with loss of the three crew. The same attacks also saw the loss of Pilot Officer P. Standfast and crew, the aircraft exploding after it had released its bombs on a tanker.

Meanwhile, C-in-C Med had requested attacks on the Corinth Canal to force Axis shipping to route through the Aegean and the hunting ground of Allied submarines and aircraft. The first heavy bomber attack on the canal was by thirty-four Wellingtons on the night of 8/9 August, with 21 tons of bombs dropped, as well as eight mines. Intense flak claimed one Wellington and damaged two others. The canal was attacked again on the 13th/14th, with 31 tons dropped on the south-east bank, some crews claiming the waterway had been blocked. Despite the seeming success, some (such as VCAS) queried this diversion of bomber effort away from more important targets such as Benghazi.

The Swordfish were successful again on the night of 17/18 August, seven aircraft attacking a convoy of five MVs plus a 10,000-ton tanker, and an escort of six destroyers. This was in what was now a favourite 'hunting ground' around Lampedusa. The tanker was hit and damaged, and one MV was claimed as critically damaged and beached. Two Blenheims went after this ship, the 5,479-ton *Maddalene Odero*, the following day and claimed to have set it on fire.

One unusual incident took place in Malta on 17 August when a flight from 249 Squadron was briefed to pick up and escort an aircraft inbound from the direction of Greece but with no more details, as it was a special flight. They duly picked up a low-flying 'twin' and flew above it en route back to Malta. On arrival at Malta the 'twin' promptly dropped into Kalafrana Bay and released a torpedo. The RAF pilots realized that it was in fact an SM.79 torpedo-bomber that they had been shepherding, but despite their best (belated) efforts they were unable to shoot it down. A very embarrassing episode and one that no doubt led to much ribbing in the bar.

Meanwhile, the Germans were expressing concern over the 'transport situation in the Mediterranean; a conference of 22 August stating: 'previous experiences have shown that the Italians are very reluctant to use their shipping. Their intention to retain their shipping for commercial use after the war when there is a shortage of shipping is obvious. In order to carry out German transports most effectively it is necessary that the Italians surrender ships to the German Commanding Officer, Supply and Transports for purely German use. (Fuhrer Conferences on Naval Affairs.)

The statistics in the document suggested that the Italians had 299 ships with total of 1,119,954 tons, which included 19 tankers (which was to prove a vulnerably small number); whereas the German (and commandeered) vessels totalled only 29 ships with 65,700 tons. It was noted that shipbuilding must be increased and that additional German ships could not be added until Gibraltar had fallen and the gateway to the Mediterranean was opened. The latter was one of the arguments used for not sending German U-boats to the Mediterranean. The same document also stated: 'Malta should be attacked and the escort service should be improved, in order to keep losses within reasonable limits.' It also looked again at Gibraltar: 'If we occupied Gibraltar we would rule the Western Mediterranean, and even the importance of Malta would be reduced to a certain degree. Co-operation with Spain and control of the Straits of Gibraltar would enable us to bring naval forces and transport vessels into the Mediterranean. This would be of decisive importance for the transport situation within the Central Mediterranean.' So, a clear understanding of the strategic need and value, but what would actually be done?

A request for radar-equipped Beaufighters as night fighters had been rejected on 26 August, as 'Beaufighters with night defence equipment not available' (signal from AOC-in-C). The same signal also addressed an increase in Blenheim strength: 'CAS proposes increase your Blenheim strength temporarily to equivalent of 3 squadrons. He expects them to be used with greatest determination against enemy L of C [Lines of Communication]. Intention is to increase present detachment with two further detachments of 16 aircraft each. Signal direct here if you can accept one additional Blenheim squadron before end of month and second about 10th September.'

The following day, Tedder signalled to London: 'Am arranging attach half Maryland squadron to Malta. Agree with Lloyd that more heavy bombers likely give best results. Feel that hammering at Naples and Brindisi on same scale as Tripoli and other African ports might well be decisive.'

On the same day Lloyd responded to the Blenheim request: 'Can accept half one additional Blenheim squadron before end of month and eight additional Marylands with present maintenance personnel and facilities. Cannot accept any more and still

Preparing cameras for a Maryland. The strategic recce flown from Malta and the Middle East provided vital information for sea and land operations, as well as identifying or tracking key shipping targets for air attack.

maintain Wellington squadron here, as limiting factor is maintenance personnel.' He went on to request 'more bombs and heavier bombs for Tripoli, as I am convinced we can make supply through it most hazardous.'

The lack of maintenance personnel is interesting and provides an insight into a key shortage – not at this stage aircraft or aircrew, but the hard-pressed ground staff to patch aircraft up to maintain serviceability rates, and also the logistics issue of bombs, and the right type of bombs. And on the 28th: 'The General [Auchinleck – Army C-in-C] is providing 150 men to assist in maintenance; all will have some degree of engineering experience. Vital factor is now one of bombs and petrol should you wish to operate more Wellingtons from here. When we have bombs and petrol suggest we operate following: 40 Wellingtons as nights are becoming longer than day, 16 Blenheims, 8 Marylands on land communication, 12 Marylands for reconnaissance striking force and reconnaissance naval bases, aerodromes and ports, 12 Swordfish, 5 Fulmars forming (under?) operations, 3 day fighter squadrons, 1 half night fighter squadron.'

The Blenheim situation was clarified in a signal of the 28th: 'To increase temporarily the Blenheim effort at Malta against enemy communications with North Africa, following arrangements are to be made:

A. 2 Group Blenheim detachment at Malta will be increased forthwith to 2 squadrons and a 3rd will be sent in if it is found possible to maintain it at Malta
B. No. 105 Squadron now at Malta will remain there and will not be relieved
C. No. 107 Squadron due to complete at Malta after carrying out operation 'status' will remain at Malta
D. A 3rd squadron detailed by Bomber Command will be held available in UK for dispatch to Malta by 10/9

E. Wastage of Blenheim squadrons at Malta to be made good from the 30 Blenheim IV reinforcements being flown out monthly to Middle East, aircraft and crews not required to meet wastage are to be flown on to Middle East

F. Bomber Command are requested to send out a Wing Commander to assist Malta in the operation of these squadrons and to send as possible ground personnel by reinforcing aircraft.

It was clear that there was to be a determined push to increase Malta's striking power as an essential contribution to the war against Axis lines of communication, which primarily meant shipping and its support facilities, as well as road routes in North Africa leading from the limited number of ports to the forward areas. The Tripoli comment above – 'more and heavier bombs' – had elicited a reply from HQ RAF ME saying that the port was perhaps not the most suitable target, which elicited an immediate retort from the Air Ministry: 'Suggest there is a grave danger in comparing Tripoli with ports at home, there is only 1 main quay 430 yards long by 150 yards wide. Total ground area of that quay is only 4400 square yards and on it the only store houses, warehouses and unloading gear in the whole port. There are 2 other jetties one 200 yards long and the petrol jetty 100 yards long. A few 1000lb bombs on the quay and jetties would not only sink ships alongside but also destroy the buildings and machinery. As regards unloading other than alongside a great deal is done. This unloading depends entirely on lighters which are limited in number and they are usually concentrated in the evenings in a very small area against the town. One 1000lb bomb in the middle of them would sink the lot. Anchorages in stream are also very limited area and whereas a 500lb bomb does not do much damage by near miss a 1000 pounder may easily disable a ship. Submit therefore that heavy bombs on Tripoli would be decisive in closing the port.' (Air Ministry to AOC Malta, 28 August 1941). In other words, shut up and get on with it!

In early September, 201 Group instituted two new patrols – Needle and Plug. The former was a daily patrol by two Swordfish from Nicosia and covering the area between Cyprus and 30 degrees east, searching for ships approaching Cyprus. The latter was a patrol by two Beauforts and at Wadi Natrun, 39 Squadron, now under the command of Wing Commander R.B. Cox, commenced operation Plug. This was the codename given to sea reconnaissance sorties carried out in search of enemy supply ships and was carried out twice a day by two aircraft flying on parallel courses. Such sorties were needed because Axis shipping was suspected of trying to avoid the aircraft based in Malta by sailing towards south-west Greece and then turning south for a dash for Benghazi. Although tasked with compiling and passing sighting reports for use in planning larger attacks, squadron aircraft also carried out bomb and machine-gun attacks on enemy merchant vessels (MVs). To reduce the effort involved in long transits to the reconnaissance areas a policy was implemented at the end of September of sending detachments of aircraft to operate from advanced landing grounds (ALGs) in the Western Desert.

Looking back at the result of the attack; Blenheim attack on a supply ship. This is an indicative shot for the Med theatre, as it is likely to be a North Sea sortie.

Night nuisance raids against Malta remained a favoured Italian tactic, and the number of daylight engagements was limited. The first significant combats in September took place on the 4th. In the morning combat the Hurricanes claimed multiple destroyed and probable, but the Italians actually lost just two fighters, while all the Hurricanes made it back, albeit some with damage. The afternoon melee took place over a Cant Z.506 rescue mission, and this time the RAF lost two fighters to the Italians one.

September 1941 saw another reinforcement run of Hurricanes to

Beaufort of 39 Squadron at Wadi Natrun; anti-shipping operations from North Africa were a central part of the strategy but depended on having bases in the right places and the back and forth of the Desert War made this somewhat variable.

Malta: Operation Status I and Status II. HMS *Furious* sailed from the Clyde on 31 August with sixty-one Hurricanes on board, arriving in Gibraltar on 7 September, where twenty-six of the aircraft were transferred to *Ark Royal*. The latter sailed on the 8th but only launched fourteen Hurricanes on the 9th as only one Blenheim guide aircraft made the rendezvous. Both carriers left Gibraltar on the 10th, the *Ark* having made a rapid turnaround. *Furious* carried twenty Hurricanes and *Ark Royal* carried twenty-six for Status II. All twenty-six were launched on the 13th, although one crashed on take-off, and met their Blenheims escorts; all made it to Malta safely. In the middle of the month there was little activity over and around Malta, but rather more as far as Malta's anti-shipping aircraft were concerned:

10th: Bombers attack Messina, damage cruiser *Bolzano*

11th: Blenheims damage *Alfredo Oriano*, which sinks on the 13th. The *Livorno* was also sunk on the 11th by the submarine *Thunderbolt*. As a side note, this had been a very bad day for Allied shipping in the Atlantic, with numerous sinkings in Convoy SC42

12th: Swordfish sink *Caffaro*, north-west of Tripoli; according to some accounts the ship had been damaged by the torpedo attack and its destruction was completed on the 13th by Blenheims of 105 and 107 squadrons.

A number of signal messages were being exchanged between the AOC on Malta (Air Vice-Marshal Lloyd) and HQ 2 Group, who were providing the Blenheim detachments, and between Malta and the Air Ministry. A signal from AOC Malta to Air Ministry dated 12 September reviewed issues with Blenheim operations, in respect to poor results: 'Main cause is lack of leaders (?) with experience and determination. Squadron Commander here is not allowed to fly which is a limitation. Other leaders have been sent on request to 2 Group. Second cause is sickness as crews not acclimatized. Sandfly and stomach troubles very serious in spite of every preventative measure. For weeks squadron crew strengths of 16 have been 3 or 4 and very seldom 5 and this by mixing crews. Mixed crews never work well together. Today for the first time for 6 weeks 8 crews are available.'

Sickness was certainly a major issue on Malta, especially for new arrivals, with Malta Dog, the infamous stomach problem, while sandfly fever was prevalent and hard to avoid. The signal continued: 'Third cause is poor standard of navigation. In north-west Europe met winds fairly accurate but winds here difficult and far less landfalls [as navigation features]. Navigators are unable to assess

105 Squadron, like most of the Blenheim detachments, had mixed fortunes during its rotation to Malta. This shot is back in the UK.

drifts in spite assistance and lectures by Maryland observers, Tried Marylands leading Blenheims not popular but successful. Had to stop owing to grave shortage of Marylands for reconnaissance. Blenheims now used for reconnaissance with Maryland crews. Remedies. First cause very difficult. Second cause to leave squadrons here for 4 to 6 months as squadron here is only now beginning to pull its weight. Casualties to be made up by crews passing through at present. Third cause cured by experience which again points to squadrons staying here. In short squadrons are sent home when acclimatized and begin to learn local conditions.'

No. 2 Group responded: 'As regards [to your message of 8/9] your remark about raw crews and no leaders, you will see the position is the same at home. We cannot be jewelled in every hole and crews must get their operational training in their squadrons. As regards [to your message of 28/9] why not fit long range tanks to a section of Hurricanes and attack schooners and ships under 1000 tons with eight-gun fighter. We do this in the Channel Stop most effectively if schooners are carrying petrol or ammunition. Experience shows the light guns or cannon fighter will set them on fire and destroy them and the aircraft invariably gets away with it. ... also tell you that fighters always accompany bombers attacking heavily escorted convoys. The fighters beat up destroyers or escorting ships while the bombers get on with the merchant ships. Combined tactics of this kind give best results at least wastage, suggest you try them.'

Sailors of the submarine HMS *Utmost* with their flag record of success; the RN and Allied submarines played a key spotting and shadowing role as well as an offensive one.

14th: *Nicolo Odero* sunk off Tripoli; with the loss of three aircraft: from 107 Squadron, Z9603 (Sergeant J.E. Mortimer and crew being killed when their Blenheim was hit by AA fire) and Z7504 (Squadron Leader F.R.H. Charney and crew being killed when hit by fire from the destroyer escort); from 105 Sqn: Z7357 (Sergeant F.B. Brandwood and crew shot down by a destroyer but the pilot was able to ditch some distance from the convoy; their position reported, they were rescued by the submarine *Utmost* the next day. Another 105 Squadron aircraft (Z9606) had been badly damaged and belly-landed back at Luqa.

16th: tanker *Filuccio* sunk off Libya by 'a crashing aircraft'.

18th: Malta was putting together a strike force to attack a very tempting target that had been located by Maryland: three 20,000-ton troopships. However, the Navy had already positioned submarines to catch these targets, and *Upholder* sank *Neptunia* and *Oceania*.

A German naval conference of 17 September reviewed the situation in the Mediterranean, and while RAF losses were high, they were influencing German thinking: 'Our North African supply shipments have recently suffered additional heavy losses of ships, material and personnel as a result of enemy air attacks by means of bombs and torpedoes, and through submarine attacks. Evidently the appeal for help made by the German General attached to the Italian Armed Forces was responsible for the order from the Fuhrer to concentrate our own air forces on escorting supply shipments, to dispatch immediately six submarines, and to speed up the transport of motor minesweepers and motor boats.'

As has been alluded to a number of times, Malta was famous/infamous for acquiring whatever passed through, which was the cause of frequent comment from HQ units. On 20 September a 'personal for AOC from AOC-in-C' was strongly worded: 'It appears from number of pilots and aircraft intended for Egypt which have failed to pass through the extremely effective filter you operate at Malta that you formed this additional night fighting flight. You have also apparently assumed that your squadron pilot establishment has been increased to the figure of 34 per squadron which you proposed. I am not convinced that in present circumstances you do require this additional unit for night fighting. I agree specializing in night fighting is necessary but why cannot one of your regularized squadrons have one flight specialized in night fighting. This is what we have had to do here [Egypt]. Am also concerned by your retention of Hurricane IIC aircraft. With present shortage of cannon Hurricanes my view is that they should be kept for night fighting. Am anxious to do best possible to keep your force on top line but active operations are also in progress in Egypt and Libya we have a more difficult and at the moment more vital defence problem that you have at Malta. At present also the main adversary in Egypt and Libya is the German repeat German [meaning – you only have Italians to cope with!].

'All squadrons in Egypt and Libya considerably below establishment of pilots and your leavings from Status do not bring them up to full strength. Consider establishment of your squadrons both and aircraft and pilots must be regularized in light of present circumstances. Please let me have facts regarding aircraft and pilots in your fighter squadrons.' (signal AOC-in-C to AOC, 20 September 1942).

No doubt having fumed for a while, and asked his staff for statistics and justification, the AOC sent his reply two days later: 'I regret you consider we see only our own little problem of Malta. We try not to filter or filch and am willing for any investigation to prove that our motives are not self-centred.' Having started with this defence, and 'our own little problem' is a telling phrase, he proceeded to provide statistics as required. He stated there were 107 fighter pilots at Malta, which at

34 per squadron was only five too many – but that missed the AOC's point that the 34 per squadron was not an agreed number. He did go on to say: 'Whether we should retain 102 pilots at 34 per squadron is another matter. Had assumed your concurrence when here. If you will state a lower figure for the squadrons, your wishes will be complied with.

'As regards aircraft, our total holding is 109, we have three squadrons each of 16 aircraft plus one hundred per cent reserve as instructed by Air Ministry – total 96. In addition, 6 are being flown to you and 7 are awaiting write-off. We have therefore not one single Hurricane over our establishment. Regarding cannon Hurricane our total holding is 11.'

'I have not been able to trace any Air Ministry statement on IE (Initial Establishment) and IR (In-use Reserve) for Malta fighter squadrons; the SD161 data confirms IE of 16 for the fighter squadrons but does not mention the IR.'

The CO of 105 Squadron (Wing Commander Sciver) was killed with his crew on the 22nd when his aircraft (Z7423) collided with the squadron's Z9809 over the target, a barracks and ammo dump at Homs. A signal from AOC Malta to the Air Ministry expressed concern over the experience level of crews: 'Wing Commander Sciver commanding one nought five squadron was killed in flying accident Sept 22 [not really correct to call it a flying accident – it was an operational loss]; with Sciver there was hope of pulling squadron together but consider it is now too late. Squadron came here at very trying time as regards climate and all crews have been sick. Only one leader in squadron and he has borne brunt of all operations carried out by squadron. With crews which have been returned England and two more who should be given a change, there are only six crews with any experience left. Remaining eight crews have not yet done an operation of any sort. Suggest squadron of eight experienced crews is sent here to absorb eight new crews or new squadron complete sending eight new crews on to Middle East.' (Signal dated 24 September 1941).

Pilots of 185 Squadron, c. September 1941. Back: P/O Allardice, P/O Jolly, Sgt Ream, Sgt Hunton, Sgt Forth, Sgt Knight, Sgt Hayes, Sgt Horsey. Middle: P/O Oliver, Sgt Bates, F/O Bailey, Sgt Cousens, P/O Lillywhite, Sgt Sutherland, P/O Reeves, Sgt Nurse, P/O Vardy. Bottom: F/L Pike, F/L Jefferson, S/L Mould, F/L Hancock, F/O Thompson.

Despite almost daily missions by Malta's strike elements, and claims made for sunk and damaged, the only recorded loss over the next few days was again to a submarine, *Triumph* sinking the *Poseidone* on the Adriatic Sea on the 23rd. Two more ships had been sunk in September; the 107 Squadron Blenheims claiming the 3,372-ton *Monselet* on the 20th and Swordfish damaging the 5,996-ton *Marigola* on the 23rd, which was then finished off by a submarine. Blenheims were again the subject of a signal to AOC Malta on 26 September: 'Arrangements made to dispatch 18 sqd with 16 fully operational crews about 5/10 to relieve 105 sqd. 6 experienced crews of 105 sqd to be returned K by sea earliest opportunity, 8 inexperienced crews to be sent on to Middle East with Blenheim aircraft. 18 Squadron will remain Malta indefinitely. Aircraft flown out by 18 Squadron will be part of monthly quota of 30 Blenheims and not repeat not additional to it.' This was an attempt to resolve the previous discussions around experience of crews and effectiveness of the Blenheim operations.

Another Malta supply convoy, Operation Halberd, with the usual full to Malta (GM2) and empty from Malta (MG2) elements, took place in late September. This was a major convoy with nine supply ships and a significant escort that had been reinforced by elements of the Home Fleet. The convoy passed the Straits in the early hours of the 25th and as usual the first two days were quiet. Enemy submarine activity was low, in part because Gibraltar's anti-submarine patrols were proving effective. So it was only when the convoy came in range of land bases that the action started. There was an increased expectation, fueled in part by Ultra intercepts, that at last the Italian Fleet may try to intervene. To that end, *Ark Royal* was prepared for an anti-shipping strike as well as its usual fleet air defence duties. The Italian torpedo-bombers appeared in the early afternoon and a hit was scored on the *Nelson* that reduced her speed to 15 knots; in the event this had no effect as that was the stated convoy speed. Shortly afterwards, the Italian Battle Fleet was reported some 75 miles from the convoy, so the designated strike force split away and headed in that direction, while the *Ark* prepared an air strike. Meanwhile, the carrier's Fulmars had already engaged the earlier attack, claiming some success. Further torpedo attacks took place, being broken up by the fighters and gunnery; the day's bombing attacks ended up costing six of the eleven attacking aircraft, for one warship damaged and one MV heavily damaged, the *Imperial Star* had to be sunk by the escorts as she could not be towed. The Italian Battle Fleet withdrew before being caught. By early morning the next day the convoy was under Malta's air umbrella and the ships made a triumphant entry into harbour.

With the increased difficulty of locating night targets, it was agreed that specialist aircraft were required. 'To increase the effectiveness of anti-shipping reccos at Malta we are sending within next

Carrier-based Fulmars performed a number of roles, although this was by no means an ideal landing on HMS *Victorious*. The Fulmar had taken over from the Skua as Fleet defence fighter, but it too was limited in it capability.

The arrival of ASV Wellingtons provided enhanced shipping support. Note: This is not a Malta unit photo.

14 days 3 long-range ASV Wellingtons with specially selected crews. Long-range ASV enables track 60 miles wide to be searched for surface vessels. Aircraft will be fitted with additional IFF to respond to Swordfish ASV so that Swordfish can home on Wellington from approx. 60 miles. An expert from Staff of Scientific Advisor on Test Communications being sent out to Malta and he will be able to give valuable help in the possible methods of employing these Wellingtons in conjunction with other aircraft. You will appreciate that ASV and similar developments must on no account be allowed to fall into enemy hands. The aircraft must never be allowed to fly near the enemy or Vichy coast.' (Signal Air Ministry to HQ RAF ME, 14 September.) On arrival the three ASV-equipped Wellingtons were designated as the Special Duties Flight (SDF) and tasked to:

1. Co-operate with RN forces based at Malta
2. Co-operate with Fleet Air Arm Albacores (828 and 830 squadrons)
3. Undertake night bomb attacks on, and night shadowing of, enemy shipping
4. Carry out sweeps along the enemy's known shipping lanes.

The Wellington VIIIs were from 221 Squadron, which had been operating the type from Docking in Norfolk since June. The detachment was under the command of Flight Lieutenant 'Tony' Spooner.

   For the co-operation with naval forces, the tactic was that the lead ship would have a 'Rooster' set (modified IFF) so that the ASV Wellington could home it on to the targets, while maintaining radio silence. The main role was the second one and for this an ASV Wellington would usually radar locate, at night, the convoy that had been located and reported in the day by, for example, a Maryland. The strike force would be some thirty minutes behind the Wellington and would be homed to the target, one of the strike force having ASV fitted. The final set-up for the attack would usually be under flares dropped by the Wellington. As ever, reconnaissance remained the key when trying to divine the Axis intentions, to monitor shipping and to find targets. For most of this period, the expert air reconnaissance was conducted by 69 Squadron, and the unit was kept very busy. For example, 30 September is indicative of a day of operations as recorded by the squadron:

- 0945–1145: Hurricane Z2332. Wing Commander Dowland. Recce East Sicilian cost, one seaplane at Syracuse, one TB.
- 0945–1135: Hurricane Z3053. Flying Officer Weetton. Recce Sicilian coast. Port Empedecle one MV and 25 small craft. Accurate AA.
- 1015–1310: Maryland BS774. Flight Lieutenant Williams. Recce East Calabrian coast, hospital ship, one 600-ton schooner, 2 MV, 2 destroyers Cape Spartivento, one MV Stile.
- 1155–1410: Maryland BS762. Flying Officer Drew. Recce Tripoli, 6 destroyers, one liner, one tanker, 5 MVs, slight AA and one CR42.
- 1300–1630. Maryland BJ427. Sergeant McDonald. Recce East Sicilian coast, 40-50 small craft and 4 barges in port between Syracuse and Augusta, one MC and one small craft Rizzuto, 2 possible E boats near Cape Spartivento, 2 seaplanes patrolling near cost at 2,000ft.
- 1630–1930: Maryland AR725. Pilot Officer Smith, Search for shipping in Tripoli area, 2 schooners East of Kerkenneh, 3 MVs and 3 destroyers near Tripoli.

This type of information, especially when compared with other reports over a number of days, enabled a pattern of activity to be put together. Were the barges and small craft part of an invasion fleet build-up? With that much shipping in Tripoli harbour, should a bombing raid be launched?

The concern over Blenheim losses was such that on 1 October Portal sent a letter to Tedder, and subsequently copied it to Lloyd: 'I am becoming rather anxious about the strain that is being imposed on the Blenheims at Malta by their constant use in low level attacks on heavily escorted merchant ships. The trouble is that one sends out a squadron composed of a few real leaders and the rest good followers, but not leaders. Soon the leaders get killed and then there is no-one with the necessary heart to take on what is, after all, an extremely tough job, and so the efficiency of the attacks wanes and morale wanes with it. It is no good imagining that all our men are heroes who can stand, indefinitely, the tremendous risks which these attacks involve. I see that in the last three months we have lost 18 crews out of a comparatively small number that have been operating and frankly I do not think we can ask one or two units to bear the brunt indefinitely. As you know, we sent the 2 Group Blenheims out because that had learned the trick of getting these ships by low bombing and I think the time has come when the burden must be spread evenly over the whole of your Command. We are sending out a new squadron to replace 105 and I must ask you to assume responsibility from now onwards for introducing a system of rotation under which all the squadrons in your Command will share, in rotation, the extra risk of these anti-ship operations. It will be for you and Lloyd to arrange between you how this is to be done.' (Letter Portal to Tedder, 1 Oct 1941).

It is interesting that the Chief of Air Staff found it necessary to intervene in this matter; it is likely that there are other background communications, perhaps from 2 Group, that raised the issue of wastage rates amongst the squadrons; Bomber Command, to whom 2 Group belonged, was always reluctant to release units. It is also interesting to note the comment about 'leaders' and 'followers'. The letter went on to say: 'Another point. The feeling among the Blenheim crews in Malta is that while it is fair to ask them to 'bump off' a merchant ship which is unescorted or weakly escorted, it is up to the Navy to deal with the very strong AA escorts that are now being provided. Is it really impossible under present conditions to put at Malta surface forces which could occasionally go out and 'beat up' the escorts? Could you not persuade Cunningham to take a hand in this?'

On the 13th, Lloyd replied to Portal: 'I am terribly sorry that there should be an impression that I have used my Blenheims constantly, in low attacks, on heavily escorted merchant ships. Actually this is not so. My Blenheim losses have worried me considerably, and I have refused to send them against heavily escorted convoys, in spite of pressure from the Navy. In fact, I sent the attached signal to Air Marshal Tedder on 18th August, stating that it was sheer murder. This signal brought back a sharp rebuke from C-in-C Mediterranean, that the statement was too strong and asked me to study Taranto, etc. I kept all that under my hat. I have followed this policy with one exception. The exception was on 12th September, when a very important convoy was sailing and it was essential to put down at least one of them. We succeeded in sinking an 8,000-ton merchant vessel, but at the loss of crews, one of which was rescued by submarine. As regards shipping sweeps, these have been made on schooners travelling from Tripoli to Benghazi. All these have been unescorted but the amount of flak from them has been terrific. The view held here is that the guns are operated by Germans, as the flak is quite unlike that on convoys.'

He included in his letter a summary of losses 'and they are very heavy':

Task	Total Sorties	Losses
Shipping sweeps and land target back-up	84	4
Shipping sweeps, not convoys	136	7
Shipping in ports	41	7
Escorted convoys	23	5
Land targets	52	2

At the same time, Lloyd copied his reply to Tedder, along with a covering letter that laid out his thoughts on Malta's strike force. 'I presume the CAS means that the two Blenheim squadrons are now being transferred to Middle East and no longer belong to Bomber Command. 107 Squadron is now here, and I understand 18 Squadron is on the way, in addition to 105 Squadron, but await confirmation of this. If this is correct, then I suggest Blenheim squadrons remain here two months at a time. I would like the programme arranged so that one squadron is relieved every month. This would allow the Squadron here to pass on its experiences to the incoming squadron. Personally, I doubt whether we should hold two Blenheim squadrons here. Two months ago I could have employed two squadrons with ease, but unescorted ships are becoming fewer and fewer. I cannot use Blenheims for shipping in the moonlight, as crews are not trained in night flying. The only targets apart from shipping are nuisance raids on Sicily and Southern Italy, munition factories, power stations, railway workshops, etc. Also targets on the Tripoli-Benghazi road which are most profitable but the Blenheim is the wrong aeroplane to that job really well. We want more than one front gun to kill those tankers, and a cannon for preference.

'I would like more Wellingtons. My signals to you have laboured this point. The ASV Wellingtons are bound to make a greater call on what I have here; otherwise there is no object in having them. There must be a striking force to follow up the find. It is true I shall have two torpedo squadrons in the Swordfish and Albacore, but many convoys are out of their range. Incidentally, if the convoys are within their range, we may as well annihilate them as play with them. Over and above convoys, there are the MT depots, and repair shops at Tripoli; the dumps and stores and such shipping as might escape through to Tripoli. I have not yet dealt with Misurata, Homs and various other staging camps to Benghazi. All of these are magnificent targets. Neither have I touched Castel Benito which is well worth a week's bombing when you want it done and you will presumably give me the tip on this, as I do not want to hit it at the wrong moment. It is a sitting target.

'Then there is Italy where we have tremendous possibilities – Naples, Taranto, Palermo, Messina, Catania – all merchant shipping, and various activities connected with it. I can do with two Wellington squadrons here, and I feel sure they will earn their keep. I do not think two Blenheim squadrons will ever do so.' (Lloyd to Tedder, 12 October 1941).

The Albacore was part of the air strike force, although it never established the same reputation as the Swordfish.

Meanwhile, a new enemy fighter had appeared over Malta, the MC.202, which in the right hands was superior to the Hurricanes. In the first air combat, on 1 October, both sides made claims that were not quite correct – as was usual and often inevitable in air combat – but the end result was in favour of the Italians, and the casualty was one of Malta's leading pilots, Squadron Leader 'Boy' Mould.

Bar to DFC to Squadron Leader P.W. Mould of 185 Squadron: 'This officer has led the squadron on 62 daylight sorties since May, 1941; in addition, he has carried out 7 night sorties. Under his leadership the unit has destroyed eight, probably destroyed fourteen and damaged seven hostile aircraft; Squadron Leader Mould has destroyed one and damaged two. By his magnificent example and courage, Squadron Leader Mould has contributed largely to the high standard of operational efficiency and morale of the squadron.' (AMB 4933 dated 3 September 1941).

Across in the Western Desert the fighter types had been taking on ground-attack operations, for which the fixed-gun armament, even the cannons of the Hurricane IICs, was not enough. And so to the dismay of the fighter pilots, bomb racks were added and the pilots were put into training in shallow dive-bombing. The first 'victims' of the new plan, endorsed by the AOC (Lloyd), were 185 and 249 Squadrons, the latter making its first such offensive sortie against Italian airfields and communication on the night of 6/7 October, with pairs of Hurricane going to

Moving torpedo amidst the rubble; the use of air-launched torpedoes increased the anti-shipping effectiveness.

Squadron Leader P.W. 'Boy' Mould DFC and Bar, CO of 185 Squadron.

185 Squadron flew three attacks against Comiso on 28 September, dropping small–calibre bombs.

68

Sunday. September 28th (cont.).

As soon as 'B' Flight had landed and refueled 'A' Flight - Co. leading again went back and handed out another dose as follows:-

14.   HURRICANES. TWELVE Hurricanes - No. 185 Squadron, took off at 09.30 hours to attack COMISO AERODROME. SIX of them (TWO sections of THREE) S/Ldr. MOULD - (Leader), P/O. LINTERN, Sgt. SHEPHARD; F/Lt. JEFFRIES, - (Leader), P/O. VIETOH and Sgt. WARDY. Each aircraft 6 x 40 lbs. G.P. and 2 x 25 lbs. incendiaries. The remaining SIX aircraft - F/O. MURCH, P/O. OLIVER, Sgt. HAYES, Sgt. NURSE, Sgt. JOLLY and Sgt. HUNTON acted as Fighter Escort. They approached COMI SO' AERODROME from the EAST at 17-18,000 feet, dived and released from 10-12,000 feet at 10.05 hours. Bombs seen to burst in N.W. and N.E. dispersal areas and amongst Administration buildings SOUTH of HANGARS. TWO small fires seen in dispersal area. P/O. VIETCH machine-gunned one large building S.W. of COMISO AERODROME and a car on the road. One bomb that hung up in F/Lt. JEFFRIES aircraft dropped when aircraft was over KALAFRANA area, reason unknown. NO opposition. ALL aircraft landed safely.

When everyone landed, it was voted a good idea to knock off for lunch; afterwards 'B' Flight with Pkey leading this time had another smack with very much the same result:-.

15.   HURRICANES. SIX Hurricane (Bombers) and SIX Hurricane (Fighters) of No. 185 Squadron were despatched at 14.00 hours to attack COMISO AERODROME. Pilots of Fighters were : P/O. BAILEY, P/O. REEVES, Sgt. LILLYWHITE, Sgt. WESTCOTT, F/O. ALLARDYCE and Sgt. ALDERSON.
      Sgt. ALDERSON returned at 14.05 hours with engine trouble. The aircraft were over the target at 14.35 hours. The first section of Bombers - F/Lt. PIKE - (Leader), Sgt. SUTHERLAND and Sgt. EASTMAN bombed the HANGARS and other BUILDINGS on the SOUTH EAST side of the AERODROME. Hits were observed on HANGARS. The second section - F/O. THOMPSON, Sgt. ELLIS and Sgt. COUSENES bombed the OFFICERS' MESS and QUARTERS on the NORTH WEST side of the AERODROME. Direct hits and near misses were observed. Bombing was carried out from 12,000 - 13,000 feet. About SIX craters were seen in the CENTRE of the AERODROME. These are thought to be the result of the TWO previous sorties. NO opposition of any kind was encountered. Weather and visibility were both very good. ALL aircraft returned.

GENE RAL NOTE :   The total weight of bombs dropped by the THREE SORTIES was 5,140 lbs. and it is estimated that 90 percent of these fell in the target area.

Sunday.   September 28th.

L.C. did the Mel Flight
I think today's activities can be best explained by Duff gen.
'B' Flight - Co. leading kicked off at dawn with the following effort:-

13.   HURRICANES. SIX Hurricane (Fighters) SIX Hurricane (Bombers) of No. 185 Squadron despatched to attack COMISO AERODROME. Pilots of the former were : F/O. THOMPSON, P/O. ALLARDICE, Sgt. STEELS, Sgt. EASTMAN, Sgt. ELLES and Sgt. SUTHERLAND. Pilots of the Bombers were : S/Ldr. MOULD, F/Lt. PIKE, P/O. BAILEY, P/O. WOODSEND, Sgt. ALDERSON and Sgt. LILLYWHITE. The Bombers approached the target from the EAST at 9,000 feet 07.15 hours, dived down to 7,500 feet on the Main Northern dispersal area and Officers' Mess. Total 1,860 lbs. (40 lbs. G.P. and 25 lbs. incendiary) burst in target area. TWO aircraft were seen to be on fire in N.W. & N. corners by the Fighters and other aircraft certainly damaged. OFFICERS' MESS appeared also to be well shaken. The enemy aircraft were clustered in their pens. Light and medium A.A. opposition, intense 4-5,000 feet barrage. NO enemy Fighters. ONE Macchi 200 seen near COMISO at 12,000 feet, made off Northward at full speed. ONE aircraft (P/O. WOODSEND) came down in the sea, 10 miles off NORTH point of GOZO. Pilot was later rescued.

Gela (railway) and Comiso (airfield). On the first night, Squadron Leader R. Barton and Pilot Officer G. Palliser had made two trip to Comiso, with Palliser commenting: 'First dive-bombing in a Hurricane. Target stood out well in moonlight. Bombs fell near dispersals and hangars in south-east corner'; and on the second sortie: 'Set off at 4.30 a.m. Much darker. Overshot target and bombed eastern side Vittorio Town, near Comiso.'

Tom Neil provided more detailed on his sortie: 'Fondly hoping that the Italian would reveal their known defensive position by shooting at me with the red balls, they did nothing of the sort, obliging me to wander about endlessly over Sicily trying to discover exactly where I was. In fact, I never did find the railway station but, by sheer good fortune, came across the railway line. I did a gentle dive in that direction and disposed of my load.'

Squadron Leader Robert Barton was awarded a Bar to his DFC in October 1941; although there was no specific citation with the award, it was for his leadership of the squadron during the summer on Malta. Aircraft of the MNFU and Fulmars of 800X were also active over Sicily that first night, with one of the Fulmars failing to return.

The reality was these were only nuisance raids with the dual aim of disturbing the peace and quiet of the Italians, and also showing the Malta garrison that it was continuing to take the war to the enemy. As with most such 'pinprick' raids, they were seldom effective, and they did suffer losses. Still, with the reduction in Italian attacks on Malta it was considered a worthwhile use of air assets.

The 18 Squadron Blenheims were soon in action. Typical of these was the mission of 17th October, when six Blenheims were escorted by Hurricanes to attack the seaplane base at Syracuse. The raid was a success in that no aircraft were lost and one intercepting fighter was shot down. However, October was another bad month for the Blenheims of 107 Squadron:

4 Oct: V5821, Sergeant D. Hamlyn, shot down by fighters, all crew safe but interned
9 Oct: V7638, Wing Commander F. Harte, mid-air with Z7644, all killed
9 Oct: Z7644, Flying Officer N. Walders, mid-air with Z7638, all killed
11 Oct: Z7618, Sergeant A. Routh, shot down by flak, all killed
11 Oct: Z9663, Flying Officer R. Greenhill, shot down by flak, all killed
16 Oct: Z7511, Flying Officer S. McAllister, crashed in Luqa circuit, two killed and one injured
25 Oct: Z7704, F/Sergeant E. Shaver, failed to return, all killed

In terms of success against ships, October started with the Dutch Navy submarine HNLMS O-21 sinking the Vichy French MV *Oued Yquem* off Sardinia on the 3rd, with another Vichy French ship, *Theophile Gautier*, falling the following day to HMS *Talisman*. The first air success was to 830 Squadron's redoubtable Swordfish, which put paid to the *Rialto* off Misurata on the 5th. The Blenheims had been out the same day on a night attack against a ship off Tripoli, claiming hits but with no loss being recorded. This was a new tactic for them though, a night attack. In one of the first attacks by the ASV Wellingtons, Tony Spooner found and attacked a supply ship on the night of the 8th, claiming it was left on fire, although no loss is recorded. There was success for 830 Squadron, with the *Paolo S Podesta* being sunk off Sicily on the 8th. The following day the Blenheims of 107 were on the hunt for shipping off southern Italy but at some point two aircraft collided with the loss of all crew, including the CO, Wing Commander F.A. Harte. The CO's aircraft also had a passenger, Lieutenant Talbot of the Royal Engineers. On 11th the Swordfish claimed two more victims, *Casaregis* and *Zena*, the latter south of Lampedusa.

Although the Italians had been keeping fairly quiet, they did make the occasional appearance over Malta, one such raid being an early morning fast strafing attack by six MC.202s on the 14th.

The raid was intercepted by Hurricanes of the MNFU, 185 and 249. One MNFU pilot was shot down, Pilot Officer David Barnwell. Hurricanes were sent out to search but no trace was found. Barnwell had moved to the MNFU from 185, and with his former unit had been awarded a DFC in September, the citation reading: 'This officer has displayed outstanding courage and determination when attacking hostile aircraft of which he has destroyed at least four by night. He has in every way set an excellent example.' (AMB 5140).

The Air Ministry News Service released a bulletin concerning this pilot. 'At dawn on 14th October a listener in at Fighter Control Room at RAF HQ Malta heard the dramatic farewell of a young fighter pilot sounding in his earphones. Twenty minutes earlier, a few enemy aircraft protected by a strong covering force had crossed the coast at low level, hurriedly and wildly emptying their machine-guns. Among the Hurricanes that pounced on them was one piloted by 19-year-old DFC Pilot Officer of a Malta night fighter unit.

'Shortly afterwards his voice came over the W/T "Tally Ho! Tally Ho! Got one! Got one!" Five minutes elapsed and the voice sounded again "bailing out, engine out – am bailing out, am coming down in sea."

'The silence which followed was not broken again. Thus did David Usher Barnwell, last of three RAF sons of the famous aircraft designer, who himself gave his live for aviation, say goodbye.' [His father had been designer of the Blenheim and Beaufort and had been killed in a flying accident while testing a new aircraft.]

'He is posted "Missing Believed Killed". Both his brothers lost their lives in service with the RAF, one with bombers and the other with night fighters.' It is hard to imagine how the news of the death of the third brother was received by the family.

'Late on the night of October 14 the disappointed crew of a RAF rescue launch brought their vessel back to moorings. It was one of the vessels which had carried out a 14–hour search for the missing pilot. With aircraft circling overhead, it had searched every yard of the area where the night fighter had come down. Once or twice hope had been raised by the sighting of pieces of flotsam or a fisherman's buoy bobbing in the choppy sea. The search went on until darkness fell, but there was no trace of the missing pilot.

'He was keen, quiet and unassuming. Chivalrous in victory, he visited the Captain of an Italian bomber he destroyed in order to congratulate him on the skill with which he had landed the burning aircraft on the sea.' (AMB 5348 dated 17 October)

In this book, we frequently refer to statistics of aircraft lost, pilot strength, and other 'mundane' numbers, but an account such as the one above helps put forward a human perspective and reality.

In August a requirement had been put forward for heavier bombs for use against ports such as Tripoli, and in due course the Air Ministry sent twelve 4,000lb bombs to Malta by submarine and three specially modified Wellingtons of 104 Squadron to drop them. It was Air Marshal Tedder's intention to use these against Naples and Benghazi, and indeed it was Naples that was attacked first, on 21/22 October, when four of these weapons were dropped. Other records show the first use was on the night of 16/17 and the target was Naples. The idea of these bombs was to knock down walls and make the interior of the target more susceptible to bombs and incendiaries.

With the departure of 105 Squadron, additional aircraft were flown in by 18 Squadron. However, a few days after their arrival the squadron lost its first aircraft; Flight Sergeant J. Woodburn and crew over Homs on the 22nd when it was brought down by frag damage from the bombs of the previous aircraft.

The Swordfish had proved a remarkable success in the Mediterranean to date, but on 16th October the reinforcements brought under Operation Callboy included eleven Albacores, flown off *Ark Royal*. A new Swordfish unit arrived on the 17th, with 828 Squadron flying from *Ark Royal* to Hal Far. The following night its well-established sister squadron, 830, added yet another score to its impressive list, damaging the *Caterina* to such a degree that she sank the following day.

Meanwhile, the Wellington detachment of 38 Squadron left and its place was taken by 40 Squadron, another of the experienced bomber units, having operated Wellingtons in Bomber Command from Alconbury. The trip out to Malta also saw the first two losses: X9974 (Pilot Officer C.G. Saunders) clipped a fence getting airborne from Hampstead Norris. The aircraft was overloaded and had ten on board; the pitot tube had been damaged and when Saunders attempted a circuit to land, the aircraft stalled and crashed, killing all on board. Wellington X9912 (Sergeant J.D. Paine) also had ten on board, as each aircraft was carrying four ground crew; the aircraft ran out of fuel near Sicily and although Paine managed to ditch, only one of those on board made it out, Leading Aircraftman R. Wade was washed ashore the following day and became a PoW. The 40 Squadron ORB recorded the move on 16 October: 'Orders were received for the squadron as a whole to move to Malta for a two-month tour of special operations duties. The squadron, now reduced to nine fully trained and two freshmen crews was to be made up to sixteen operational flight crews.' On 23 October, Wing Commander Stickly led the first eight aircraft from Alconbury, followed by a second eight on the 25th, although not all of these arrived in Malta.

Philip Dawson had just returned to flying after being in an aircraft crash and was one of those due to go to Malta: 'We were told that the detachment would be for about three months and that we should be home by Christmas; the reason we were going was that the Wellington II had a greater bomb load than the ICs and a major effort was needed to support the Crusader offensive. Aircraft were flown to Heston in order to have beam guns fitted and then we deployed to Stanton Harcourt as the starting point for a direct route to Malta. It was soon discovered that the take-off run at Stanton was insufficient for an overloaded Wellington, we had overload fuel tanks, extra guns, six aircrew, four groundcrew and spare parts on board; the solution was soon to hand when a swathe was cut through the offending trees thus giving us an acceptable run!

'Once airborne we set course over Brighton, flying between two searchlights being used as markers, and then off across France; it was easy to see when we crossed into Vichy France as all the lights were on as if it was peacetime. We arrived off Malta just before dawn and had to circle Filfla Island until it was day and we were able to land. I logged eight hours twenty-five minutes for that trip.' (*personal communication*).

Eric Barfoot was also en route to Malta via Gibraltar, leaving Hampstead Norris on 5 November: 'The night was cold and raw. A short, chubby WAAF Corporal cook gave us each a packet of sandwiches, a bar of chocolate, an orange and a very wet kiss. Tears were streaming down her face.' Wellington Z1041 'L for Leather' was brand new and was piloted by Squadron Leader J.H.T. Simpson, and Eric was fresh out of training and would act as second pilot for the flight – destination Egypt, via Gib and Malta. After a brief stop at Gib, the crew flew to Malta on 7 November: 'Refreshed and refuelled, we took off for Malta. En route the African coast occasionally came into view as we flew close under cloud cover for protection. However, after seven tedious hours the skies cleared and a sharper lookout was needed. The coast was now visible and the Italian island of Pantelleria was not too far away. Then we saw it. It was an Arado flying boat on the starboard beam. According to the 'book' it was much slower than us and lightly armed, so we turned to attack. However, I was soon to wish that we had a reverse gear, three more Arados were coming along behind. Discretion overcoming valour, tempting us to use our superior speed and to leg it for Malta. We succumbed to the temptation and finally landed on a well bombed airfield [Luqa] after a flight which had lasted 8 hours and 55 minutes.' The Wellington moved on late on the 8th and duly arrived at Fayoum to join 70 Squadron. (*pers comm*).

The offensive mindset was such that the Navy's Force K moved to Malta on 21 October. The positioning of this force of two cruisers (*Aurora* and *Penelope*) and two destroyers (*Lance* and *Lively*) was intended as a rapid strike force to attack convoys. October's anti-shipping record was poor for the Blenheims; heavy losses and only one success, sinking the 2,415-ton *Achille* on the 23rd. The earlier comment about Blenheims not operating at night was soon turned into a request for just such operations, with the Lloyd request that Luqa 'consider the operation of a limited number of Blenheims of 18 and 107 squadrons for operations at night. The aircraft would only operate on first class moon conditions when the target could be seen distinctly. Feasible targets are shipping. These are very easy targets under the right conditions of moon, and very effective attacks can be made at a low altitude with very little risk. Wing Commander Hart was experimenting with this method of attack shortly before he was reported missing [9 October], and he achieved considerable success with moonlight attacks.'

Lloyd went on to explain why this was so urgent: 'At the present moment, it is very important that we continue our pressure in Sicily and Italy, and also in Libya; consequently, there is a very great scope for the use of Blenheims in this role. I suggest that about six crews in each squadron should be employed for this role, and since night flying here under ideal moon conditions is very easy, it is very likely that little training will be necessary.' (Letter HQ RAF Mediterranean to RAF Luqa, 23 October 1941).

The response came on the 31st and provided more detail as to targets and tactics: 'The ultimate role of these crews will be primarily to interfere with road movement between Tripoli and Benghazi. It is important that these crews are determined in that we must interfere with any night movement on road communications. Aircraft are to carry the maximum number of 40lb bombs fitted with parachutes together with 250lb bombs fused instantaneous. Aircraft must therefore operate at about 400ft for the 40lb bombs and at 1,000ft for the 250lb bombs.

'So that crews may attack their targets with a certain degree of accuracy, certain moonlight targets are being arranged in Sicily for training. When these twelve crews are sufficiently proficient to attack transport on the road between Tripoli and Benghazi, will you please inform this HQ. It is important that interference with the enemy movement at night is made at the earliest possible date. The intention is to use these twelve crews by night during the moonlight period which time they will operate two nights out of three.' (Letter RAF Luqa to HQ RAF Mediterranean 31 October 1941).

On the night of 21/22 October Wellingtons from Malta attacked Naples, dropping 34 tons of bombs, including four of the 4,000lb bombs that had been delivered to Malta by submarine. This was one of six raids on Naples in October. The opportunity was also taken to drop a new leaflet on the population of Naples, which read as follows: 'Neapolitans. We British, who have never been at war with you before, send you this message. We bombed Naples tonight. We did not want to bomb you Neapolitans. We have no quarrel with you. All we want is peace with you. But we are forced to bomb Naples because you let the Germans use your port. So long as ships continue to leave Naples with German arms and German supplies for the Germans in Libya your city will be bombed again. Tonight's bombing is only the first drop of the coming storm. Therefore, if you want to save yourselves:

Your dockers must refuse to load ships for the Germans.
Your sailors must refuse to sail ships for the Germans.
You must go yourselves to the docks and scream at your dockers and sailors to cease work.'

The dropping of propaganda leaflets, 'nickelling' as it was called in Bomber Command, was common on many bombing missions, although it was rare in the Middle East for a purely leaflet 'raid' to be made. Despite the attacks on Naples, it was Benghazi and more Benghazi that was the routine for as many bombers as the air commander could summon up; even the Marylands of the SAAF units, such as 12 Squadron and 21 Squadron, started flying missions to attack the port, the first such being by 21 Squadron on 14 October, high-level bombing targeting the harbour installations to disrupt offloading activities. Tedder had requested Flying Fortresses, and a small number of these arrived at the end of October, with two bombing Benghazi on 8 November – not a great introduction as one ran out of fuel and force-landed.

The only confirmed success that Philip Dawson had in the anti-shipping role came on the night of 31 October when, flying his usual Z8404, he was one of four Wellingtons tasked, in company with a flare-dropping aircraft of 69 Squadron, to attack a small convoy of three ships (one warship and two MVs) that had earlier been located by a 69 Squadron aircraft.

'We reached the rough area and then the flare-dropper began to do his stuff; it was a good moonlit night and I saw three ships in the moonpath and so set up for a run against the larger of the MVs. Having made three runs at 6,000ft it was impossible to make a good attack because of the evasive tactics of the ships. We tried again at 3,500ft, the minimum height for using the bombsight, but again had no luck. We then decided to make a diving attack, from 3,500ft down to about 150ft over the target. The warship seemed to have only one good gun on the stern and this kept shooting over our starboard wing. The bomb aimer had to guess the release – and got it right as two bombs struck the ship. Another of the Wellingtons also hit this target and when a reconnaissance sortie spotted the convoy the following day it was down to two ships.' The ship loss records do not list any losses to aircraft for this date.

Of significance to Malta's offensive role was the arrival on 30 October of 148 Squadron's Wellingtons. There were plenty of targets north and south, and the bombers of 205 Group in Egypt were too far away, so it was logical to put operational Wellingtons on Malta. The only suitable base was Luqa and so they duly took up residence, flying their first mission on the night of 31 October, led by Squadron Leader Foss.

Gibraltar had become increasingly busy, and its runway had been determined as inadequate at the beginning of 1941, although action to remedy this was somewhat slow. It became increasingly urgent from April with the increased use by transit aircraft, especially Wellingtons, from the UK. A runway extension plan had been put in place in April, but in October the scale was greatly increased with a decision that the runway was to be extended to a length of 1,550 yards and with a width of 150 yards. Lord Gort signalled the War Office that this would be a major engineering feets requiring 500,000 tons of filling, and building the runway 500 yards into the sea, an estimate later increased to 570 yards into the sea. The work duly commenced, and Gib ended up with the 'into the sea' runway for which it became well known. Additional facilities were built at the same time as up to that point 202 Squadron had only one slipway, and a maintenance hangar had only been

The facilities at Gibraltar continued to grow, with extensions to airfield and naval facilities. This is an early 1944 aerial, note Catalinas on the slipway to the left.

completed on September. The squadron remained the main operational RAF unit, with its routine of AS patrols and reconnaissance. These met with occasional success. The Italian submarine *Galileo Ferraris* was damaged by a Catalina out of Gibraltar on the 25th and was scuttled by her crew.

No. 205 (Heavy Bomber) Group was formed in October 1941 at RAF Shallufa in place of 257 (HB) Wing, and initially comprised five Wellington squadrons, all in the Canal Zone, two at Shallufa (37, 38) and two at Kabrit (70, 148) and one at Fayid (108). The group was not placed under the jurisdiction of AHQ Egypt but remained directly under the hand of the AOC-in-C. As we have seen throughout this account so far, the Wellington squadrons operated detachments from Malta, as did UK-based units. As part of the overall campaign, the bombers of 205 Group were kept busy on strategic targets, with ports remaining the top priority in an effort to stem the flow of supplies. This meant Benghazi was 'visited' on a regular basis, so regular in fact that some squadrons referred to it as the 'Mail Run'. In the period mid-June to mid-October, the Germans recorded 72 heavy air raids on Tripoli and 102 on Benghazi.

One of the major problems faced by the offensive forces on Malta was shortage of munitions and fuel and this had an adverse effect on the scale of operations; the most common weapons being dropped by the Wellingtons were the 250lb GP bomb and 250lb SAP; no special anti-shipping bombs were available and a number of weapons that dated back to the latter part of the First World War were also called into service. Many of these bombs could only be tail-fused and so reliance was placed on the weapon actually penetrating the deck of the target as without nose fusing they would not go off on impact

Tedder issued a new set of operational instructions giving target priorities for the Malta Wellingtons:

- Sustained light scale nuisance raids on Naples area, docks and shipping
- Sustained heavy raids on Tripoli
- One heavy attack on Castel Benito (to prevent the Italians moving aircraft east of that place).

The Wellingtons attacked Castel Benito twice in early November, on the nights of the 2nd/3rd and 5th/6th, claiming the destruction of twelve aircraft on the ground during the first mission. One Wellington of 40 Squadron was lost on the night of 2nd/3rd during an attack on Castel Benito airfield. Wellington X9763 was shot down by a night fighter and Sergeant G.D. Colville and his crew were all killed. Flight Sergeant C.A. Armstrong of 40 Squadron received the DFM, with the citation reading: 'This airman is an extremely skilful and courageous pilot who has completed many sorties. Throughout, he has displayed the utmost determination to press home his attacks to the full whatever the opposition. On one occasion, in November, 1941, he bombed the aerodrome at Castel Benito, setting aircraft on the ground on fire. He then descended to 200 feet and machine-gunned the aerodrome. On another occasion, he participated in an attack on shipping at Patras in unfavourable weather. Despite the prevailing low clouds, he descended beneath them and released his bombs which burst on the quay, near which three merchant vessels were moored. In an attack on Misurata, his bombs started a large fire. Despite heavy anti-aircraft fire, he descended to 250 feet and machine-gunned transport on the road.' (AMB 6957 dated 14 May 1942)

Tedder also provided priorities for the Blenheims:

- First priority: southbound shipping with special effort against ships en route to Benghazi
- Second priority: Tripoli–Benghazi land communications
- Third priority: one daylight attack on Castel Benito, if the target appeared to be promising.

Counter-air operations thus remained a prong of the air strategy. The Malta squadrons were making their contribution to the *Crusader* offensive by bombing supply centres in Italy, particularly the docks and rail facilities at Naples and Brindisi, as well as targets in Libya. AMB 5501 of 2 November stated: 'Large formations of heavy bombers again pounded Naples and Palermo throughout Friday night, dropping many tons of bombs in attacks lasting from before eight o'clock until two o'clock in the morning. The weather was bad over Naples early in the raid, and the pilots reported freezing conditions more appropriate to Northern Europe than the Mediterranean.

'At Naples, a torpedo factory was again hit by heavy bombers, and hits were made on an airframe factory and the railway station. At Palermo, power stations, the dry dock and moles at the seaplane base were severely hammered. All our aircraft returned safely, despite attempts by enemy night fighters to intercept them over Naples.'

Although most of the airfield attacks were carried out at medium level, there were occasions when the crews went in at low level; one such was 2 November, a fine moonlit evening when sixteen Wellingtons from Malta bombed and strafed Castel Benito. Philip Dawson was still flying his favourite Z8404: 'We went over the airfield with all guns blazing, our front gunner saw a truck moving over the airfield and opened fire on it. One poor Italian aircraft arrived in the area with its lights on and a number of Wellington gunners latched onto him and let rip. The airfield was very poorly defended, we had the impression that it had one machine gun in each corner and that was about it.' (pers comm).

The attack force was twenty-one Wellingtons and they dropped 30 tons of bombs, causing damage to hangars and buildings, and with 'twelve or more enemy aircraft left burning on the ground. Four enemy fighters attacked the Wellingtons which shot down one CR.42.' (Middle East Int Summary). One Wellington failed to return. A further 25 tons were dropped on the same target by eighteen Wellingtons on 5th/6th November.

A 69 Squadron Maryland picked up an Italian supply convoy on 8 November and reported its composition and position to Malta. The convoy of ten merchant ships with six escorting destroyers were in two groups, and Force K set sail to intercept, which it did off Cape Spartivento. The Naval Situation report stated: 'H.M. Cruisers *Aurora* and *Penelope* and the Destroyers *Lance* and *Lively*, acting on the report of a Maryland aircraft, proceeded on the evening of 8th to intercept a southbound convoy in the Ionian Sea. It was a bright moonlight night and, after the first sighting, our force was able to work round so as to have the enemy silhouetted against the moon. As the range closed the convoy was found to consist of four destroyers and eight merchant ships, with a second convoy of two destroyers and two merchant ships joining them. Fire was opened at just under 6,000 yards range, and the first salvo hit a destroyer.

'Two destroyers were sunk in a few minutes and a third was badly damaged. An ammunition ship was hit and blew up. At least twelve torpedoes were fired by the enemy and of four fired by H.M. ships three scored hits. A total of nine merchant ships was sunk and a 10,000-ton tanker was set on fire and is considered a total loss. Our ships suffered no damage or casualties, and took no prisoners. They were ineffectually attacked by torpedo-bombers during the morning.

'H.M. Submarine *Upholder* after the engagement sighted two Trento class cruisers (8-inch guns), which had apparently been covering the convoys, and six destroyers escorting a damaged one. She sank one destroyer and hit another, which was last seen in tow with the stern under and the fore part out of water.' An excellent example of air and sea co-operation. The 'Battle of the Duisburg convoy' had been a bad day for Axis shipping, with confirmed losses of two tankers, *Conte di Misurata* and *Minatitlan*, four troopships, *Maria*, *Sagitta*, *San Marco* and *Duisburg* (the latter two German ships), the cargo ship *Rina Corrado*, and two destroyers, *Libeccio* and *Fulmine*, all sunk by shelling.

The Blenheims started November with the sinking of the *Anna Zippitelli* on the 5th. Aircraft of 18 Squadron were the main detachment in November and unfortunately they also suffered heavily:

5 Nov: Z7801, Sergeant H. Vickers, shot down by convoy escort, all killed
5 Nov: Z7922, Sergeant R. Morris, shot down by convoy escort, all killed
8 Nov: Z7985, Flight Lieutenant G. Pryor, shot down by convoy escort, all killed
19 Nov: V6060, Sergeant D. Buck, shot down by convoy escort, all killed
19 Nov: V6492, Sergeant J. Woolman, shot down by convoy escort, all killed
19 Nov: Z7860, Sergeant H. Hanson, probably shot down by convoy escort, all killed

No. 107 Squadron was still operational and also suffered another loss on the 8th, Sergeant W. Hopkinson and crew being killed on same convoy attack as 18 Squadron.

On 12 November the Malta fighter squadrons mounted an attack on Gela airfield, the plan being concocted, and led by, Wing Commander Alexander Rabagliati DFC* (the bar having been awarded in October 1941 with no specific citation) and Wing Commander Mark Brown. The plan involved 126 and 249 providing as many aircraft as possible, some as fighter cover and some as ground attackers. The first wave of four took off at 0630 to strafe the airfield defences ahead of the bomber wave of four Hurribombers, the two wing commanders being joined by Pilot Officer Tedford, the fourth aircraft having to return early. By the time they arrived over the target the defences were more alert than suppressed, and Wing Commander Brown was soon shot down. Before this happened they had strafed a number of aircraft on the ground, and Rabagliati also shot down a Stuka. Next up was the main wave, with eleven Hurribombers escorted by ten other Hurricanes. The formation was intercepted near the target, a Hurricane of 126 being shot down, the pilot becoming a PoW.

Hurricane with 250lb bombs; the Hurribomber role was popular with pilots in that they could go and hunt the enemy, but it was unpopular with the fighter purists!

More Hurricanes arrived on 12 November, *Ark Royal* and *Argus* launching thirty-seven aircraft of 242 and 605 squadrons. The former was equipped with IIBs and had been operating offensive missions over France from North Weald and Manston prior to a spell at Valley to prep for the trip to Gibraltar aboard *Argus* and then on to Malta. Three aircraft were lost on the ferry, and a fourth crashed on landing, but the reinforcement of aircraft and pilots was significant. However, they were still old and worn Hurricanes and with the advent of better Italian fighters, the balance of combat performance was in favour of the Axis air force, and the situation was about to get worse.

The Axis forces scored one major success against Force H, when *U-81* sank *Ark Royal* as it was returning to Gibraltar on the 13th. This carrier had been claimed as sunk many times before, but this time it was true. This was one of the first German submarines to manage to break through the Straits into the Mediterranean, one of Gibraltar's roles being to keep the entrance to the Med sealed. However, in the period September to December 1941, twenty-six U-boats made the passage.

The Navy had some revenge, sinking *U-433* on the 16th and *U-95* later in the month, the latter by a Dutch submarine.

The German Naval C-in-C conference of 13 November stated that: 'The situation regarding transports to North Africa has grown progressively worse, and has now reached the critical stage. It is pointed out that the Naval Staff has always fully recognized the dangerous situation caused by British naval superiority in the Mediterranean, and constantly emphasized the need for speedy introduction of the proper German measures. Today the enemy has complete naval and air supremacy in the area of the Mediterranean. Malta is continually being reinforced. Patrols in the Straits of Gibraltar have been intensified, evidently as a result of German submarine operations. The Italians are

MALTA COMMAND
(Under the operational control of H.Q., R.A.F., M.E.)

Location.	Unit.	Equipment.
Dingli	A.M.E.S. No. 504	—
	A.M.E.S. No. 242	
	A.M.E.S. No. 241	
Hal Far	R.A.F. Station	Magister.
	Station Flight	Swordfish.
		Seal.
		Gauntlet.
	No. 185 (F) Squadron	Hurricane.
Kalafrana	R.A.F. Station	—
	Inter-Command W/T Station	
Luqa	R.A.F. Station	—
	No. 104 Squadron (On detachment)	Wellington II.
	No. 69 (G.R.) Squadron	Maryland.
	No. 40 Squadron (On detachment)	Wellington II.
Magdalena	No. 502 A.M.E.S.	—
Takali	Station H.Q.	—
	No. 126 (F) Squadron	Hurricane.
	No. 249 (F) Squadron	Hurricane.
Ta Silch	No. 501 A.M.E.S.	—
Valetta	H.Q., Mediterranean	—
	Base Accounts Office	—
	Base Personnel Office	—
	Met. Station	—

SD161 Location of Units for Malta Command, November 1941.

not able to bring about any major improvements in the situation, due to the oil situation and their own operational and tactical impotence.'

Air and naval anti-submarine patrols were stepped up from November, primarily to ensure that the Straits stayed closed and thus prevent German U-boats entering the Mediterranean in strength. December saw the disbandment of 200 Group and the formation of AHQ Gibraltar, in recognition of the increased air effort. One reason for the intense operations in October and early November was the preparation for the major Allied offensive in the Western Desert; Operation Crusader was launched on 18 November.

The Italians had essentially ceded the air to the RAF and had throughout the summer failed to keep up the pressure on Malta, enabling the island to build up its defensive and offensive capability. Rommel was complaining constantly about the lack of supplies, even though the Italian merchant marine made consistent – and generally unsuccessful – efforts to run supplies. By November the Italians had started to increase the number and scale of attacks, primarily with hit-and-run fighter

The loss of the carrier *Ark Royal*, sunk by U-boat on 13 November.

raids, and from time to time with escorted bombers. On 22 November ten Italian Stukas, escorted by more than sixty fighters, were tasked against the RAF airfields. This resulted in some of the most intense air battles for some time. The Italians claimed to have been intercepted by forty or more fighters, claiming eight shot down. The RAF put up twenty-one Hurricanes of 126 and 249, with pilots making claims for two destroyed, three probables, and four damaged for no loss.

Pilot Officer Henry Lardner-Burke of 261 Squadron received the DFC, with his citation reading: 'In November, 1941, this officer was the pilot of one of 4 aircraft which engaged a force of 18 hostile aircraft over Malta and destroyed 3 and seriously damaged 2 of the enemy's aircraft. During the combat Pilot Officer Lardner-Burke, who destroyed 1 of the enemy's aircraft, was wounded in the chest and his aircraft was badly damaged. Despite this, he skilfully evaded his opponents and made a safe landing on the aerodrome; he then collapsed. Throughout the engagement, this officer displayed leadership and courage of a high order. He has destroyed 5 enemy aircraft over Malta.' (AMB 5722 dated 2 Dec 1941).

The debate over Malta's night fighter capability continued, and on 18 November, Air Commodore W.A. Coryton (Director of Overseas Operations) wrote to the VCAS on the subject: 'Whilst I agree that the aircraft and personnel for a night fighter unit at Malta can only be taken out of the three existing fighter squadrons, I do consider our future plans should allow for a separate night fighter unit being established at Malta. Whilst there is only Italian opposition, three fighter squadrons are adequate at Malta but their whole effort will be required for day work alone if the Germans come back to Sicily. A separate night fighter unit will then be urgently needed. I feel Malta has already reached saturation point in the number of aircraft which can be maintained from a supply point of view and which can be efficiently operated from there. Blenheims at Malta are paying very diminishing returns. If it is necessary from a supply point of view, we could well forage a flight of Blenheims for the purpose of establishing a night fighter flight.'

It was an interesting thought to use the Blenheim for the purpose, but for now the focus was still on anti-shipping work for them. He also agreed that 'from the morale point of view' there was benefit in conceding to Malta's request to give the unit a squadron number. Despite these seeming

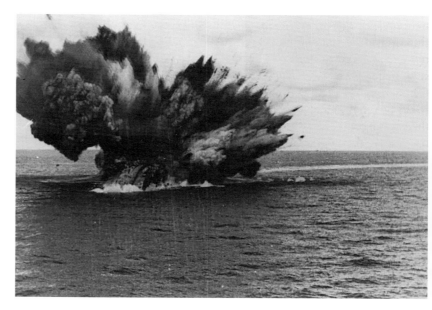

The loss of HMS *Barham*. The anti-shipping war was not all one way; the Royal Navy, with its Allied contingents, played a dominant role in the Mediterranean with both strategic naval operations and escort duties.

adverse comments, the Blenheims claimed two more ships in the last few days of November, the small (2,093-ton) Italian tanker *Berbera* (28th) and the 3,476-ton *Capo Faro* (30th), while the Malta Wellingtons claimed the *Priaruggia* during at attack on Benghazi. In terms of shipping success, however, the major victory went to the *U-331* when it sank the battleship HMS *Barham* on the 25th. The increased presence and threat from German submarines led to increased anti-submarine patrols by RAF aircraft, from Malta and Alexandria in particular.

The Blenheims went after a convoy on 29 November. The formation consisted of four aircraft from 18 Squadron and two from 107 Squadron. One crew was awarded immediate gallantry awards for its actions on this and an earlier mission in November. The joint citation for Flight Lieutenant Edmunds (DFC) and Sergeant Hedin (DFM) of 18 Squadron reads: 'In November, 1941, Flight Lieutenant Edmunds and Sergeant Hedin were the pilot and navigator respectively of an aircraft which carried out an attack on shipping east of Tripoli. In spite of extremely unfavourable flying conditions Flight Lieutenant Edmunds persisted in his mission and, ably assisted by Sergeant Hedin who skilfully navigated the aircraft over 200 miles of the sea to the target area finally attacked and scored hits on a large vessel and an escorting destroyer. Two days later, Flight Lieutenant Edmunds, with Sergeant Hedin as navigator, led a low flying attack on shipping in Navarini Bay. In spite of intense fire from the shore, several hits were scored on a 6,000-ton tanker which was set on fire. The skill and determination shown by Flight Lieutenant Edmunds, combined with the skilful and accurate navigation displayed by Sergeant Hedin, were largely responsible for the success achieved.' (AMB 5880 dated 19 December 1941). The latter attack had destroyed the tanker *Berbera*.

The ASV Wellingtons were still providing invaluable service, and Tony Spooner in particular was proving himself to the be the ASV equivalent of Warburton. He flew long missions and was determined to find, track and home strike aircraft to any worthwhile target. His work was recognized in the award of a DFC: 'One night in November, 1941, this officer was the captain of an aircraft co-operating with our naval forces in the Ionian Sea. Extremely unfavourable weather conditions prevailed, clouds being down almost to sea level but, in spite of this, Flight Lieutenant Spooner carried out a search extending for some 300 miles of open sea. Flight Lieutenant Spooner succeeded in locating 2 convoys, each consisting of a merchant vessel and a destroyer, and it was entirely due to his skill and persistence in the face of great odds that a naval force was directed to the target and thus able to destroy the convoys. In October, 1941, Flight Lieutenant Spooner attacked an 8,000-ton enemy merchant vessel, setting it on fire. Two nights later, he shadowed a convoy which was subsequently attacked by our naval aircraft and 3 merchant vessels were seriously damaged. During October and November, 1941, this officer was successful in locating 3 enemy convoys and, as a result of attacks by our aircraft, several enemy ships were set on fire and others were damaged. In the latest attack, which was on 4 ships, only 1 was to be seen the next day. Throughout, this officer has displayed exceptional skill and determination.' (AMB 5933 dated 24 December 1941). One of his longest sorties was flown on the 30th, during which he homed various attack formations to the convoy he had found; the only confirmed success was to Blenheims of 18 Squadron, sinking the *Capo Faro*.

The coastal tanker *Speranza* was damaged in an attack on Benghazi to such an extent that she was scuttled a few weeks later, another tanker out of commission. By late November the Axis fuel supply situation was becoming critical and an attempt was made to use Ju 52s to fly fuel from Eleusis (Greece) to Derna; a concentrated series of attacks on Derna destroyed many of these transport aircraft. The success against shipping was accompanied by Rommel's constant complaints to anyone who would listen. Despite Hitler's continued indifference to the Mediterranean theatre, he did listen to Rommel when it tied in with his master plan for the war with Russia, in this case take the Middle East and strike up into Russia from below. The inevitable consequence of this, and the Russian winter enabling air assets to be redeployed, was the return of the Luftwaffe to Sicily, and the next crisis for Malta.

June had brought renewed 'debate' between naval (Cunningham) and air (Tedder and Longmore) commanders as to the creation of a 'Coastal Command for the Mediterranean'. The crux of the debate was around the importance of a dedicated and capable force that could contribute to the air-sea war. Cunningham summarized his thoughts: 'It is my considered opinion that an Air Command (called a Coastal Command or any name if that one is unacceptable) is at once needed, designed to operate against sea-borne enemy forces; that this force should be controlled and operated by the Royal Air Force but in closest collaboration with myself, and that it must have its own units which will not be removed for other duties without prior consultation. To this Command would be attached all disembarked Fleet Air Arm units which could be organized and handled by a Naval Officer working with the Air Force Commander of the Command.'

Tedder replied that in essence he agreed and was building 201 Group to serve this role, but that, unlike in the UK, naval operations could not be 'properly considered as a self-contained activity separate from the main air and land operations in the Middle East.' He was more inclined to an 'all arms' command but stated that: 'We will spare no effort to meet the Navy's requirements, but specifically to segregate air forces for special duties and thereby preclude concentration of air effort is at the present time playing into German hands.' (*The RAF in Maritime War, ibid*).

That did not end the exchange, which continued for some months, but with Tedder holding fast to his position. It eventually went to Admiralty and Air Staff level, but the only result was that 201 Group became 201 (Naval Co-operation) Group, albeit with a more focused definition of its tasks: 'The primary functions of No. 201 (NC) Group were to be the conduct of operations at sea and co-operation with the Mediterranean Fleet as required by C-in-C Mediterranean [although operational control rested with AOC-in-C Middle East – Tedder]. If necessary one or more units of the Group might have to be employed on tasks other than those of their primary functions, but except in emergency this would not be done without prior reference to the C-in-C Mediterranean or his representative.' (*The RAF in Maritime War, ibid*). The strength of the group was:

- Three GR squadrons (39 Squadron Maryland/Beaufort; 203 Squadron Blenheim; 13 Hellenic Squadron Anson)
- Two flying boat squadrons (230 Squadron Sunderland; 2 Yugoslav Squadron Dornier)
- Two long-range fighter squadrons (252 and 272 squadrons Beaufighter)
- Operational control of the RN Fulmar Flight.

By the end of October 39 Squadron had moved on, but 73 Squadron (Hurricanes) and 700 Squadron FAA (Fulmar, Walrus) had been added, along with a newly-formed Sea Rescue Flight. In addition to its role in the Med, the group also covered Alexandria, and the Delta area, and the Suez Canal. Again, space precludes our account going into details of Axis operations against Alexandria or the canal.

Between June and October 1941 the Axis convoys to North Africa lost an estimated 220,000 tons of shipping, of which 115,000 tons were claimed by aircraft, and, more importantly, 90 per cent of that was on outbound – loaded – legs of the journey, denying supplies to the North African combat troops. Malta's aircraft had played a major part. An AHB estimate showed that of 186,564 tons of

Beaufighter detachments to Malta were always most appreciated, especially as escort for anti-shipping sorties, although they also operated in the long-range fighter role.

stores were sent to North Africa in September–October, of which 24.4 per cent (45,437 tons) were sunk by Malta-based aircraft. Of the total delivered in those two months only 43,446 tons were destined for German forces – against a monthly requirement for 40,000–50,000 tons. As a direct result, Rommel's planned attack on Tobruk was twice postponed, which led to Hitler's decision to deploy Fliegerkorps II from Russia to Sicily.

It was an incredible achievement. Such was the success of these attacks that Rommel's complaints about the lack of supplies convinced the German High Command that Malta had to be destroyed. The Luftwaffe returned.

The loss of shipping at sea and in the departure and arrival ports (as here) was truly devastating to the Axis cause in North Africa. The same was true of Malta, where the arrival of even a single supply ship could make a significant difference.

Chapter 5

Luftwaffe Round Two: December 1941 to May 1942

I n October Albert Kesselring had been appointed as C-in-C South and in his memoirs recalled his briefing during a meeting with Hitler, Goering and Jeschonnek: 'The unfavourable situation of our supply line to North Africa, I was told, must be remedied by the neutralization of the British sea and air key-point, the island of Malta. When I objected that we ought to make a thorough job of it and occupy Malta, my interruption was brushed aside with the flat statement that there were no forces available for this.'

Kesselring arrived in Rome on 28 November 1941 and was soon even more convinced that: 'Every day showed more plainly the naval and air supremacy of the British in these waters. Meanwhile Malta had assumed decisive importance as a strategic key-point, and my primary objective at the beginning was to safeguard our supply lines by smoking out that hornet's nest. Time was required to build up the ground organization in Sicily, to bring forward our air formations and the supplies needed to smash Malta's naval and air bases, as well as to secure the co-operation of the Italian air force for our offensive. For the moment it was impossible to do more than reinforce the air umbrella over the most indispensable convoys.' (The Memoirs of Field-Marshal Kesselring).

Fuhrer Directive 38 was issued on 2 December where Hitler: 'commanded that sections of the Luftwaffe now released from the East, to the strength of about one Fliegerkorps and the necessary air defence forces, be transferred to the South Italian and North African Area. I put Field Marshal Kesselring in command of all the forces to be used for this task, as C-in-C Southern Area. His tasks are:

1. To achieve air and sea mastery in the area between Southern Italy and North Africa and thus ensure safe lines of communication with Libya and Cyrenaica; the suppression of Malta is particularly important in this connection
2. To co-operate with German forces operating in North Africa and with the forces of her Allies
3. To paralyze enemy traffic through the Mediterranean and to stop British supplies reaching Tobruk and Malta; this is to be effected by close co-operation with German and Italian naval forces.'

The clear objectives were then somewhat messed up by Hitler adding that Kesselring 'is a subordinate to the Duce from whom he will receive instructions for the task as a whole via the Italian Supreme Command.' Kesselring's Luftflotte 2 was moved to the Mediterranean, with Malta as a primary target. By mid-December the Axis air strength in Sicily totalled 250 bombers and 200 fighters. On a good day, Malta could muster maybe sixty to seventy fighters (Hurricanes, including older and worn-out models) and, for attack, maybe sixty bombers. On the plus side, Malta had learned the hard way how to survive an air pummeling and wherever possible the infrastructure had been protected, and repair and recovery was efficient ... but would it be enough?

Thus, in December 1941, an air armada of some 600 aircraft (German and Italian) was assembled in Sicily under the command of Kesselring with orders to destroy Malta to safeguard Axis shipping.

The arrival of II Fliegerkorps from Russia, with strong bomber elements as well as 109s of JG 53 (three Gruppen) along with II./JG 3 gave the Axis forces a massive superiority over Malta's air capability. The airfields in Sicily were crammed with aircraft, a tempting target for the British but with little capability to make significant attacks. The new air campaign was launched in late December, the initial focus being Malta's airfields, with Hal Far, Luqa and Ta Kali being subjected to heavy attack. With the arrival of large numbers of aircraft and experienced crews it looked inevitable that Malta would be overwhelmed.

Petrol remained the key to operations in North Africa and on 1 December the Blenheims scored a brilliant success with the sinking of the 10,540-ton tanker *Iridio Mantovani*. This was a joint air–sea operation that also involved Force K, and

Albert Kesselring (centre) had been appointed C–in–C South in late 1941: 'The unfavourable situation of our supply line to North Africa, I was told, must be remedied by the neutralization of the British sea and air key-point, the island of Malta. When I objected that we ought to make a thorough job of it and occupy Malta, my interruption was brushed aside with the flat statement that there were no forces available for this.'

the cruiser *Aurora* was involved in the sinking. The *Aurora* also shelled and sank the destroyer *Alvise da Mosto* the same day. For the next two weeks, aircraft achieved no sinkings despite a number of attacks being made, the only successes being by surface ship and, more particularly submarines. A Blenheim of 107 Squadron was lost during an anti-shipping sortie on the 4th. The target was Messina and the squadron was after ferry boats, and trying out the new forward armament fitting. Sergeant R.G. Kirby (Z7775) was last seen being pursued by three fighters; he was shot down and the only survivor was Sergeant J. Hughes, who became a PoW. That night, the Wellingtons of 40 Squadron were back at Naples, losing R1066 (Flying Officer D.F. Hutt) to fighter attack. The two pilots survived as PoWs and the other four crew were killed. For a while the Blenheims had taken on an

increased role in attacking land targets, and it was on one such target on the 8th that 18 Squadron lost two aircraft. The target was Catania airfield and the four aircraft went out at sea level to avoid detection. At some point someone in the formation called that an aircraft had been sighted, and when the formation broke away two of the Blenheims collided. They were Z7613 (Pilot Officer J.A. Barclay) and Z9719 (Sergeant W.J. Cumming), and all six aircrew were killed.

Although Italian attacks on Malta had been infrequent, certainly in terms of scale and effectiveness, they were still being totalled up and on 1 December an Air Ministry press release announced

A 109 pilot poses in his life vest; the chances of being picked up in the area between Sicily/North Africa and Malta were reasonably good, as both sides operated rescue services.

'Malta's Thousandth Air Raid'. This is phrased as a success and praises the people of Malta and their resilience. While it is an undoubted piece of propaganda, and thus had its 'errors', it is also essentially true in its recognition of how resilient the Maltese had proved to be (and it was not over yet) in the face of air attack.

'The present reactions of these experienced islanders to the siren is interesting. Familiarity with raids has not bred contempt. Rather have the Maltese become air raid connoisseurs. Nowadays they know that a daylight raid is likely to be high and hurried, for the air above is not long safe for enemy aircraft even 4 miles up, as the climbing Hurricanes roar out to meet the approaching enemy. The prudent take shelter, for they know that a bomb, even if aimed at a military target from very high up, is liable to go astray. The narrow streets between the tall buildings gradually empty. From one edifice, which was a knight's palace two centuries ago, files a 'crocodile' of trim, white-bloused schoolgirls winding its way towards the appointed shelter. The girls are chattering gaily and unhurried.

'When a formation of fast-flying fighters made a hurried swoop on an aerodrome, the shelters quickly emptied and crowds stood at vantage points and watched the Hurricanes tearing in to the Macchis. They were aware that the Italian fighters would at best fire a few furtive rounds. When the snarl and whine of engines faded northwards and the stuttering of the machine guns died away over the sea, they returned to their homes, elated. They have seen Malta's defence grow from a few lionhearted Gladiators and they are confident and content.' All good PR stuff!

'There are two meatless days a week in Malta now, but otherwise food appears to be plentiful. Some of the bombed shops are barricaded and there are defiant 'Vs' on the boarded windows. Temporary premises are already springing up among the ruins. The cinemas are open and well patronized, and a 'country fair' with stalls and boxing booths has just opened.' (AMB 5759 dated 1 December).

The siege of Tobruk was lifted on 9 December and the Allied advance continued, with pressure by air attack on the key port of Tripoli increasing. With the Allies moving forward, the desert airfields were now able to support coastal shipping, as well as adding firepower to attacks on Axis shipping and associated installations.

Air Ministry Bulletin No. 5759

MALTA'S THOUSANDTH AIR RAID

Malta has just had its thousandth air raid warning.

The present reactions of these experienced islanders to the siren is interesting. Familiarity with raids has not bred contempt. Rather have the Maltese become air raid connoissours.

Nowadays they know that a daylight raid is likely to be high and hurried, for the air above is not long safe for enemy aircraft even four miles up, as the climbing Hurricanes roar out to meet the approaching enemy.

The prudent take shelter, for they know that a bomb, even if aimed at a military target from very high up, is liable to go astray.

The narrow streets between the tall buildings gradually empty. From one edifice, which was a knight's palace two centuries ago, files a "crocodile" of trim, white-bloused schoolgirls winding its way towards the appointed shelter. The girls are chattering gaily and unhurried.

As soon as the steady note of the "Raiders Passed" has gone the girls scamper back to school, sedately followed by the mistresses. Malta goes about its business again.

Extract of press release covering Malta's 1,000th air raid warning, 1 December 1941.

Although defensive operations at Malta remained fairly quiet, offensive activity was high, with sweeps by the fighter types, and bombing missions by everyone else. During the week of 9 to 16 December a special effort was made against Axis shipping in ports, as recce had seen concentrations at Patras (Corinth Canal), Argostoli (Cephalonia) and Catania and Trapani in Sicily, as well as warships at Taranto. Blenheims attacked Argostoli on 11th, 13th and 16th. For the Blenheims, losses continued to mount, with the harbour at Argostoli, on the Ionian Island of Kefalonia, proving particularly trying. Blenheim Z7802 (Flight Lieutenant E Edmunds and crew) of 18 Squadron were lost on the 11th, one of three aircraft after shipping and probably shot down by flak.

Life goes on; the resilience of the people of Malta was vital, and great efforts were made to keep food supplies as regular as possible, albeit not very varied.

The Blenheims were back at the same target on the 13th, and this time three aircraft were lost, two from 107 Squadron and one from 18 Squadron. The target was a small group of MVs – but there were also five destroyers present and air cover in the shape of 109s. The 18 Squadron Blenheim (Z7858), Sergeant F.W. Jury, was chased and damaged by a 109 when exiting the target area, eventually ditching close to Malta where the crew was picked up by a Maltese fishing boat. Of the other two lost, Sergeant R.D. Gracie (Z7368) and crew were shot down and killed, and Sergeant S.J. Lee (Z7800) and crew survived being shot down and were taken prisoner. Patras was attacked on the 11th/12th by nineteen Wellingtons,

A possibly posed PR shot of Maltese boy with the Union Jack (and his dog), in token defiance!

the target being three large MVs and a number of smaller ships; the weather was poor but the crews reported damage to at least one MV. The main attack on Taranto was the night of the 15th/16th, with twenty Wellingtons dropping 30 tons, including three 4,000lb bombs, as well as 32,000 leaflets. The defenders put up a thick smoke screen, so results went unobserved.

Meanwhile, in another of the Royal Navy's classic battles, this one off Cape Bon, Tunisia, a naval force from Gibraltar and Alexandria, although also recorded as Malta Force Group I in some records, intercepted the Italian cruisers *Da Barbiano* and *Di Giussano*, which had been involved in trying to run petrol to Tripoli, such was the desperate fuel situation. In a sharp night action both cruisers were sunk. However, the next few days brought very mixed results, with the ending balance very much in favour of the Axis forces. On the 14th the cruiser *Galatea*, Admiral Vian's flagship, was sunk by *U-557*. The following day the fleet sailed again to escort the supply ship *Breconshire* to Malta;

the ship arrived safely on the 18th. Force K left to hunt for an Italian convoy, only to stumble into a minefield with disastrous consequences. No fewer than four ships hit mines. The cruiser *Neptune* was sunk and cruisers *Aurora* and *Penelope* damaged, while the destroyer *Kandahar* was also sunk. Both sides made extensive use of mines, both in open water and in harbour areas; they were easy to lay and hard to track, but this was the worst incident in the campaign.

On the 17th Air Vice-Marshal Lloyd broadcast to the garrison and people of Malta: 'We are on the eve of even greater events, in which Malta will play a still greater part in the defeat of our enemy. We are in a very commanding position. We dominate this part of the Mediterranean. We strike at the enemy where it hurts him most. And it hurts him grievously. Malta has very reason to be proud of the part she has played in this war. The full story has yet to be told. When it is told it will amaze people. The best, however, is yet to come. God speed that day.'

On the same day, Malta's FAA units claimed their first success for some time, sinking the tanker *Lina* to the west of Tripoli. Indeed, December had been the worst month for some time in terms of Axis shipping sunk; in part this was because there were fewer convoys, which was one reason for increased attention on harbours. Overall, the month was much better for the Axis, and the British fleet suffered more bad news on the 19th when an Italian human torpedo attack was made on Alexandria harbour, severe damage being caused to the battleships *Valiant* and *Queen Elizabeth*. What the Italian battle fleet had been unable to do – essentially destroy the British fleet – had been achieved by a minefield and by charges laid by human torpedoes. For a while even greater reliance would have to be placed on aircraft to interdict the Axis supply convoys.

By mid-December 1941 Luftwaffe recce aircraft, usually Ju 88s, had started to appear over Malta again, and on the 19th the first combat took place, when an early morning recce Ju 88 was followed up by three Ju 88s seeking to attack recently arrived ships. They were intercepted by 249 Squadron, which claimed one shot down, with one Hurricane damaged. The air raids had also destroyed at least two of 40 Squadron's Wellingtons, while a third Wellington, from 104 Squadron, was damaged on landing. The aircraft had been on a mission to Tripoli and on return the pilot had landed on the wrong side of the flare path, but in part this was due to the path having been adjusted because of damage to the runway. Malta and its crews were 'out of practice' in dealing with damaged airfields and accurate attacks; they would soon have plenty of opportunity – and need – to improve.

The action heated up the next day with four Ju 88s aiming at ships in the harbour; they were intercepted by 249 Squadron and Pilot Officer Palliser claimed one shot down. The Hurricanes then tangled with the strong escort of Bf 109Fs of JG 53 and MC.202s. In the ensuing combat three Hurricanes were shot down and two pilots

Gunter von Maltzahn of JG53 was an experienced and highly successful fighter pilot by the time his unit moved to Sicily, claiming first victory over Malta on 19 December, a Hurricane.

killed (Sergeant Moren and Pilot Officer Cavan), while 249 claimed one fighter destroyed and one damaged. It was a similar story the next day, with a small number of bombers and a strong fighter escort tangling with Hurricanes of 185 and 249. Each squadron lost one Hurricane, but claimed two in return.

And so it continued for the rest of the month; the relative peace and quiet of Malta was over, and the RAF was facing superior enemy fighters and combat-experienced German pilots. The Germans were now appearing multiple times a day, four on the 26th and five on the 29th; the latter proved to be a bad day with three combats during the five raids. The first combat was mid-morning, and started badly when two Hurricanes clipped wings after take-off; one pilot was killed and one parachuted into the sea. The other fourteen pressed on and engaged the formation, claiming one destroyed and one damaged, for the loss of three Hurricanes damaged.

It was 185 Squadron's turn next, its scramble at 1430 resulting in claims of one shot down and three damaged, for the loss of one Hurricane. The last combats of the day occurred when 249 Squadron scrambled to take on some 109s that were attacking the Gozo ferry; the 109s claimed two Hurricanes, with both pilots killed (Sergeant R. Lawson and Flight Lieutenant Brandt) for the loss of one of their own. In terms of aircraft losses at Malta, the worst day was the 29th, with at least nine Wellingtons written off in air raids, six belonging to 40 Squadron and two still on the books of the OADU as they were on delivery. The only casualties were with X9907, whose crew was in the process of boarding the aircraft; the pilot, Sergeant F.J. Sunley, was killed and all the others injured.

Aircraft losses, write-offs and damage put pressure on availability, but not yet to any critical nature, and damage to airfield facilities was still minimal. The loss of pilots had been high and something that the squadrons had not suffered for some time.

In the latter part of the month the Blenheim units continued to lose aircraft:

22nd: 107 Sqn: Z7915 (Sergeant R.F. Henley); one of six aircraft tasked, in pairs, to attack targets of opportunity on the road west of Sirte, the type of task the North Africa-based Blenheims had been doing for some time (and suffering losses). A convoy was found and attacked, but Henley's aircraft was hit by ground fire and crashed into the sea, with all three crew killed.

107 Sqn: Z7848 (Sergeant E. Crossley); one of three aircraft attacking shipping off Zuara; it was reported that the Blenheim clipped the mast of one of the ships and flipped into the sea; all killed.

18 Sqn: Z7796 (Sergeant O.V. Summers); on an anti-shipping patrol when jumped by a fighter and shot down into the sea; all killed.

Z9816 (Pilot Officer K.W. Wyatt); anti-submarine patrol off Tunisian coast. Landed on Kirkenna Banks in poor visibility and crew picked up and interned (released after Operation Torch in November).

Also this month a DFC was awarded to Squadron Leader George Powell-Sheddon, attached to AHQ Malta, with the citation reading: 'This officer has been engaged on operations almost since the war began. He served with a fighter squadron in the Middle East theatre of war until June, 1940, when he returned to this country and took part in the Battle of Britain. In July, 1941, Squadron Leader Powell-Sheddon was posted to Malta where he formed the night flying unit which has since performed sterling work in the night defence of Malta. By his great and energetic organizing ability, together with his courage and initiative in the air. Squadron Leader Powell-Sheddon has contributed materially to the successes obtained. He has destroyed at least 5 enemy aircraft 3 of which were destroyed by him during the Battle of Britain.' (AMB 5841 dated 12 December).

The attacks intensified in January and the defenders were gradually being beaten down, the number of fighters reducing to a handful each day, flown by exhausted pilots. The weather in January meant that only Luqa, which had a surfaced runway, could be guaranteed as operational. Although some offensive missions were flown in January, to all intents and purposes by February any effective offensive was over. In early 1942 Malta was pounded heavily and enemy fighter patrols around the island made anti-shipping strikes virtually impossible, which made anti-shipping operations from North Africa even more critical.

So what happened in January?

On 1 January a DCAS note to CAS was upbeat but also cautious: 'Up to date Malta has been of the greatest strategical importance to us as a stepping stone for the vital flow of air reinforcements to the Middle East, and as a base to harry the enemy's vital sea communications between Italy, Greece and North Africa. In fact, the enemy's virtual collapse in North Africa during Crusader operations can be primarily described as due to the interruption of enemy sea communications by naval and air forces based at Malta. There can be no doubt that provided we can hold Malta it will play an equally important part in any operations which are conducted in the Central and Eastern Mediterranean area. For the defence of our western flank in North Africa Malta will certainly remain of the utmost importance.'

He went on to describe the growing threat and 'possibility of heavy attacks on Malta'. He summarized defences as 'three fighter squadrons and two lodger fighter squadrons without ground personnel. The anti-aircraft defences consist of 112 heavy and 20 light AA guns. The operation of fighter aircraft suffers by virtue of the limited number of aerodromes from which they can operate, and from the small amount of space for organizing defence in depth. Unless they were considerably reinforced they might be immobilized by a series of heavy air attacks. In fact, the destruction of runways alone might keep our fighters grounded.'

The war had also seen a major strategic change in December with Japan entering the conflict, which would have a major impact on the British ability to provide reinforcements, or even maintain force levels, in the Middle East. The Fleet was the first to lose forces to the Japan war, which led to CAS claiming that 'naval control of the Eastern Mediterranean had virtually ceased to exist and would have to be replaced by air control.' The Chiefs of Staff approved an increase in air assets and the dispatch of seven squadrons (two Beaufort, one GR Hudson, one Wellington, one Beaufighter, and two USAAF B-24 Liberator squadrons), all connected directly with the air-sea war, and none destined, at least initially, for Malta. As units arrived this also led to an expansion of 201 (NC) Group.

The year started well for the defenders of Malta, with a raid on 3 January losing two Ju 88s, primarily due to the Hurricanes

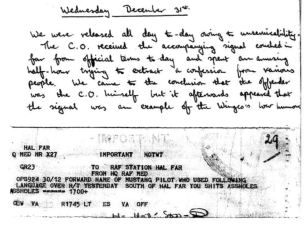

The 185 Squadron diary is a mine of fascinating snippets that seem to very rarely survive but which add human face to the usual official accounts.

having scrambled early and thus getting a height advantage. However, the attackers did well in that they destroyed at least nine aircraft, six Wellingtons, two Whitleys (138 Squadron) and a Blenheim. On the same day, Air Vice-Marshal Bottomley highlighted the problems caused by the weather: 'We have had a terrific amount of rain this year, and have had a tremendous job with bogged aircraft. I dislike seeing our airmen working in the open in mud up to their ankles when it could have been avoided with a little thought and vision.' By this he meant that essential airfield surfacing work had not been done, such as perimeter tracks and dispersals. He continued: 'I have had to send one squadron of Wellingtons to Egypt. It is no longer safe to keep a lot of Wellingtons about when I cannot disperse as much as I want. I have the dispersal, but the standings are so wet that I cannot get aircraft out when I put them in.' So, not so much driven away by enemy attacks but by the rain! Although not connected by subject to the rest of the message, his last paragraph made sideways reference to the invasion threat: 'I have thoroughly learned and assimilated the lessons of Crete, and I trust I shall be able to apply them here.'

The latter comment may have been connected with a signal the same day from the Joint Intelligence Sub Committee (JIC) in London on 'an Axis Attack on Malta' that stated: 'We believe a combined operation against Malta would be of such difficulty that it is improbable that the enemy would attempt it, at any rate until he could judge whether the attempt to neutralize Malta by air attack is likely to succeed.' It also stated that by 1 February it expected the Luftwaffe strength for any

attack would be 550 aircraft, along with 320 Italian aircraft, and 'once the necessary shipping and assault craft and transport aircraft were made available, and subject to events in Russia, the Germans could mount a force of say – 1 parachute division, 1 airborne mountain or infantry division, at least 2 infantry divisions brought by sea. These formations might be available by the beginning of March if events in Russia allow. On the other hand, Italian formations could be made available immediately. The Italians have at least six small parachute 'battalions' which have had considerable training. Italian parachute troops have probably much higher fighting value than normal Italian infantry units.' The general perception remained that an invasion was unlikely, although anti-invasion measures continued to be made.

Wing Commander Rabagliati was offensive-minded, and to send a message to the Germans that they were not safe on their bases, he led an early morning four-ship attack

Recce photo of Castel Vetrano, Sicily, 3 January 1942, showing large numbers of aircraft, mainly torpedo bomber Z.1007s and SM. 79s and transport Ju 52s and SM.82s.

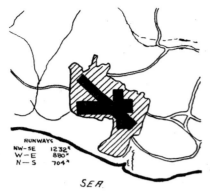

RUNWAYS
NW-SE 1232'
W-E   880'
N-S   704'

SEA

Hal Far Plan February 1942.

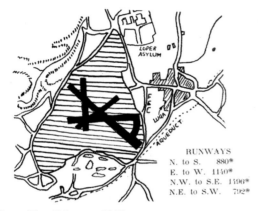

RUNWAYS
N. to S.   880*
E. to W.   1140*
N.W. to S.E. 1196*
N.E. to S.W. 792*

Luqa Plan February 1942.

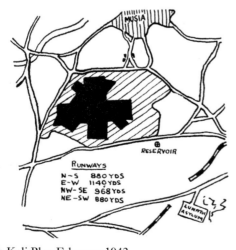

RUNWAYS
N-S   880 YDS
E-W   1140 YDS
NW-SE 968 YDS
NE-SW 880 YDS

Ta Kali Plan February 1942.

on Comiso airfield, the main base of KG 77 (Ju 88) and JG 53 (Bf 109). The Hurricanes each carried eight 20lb fragmentation bombs, the idea being to cause area damage to aircraft and soft installations.

The Blenheims were also active against enemy airfields, with ten aircraft, a mix of 18 and 107 squadrons, attacking Castel Vetrano on the 4th, a recce sortie having reported a very tempting target – seventy-five transport aircraft (Ju 52 and SM.82) 'packed closely together'. 'The attack was made in three waves, the Blenheims bombing from between 20 and 100 feet, and destroying over 30 aircraft and seriously damaging many others without loss to themselves. On the following night nine Wellingtons repeated this attack, setting a further 14 aircraft on fire and blowing up a petrol dump.' (*The RAF in Maritime War*)

Three squadrons (126, 242 and 249) scrambled in the early afternoon, some to protect the convoy and others to protect Malta. The enemy formations comprised seventy or more bombers and fighters. Although only one of the bombers attacking the convoy was claimed, the attack was disrupted and thus ineffective. The attack on the airfields at Ta Kali and Hal Far were more successful, destroying or damaging a number of aircraft and killing and wounding a number of service and civilian personnel.

On the same day, Royal Navy submarines sank the troopship *Citi di Palermo* near Cape Dukato, the first major sinking of 1942, but the start of what was to be a bad year for Axis shipping. The first aerial success came two days later when four Swordfish of 830 Squadron damaged a cargo ship south of Pantelleria. On the same night an Albacore of 828 Squadron sank the 5,741-ton *Perla*; the attack had been led in by one of the ASV Wellingtons, which also noted that the ship was stationary after the attack, with an escorting destroyer taking off the crew. This first success of the year for the joint ASV Wellington–strike force tactic, proved the concept, and in the seven-week period from 1 January to 24 February, thirty-two torpedoes were launched during such attacks with, it was claimed, a high success rate of twenty-three hits, although this seems unlikely even for well-trained crews in ideal conditions. However, the fact that, of fifty-nine sorties flown, only seven failed to find their targets was indeed a major improvement on previous night actions.

On 6 January, the Air Ministry sent a signal to AOC Malta: 'Reports of air attacks on Malta during last few days suggest enemy is exploiting short distance between Sicily and Malta to make interception difficult. Apparent some cases also where fighters which make contact do not destroy enemy aircraft. Similar experiences in fighting over English Channel have emphasized importance of following points. (A) Time lag in transmission of RDF plots from station to filter room must be cut to minimum. (B) Time taken to filter and repeat to operations table must be cut to a minimum. (C) Quick issue of orders from Ops Rooms to squadrons essential. (D) Quick take off of fighters developed to maximum, aim should be 2 minutes. (E) Guns and gun sights carefully harmonized and checked every 48 hours. Remove extra tanks from aircraft employed in interception duties over the island.'

The latter part of 1941 saw an increase in the number of Axis submarines operating in the Mediterranean, and it was estimated that there were seventy Italian and twenty German submarines operating in the eastern area, one of their main tasks being to intercept Allied coastal convoys that supported land operations, as well as intercepting any shipping out of Alexandria, including convoys to Malta. Between 20 December and 20 January, AS aircraft operating out of Egypt made seventeen submarine sightings and carried out twelve attacks. Squadron Leader Garside of 230 Squadron scored an early success in 1942, sinking *U-577* on 9 January; in the space of a few weeks this experienced Sunderland captain made four more attacks on U-boats, although without any definite results. The 230 Squadron record book for January and February 1942 shows little operational activity in terms of U-boat sightings and attacks – other than the exceptional activities of Squadron Leader Garside and his crew. Between 9 January and 7 February this officer is recorded as having made attacks on six submarines, all while flying Sunderland W3987:

9 Jan: Dropped three DCs in first attack and threw out flame float, dropped four 250lb AS bombs in second attack. Huge bubble appeared and large patch of oil with bubbles continuing to come up; the 'submarine was undoubtedly destroyed'.

27 Jan: In first attack dropped a single AS bomb, in second attack dropped three DCs set at 50ft followed by a third attack with three DCs set at 100ft.

29 Jan: In a dive attack dropped eight AS bombs in a stick from 600ft, straddled conning tower. After the spray had subsided the submarine had gone, a second or two later the stern rose vertically out of the water and slid under. An oil patch appeared and spread 400 by 200 yards.

6 Feb: Eight AS bombs were dropped in a straddle over the centre of the submarine, after the spray subsided the submarine was seen to have broken up and the disconnected sections were momentarily seen above the surface but the wreckage quickly sank.

7 Feb: At 0039 a submarine crash-dived before an attack could be made. The Sunderland loitered and at 0200 an ASV contact was picked up; eight AS bombs were dropped in a dive attack, the last bomb bursting near the stern of the submarine. The submarine turned and dived, leaving a yellow streak. ASV picked up another contact at 0307 and this was attacked with 750 rounds of machine-gun fire. (*228 Sqn ORB*)

This fine record was recognized with a DFC to Wing Commander Kenneth Garside: 'This officer has served with the Squadron for the past two and a half years. He has completed over 100 sorties, including attacks on enemy submarines at night. In one of these attacks his aircraft came under enemy machine-gun fire whilst flying at low level. Wing Commander Garside has performed much valuable work both operationally and in the training of new pilots.' (AMB 7113). It could be argued that the DFC was not really enough and that a DSO would have been more appropriate,

Although the Sunderlands made numerous attacks in January, all of which helped keep the Axis submarine threat in check, the first confirmed sinking was by Swordfish of 815 Squadron, which surprised and sank *U-577* on the 15th.

'Most important event of the month was the arrival of convoy of three ships totalling 21,000 tons on the 19th.' So wrote Governor Dobbie in a signal to the Secretary of State for the Colonies, which was his normal reporting chain. 'This was most welcome after nearly four months without convoys and has greatly encouraged us all. I will report further when unloading is complete, but the convoy brought valuable replenishments of wheat, coal, kerosene, and other commodities.' He also reported on raids and casualties: 'Raids have greatly increased in frequency during the past month. There were 150 alerts during the day and 103 at night. These included 68 raids by day and 64 by night during which bombs were dropped. 91 persons were killed and 89 seriously injured.'

Dobbie also referenced the problems of unloading ships with so many air raid alerts, and the new visual warning system. 'This has been achieved by posting naval lookouts on the Palance Tower, and giving special signals by flag and sounding of the hooter in the dockyard, known as the Typhoon, when raiders are likely to approach, or guns to fire over the Grand Harbour.' It was crucial to gets ships unloaded before air attack destroyed the hard-fought supplies.

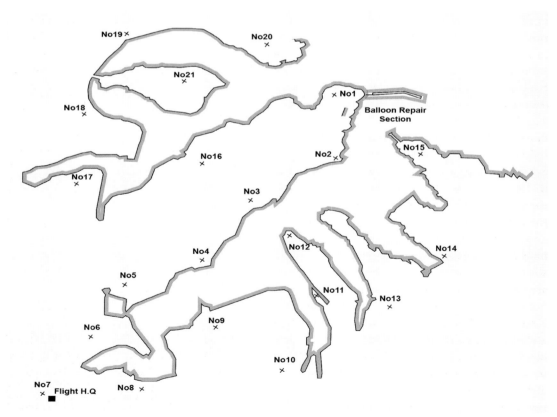

Map of balloon sites around Grand Harbour; this area relied heavily on the balloons and guns for its defence, until later in the period when effective fighter interception meant that few bombers ever got this far.

A signal from the AOC to HQ RAF ME of late January (the actual date is unclear) addressed the question of fighters for Malta and problems with the radar (GCI). 'First problem here is fighter defence. Do not hold tools for jobs. Must stop day bombing. Hurricane 2 has no performance to deal with problem. 109 always have advantage in height and performance. Hurricane cannot take on Junkers 88 under these conditions without grave risk and always at a disadvantage. Spitfire 5 can only make height in time to take on fighters. Bombers carry much armour and cannon is necessary to kill, consequently Kittyhawk is best aircraft available to deal with them. With Spitfires and Kittyhawks, bombers will find escort inadequate and so will be forced to greater heights and thereby reduce effectiveness of bombing. Ultimate answer to defence of this Island is 3 squadron Spitfire 5s, 2 squadrons Kittyhawks and ½ squadron Hurricanes for night defence. Immediate answer is 2 Kittyhawk squadrons in exchange 2 Hurricane 2 squadrons. Kittyhawks can only operate from Luqa with its runway as Hal Far and Ta Kali too rough. Will reduce number of aircraft at Luqa by various means before Kittyhawks arrive.' An interesting discussion, but it does not appear that Kittyhawks were seriously considered, or at least none ever arrived and the discussion appears to have ended.

The signal continued: 'Second problem is GCI which must work. Require scientist for advice on sighting instances and calibration as all attempts have proved fruitless. Must have good experienced controller immediately for general improvement. Please loan S/Ldr Dakin for 1 month, now on loan Western Desert. Consider we can learn what is wrong and put matter right in that time. If you agree, request he is flown here direct.' (Signal AOC Mediterranean to HQ RAF ME, January 1942).

According to the SD161 Location of Units for November 1941, Malta had five AMES units, three of these were at Dingli (241, 242, 504), one at Magdalena (502) and one at Ta Silch (501). The first station on Malta had been 242 at Dingli, established in March 1939. The stations were later referred to as COL (Chain Overseas Low) and COH (Chain Overseas High) and they reported in to the Filter Room at Lascaris. One of the problems for the Malta stations was the short warning time, as Sicily was so close. The signal quoted above does not specify what the problems were, and the author has been unable to find any more details, or even a reply to that signal.

Two comments recorded in the 249 Squadron history *249 at War* are very apt; the first concerned the seemingly mundane issue of the lack of petrol and oil bowsers for turning aircraft around. A simple but important issue, and Malta's groundcrew had always prided itself on the speed with which they refuelled and rearmed their aircraft. The comment was that most such bowsers had been destroyed or damaged in recent air raids and that 'make-do' bowsers had to be constructed. The other comment concerned the inability of the Hurricanes to catch their faster opponents – Ju 88s and 109s – and even if they did catch the 88s the hitting power of the machine gun-armed Hurricanes was not enough to cause critical damage in the short period in which the

Location.	Unit.	Equipment.
Dingli	No. 504 A.M.E.S.	—
	No. 242 A.M.E.S.	—
	No. 241 A.M.E.S.	—
Gozo	No. 521 A.M.E.S.	—
Fanuma ..	No. 256 A.M.E.S.	—
Hal Far ..	R.A.F. Station	Magister. Swordfish. Seal. Gauntlet.
	Station Flight	
	No. 185 (F) Squadron	Hurricane.
Kalafrana ..	R.A.F. Station	—
	Inter-Command W/T Station ..	—
Luqa ..	R.A.F. Station	—
	No. 40 (B) Squadron	Wellington IC.
	No. 69 (G.R.) Squadron	Maryland
	No. 21 (B) Squadron	Blenheim.
	No. 107 (B) Squadron	Blenheim.
Maddalena ..	No. 502 A.M.E.S.	—
Takali	Station H.Q.	—
	No. 126 (F) Squadron	Hurricane.
	No. 249 (Gold Coast) Squadron ..	Hurricane.
Ta Silch ..	No. 501 A.M.E.S.	—
Valetta	Air H.Q., Malta	—
	Base Accounts Office	—
	Base Personnel Office	—
	Met. Station	—
	No. 841 A.M.E.S.	—

SD161 Location of Units entry for Malta, March 1942.

enemy could be tracked. The cannon–armed Mark IIs had a better chance of causing damage. One of those to comment was Flight Sergeant Etchells: 'On several occasions, as I recall to my disgust, I saw an odd Ju88 unescorted and just asking to be shot down, but with all power on and nose down by 15 degrees, it was able to increase the distance between us.' He also commented: '… a lot of our time was taken up by attempting to survive in well-used Hurricane Is and IIs. We were very aggressive as a fighter squadron, but soon learned that it was more necessary to keep a good lookout behind and above, than looking for victims, as the 109s in particular had many thousands of feet advantage over us, plus an enormous speed advantage.'

The return of the 109s flagged up once more the inability of the Hurricanes to cope with the German fighters, although most losses had actually been to ground strafing and not air combat. In January, Tedder sent his SASO (Group Captain Basil Embry) to Malta to review the fighter situation and come up with recommendations. On 29 January, a summary and recommendations was produced.

He first of all deals with the inadequacy of performance of the Hurricane IIBs (12 guns) to deal effectively with enemy fighter escorted bombing raids, and recommends their substitution by Spitfire V and Kittyhawks. 'The existing strength of three squadrons of Hurricane IIBs and two squadrons of IIBs/IICs should be replaced by three squadrons of Spitfire Vs (2 cannon, 4 Brownings) and two Kittyhawk squadrons (6 × 0.5in guns). It is obvious that if our fighters in Malta are expected to intercept and effectively engage enemy bombers (preferably before they drop their bombs) it is necessary that they should be of a type that allows them, within the time of the first warning plot received of the approach of an enemy raid, to attain not only the height of the enemy bombers and their close escort fighters, but also allows time for a proportion of our fighters to attain 'high cover' at a considerably greater altitude as protection from high flying Me.109s jumping on our fighters lower down as they get stuck into the bombers.

Embry also remarks upon the fact that 'if our fighter pilots in Malta operate too long on Hurricane IIs it is bound to have an effect on their morale. Our experience during the Battle of Britain, as also during our fighter-bomber operations over France last year, is that nothing tends to lower morale more than for our pilots to be called upon to fly inferior performance aircraft longer than is necessary, or to called upon to operate against 109s perpetually at a great height disadvantage.' Embry's recommendation for replacement of existing fighter aircraft at Malta is, of course, a council of perfection and not an easy one to accomplish.'

All excellent, and one could say obvious, points that were already well known, but Embry was a very respected combat leader and his opinions would carry great weight – although the availability of aircraft when everywhere there were shortages and crises would play a major role in what could actually be done.

The summary continued to highlight why the need was particularly pressing at Malta: 'Nevertheless, in spite of the fact that presumably the Hun, when he feels inclined, can probably put out of commission the aerodromes at Malta and a large number of our fighters too, it is felt that something should be done to replace the inadequate Hurricane IIBs by Spitfires, if only by one squadron. The provision of only one squadron of Spitfires would enable some semblance of 'top cover' to be achieved as protection from above for the remaining Hurricane squadrons.'

Therein lay the nub of the air combat issue … he who has the height, has the advantage. And with the 'lumbering' Hurricanes, despite attempts to strip out some weight, and the short notice of attack, there was little chance of achieving that height advantage. The option of standing patrols was not viable as there were not enough aircraft, or indeed fuel.

Embry also commented on the lack of air-to-air gunnery training and recommended that drogue equipment be made available for fitting to some fighters for training. It was all very well catching up with the enemy aircraft, but if you could not bring effective fire to bear then it was all a bit of a waste of time, which was also the reason for discussion on aircraft armament. Cannon were now the preferred weapons, although the 0.5in machine guns of the Kittyhawk were considered more effective than the 0.303in Brownings of the Hurricane IIB.

A very important part of his visit was to look at the RDF, and more particularly the operations room, and see where they could be improved. On RDF he recommended some equipment changes, including provision of a GCI set, but on the ops room, he was more damning: 'It would appear that a not very high standard of Operations Room 'discipline' prevails in Malta. It is obviously essential that the Controller should control his aircraft in the proper and standard method of vectoring them to make interception with the enemy and not by Jim Crow aircraft who do not know anything like the whole picture as it is known or should be known, by the Controller in his Operations Room. I suggest that much would be obtained by sending out to Malta a strong Senior Sector Controller with the acting rank of Wing Commander or Group Captain, well versed in correct Operations Room discipline, procedure and technique to establish their Room and control on a sound basis.' (Group Captain Bouchier, DDF Ops, summary of Embry report, 29 January 1942).

The aircraft mix was discussed again in a note from DCAS to CAS: 'The Kittyhawk has not the necessary ceiling to provide high cover nor has it the speed of climb to ceiling which is so necessary for interception in the island where there is so little defence in depth. The Hurricane is certainly outclassed by the Me.109s and cannot be considered for anything save night defence. The Spitfire and Kittyhawk are both unsuitable for night defence.'

He went on to state that five Spitfire V squadrons plus one Hurricane IIC squadron 'may be considered the ideal defence' but that problems of spares and support for Spitfires meant that 'we should be wise to accept a proportion of Kittyhawks' and so recommended reducing Spitfire squadrons to three and adding two Kittyhawk squadrons. CAS replied: 'I agree, but we must gamble on the Spitfire being a success i.e. we must lose no opportunity of stocking Malta with the men and material that would be required if the Spitfire proved successful immediately.'

On 24 January the AOC was stating that the Marylands 'are no longer earning their keep and not worth the cost expenditure on them for results achieved.' His concern was a lack of serviceability, a lack of spares, and they 'go continually unserviceable just before or shortly after take-off.' The need for reconnaissance had not diminished and he was using part of his Blenheim force in place of Marylands. 'The Marylands must go as I cannot rely on them for the vital reconnaissance requirements in this area … does not appear to be any suitable replacement of the equivalent performance; suggest long range Mark 3 or 5 Hudsons as replacement with reluctance in view of enemy activity and must keep it to open sea; for areas where enemy interference likely propose PRU Hurricane or Spitfire or Mosquito. Summary, re-equip 69 Squadron with 9 LR Mark 3 or 5 Hudson and 6 PRU Hurricane and/or Spitfire and/or Mosquito.' (Signal AOC Malta to HQ RAF ME, 24 January 1942).

The reply was sent on 12 February. 'We are pushing on fitting extra tanks to Baltimores for you which will progressively replace Marylands. Have been advised by Air Ministry that six non-tropicalized PRU Spitfires will leave as soon as weather suitable. You may retain first two but others are to be passed on here without delay.' Malta had a reputation for 'acquiring' aircraft – and crews – that were meant to go on to Egypt. The signal ended: 'Our two PRU Hurricanes are being withdrawn primarily on your statement that they are old and unfitted for PRU work over long stretches of sea.'

Meanwhile, January saw the introduction of a new role for 39 Squadron with the start of torpedo training. At the beginning of the month, 'B' Flight went to Shandur, in the Canal Zone, for a torpedo familiarization course while 'A' Flight continued the task of sea reconnaissance until its turn came for conversion. The FAA had already proved the value of the air torpedo in this theatre of operations, and soon the Beauforts and Wellingtons would add appreciably to this capability from Malta and North Africa.

The main torpedo used was the British Mk 12, which weighed a basic 1,505lb plus 445lb of TNT in the warhead. Designed as a naval weapon, it was not intended for air-dropping, but nevertheless had already proved effective in this mode of delivery. The normal setting of the torpedo was 40 knots for ranges up to 1,500 yards, or 27 knots up to 3,500 yards – although these latter parameters were seldom used. Running depth was preset and detonation was either magnetic or contact. The usual height for a drop was 75ft (±15ft) at a speed of 140 knots (-10 or +20 knots) and in level flight – rigorous requirements – but the torpedo was a temperamental weapon and required accurate delivery. Such accuracy had to be achieved while considerable judgement of target range, heading and evading action was also required, and so it was generally considered that eight or nine simultaneous drops were needed to ensure a single hit. Approaches to targets were to be made at ultra low level since flying at wave-top level had its own dangers – especially with a flat sea surface giving a poor horizon. On the final run-in, the aircraft was to be climbed to the minimum acceptable torpedo release height (60ft) and the drop made at 1,500 yards. The aircraft was then to be held down as the ship loomed larger and larger until, at the last moment, it was to execute a quick hop over the superstructure and flash away down on the wave tops at the far side – at the same time hoping to see a tell-tale smoke and water column from the victim, scanning the sky for other members of the formation – and any sign of the inevitable opposition in the shape of Bf 110s and Ju 88s.

A great many of the pre-planned strikes were intended to have an anti-flak and anti-air escort of Beaufighters but in practice this frequently failed to materialize for one reason or another. On the occasions that the Beaufighters were present, the anti-flak aircraft flew in before the torpedo Beauforts and beat the hell out of the escort vessels in an effort to reduce the barrage facing the Beauforts during the vulnerable dropping phase.

Having completed its torpedo conversion, 39 Squadron participated in an attack on a convoy on 23 January. On the afternoon of the 22nd, a submarine had spotted a convoy leaving Taranto Bay and reported a 13,000-ton troopship – the liner *Victoria*, described by Count Ciano 'as the pearl of the Italian merchant fleet'– with four MVs and a strong escort. An ASV Wellington picked up the convoy that night, and 201 Group put together a very strong reconnaissance and strike force. The recce element comprised nine Blenheims (203 Squadron), two ASV Wellingtons (221 Squadron) and a Maryland (39 Squadron), all operating out of Berka. The strike force comprised eighteen Wellingtons (28, 48 and 108 squadrons) at El Adem; nine Blenheims (55 Squadron), eight Albacores (826 Squadron) and three torpedo Beauforts (39 Squadron) at Berka; thirteen Blenheims (11, 14 squadrons) at Benina; two Fortresses (220 Squadron) at Fuka, plus five Beaufighters (272 Squadron). Additional forces were assigned from Malta, but not relied on in case they were unavailable due to enemy closure of their airfields.

At 0940 on the 23rd a Blenheim recce picked up a convoy of one battleship, four destroyers and one MV, while over the next hour or so other reports were received of various naval forces, which gave the planner problems in assigning attackers as there was confusion as to the accuracy of the reports. Various small attack forces were sent out, but no contacts were made until later afternoon/early evening, the first by a Fortress, claiming near misses on a battleship, and then by three Blenheims. The last two attacks both targeted the liner, with the Beauforts attacking around

1730 and the Albacores an hour later. The Beauforts (piloted by Flight Lieutenant Taylor, and Pilot Officers Grant and Jepson) led an attack on a large MV. The convoy was made up of MVs escorted strongly by battleships, cruisers and destroyers, making some twenty-thirty ships in all. Although an intensive flak barrage was thrown up on all sides, the Beauforts held their course and dropped their torpedoes from 1,500 yards; all were seen to be making good tracks and a dense column of smoke was seen to come from the liner, indicating at least one hit. Thus crippled, the liner was attacked again later on the day by the Albacores of 826 Squadron.

Water plume from a torpedo hit on an MV. (*Don Tilley, SAAF*)

At around 2000 hours, an ASV Wellington picked up the convoy, with fourteen strike Wellingtons also in the air, of which seven found the ships some 160 miles west of Tripoli. They dropped 35 × 500lb bombs and claimed near misses. Nine Albacores and Swordfish out of Malta were unable to find the convoy. Meanwhile, a Malta ASV Wellington had started shadowing and called up seven Wellingtons from Malta, which dropped 21 × 500lb bombs, claiming hits; the final Malta attack was by Swordfish, with Lieutenant Commander F.H. Hopkins claiming a torpedo hit on the liner. So, three squadrons claimed to have a role in – or credit for – sinking the liner! What was certain was that the fatal damage was caused by torpedo.

The Wellingtons of 38 Squadron had been assigned a torpedo role from December 1941, the motivation being the need for a longer range aircraft torpedo aircraft and one capable of carrying two torpedoes. Standard aircraft required a number of modifications, such as removal of the nose turret and changes in the bomb bay to allow two of the standard Mk 12 torpedoes to be carried. The first practice drop was made by 38 Squadron's commanding officer, Wing Commander John Chaplin, on 20 December, and having proved the basic soundness of the concept, an intensive training period took place in the first few months of 1942 to refine the technique.

The first operational sorties took place, but without success; further tactical changes were made with the aircraft being given long-range fuel tanks and, by operating from some of the forward airfields, attacks being made on harbours in Greece. The squadron was soon sending detachments to forward airfields for anti-shipping work. Typical of this was that recorded in the ORB for 23 January: 'Five aircraft required to attack convoy endeavouring to reach Tripoli, and to destroy the escorting battleships. Aircraft to operate from El Adem – four aircraft from B Flight and one from A Flight left Shallufa for El Adem. In addition, two other A Flight aircraft left for El Adem to operate from there and delivered torpedo attacks on the convoy.' Also typically, this mission was cancelled the next day, although the aircraft remained on standby at El Adem for a few more days. In the meantime, more aircraft were being sent to Heliopolis to be modified for torpedo dropping and crews were practising night torpedo attacks against HMS *Sagitta* in Suez Bay. As more aircraft became available, the squadron sent a detachment, of only two aircraft, to Malta – the first such leaving for the island on 27 February.

Back to Malta: The 25th January was a bad day for the island's defenders. Two supply ships sailing from Malta were provided with Hurricane air cover, and with more than twenty aircraft this was a sizeable force. However, they were bounced by 109s and in short order seven were shot down, although only one pilot was killed. Others were damaged when the 109s strafed Hal Far. The Germans suffered no losses. This was the same day that the reliable *Breconshire* was back again bringing fuel and general supplies.

There had been discussion for some time that Malta's fighters could launch night rovers over enemy airfields in Sicily, to catch the enemy bombers before they could head off to Malta. The first such attack by 1435 Flight took place on 25 January but tragedy struck even before the attack was launched. Alex Mackie was air testing his Hurricane when he was bounced and shot down; he was killed in the crash. During January Malta had been on the receiving end of nearly 2,000 enemy sorties, 591 of those being bombers and 1,145 fighters; these figures were to increase in February.

The Axis forces in the Desert had come to rely on supply runs made by Ju 52s – an incredibly wasteful and, for much of the time costly, operation, but nevertheless an important one for key supplies, including fuel and critical spares. The 'air bridge' was very dangerous while Malta's fighters had some freedom to go after targets rather than struggle to defend their own airfields, and losses of Ju 52s had been high, However, with the return of the Luftwaffe to harass Malta and effectively seize local air superiority, the threat all but vanished and the Ju 52s made successful supply runs. This was aided by the fact that Rommel was back on what was the shortest and easiest such route, and also was minimizing his fuel consumption in his defensive position. As so often in the Desert War, the campaign was one of supplies, especially fuel, and airfields.

Shipping remained the only effective way to get large quantities of supplies to Africa to support an offensive, but within weeks of receiving increased supplies Rommel was on the move and driving the Allies backwards at a rapid rate. Capturing airfields on the way, but very few supplies, and ably supported by the reinforced Luftwaffe, the panzers seemed unstoppable and the Germans moved on Egypt. The loss of airfields across North Africa had an impact on the war in the central Mediterranean, making it harder for the RAF to interdict supply convoys. Success or failure – for both sides – was on a knife edge; Rommel needed large quantities of supplies, especially fuel for his panzers, and having failed to capture Allied dumps he was in a difficult position. To a large extent it was about to become even more a war over fuel supplies.

The anti-shipping campaign was thus to play a significant, indeed perhaps crucial, part in the Allied success; never was logistics more critical – or more vulnerable. Even though there had been little confirmed success by aircraft in January, although the Navy's submarines were proving effective, the constant patrolling and the various attacks had contributed to Axis shipping taking longer routes. It was about to get worse for the Axis supply ships, as more RAF aircraft assumed an anti-shipping role. In the back-and-forth of the Desert War, Benghazi was back on the target list again in late January, having fallen to Rommel's advance on the 28th of the month. If Rommel was able to get supplies unloaded at Benghazi, then much of his logistics problem would be resolved, because of reduced distances to forward areas. Preventing this, by attacking convoys, ships in port and the port facilities, was therefore crucial.

No. 205 Group Operation Order A.282 tasked the group's squadrons with a minelaying task, one of the unsung but crucial parts of the anti-shipping campaign:

A. Form B.No. 9.
B. 4th February 1942.
C. The enemy are known to be using Benghazi as a supply port for its units operating in the Benina area.

D. To lay mines in the approaches to Benghazi Harbour.
E. Night 4th/5th February 1942
F. 10 aircraft, 148 Squadron, 12 aircraft, 37 Squadron, 8 aircraft, 38 Squadron
G. i.   6 aircraft 37 Squadron are to attack the Central Mole defences and Guiliana point defences
   ii.   2 aircraft 148 Squadron are to attack Benghazi Town.
   iii. 1 aircraft 148 Squadron is to attack Berca Main landing ground.
   iv.   1 aircraft 38 Squadron is to drop flares on the east side of Benghazi Town.
   v.   7 aircraft 148 Squadron and 2 aircraft 38 Squadron are to bomb Benghazi Town east of a line
       drawn through B.10 and P.10 target map B.2.
   vi.   6 aircraft 37 Squadron are to attack Berca Main landing ground.
   vii. 5 aircraft 38 Squadron are to plant Cucumbers in the areas notified to OC 38 Squadron.
K. All aircraft are to operate from, and return to, LG.09.
L. For i. time of attack is 2330 hours
   For ii and iii time of attack is from 2335 to 2345 hours
   For iv the time of attack is 2350 hours
   For v and vi time of attack is from 2350 to 0030 hours
   For vii time of attack is 0005 hours

(37 Sqn ORB)

Although the stated primary mission was laying mines, only five of the thirty aircraft were actually laying mines – the reference to Cucumbers. Minelaying was referred to as gardening and the aim was to plant (lay) vegetables (different types of mines having different vegetable names). Similar op orders for minelaying or bombing were frequent in the period February to April, and this one is included as indicative of this type of mission.

On Malta, the AOC was deeply concerned about his fighter pilot strength, and on 6 February signalled the Air Ministry, for the attention of DCAS: 'Feel you should know fighter position here. Total pilots including sick and non-effective each squadron is as follows: 126 – 18; 185 – 22; 242 – 15; 249 – 17; 605 – 15. Total 87 pilots. For night flying flight 1435 Flight 11 pilots. Grand total 98 pilots. Total holding of Hurricanes inclusive of repairable is 92. Have not received one single pilot to replace casualties since my arrival here. A few have arrived to replace those due for change. Except for 242 and 605 squadrons, all pilots have been here for 8 or 9 months and they are stale. I have not more than 20 pilots of over 200 hours operational flying. Had arranged exchange with Middle East but that is now off. New blood is required, would it be possible to send 30 pilots by flying boat. Only fully experienced pilots are of any use.'

Spitfires were still the subject of exchanges in early 1942 and on 10 February the AOC wrote: 'Have number of Spitfire pilots here all certain that Spitfires can be operated from Ta Kali provided certain filling and rolling is done. Work will take 14 days. Pilots state bad aerodrome with no runways being used in England without difficulty and see no objections to Ta Kali. Ta Kali runway will mean aerodrome unusable for about 6 months. Cannot accept it in view of present enemy strength. Alternative is to build two runways Ta Kali dispersal area in directions prevailing wind, work to take 8 months. Am doing this. Ta Kali will then be all-weather aerodrome. Labour difficulties but must force it through. Material available except grave shortage motor transport petrol but must overcome that also. Propose therefore 3 squadrons Spitfires Ta Kali. Night fighter squadron Hal Far. 2 squadrons spitfires Luqa. Army will complete present Luqa work end March which will be tremendous advantage and with dry weather approaching dispersal will be facilitated. One squadron Wellingtons to remain Luqa, also reconnaissance squadron. Blenheim squadrons to Hal

Sketch map of the dispersals and connecting taxiways between Luqa–Safi–Hal Far. This connectivity and the extensive nature of the dispersals was an important part of the overall plan of keeping Malta operational.

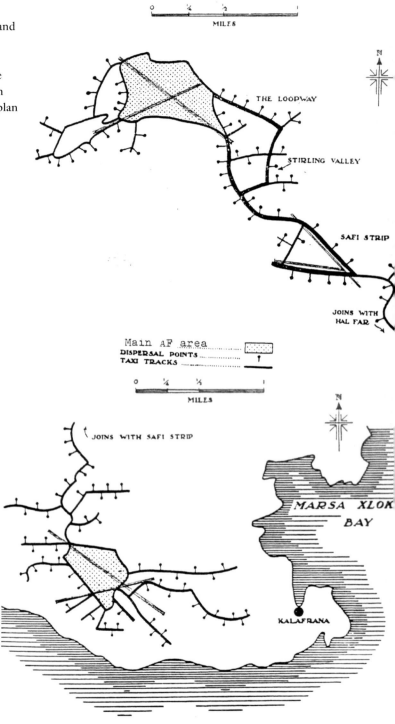

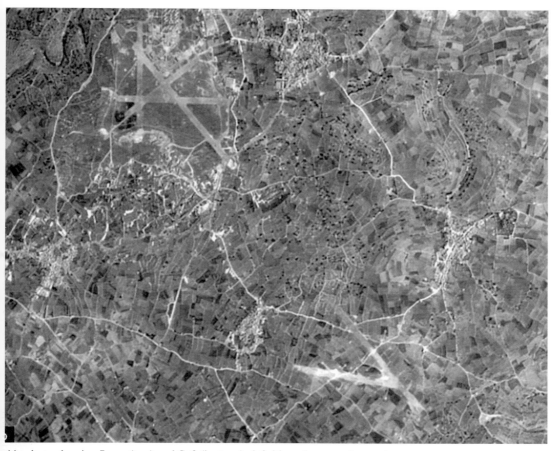

Air photo showing Luqa (top) and Safi (bottom) airfields and connecting taxiway.

Far when present extension completed. Taxi track Luqa–Safi–Hal Far being relaid by soldiers and will be excellent surface middle March. This will give further dispersal Luqa and Hal Far. In view maintenance difficulties and little difference in performance must agree Hurricane Charlie in preference Kittyhawk.' (signal AOC Malta to HQ RAF ME, 11 February 1942). It seems to have been accepted that Kittyhawks were not needed, and anyway, every available Kittyhawk was needed by the Desert Air Force, where they were the main operational type.

The Blenheims of 21 Squadron had moved to Malta from Watton in December, having previously only operated on the island as part of the routine detachment rotation. The squadron lost its first two aircraft on 14 January during an anti-shipping patrol, all six crew being killed (Z7342 Flight Lieutenant H.F. Dukes-Smith). A second aircraft was lost on the 29th, Z7271 being damaged by fragmentation from the explosions caused by the preceding aircraft. The target was a series of buildings on the coast road near El Zauir; Flight Lieutenant E. Fox and his navigator were killed, while the gunner survived to become a PoW. February was a disaster for the squadron, with seven aircraft lost and nineteen aircrew killed in the first half of the month.

4 Feb: The target was Palermo harbour but in poor weather in the target area, two aircraft flew into high ground (Z7341, Sergeant M. Houston; Z9824, Flight Sergeant J.K. Ibbotson) with only

In this mid-1960s high-level air photo the links between Luqa (top) and Safi (bottom), are still very clear, although it has grown in size, especially with its long main runway.

one survivor; Z9812, Flying Officer F.J. Workman was hit by flak and crashed, and Z9806, Wing Commander W.R. Selkirk clipped the sea and crashed, the gunner managing to escape and be taken prisoner.

6 Feb: The formation was on an anti-shipping strike off Libya when they were bounced by 109s near Filfla Island, Malta; three aircraft were shot down and all nine crew killed; Z7308, Squadron Leader R.R. Stewart; Z9822, Pilot Officer J.G. Grieve; and Z9725, Flight Sergeant G.R. Cameron.

11 Feb : Z9823, Sergeant J.H. Stubbs shot down near Filfla, all killed.
A signal of 22 February stated: '21 Squadron Blenheim shaken as result of losses here the best of squadron has gone. I feel I shall get nothing out of them until they are made up to strength with crews. This will take time and meanwhile the squadron is a liability to me and I cannot rely on it for any work and am therefore sending the squadron on to you [Middle East].' (Lloyd to Tedder).

Hurricane Z2402 of 185 Squadron; this Hurricane was lost on 5 March 1942.

The squadron was transferred to the Middle East on the 22nd, the same day that 37 Squadron's Wellingtons arrived.

On 20 February the AOC reported (to HQ ME) that he had seventeen Blenheim IVs on site, all of which would be serviceable by the end of the month, but he only had six 'serviceable' crews. 'Am most anxious to hold no aircraft unless they are being used. Suggest I keep 12 Blenheims and 16 crews. Can you let me have 10 crews? Some must be experienced as 21 Squadron have lost their best. If you send me 10 crews I want 5 more crews to ferry my surplus Blenheims on to you. Also hold 4 Blenheim fighters with crews these will be flown to you as soon as serviceable.' (Signal AOC Malta to HQ RAF ME, 20 February 1942).

Meanwhile, on 13 February the German C-in-C sent a signal to Hitler: 'The most significant factor at this time is that not a single heavy British ship in the Mediterranean is fully seaworthy. The Axis rules both the sea and the air in the Mediterranean. However, enemy submarines still menace our shipping, and there is still a shortage of transport vessels and escort forces, and the oil situation continues to be critical.' There was no mention of any air threat or, for once, the need to deal with Malta. As we will see from a report a month later, the Germans saw they had a window of a month or so for these favourable conditions. The failed convoy MW9 from Alexandria on the 9th was evidence of this dominance. None of the three merchant vessels made it to Malta; *Glen Campbell* was damaged and returned to Tobruk, while *Clan Chatten* and *Rowallan Castle* were so seriously damaged that they had to be sunk by the escort ships. Nevertheless, it was not all one way, and Malta's Albacores scored successes on the 3rd (*Napoli*) and 14th (*Ariosto*) of the month, both recorded as being shared with a submarine. However, overall February was another month in which most enemy shipping was sunk by submarine or surface vessel.

Malta's airfields were plastered in February, with Luqa the main target being on the receiving end of 142 attacks of varying magnitude. As this was also the main bomber airfield it was clear that it was no longer a suitable location for Wellingtons, and to reduce the numbers, 40 Squadron was effectively disbanded on 15 February, its remaining aircraft and crews in Malta and Egypt being assigned to 215 Squadron and moved to India. The UK element of the Squadron became 156 Squadron. However, it ended up back in Egypt, and on detachment again to Malta, later in the year.

The OADU was continuing to deliver Wellingtons to Malta and beyond. During the first few months of 1942 it had suffered a number of losses during the transit from Gibraltar, with the aircraft either intercepted and shot down, suffering engine trouble, or crashing as a result of navigation errors. On 15 February four aircraft were destroyed at Luqa during an air raid, with one airman, Corporal J. Webb of 40 Squadron, killed when he was taxiing one of the aircraft. Five more Wellingtons, assigned to the OADU, were lost on the 16th/17th on the run from Gibraltar, and another nine Wellingtons of OADU were lost to various causes during the remainder of the month.

It is very rare, and always interesting, to come across strongly worded messages between commands; one such letter to Air Vice-Marshal Bottomley concerned Wellingtons arriving from Gibraltar: 'Our relations with 200 Group are amicable. We have no intention to bicker or to quarrel. I feel, however, that when they do stupid things, they must be told in no uncertain manner. I was furious when I sent the 'lunatic' signal [I have not found a copy of that one!]. I slept on it and changed 'criminal' to 'lunatic' and in my view the 'raspberry' was fully justified. Whatever the risk, the state at Gibraltar, and whatever the orders from Air Ministry, I consider it lunacy to send young crews on a long flight over the sea to a very small island where they must do their first night landing. The staff are very foolish.' (Letter dated 3 January). A significant number of Wellingtons failed to make it safely to Malta, or had incidents on landing, and it would seem the 'raspberry' was indeed justified.

Lloyd sent a somewhat despairing signal to Tedder on 23 February: 'February 22 clearly showed inadequacy of our fighter force here. Continuous alerts. Attacks on our aerodromes all day. Apart from material damage to buildings, aircraft, aerodromes and runways which is very serious, loss of working time very grave. Loading of mines on to 37 Squadron aircraft, for example, had not been completed by nightfall. It also largely accounts for bad serviceability among fighters and reconnaissance aircraft. I could get only one reconnaissance aircraft all day. Had two ASV Wellingtons at beginning of day but by night only one, which is not enough for an operation of the importance of that pending last night. Our few fighters did gallant work but the pace and numbers too hot for them, also when they did get in machine gun fire did not kill. Enemy fighters in great numbers and

Gibraltar was the staging post for Wellington to and from Malta (and the Middle East); here a 40 Squadron Wellington poses with the distinctive Rock of Gibraltar in the background.

in pairs were sweeping round Island so that in addition to attacking bombers, Hurricanes had to escort out and in reconnaissance aircraft. Sea rescue unable to rescue pilot shot down close to Island owing to impossibility of providing adequate cover for High Speed Launch. All attacks well escorted together with high cover.'

Having described the problem, he went on to define the solution, all of which points had been made before: 'Am confident if we could shoot down a score this daylight nonsense would stop. To do this must have Hurricanes with cannons as it is very distressing for our pilots to see bombers go off carrying so much lead [lack of lethality of the 0.303 in machine guns]. Must also have Spitfires in adequate numbers for high cover. Same sort of thing on slightly reduced scale continuing today [23rd].'

Another signal of the 23rd concerned Spitfire VB supply and pilot quality: 'Sixteen Spitfire VBs, fitted with tropical equipment, VHF, IFF and long range tanks, are to be provided to be shipped to Gibraltar. They are to take priority over any other Spitfire VB commitment to the Middle East. Sixteen pilots are to be provided by Fighter Command; these pilots are to be of the highest quality and specially selected.'

The pilot quality issue seems to have gone back and forth for the next few weeks, and on 18 March DCAS wrote to Lloyd: 'I need hardly assure you that your need for operationally experienced pilots is fully appreciated here. Great emphasis was laid by CAS, AMF and myself on the necessity for selecting really first-class pilots to meet the commitment.' It closed by reminding Lloyd that Fighter Command squadrons were being continually drained to reinforce overseas commands and was only able to do so because of the reduced tempo of ops at home.

Among the many documents produced around this time, a paper prepared for the Air Ministry to 'examine the existing method of finding fighter pilots for reinforcing Malta, the Near East and the Far East, and to suggest a better way' provides an excellent insight into the challenges faced by the RAF in providing (and sharing) operational pilots. The report by Group Captain Bouchier was issued on 27 March 1942 and its damning final statement baldly states: 'From every angle it is looked at, the present method has the air of compromise and the manner of makeshift about it.'

The central problem was that AOC Fighter Command would receive an order from the Air Ministry that '32 fighter pilots are urgently required to reinforce Malta' and, of course, that they must be 'good and operationally experienced', which might include a requirement for at least 150 hours' operational flying. The message was then passed on down until it reached the operational sector stations, with each squadron being perhaps asked to provide two suitable names. Bouchier aptly summarizes this: 'Much could be written of the preliminary telephoning that goes on [between the Wing Commander Flying] when Squadron Commanders first receive this bad news. 'Is it possible, Sir, for the Squadron as a Squadron to go out? – this is the second request in a week to produce 2 operational pilots for posting, and last week they took one of my Flight Commanders also – couldn't we go out as a Squadron – the Squadron's full out to go – or better still go out as a Wing?"' He concludes that the inevitable result tends to be the pilots put forward are the ones that are easiest to lose – the last arrivals, those who maybe have not quite 'clicked' on the squadron – all operational and proficient of course. He also alludes to the esprit de corps aspect of squadron morale of pilots that fly as a squadron, and it is clear that his solution to the problem is that reinforcement should be by squadron and not by groups of pilots.

The challenges of getting fighters to Malta was a frequent subject of discussion in Fighter Command as well as HQ Middle East. On 24 February, Air Marshal Sir Sholto Douglas was involved in the problem of fighter supply from carriers. He wrote to CAS: 'Hitherto, an essential feature of these operations has been the provision of a navigating aircraft which takes off from Gibraltar, makes contact with the carrier at the flying off position, collects the flown off fighters and then leads them to Malta.'

He goes on to say that it is not really working and that the navigation aircraft sometimes misses the flying off point or in some cases is not available: 'There is a hold up in the provision of Blenheim aircraft and (more important) skilled Blenheim crews to undertake this escorting duty for fighters. I have, therefore, been asked to consult you on the possibility of Spitfires with long range tanks completing the journey from the flying off position to Malta without the aid of a navigational aeroplane. The basic factors bearing on this problem are as follows:

1. The Naval authorities are unwilling to take the carrier further than about 3 degrees East. This means the fighters have to complete a journey of some 600 miles
2. A Spitfire with long range tanks is calculated to give a range of 1,000 miles at 155 miles per hour (ASI). At 20,000ft this ASI will be equivalent to approximately 200 miles an hour cruising speed.
3. The best track for fighters between the flying off position and Malta calls for a slight dog-leg in the neighbourhood of Cape Bon.'

The letter went on to discuss the problems of single-seat navigation, as, in theory, the Blenheim had a professional navigator on board to do this! In essence the plan would be to rely on DR (deduced or dead reckoning) for the first part of the route and then DF (direction finding) and RT for the final part.

'The fighters would have to fly the first 450 miles on DR alone. I do not think this latter factor is very important, given trained pilots properly instructed and practiced in long oversea flights. The prevalent winds being from the NW should blow the aircraft on to the North African coast. It would probably be justifiable if the fighter leader kept the coast in sight.

'As soon as Cape Bon is turned, the fighters should get within VHF DF range of Malta. Thereafter the task should be easy. The only danger will be jamming, and this we know is likely to be difficult except, perhaps, in the immediate vicinity of Pantelleria.'

Eight Hurricanes (six of 249 and two of 126) had scrambled at 1135 on the 22nd to intercept one of the raids, which, as was typical, was a small number of bombers (three Ju 88s) with an escort of Bf 109s (six from JG 3). The two sides met at 16,000ft over Filfla Island and a number of inconclusive engagements took place, in which at least three Hurricanes were damaged. As stated in the AOC's signal, the Hurricane pilots were claiming hits on enemy aircraft but failing to bring them down. On 24 February the Germans were back again; among the losses that day were two 249 Squadron Hurricanes that were pounced on by four 109s, with Squadron Leader Turner crash-landing at Luqa and Pilot Officer Tedford calling that he was wounded and bailing out, although he was not subsequently found.

Malta operations room with status board – with heading 'this board must be kept up to date' – and despatch rider waiting for instructions.

Two days later the squadron was stripped of its Hurricanes and many of its pilots ahead of its re-equipment with the first batch of Spitfires. The squadron transferred aircraft and pilots to 126 Squadron in preparation for receiving Spitfires, news that was well received, except by those who stayed with the Hurricanes.

The increased scale of night attacks was also causing concern, and whilst the 'cats eye' Hurricanes had some success, it was clear that AI (radar) night fighters were needed. A signal of 25 February stated that: 'In order to minimize the scale of German night attack on Malta it has been agreed that AI Beaufighters can be operated from the Island provided that most strict orders are issued to all concerned that they are not repeat not to operate more than 30 miles from Malta. Suggest you send four AI Beaufighters to Malta forthwith.' (signal Air Ministry to HQ RAF Middle East, 25 February). The HQ signalled in early march that Malta could not yet accept them 'until reorganization operational facilities completed'.

February had also reinforced the challenges of protecting coastal convoys, with two of the three MVs in Alexandria to Tobruk convoy (Operation Onset 20–22 February) being lost; air cover was provided but nevertheless the convoy suffered air attack. We have tended to focus, for space reasons, on the cross-Mediterranean convoys, but the coastal convoys – or single runners – were also key elements of the overall supply situation. Equally important were troop movements by sea, such as the two successful convoys run from Egypt to Cyprus under air cover: Operation Installation (12–17 March) and Operation Scalford (29 March–7 April).

The lack of naval cover had led to an increase in 201 (NC) strength, which by late February comprised two Beaufort squadrons (39, 47), two Blenheim squadrons (55/18, 203, which also had Hudsons, 13 Hellenic), two Beaufighter squadrons (252, 272), three FAA Swordfish squadrons (700, 815, 826, which also had Albacores), one Sunderland squadron (230), one Hudson squadron (459), one Fortress squadron (220), two Wellington squadrons (221, Sea Rescue Flight), and one Dornier squadron (2 Yugoslav). At around the same time, 235 Wing was created at Fuka to act as the command and control of units deployed to forward areas, such as Bu Amud. Increasingly, the group co-ordinated activity with Malta when major convoys were found; such was the case when on 20 February a Tripoli-bound convoy was located. Operational control was given to 235 Wing and it assembled a strike force that comprised North Africa and Malta elements. From North Africa came twenty Blenheims (18/55, 14, 203 squadrons), six Beauforts (39 Squadron), twenty-nine Wellingtons (one ASV from 221 Squadron, three torpedo of 38 Squadron and twenty-five bombers from 205 Group), plus two Fortresses of 221 Squadron and a single Liberator of 108 Squadron; the Malta force was boosted by detaching six Wellingtons of 37 Squadron.

The convoy, in two groups, was picked up by a Malta Wellington on the night of the 21st, but the planned shadowing aircraft, the sole Liberator, crashed on take-off. However, the convoy was picked up by a Maryland at 0725 on the 22nd, which reported eight MVs, two battleships, five cruisers, fifteen destroyers, and an escort of 109s. The first attack group, five Albacores from Malta, failed to find the target, as did one of two Fortresses sent out from LG05 to shadow the convoy; the other one made an attack with 500lb bombs but was heavily engaged by flak and fighters and had to abandon its shadowing task. Next up was a formation of Beauforts, which failed to find the target before reaching their fuel limit. Two formations of Blenheims left Bu Amud, the closest airfield to the target, but again had no luck in finding the target, and one aircraft went down in the sea. The afternoon attempt by 14 Squadron from Gambut started badly when four of the seven Blenheims returned early with engine problems and the remainder made no contact; so for twenty-nine aircraft sent out only one – the Fortress – actually made an attack.

A final attempt at a night attack by Malta Wellingtons also resulted in only one aircraft finding and attacking the target. Tedder attributed the failure by stating: 'By one means or another Malta's striking force was effectively neutralized and the convoy was routed just outside the effective range of our day air striking force from Cyrenaica.' This reinforced the importance of Malta as a strike base, and how important it was for the Allies to keep it open and for the Axis to close it.

March was to prove a very hard month for Malta; enemy sorties increased to nearly 5,000, which meant that bombing or air activity was frequent day and night. Despite all the recent arrivals, the average daily RAF fighter serviceability was only twelve aircraft. The intensity of air attacks is reflected in the fact that the RAF lost forty-six aircraft on the ground and only twelve in the air (with nine pilots killed, a higher ratio than usual). In addition, twenty-eight personnel were killed on the ground and a further thirty-four were injured. The Wellingtons of 37 Squadron scored an early success with an attack on Palermo harbour on the night of 2 March. The attack seems to have been particularly accurate and to have been responsible for sinking 13,000 tons of shipping (three ships, *Cuma*, *Tre Marie* and *Securitas*). One of the Wellingtons was written off in a landing accident back at Luqa but with no injuries to the crew. The squadron was not so lucky a few nights later (8th/9th) when two aircraft collided on take-off (Z9038 and EV483), with five killed, six injured, and only one surviving unhurt. The devastating nature of the accident was a result of the mines exploding. The squadron lost two more Wellingtons on the 9th – destroyed in an air raid on Luqa … so much for the promising start! Some records suggest that seven Wellingtons were destroyed in total and another four damaged. For 37 Squadron it was essentially the end; it flew its last op on the nighty of 13th/14th and its detachment formally ceased the following day.

Although Malta's strike effort was curtailed when the island was under intense attack, there was usually an increased effort from other air elements in range of shipping and port targets. As we have discussed before, the main strategic bombing force was 205 (Heavy Bomber) Group. This was formed in October 1941 at RAF Shallufa in place of 257 (HB) Wing, and initially comprised five Wellington squadrons, all in the Canal Zone, two at Shallufa (37, 38), two at Kabrit (70, 148) and one at Fayid (108). The group was not placed under the jurisdiction of AHQ Egypt but remained directly under the hand of the AOC-in-C. As we have seen throughout this account so far, the Wellington squadrons operated detachments from Malta, as did UK-based units. As part of the overall campaign, the bombers of 205 Group were kept busy on strategic targets, with ports remaining the top priority in an effort to stem the flow of supplies. That meant Benghazi was 'visited' on a regular basis, so regular in fact that some squadrons referred to it as the 'Mail Run'. In the period mid-June to mid-October, the Germans recorded 72 heavy air raids on Tripoli and 102 on Benghazi.

The heavy bombers, primarily Wellingtons, took on some of the longer-range targets such as Benghazi. It was important that, even if a ship had reached harbour, both it and its supplies were still under threat.

The capability of 205 Group had been increased by adding more squadrons, but also by re-equipping units such as 108 Squadron with the B-24 Liberator, which had taken place towards the end of 1941. The Liberators were used for both reconnaissance and bombing missions. However, it was not only the 'heavies' that took part from North African bases; the Blenheim squadrons in the Western Desert were very much part of the anti-shipping and supply war, and while the scale (and loss) was less than that suffered by the Malta-based units, their participation was important, and at a cost. A typical mission was that of 22 February when Blenheims were part of a strike force tasked against the Italian fleet, which was providing distant cover for a convoy. One Blenheim of 14 Squadron was lost, Z9657 flown by Flight Sergeant Sergeant L.W. Jones and crew. A Wellington of 148 Squadron was lost the same night when tasked against the convoy; Sergeant R. Hamilton suffering an engine failure in Z8360 and having to crash-land behind enemy lines, all the crew becoming PoW. This is just an illustrative example of the missions flown from North Africa that were very much part of the overall Mediterranean War. We will allude to such missions from time to time, but space in this account precludes comprehensive coverage.

On 5 March Lloyd signalled Tedder: 'Daylight attacks on aerodromes very serious. Little work being done due to continuous alerts. Much minor damage to aircraft sufficient to make them unserviceable for night operations. They are repaired next day and then hit again. Deliveries are serious problem as they are damaged if they stay here during day. The longer they stay the more damage. Have 17 Wellingtons in this category including those damaged on landing on arrival here with further minor damage due to air action. To avoid this, Wellingtons are being passed through same night as arrival with relief crews. This is difficult with continuous intruder raids but we can take it. Must have more fighters as soon as possible. Delay in Spitfires is annoying. Can you hasten dispatch your squadron Hurricane Charlies? Can you hasten collection of Blenheims?'

A short message but one that flags up a number of key issues. Malta only existed strategically for its ability to attack the enemy lines of communication between European bases (now stretching from France to Crete) and North Africa. Every piece of equipment, every man and all supplies had to move from Europe to North Africa, the majority by surface vessel, and had to be gathered at a limited number of port facilities in both locations, which made those places key choke points and targets. Once in North Africa everything had to move along the main coastal road from the supply ports to dumps and to units. Every campaign is to a greater or lesser extent one of logistics, the Desert War more so than most. It has often been called a 'war of airfields' but it is more accurately a 'war of logistics', with airfields playing a major role in defending one's own supply lines while striking at the enemy's lines. If Malta could not attack then it was a drain on resources, but in order to attack it had to protect the infrastructure and equipment needed for attack. The comment on passing aircraft on is also a key one; as we highlighted in the first book in this series (*The Desert Air Force in World War II: Air Power in the Western Desert 1940–1942*, Ken Delve, 2017) the offensive capability of 205 Group from its bases in Egypt depended on the Wellingtons arriving via Malta. Every Wellington destroyed or damaged, or delayed in Malta, reduced the striking power of the group and thus its impact on the campaign.

After numerous requests and an agonizing wait, the first Spitfires arrived in Malta on 7 March under Operation Spotter/Quartet. Fifteen Spitfires plus seven Blenheims landed at Ta Kali; groundcrew took over the Spitfires and rapidly turned them from ferry fit to combat fit. The Spitfire had 90-gallon slipper tanks fitted for ferry purposes that provided the necessary range from the 'safe' launch points for the carriers. External tanks were a great way of providing extra fuel for ferry flights

and even for routine combat ops –
as long as they could be dropped
when contact was made with the
enemy. First combat patrols were
flown on the 10th, the Spitfires
climbing to 19,000ft to provide
high cover against fighters, while
the Hurricanes were to focus on the
bombers, the same tactic that had
been employed successfully in the
Battle of Britain. A Ju 88 formation
was after Luqa and was intercepted
after bombing; the first confirmed
Spitfire victory over Malta went
to Flight Lieutenant P, Heppell,
shooting down a 109 of JG 53.
Other attackers were damaged and
one Hurricane was lost. The same

Spitfire take-off from HMS *Eagle* on 7 March – the first Spitfire
reinforcement ferry to Malta.

day also saw the first Spitfire loss, Pilot Officer Ken
Murray (AB343) being shot down. The next few
days remained intensive, with losses on both sides
and increasing amounts of damage to the airfields.
On the evening of the 18th, Ju 88 formations with
strong escorts attacked Luqa and Hal Far again,
dropping 14 tons of bombs. Eleven Hurricanes
and four Spitfires scrambled and were, as usual,
heavily outnumbered. One Spitfire of 249 and two
Hurricanes of 185 were shot down; *HSL128* went
out looking for the downed pilots and picked up
185 Squadron's Pilot Officer Lester.

After the Wellington success at the beginning
of the month, there was little good news on the
anti-shipping front for Malta. The only other
success was the sinking of a freighter by 830
Squadron on the night of 17/18 March. However,
the anti-shipping campaign was being more
heavily prosecuted from Middle East bases, with
Blenheims and Beauforts. March was to see the
first classic torpedo strike by 39 Squadron in the
Mediterranean. Eight Beauforts led by Flight
Lieutenant A.M. Taylor took off on the afternoon
of 9 March to search for a convoy reported to be
heading for Tripoli. At 1640 the formation located
the convoy of four MVs, three cruisers and six or
seven destroyers at position 3325N 01746E (approx.
170 miles north-east of Tripoli), steering a course

Pilot listing for 185 Squadron, March 1942,
now under the command of Squadron Leader
Mortimer Rose; the bottom part is interesting as
it shows the formation used by the squadron.

of 045 degrees at some 10 to 12 knots. The convoy had an air escort of three Ju 88s plus at least one Bf 110. The Beauforts should have had an escort of Beaufighters but this had failed to turn up at the rendezvous and Taylor had elected to press on without it. Approaching the convoy, he called the formation into line astern and commenced his attack run. He elected to make his main attack against the cruiser force, which was considerably in front and to port of the main body of the convoy and therefore more vulnerable. All eight aircraft made successful drops, with one torpedo aimed at the largest MV and the other seven at the cruisers. Forcing a way through the barrage of flak, the formation emerged on the far side of the convoy – to be met by the escorting Ju 88s and Bf 110s. This time, however, it was to be the Beauforts' day; one Ju 88 was shot down by Flying Officer Bee's aircraft and, not to be outdone, Flying Officer Leaning's gunner damaged an Bf 110. All eight Beauforts broke through the defences and flew back to North Africa, four making night landings at Bu Amud and four at Sidi Barrani.

The outcome of the strike was one MV hit, one cruiser hit, one destroyer hit and possibly sunk, one Ju 88 destroyed and one Bf 110 damaged – all for the cost of one Beaufort slightly damaged. The squadron received a signal of congratulations from the C-in-C Mediterranean and Alistair Taylor was granted the immediate award of the DFC. It was a very successful strike, although unusual in the small degree of damage suffered by the Beauforts. The citation for the DFC to Flight Lieutenant Taylor stated: 'This officer has proved himself to be a capable and courageous flight commander. Late in January, 1942, the formation of which he was the leader attacked an Italian convoy which was protected by a battleship and a number of cruisers and destroyers. Flight Lieutenant Taylor led his formation through a fierce barrage and himself scored a hit on one of me merchant ships. Subsequently, in March, he led an attack on another convoy when a cruiser, a merchant vessel and a destroyer were torpedoed by the formation. A Junkers 88 was also destroyed on this occasion.' (AMB 6609 dated 4 Apr 1942).

A German naval report of 14 March was clear that the 'favourable situation in the Mediterranean, so pronounced at the present time will probably never occur again.' The report was urging immediate action. 'The Naval Staff thinks it is desirable on the part of the Fuhrer to issue orders that preparations for an offensive against the Suez Canal be begun. The need for the occupation of Malta is pointed out. Advantage should be taken of the present state of its defences, greatly weakened by German attacks. If Axis troops do not occupy Malta it is imperative that the German Air Force continues its attacks on the island to the same extent as heretofore. Such attacks alone will prevent the enemy from rebuilding Malta's offensive and defensive capabilities. If our attacks are not continued, the enemy will immediately and hurriedly begin to rebuild Malta.' Dead right – and from the British point of view it was decisive that neither of the options were followed, and Malta was indeed able to build up once more ... but that is still a few weeks away.

The AOC in Malta sent a signal to HQ ME on the evening of 19 March: 'In view of vital importance maintaining fighter escort with additional Spitfires and 229 Squadron must banish Wellington effort from here for time being. Fighter repairs must be on 24-hour shift. Must get on top of German effort before taking Wellingtons again. May ask loan of Squadron short periods for special jobs. Regret this very much. Am sure it is right at present. Will give us far greater dispersal and more room in which to operate.' He was referring to mix of engineering effort, and Malta was invariably short of engineering support and equipment, and protective dispersal requirements.

Ta Kali was hit by a heavy raid by sixty or more Ju 88s on the evening of 20 March, causing severe damage – gone were the days of small numbers of ineffective Italian bombers. The following morning the Germans were back with another heavy attack. The defenders had little to offer as damage to airfields reduced their ability to mount sorties, as did the lack of serviceable aircraft. The Luftwaffe was not done with Ta Kali for the day, and a second even larger raid (200+) dropped another 182 tons of bombs on the airfield and surrounding areas. It is estimated that more than 1,500 bombs hit the airfield area, destroying or seriously damaging every major building. The following day nine Spitfires, and two escorting Blenheims, landed, having been part of the first phase of Operation Picket.

The supply situation on Malta was dire and unless a convoy could be run the consequences were likely to be critical. In late March Cunningham assembled an Alexandria to Malta convoy that comprised four supply ships plus a significant naval escort. The overall plan included suppression of as many as possible of the air bases that could send bombers to attack the convoy, and that included bases in Africa and on the islands of Rhodes and Crete, as well as Sicily, when (and if) the convoy closed on Malta. The convoy sailed from Alexandria on 20 March. Malta was trying to prepare for the arrival of its next batch of Spitfires, repairing airfield surfaces and dispersals and trying to work out a defence plan to protect the new arrivals, and the remaining resident aircraft, from immediate attack. More raids arrived on the 21st, adding to the damage on the airfields (and elsewhere) and destroying or damaging more aircraft on the ground.

Meanwhile, convoy MW10 had had a tense but undisturbed day, clearing the first danger zone – south of Crete – without being attacked from the air. They had been spotted, however, so an attack was only a matter of time. Air attacks, primarily by Ju 88s, started on the morning of the 22nd and coincided with the appearance of an Italian surface force. The convoy commander elected to send the supply ships and their close escort on to Malta and then turn to engage the surface fleet and prevent it getting in range of the supply ships. The two naval forces manoeuvred for the rest of the day without any significant engagement, and at dusk the British warships withdrew towards Alexandria so as to be out of the danger zone of air attack before daylight. The supply ships and close escort were pressing on to Malta and suffering air attack.

Mr Slinn, a crewman on the *Pampas*, provided a detailed account of his experience of the air attacks. 'We were bound from Alexandria to Malta with a general cargo of 8,000 tons. The ship was armed with 4 Oerlikons, 2 Hotchkiss, 2 Lewis, 2 Marline, 1 12-pounder HA, a 4in BI, a Harvey Projector and 2 PAC rockets.' This was a significant amount of self-defence armament for a merchant ship and indicative of the threat, especially the air threat. 'The crew, including 9 naval and 4 military gunners, numbered 58 of whom 3 men were injured. We left Alexandria on Friday 20th March at 0630.' He then listed the other ships in the convoy and the significant warship escort, and 'up to 0930 on the 22nd we had an air escort of Beaufighters, after which time they left us. At 1000 on the 22nd the battle began. The first attack was delivered by Italian torpedo aircraft and this was repelled. The second attack, about a dozen bombers, came over just before lunch, these also being Italian torpedo bombers. We had a lull for half an hour, during which we had our lunch, and after that the attacks were almost continuous.'

Admiral Vian signalled a warning of dive-bombers approaching, and at about the same time steamed off with most of the escort as the Italian battle fleet had been sighted. 'Leaving the convoy with 4 Hunt Class destroyers only to meet the dive-bombers. Our ships laid a thick smoke screen as they left.' At 1610, Admiral Vian signalled that the Italian fleet had been repelled, and HMS *Cleopatra* rejoined the supply ships. 'The dive-bombing had continued throughout the afternoon and evening until dark, all the merchant ships put up a terrific barrage, the *Breconshire*, being fitted with pom-poms, and no hits were scored by the enemy. Our gunners shot down one Savoia bomber at about 1600. It came in low over the *Talbot*, and straight for us at a height of about 50 feet. We fired, but it continued on its course so that we could not miss. We could see the bullets pouring into him, he banked, did not release his torpedo, but went straight down into the sea.'

So far, so good for the convoy. But overnight the weather turned bad and in rough seas the ships had to disperse. 'During the bad weather, we lost the destroyer, and at daylight on the 23rd were alone, when at 0730 we were attacked by a formation of Ju.88s. The enemy scored two direct hits on our ship, the first bomb falling on No. 1 Hold and the second on No. 2 Hold, which was full of benzine, but fortunately neither bomb exploded. Ten minutes later another plane dived at us and released a salvo of 5 bombs under our stern which almost lifted the ship out of the water, and after that were subjected to a machine-gun attack by a Messerschmitt, which wounded 3 of our crew at the guns.'

The ship had been very lucky, two hits but both unexploded, and a salvo close but again causing no damage. The fact that the attacks started almost immediately after the Beaufighters left, caused ACAS to comment: 'The Beaufighter could have dealt effectively with all the enemy aircraft employed. I am, therefore, prompted to ask whether it would be possible to fit a Beaufighter with an extra tank to increase the period during which it could escort our convoys in the Mediterranean.' A hand-written note on the signal said: 'I will look into the possibility of doing this.'

Of the supply ships, the first two, *Pampas* and *Talabot*, entered the harbour in the early morning of the 23rd. *Breconshire* was hit a number of times and eventually had to drop anchor, while *Clan Campbell* was sunk. Having been left dead in the water some 10 miles from Malta, *Breconshire*, and her 10,000 tons of supplies, was a sitting target. Attempts were made on the 24th and 25th to tow the ship to harbour and when that failed to use HMS *Plumleaf*, a tanker, to try to pump off the valuable fuel cargo. Throughout, she was given a strong 'escort' that was there to provide AA cover. On the evening of the 26th a Ju 88 put four more bombs into the *Breconshire* and fires raged – but still she didn't sink. However, by the following morning it was clear she was doomed, and as the cargo exploded she finally sank. As a footnote, she was salvaged in April 1954, but only to be towed to a scrapyard in Trieste to be broken up.

For the two ships that reached harbour the trials were not yet over, as the Luftwaffe continued to attack them in an attempt to prevent stores being unloaded. In an air assault on the 26th, the Luftwaffe disposed of the ships. As Mr Slinn recorded: 'We had continual daylight bombing in the Grand Harbour from the 23rd to the 26th March. On the 24th, out of 8 hours working time, we lost 4 hours 36 minutes for unloading owing to the bombing. We also lost time in unloading as several of our derricks had been put out of action. On the afternoon of 26th there was a fierce attack by Stukas and the *Pampas* was hit. A bomb went down the funnel and burst at the base, wrecking the

German recce shot of ship burning in Grand Harbour; reaching port was no guarantee of safety, indeed, ships in Grand Harbour attracted Axis raids and the rush was on to unload supplies before a ship was hit.

accommodation amidships and setting it on fire. We returned to the ship and fought the fire, but found that the holds were filling and the engine-room was soon flooded. The vessel must also have been damaged also by the many near misses which fell around her and at about 1600 hours she touched bottom and we had to abandon her.'

The M/S *Talabot*, a Norwegian merchantman of 6,798 tons, on her second Malta run, the first having been in May 1941, was hit, a bomb exploding in her engine room. The fire quickly spread to the stores, including ammunition, and in an effort to prevent a catastrophe that could have caused major destruction to the port facilities, the captain ordered her to be sunk to flood the holds. Captain Albert Toft later stated that the cargo was 600 tons of ammunition, 600 tons of benzine, 200 tons of paraffin, and 880 tons of coal, as well as some quantity of wheat and flour.

The excellent website www.warsailors.com includes a summary of Captain Toft's account: 'Everything went well until the morning of March 22, when dive bombers and torpedo aircraft attacked. All of Talabot's guns were in use that morning, then there was a pause in the attacks until about 14:00 when the main attack came. 5 attacks took place with Talabot as target, the bombs raining around her, some exploding very close to the side of the ship. At about 4 o'clock that afternoon the admiral signalled that enemy surface vessels had been spotted, and that the escorts were going to attack, then left after having protected the merchants with a smoke screen. 6 destroyers were now accompanying the convoy. An hour later, Talabot was again attacked by aircraft, 6 Stukas, resulting in an injured gunner and signalman, and at the same time the captain spotted a torpedo aircraft coming in extremely low, but he says no torpedo was dropped, though the plane narrowly missed the ship with one of its wings, closely followed by the shells from Talabot's Breda guns, until it crashed in the sea about 100 meters away. While all this was going on, they could still hear the sounds of the naval battle taking place out of their view to the north of them, and some projectiles were seen to strike the water close by them.

'At 7 o'clock, the Commodore signalled for them to steer in a true 260° course for 2 hours, then follow the instructions in 'Operation B', and when Captain Toft broke the seal of the envelope containing the instructions for this operation he learned that each ship was to continue independently to Malta at maximum speed, with 1 destroyer as initial escort; another arrived later. The night was quiet, but as soon as day dawned they were attacked by bombers again. The night before, a damaged destroyer had come alongside Talabot, and this provided some extra protection so that together they managed to keep the aircraft at bay. Also, 2 British fighter planes appeared at this time to help in the defense. When another group of aircraft showed up just before they reached Grand Harbour they just waved and smiled, assuming they were friendly aircraft, but they were wrong. Intense firing ensued, but again they avoided being hit. At 09:45, the pilot came on board, but they were not made fast until around 5 that afternoon (23rd), all the while enduring continuous air attacks. Lighters were placed from the ship to the quay to be used as gangways for the stevedores and crew to go to the shelters during attacks.

'They unloaded cargo for two days, constantly interrupted by attacks. On the 3rd day, the bombing started very early in the morning and increased in intensity as the day went on. At noon, 30 Stukas came out of Sicily and turned the harbour into a flaming inferno. The captain says they were in a shelter in the harbour at about 14:00 when he saw Talabot being hit by a bomb. He stormed out of the shelter in order to get to his beloved ship, barely being missed by a bomb, whereupon the engineer dragged him back into the shelter, but wild horses couldn't keep him in. Examinations showed that the bomb had hit Talabot on the port side of the boat deck, had gone straight through the electrician's cabin, the shelter deck and main deck, and had exploded in the engine room where a fire had started. All the cabins had been blown to pieces by the sheer force, another bomb had hit just outside the side of the ship, and in hold No. 1 the contents had been tossed around and dropped helter skelter. After a while, Captain Toft realized he had no choice but to ask a cruiser located on the other side to shoot a hole in the side of the ship and into the engine room so that it would fill with water. At the same time the surrounding area was evacuated, as there was imminent danger of Talabot blowing up. Word came from the cruiser that no such hole could be shot without permission from the admiral. Shortly thereafter a message was received from the admiral that he could not give such an order, but he could put explosives at the captain's disposal, as well as all the assistance he would possibly require, but he himself had to do the job. Meanwhile, the fire had spread to hold No. 1 where the benzine was stowed. The explosives arrived, Captain Toft went to his cabin to collect some personal effects; pictures of his wife and children, his diary etc. before leaving the ship. By then the deck was so hot that "it sputtered under the soles of my shoes".

'The next morning *Talabot* was a total wreck, but the water level was well above the cases of ammunition so there was no longer any danger of an explosion. On March 27 the Norwegian flag was lowered and the British naval flag put up. 2 days later *Talabot*'s men (and 1 woman) were ordered to sail for the U.K. on the British cruiser *Aurora*. The captain ends his story by saying: "One incident I shall never forget. Just before I was about to leave the ship for the last time, our brave little mess girl Margit suddenly came up to me. It was in the middle of an air attack and she was holding the ship's frightened little cat. Neither the cat nor we could accomplish any more. We were the last to disembark – Margit, the cat and I."'

I include the account above in some detail in recognition of the work of the merchant sailors of many nations, who were the lifeline of Malta, and of the dock workers who risked their lives to ensure that the supplies that reached the island made it ashore. Sadly, on this occasion fewer than 2,000 tons of supplies made it ashore from the supply ships. It was a major victory for the Luftwaffe and a blow to Malta's morale. On the upside, if there was one, the ships had sunk in the harbour or close by, and so over the ensuing weeks an additional 3,000 tons of supplies were salvaged.

A signal of 26 March sounds humorous now but at the time highlighted the frustration of Malta and its lack of supplies: 'The Wellington which arrived last night from Middle East brought 750 pounds of NAAFI goods, chief items were soap, toothpaste, razor blades and Brylcreem. Consider this absolutely reprehensible when we have aircraft grounded for lack of so many spare parts; for example, four Hurricanes are grounded for lack of Colbert rivets. We are fighting for our existence here and Brylcreem is the last thing we need.' (signal HQ RAF Malta to HQ RAF ME).

The Army would have found this amusing, as they frequently referred to the RAF as 'the Brylcreem Boys!'. The response back was that the aircraft had already been preloaded and that other aircraft with the required spares were on the way. In the midst of crisis of Malta, it is always interesting to come across this type of exchange – but sadly most are buried in dreary files that historians do not peruse! Seemingly unnecessary items could actually be useful; such as when 'Titch' Whiteley included lipsticks in the items he brought back from a UK trip (April 1941). Said lipsticks were touted around the matrons and nurses on Malta by George Burges and he returned with the prize the squadron wanted – castor oil. As Whiteley explained: 'The Squadron was desperately short of hydraulic fluid. I knew how to dispense this fluid provided I could obtain castor oil.' Hence the barter of lipstick – not obtainable on Malta – for something the nurses could find – castor oil. So, many a Maryland owed its flight to lipstick!

The same day saw Hal Far being given similar treatment to that of Ta Kali a few days before; Heavy raids on the 26th caused extensive damage and killed twenty-nine people on the airfield. To the credit of the damage parties, and the pilots, Hurricanes were using the airfield again by the afternoon. As recounted above with the supply ships, this was also the day that the Luftwaffe focused on destroying shipping in the harbour, and in addition to the supply ships lost, the cruiser *Penelope* was also heavily damaged.

A press release covered the 'Big Malta Air Battle': 'Malta's Spitfires and Hurricanes shot out of the sky a formation of 30 Ju.87 dive bombers on Wednesday afternoon. At least half of them either did not return home, or landed riddled with cannon shell splinters and machine-gun bullets. It was one of the biggest air battles ever fought on the island. Flying at about 7,000ft the enemy bombers zig-zagged down from Sicily to attack a ship lying off the coast. They came in pairs, line astern. Stepped above them were the usual protecting Messerschmitts. 'This was just the chance for which the Spitfire and Hurricane pilots had been waiting. They seized it. Before the Stukas had a chance to do their dive on the ship, the British fighters swooped on them, breaking up the formation. So rattled were the Nazi pilots that all their bombs fell wide. The ship did not sustain damage even from a near miss, and, in spite of the Messerschmitts, at the end of the 15-minutes whirlwind battle our fighters were unscathed.' The press release stated claims for three destroyed (two 109s and one Ju 87), six probables (all Ju 87s) and eight Ju 87s damaged.

'There is good reason to believe that several of the dive-bombers crashed into the sea, but our pilots, outnumbered, were so busy engaging in combat – first one and then another – that they had no time to follow each of their adversaries down.' (AMB 6558 dated 26 March). The press release also highlighted a second attack by 30 Ju 87s on shipping in Grand Harbour: 'The enemy pilots had to run a gauntlet of the intense anti-aircraft harbour barrage. Many were deterred and a large number of the bombs fell harmlessly in the water.'

On the 27th – and much to their dismay when they saw the state of Malta – the Hurricanes of 229 Squadron arrived. Having been in the Middle East since spring 1941, equipped with Hurricane Is and IIs, the squadron turned up at Hal Far to join the fray, although it was disbanded a few weeks later!

Governor Dobbie sent an update signal on 30 March stating: 'During the period 21st February to 20th March there were 255 alerts, including 74 raids by day and 56 raids by night. 122 people were killed and 175 seriously injured. Raids have been progressively increased in intensity culminating in attacks on ships at Malta.'

HMS *Penelope* enters harbour having been damaged in air attack.

He also stated that the palace had been hit and that his office had been damaged, and the 'Palace Banqueting Hall' destroyed (it conjures an image to me from the film *Carry On Up the Khyber* when the British carry on their dinner party in the residency while it is being attacked by tribesmen!) More significantly, he noted that 'the large reservoir near Ta Kali aerodrome containing one third of our present water reserve was breached on 22nd March and emptied. Greater economy of water during the summer will be required.' This was likely not an intentional target but it would have been interesting had the Germans actually targeted what was a critical and vulnerable part of Malta's infrastructure.

In the eastern Mediterranean, the anti-submarine war had heated up again, in part because of increased Allied coastal convoys supporting land operations. In February and March an average of five or six daily patrols were flown; this increased to an average of eleven the following month. On 22 March a Blenheim of 203 Squadron out of LG39 caught *U-73* on the surface some 50 miles north-west of Derna and, although the U-boat crash-dived, Pilot Officer Beresford-Peirse dropped four 250lb anti-submarine bombs that were close enough to cause severe damage. Indeed, the U-boat was lucky; unable to dive, it made its way back to port, and was very vulnerable while doing so.

On the 27th, two Sunderlands of 230 Squadron made separate attacks on a submarine near Bardia; the first attack by 250lb bomb and DC claimed no hits, but the second aircraft dropped eight bombs and claimed the submarine destroyed, although this was later reclassified as 'probably damaged'. Swordfish were also active in the role in March, with an 815 Squadron aircraft claiming on 11 March that an attack near Mersa Matruh with DC caused the submarine to stop and submerge slowly; this was only classified as 'probably slightly damaged'. March also saw the operational debut of another Wellington unit in the Middle East; 221 Squadron had arrived at LG39 in January (although a detachment remained at Luqa for some time) equipped with Wellington VIIIs carrying ASV.

Kesselring held a conference at II Group HQ to finalize plans for the neutralization of Malta: 'The basic idea of II Group's orders was to surprise and neutralize the enemy's fighters, or at least to cripple them so much that they would not be any considerable danger to the ensuing bombing assault, while the three airfields were to be attacked at short intervals with heavy bombs, light anti-personnel bombs and machine-gun fire in order to destroy the aircraft on the ground and to render the runways at least temporarily unserviceable. Daylight attacks were to be concentrated and incessant, and given such powerful fighter protection that the British fighters would be kept away from our bombers and pursued until they were wiped out. At night continual nuisance raids by single aircraft were to hinder clearing up the wreckage and repairs. An additional part of the programme was the sinking of the few supply ships making for the port by dive-bombing attacks, and the blocking of the harbour entrance by dropping mines.' (Memoirs of Field Marshal Kesselring).

The April assault actually started on the 1st, and across the four fighter squadrons, the defenders could only muster nineteen Hurricanes and eight Spitfires at the start of the day; indeed, by this time the few Spitfires were being operated on a 'take it in turns' rosta between 249 and 126 squadrons. The main target was Hal Far and the airfield was temporarily unusable because of craters, but these were filled rapidly and the surface made usable again. The main assault began on 2nd April and was to last for about six weeks. According to Kesselring, it was a great success. The next day, 3rd April, it was the turn of Ta Kali and, once again, the airfield was rendered temporarily unserviceable and a number of aircraft were destroyed or damaged. However, this piecemeal method of attacking airfields in turn was a failure, as it gave each airfield time to recover between attacks, and left some serviceable from which aircraft could still operate. Three Wellingtons with OADU crews were lost in ground accidents on the 4th, two colliding with each other and the third hitting a parked aircraft. None of the crews were injured, but this type of loss was infuriating as it cost valuable aircraft and time to clear up, although the engineering staff sometimes appreciated the unexpected plethora of spare parts once the aircraft was declared DBR (damaged beyond repair) and subsequently SOC (struck off charge). The loss of three aircraft on delivery flights meant that the squadrons waiting to receive them would continue to be short of aircraft.

It was Luqa's turn on the 6th, and in this case the airfield suffered a repeat attack the following day, with a second raid on the 7th also hitting Kalafrana. This day also saw a particularly destructive raid that flattened large areas of housing and caused numerous casualties. The Sliema area was hit again the following day. By the 9th the harbour and dockyards were a sorry state and were all but unusable; one of Malta's 'reasons for being' – an offensive naval base –was being rapidly extinguished. Even the 10th Submarine Flotilla, which had been establishing an excellent reputation in previous months, was finding it all but impossible to operate from Malta. Her most successful boat (HMS *Upholder*) and commander (Lieutenant Commander M. Wanklyn VC DSO**) sailed for patrol on the 6th but after a report on the 10th was never heard from again. The role of Allied submarines in the Mediterranean war has seen only occasional reference in this account, but that is due to space, and a focus on air operations, rather than an intent to minimize or diminish the role they played. During my RAF career in the 1980s I only once took up the offer of a trip in a sub, and that was little more than a 'trip around the bay' – an experience that convinced me that submariners were indeed a different breed … and welcome to it!

The numbers of RAF fighters dwindled every day despite the best efforts of maintenance crews; the attrition rate on aircraft was unsustainable. Malta had enough pilots but nothing for them to fly. One of the 'victory measures' in the Battle of Britain had been that pilots who had their aircraft damaged in combat could often bail out or crash land and be back on the squadron, where a steady stream of replacement aircraft kept the defences more or less intact. This was simply not the case in Malta. As an example of the role of the Marine Craft Unit in 'returning pilots to service', in this period *HSL128* found and returned three fighter pilots: 2nd April, McCleod (Spitfire), 9th, Pauley (Hurricane), and 14th, Kelly (Spitfire).

Both Luqa and Hal Far were hit hard on the 11th, with the destruction of nine aircraft (plus four damaged) at Luqa, and six Hurricanes destroyed at Hal Far. Small numbers of bombers appeared, as they did most days, but more dangerous were the seemingly ever-present fighters, which pounced on any air movement, as well as strafing any suitable ground targets. Both airfields were again targeted on the 12th, with more destruction to infrastructure and more aircraft lost, three Wellingtons being burnt out at Luqa (some records suggest the 14th and four Wellingtons).

Malta was still trying to maintain its reconnaissance role, with 69 Squadron still

Because of its location close to the Harbour, Sliema was hit frequently.

sending off its Marylands. In view of the threat of marauding fighters, the Marylands were usually provided with fighter cover on their departure and return; three of 249s Spitfires gave cover to a Maryland leaving Luqa on the 14th and were bounced by 109s, which shot down Pilot Officer Kelly. He was quickly picked up by *HSL128*, which also recovered the body of a Beaufort crewman (Beveridge) the same day. The Spitfires covered the return of the Maryland later in the day, again tangling with 109s, and claiming one destroyed and one damaged.

The recce information was not only for use by Malta aircraft but was part of the overall strategic picture of shipping at sea and in port in the central Mediterranean, and with less offensive capability in Malta, other units undertook attacks based on the 'intel'. No. 205 Group was kept busy and in April a significant number of ops were flown, and losses mounted, especially when Benghazi was the target. During April the group suffered a number of losses on Benghazi ops:

4th/5th: 70 Sqn Wellington AD632, Sergeant G.T. Salmon and crew PoW. The same night also saw 38 Sqn Wellington DV419 lost on a shipping sweep, Pilot Officer R. Langley and crew being killed.

7th/8th: 37 Sqn Wellington DV411, Warrant Officer C.H. Tourville. Crashed shortly after getting airborne from LG09; all killed.

7th/8th: 38 Sqn Wellington AD604, Flight Sergeant T.A. Holdsworth. Attacked target successfully but on return suffered engine failure and crashed near Mersa Matruh; 3 killed and 3 injured.

11th/12th: 37 Sqn Wellington DV420; Damaged by flak and undercarriage collapsed on landing; one injured and aircraft written off.

18th/19th: 37 Sqn Wellington AD642, Sergeant B.R. Steward. Sortie was aborted because of bad weather and aircraft crashed close to LG09 while searching for the airfield; all killed.

19th/20th: 70 Sqn Wellington T2842, Pilot Officer R.A. Sharp. Pilot disoriented when instruments failed, crew bailed out and one subsequently died of injuries.

25th/26th: 70 Sqn Wellington Z8984, Sergeant P.R. Darby. Hit by flak over target and one killed, rest bailed out and became PoW.

27th/28th: 70 Sqn Wellington Z8787, Sergeant L. Holliday. Attacked target but on return flight port propeller flew off; crash-landed with only one injury, but aircraft written off.

It was a similar picture over the next few months.

On the 19th Malta had received a small but welcome reinforcement from North Africa, with the arrival of seven Hurricanes. Churchill requested and was granted use of the American carrier USS *Wasp* and with its much greater capacity this ship took fifty-four Spitfires to within range of the island on 20 April under Operation Calendar. Getting access to this American carrier was a major achievement by Churchill and an indication of his strong relationship with President Roosevelt. Two Spitfire squadrons, 601 and 603 squadrons, were flown off the *Wasp*. Forty-seven of the fighters made it to Malta but the Germans were ready and within hours air attacks had reduced the total to eighteen serviceable.

Lloyd gathered crews at the Xara Palace so that he could address them and give them a pep talk. As a bomber man, and also correctly in terms of Malta's role, he initially stressed the importance of the island as a base for attack (the sword), but then stated that at the present time the shield was needed to protect the sword, and the fighters and AA were that shield. According to some present, he then criticized the German tactics as being ineffective, a stance that the new arrivals in particular thought somewhat at variance with the reality they were seeing.

Three days later the fighters flew their first air defence sorties, accounting for a number of Bf 109s. Axis intelligence had been caught unawares but within days the intensive air bombardment had put the Spitfires out of action. 'Spitfires arrived Luqa and Ta Kali 20th but unfortunately followed 90 minutes later by raid, 40 tons on Ta Kali, 12 tons on Luqa. Put every serviceable Spitfire into the air. Subsequently total tonnage dropped Luqa and Ta Kali during 20th after arrival Spitfires 48 tons Luqa, 98 tons Ta Kali; 21st 125 tons Ta Kali and 28 tons Luqa; 22nd 154 tons Ta Kali and 46 tons Luqa. Both places a complete shambles, in spite soldiers working day and night. Have made every effort to get Spitfires off ground but after arrival Spitfires following sorties made for each of three raids a day: 20th – 6 and 15; 21st – 10, 12 and 10; 22nd – nought and 6. We shall be able to maintain an effort 6 or 8 Spitfires each sortie with luck. Enemy escorts heavier. We have lost eight in combat and nearly all are hit, some seriously. 9 Spitfires destroyed on the ground and 29 damaged sufficient to affect serviceability.' (HQ RAF ME to Air Ministry 23 April).

So even the arrival of nearly fifty Spitfires still only enabled six or eight to face each of the large-scale raids, and attrition would likely mean even fewer within a matter of days.

The Germans had sent almost 300 bomber sorties to Malta on the 20th, most from early afternoon onwards when the Spitfires had arrived. Only a small number of defending fighters were available and they did the best they could to break up attacks and enable the fuel-hungry Spitfires to land.

Sergeant Hesselyn witnessed Daddo-Langlois bringing his damaged Spitfire in to land, having lost a wingtip in a collision with a 109: 'I noticed one Spit with its wingtip sheared off. He was flying low down with a bunch of 109s above, and was whistling around the circuit, waiting a favourable moment to come in and land. His damaged wing was plainly visible from the ground. About 18 inches of it was missing, and instead of the usual elliptical section of a Spit wing, it looked rather like the square-cut wing of a 109E. Eventually the Spit came in, but was hit. It went running past dispersal when the pilot whipped up his undercart, and skidded the aircraft along on its belly … It came to rest in a cloud of dust … I saw Raoul Daddo-Langlois leap from the cockpit of the Spitfire and make a bee-line for dispersal. Machine-gun bullets ploughed into the ground all around us, and a cannon shell burst within a few yards of Buck Brennan, but luckily we were not hurt.' (*249 at War*, *ibid*). The evening raid involved around 100 bombers, many Ju 88s, with thirty or so 109s as escort. The defenders' response was six aircraft of 249 from Ta Kali and six from 126 Squadron from Luqa. Combat ensued and, heavily outnumbered, the defenders managed to claim fleeting hits on a number of aircraft, some of which they claimed destroyed or damaged. Two Spitfires of 126 Squadron were lost. Hesselyn was himself a successful pilot on Malta, being awarded a DFM, with the citation reading: 'Sergeant Hesselyn is a skilful and gallant pilot. Undeterred by odds, he presses home his attacks with outstanding determination. He has destroyed five enemy aircraft, two of which he shot down in one engagement.' (AMB 7045 22 May 1945)

As a side note, a signal of 11 May from VCAS responded to comments from Malta as to the new squadrons and provided an explanation of 'why two crack 11 Group fighter squadrons were not sent to Malta, it is necessary to recapitulate Fighter Command's commitments at that time to provide additional pilots for overseas … C-in-C, therefore, correct in starting he was 'limited' in his choice of the two squadrons to go to the Middle East, and he chose the two best, namely 601 and 603.'

Much of the correspondence appears to be missing, but the implication is that someone on Malta did not consider these the best squadrons that could have been sent! The VCAS signal

Spitfires of 249 Squadron at Ta Kali.

continued: 'Obviously if two hardly operational squadrons are chosen or sent, it may be better to hand pick a mixed bag from throughout the Command, although I doubt it. The team spirit is a great factor in fighter squadrons [as Bouchier had pointed out in his earlier paper], and I am sure the two comparatively weak squadrons that have been sent will rise to the occasion.' He stated that if squadrons are put on standby to deploy for too long then they may be 'milked' of the most experienced pilots.

The ground crew worked their usual miracles as they tried to get aircraft serviceable by robbing parts, and eventually managed to declare twenty-six operational Spitfires as 21 April started, plus around eight Hurricanes, a total fighter strength of thirty-four. This was a great achievement but was a disaster in terms of survivability of delivered aircraft, and thirty-four serviceable by no means meant that number could rise to meet any attack. When the first raid appeared in the early morning, Malta sent up nearly 50 per cent of its strength, ten Spitfires and five Hurricanes. The second, slightly larger raid, which included Stukas, arrived just after midday and was engaged by a number of Spitfires. The final raid comprised eighty bombers and forty fighters, and as with the previous raids they aimed at the main airfields and Grand Harbour. Spitfires of 249 went up to intercept. During all three raids the losses on both sides were low, but the damage and destruction of aircraft on the ground continued to erode the defenders' combat capability.

Also, the presence of the Spitfires attracted the heavy weight of attack that also had an impact on other residents. Ten Wellingtons of 148 Squadron arrived on the 21st as the next bomber detachment from 205 Group, losing one the same day in an air raid. The signal of the 24th also addressed this: 'Wellingtons well dispersed and protected but have lost two with direct hits and two more damaged. 87s dive at each individual Wellington. Wellingtons not fortunate night of 21/22. Runways only serviceable at 2300 hours after filling three holes each with 100 tons and badly holed dispersal tracks. Only able to mount one sortie.'

No. 148 Squadron had been reduced to only two aircraft by the 26th, most were destroyed on the ground but two (BB483, Flight Lieutenant A. Hayter, and DV573, Flying Officer R. Harper) were lost in a night-time attack on Comiso (23rd/24th). The only survivor was Anthony Hayter, and he became a PoW and ended up at Stalag Luft III. He was one of those involved in the Great Escape, and was captured and shot by the Gestapo on 6 April 1944. The squadron was recalled to the Middle East on the 26th.

There were four more major raids on airfields in April, and while targets were mixed, the primary target each day appears to have been: Luqa (22nd, 25th and 27th), Ta Kali (22nd, 23rd) and Kalafrana (26th), Grand Harbour (24th). It was a similar story on each day; formations of bombers with a strong escort met by diminishing numbers of fighters, combats and claims on both sides, and attrition of aircraft on the ground. That attrition also included equipment, with some items becoming very scarce. Needless to say, there were also casualties on the ground. The hard work of the ground staff would have been impossible without the protection that aircraft and men received in the increasingly effective pens around the various airfields. This passive defence measure meant that only a direct hit from a bomb could cause fatal damage, and the pens were not always easy to pick out, as most were made of local stone or 'bits and pieces' that often looked just like other parts of the airfield. Everyone took part in building and maintaining the pens. The first few months of 1942 had seen significant increases in the number of protective pens, from 240 at the start of January to 285 by 1 March and 358 by 30 April. The breakdown of assignment of pens was:

Date	Total Pens	Fighter	Bomber	Recce	FAA	Bowser/Roller
1 Mar 1942	285	170	14	31	31	0
30 Apr 1942	358	205	27	67	34	25

'The task of building dispersal roads and pens for aircraft was achieved largely through Army work forces, provided mainly by the Infantry Battalions. An indication of the effort required is given by the fact that an open pen for a Wellington requires 3,500 tons of stone. Such a pen, which measures 90ft × 90ft with 14ft high walls, took 200 men 28 days to build. Stone proved more effective than earth-filled petrol cans which were used initially, but the latter could be erected more quickly (21 days for a Wellington pen). A fighter pen required one quarter of the effort of that for a Wellington pen.' (*Battle Casualties from Air | Bombing of Malta Airfields 1942*, Operational Research Branch 1988).

   The scale of Army support was impressive; in April there were 660 men working at Luqa/Safi, 870 at Ta Kali and 650 at Hal Far, with the main activity at each being the building or improving of pens. In June the numbers at Luqa/Safi went up to 945 but at others the number came down. 'Significant working parties were also maintained during the hours of darkness. For example, at Ta Kali on the night of 13th/14th April, over 300 Army personnel were working on the airfield. Night repair work was in fact vital to the continued operation of the airfields and was carried out with the aid of arc lights. The removal of damaged aircraft from runways and taxiways proved a major problem. Tanks and bren carriers were used to tow such aircraft to repair areas or scrapyards.' (*Battle Casualties from Air Bombing of Malta Airfields 1942*, Operational Research Branch 1988).

   In addition to pens for aircraft, shelters for personnel were also crucial: 'There is no doubt but that without the extensive shelter accommodation provided throughout the Island, casualties would have been massive, and operations could not have been maintained.' For the service personnel this involved slit trenches, with 5ft or so of top cover, close to pens and other work areas, so that on an alarm sounding anyone in the open had a good chance of reaching

'The task of building dispersal roads and pens for aircraft was achieved largely through Army work forces, provided mainly by the Infantry Battalions.'

cover. They provided good protection and even near misses were usually ineffective: 'For example, on 9th May, a 500kg bomb exploded 29ft from a slit trench full of pilots and ground crew and there were no casualties.' Other shelter types were also provided, including rock shelters. The civilian population also had shelters of various types, the largest being the disused Floriana railway tunnel, capable of holding 3,000 people, whereas the Valetta scheme had five underground tunnels, each 2,000ft long and 600ft apart, with access from linked gradient ramps. Some direct hits on shelters did cause loss of life, such as one at Hal Far built partly above ground that was hit on 25 March with the loss of twenty-three of the twenty-five occupants.

A heavily pockmarked Ta Kali after the April attacks; photo is dated 29 April.

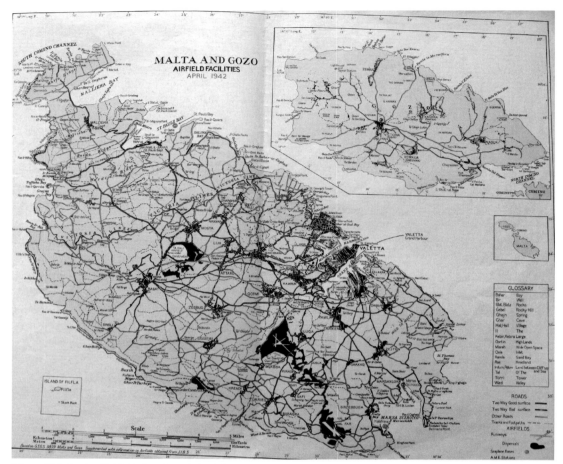

Map of Malta April 1942 showing airfield facilities, Ta Kali is shown as under construction as major work was under way; the runways at Krendi are shown, although that airfield too was still under construction.

April had brought more than 6,700 tons of bombs raining down on Malta, with the docks receiving 3,156 tons and the three airfields receiving 2,395 tons (Luqa 804, Ta Kali 841, Hal Far 750), which was more than three times as much as the March figure of 2,147 tons. April was the worst month for casualties, with 300 civilians killed and a further 630 wounded. Twenty-four service personnel in heavy AA sites were also killed (and a further eighty wounded) – this was by far the highest number of casualties at these gun sites. A workshop at Kalafrana was hit on 18 April, causing five deaths, the highest number of RAF ground fatalities in a single incident in April, although the worst day had been 24 March at Hal Far with fifteen deaths when two shelters were hit. The threat had reached such proportions that, reluctantly, the remains of the 10th Submarine Flotilla left Malta for Alexandria. To all intents and purposes Malta was now just 'hanging on' and all its offensive capability had been negated.

Meanwhile, air operations remained hectic. 'We scrambled at three o'clock, climbing south of the island getting to 26,000 feet with the sun behind us. Wood called up and said: "Hello Mac. There's a big plot building up but it's taking time to come south. Keep your present angels and save your gravy. I will tell you when to come in." We stooged around until he gave us the word. Then we sailed in …

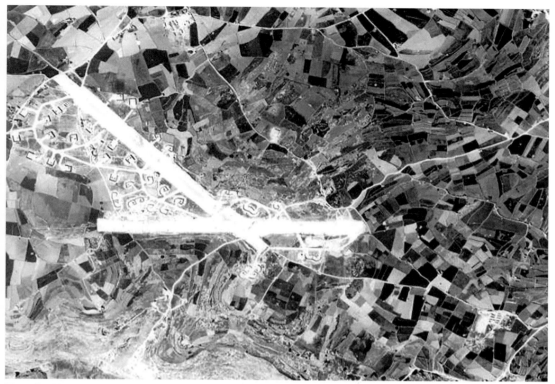

Krendi with its two runways and extensive and convoluted dispersal areas.

'Suddenly, glancing behind, I saw four 109s coming down on me. Three of them overshot. The fourth made his turn too wide and I got inside him. I was slightly below when I attacked from 200 yards, firing perhaps 20 feet ahead of him in the hope that his aircraft and my bullets would arrive at that spot simultaneously. They did. I kept on firing as I was determined to make certain of him. He caught fire. Black smoke poured out, he rolled on his back and went into a vertical dive and straight into the drink.

'As he crashed it struck me suddenly that there might be something on my tail. In my excitement I had forgotten to look but luckily none of the other 109s had dived down on me. Wood now reported that the 88s were diving on Takali, and I pulled up to 10,000 feet. The next instant the 88s were diving past my nose and the other boys were coming down from above to attack them. I picked out one and went for him and as I pressed my gun button his rear gunner opened fire. I had fired for about a second when my port cannon packed up. Luckily I was travelling fast. This prevented my aircraft from slewing from the recoil of my starboard cannon as I was able to correct with rudder. I concentrated on the 88's starboard motor and wing root and could see my shells hitting. Bits were flying off him and flames began spreading as he continued in his dive; he was well ablaze when he crashed.

'Returning to land I had my first experience of being beaten up in the circuit. A great pall of smoke and dust from the bombing was hanging over Takali. I made a couple of dummy runs over the airfield and could see that the landing path was well cratered. Just then I sighted six 109s above at 5,000 feet, waiting to pounce. The other boys were kicking about the circuit waiting to try and get in. I beetled up Imtafa valley, skipped round some windmills at the top and swung down a valley on the other side. Again and again the 109s dived down from above and attacked me. Again and again I thanked my stars that the 'Spit' was such a manoeuvrable aircraft. Each time I was attacked I turned violently and their shells and bullets whipped past behind me. It was a nerve-racking business. With all the violent turning and twisting I began to feel very sick. My neck ached from constantly twisting from side to side, looking back and from holding it up while doing tight turns against the extra gravity force. Eventually Mac said that we were to go in and he would cover us.

'I started a normal circuit about 300 feet above the airfield, put my wheels and flaps down, did weaving approach and, as my wheels touched ground felt a sigh of relief. I taxied to my pen, forgetting to put up my flaps. All I could do when I got there was to lie back in the cockpit and gasp for breath. The ground crew had to help me out of my aircraft and, dazed and dizzy, I groped my way along the wing out of my pen.

'I met Laddie as I was wandering over to dispersal. Both our tunics were soaked with perspiration. We looked up to see how Mac was getting on. He was making his approach about 50 feet up when suddenly two 109s darted out of the sun. Their shooting, however, was poor and whipping up his wheels Mac turned sharply into them. The 109s overshot him, carried on and beat up the aerodrome. Mac made a quick dart, put down his wheels and managed to get in. He landed with two gallons of petrol – at the pace we were using it, sufficient fuel for only another two minutes in the air. I had had five gallons; the others about the same.' (*New Zealanders with the RAF*)

In one of his reports, Air Vice-Marshal Lloyd noted: 'Conditions had become extremely difficult. The poor quality of the food had not been noticed at first, then suddenly it began to take effect. In March it had been clear enough but in April most belts had to be taken in by two holes and in May by another hole … Our diet was a slice and a half of bread with jam for breakfast, bully beef for lunch with one slice of bread, and except for an additional slice of bread it was the same fare for dinner. There was sugar but margarine appeared only every two or three days; even drinking water, lighting and heating were all rationed. And things which had been taken for granted closed down. The making of beer required coal so none had been made for months. Officers and men slept in shelters, in caverns and dugouts in quarries … Three hundred slept in one underground cabin as tight as sardines in a tin and two hundred slept in a disused tunnel. None had any comfort or warmth. Soon, too, we should want hundreds of tons of fuel and ammunition …'

Gliders were noticed on airfields in Sicily and it was clear that the Germans were preparing the final assault. However, the campaign in Russia had stalled and the Luftwaffe was required to go and support the 1942 offensive, with some also transferring to North Africa to bolster Rommel for his final push on Egypt. So, although some Luftwaffe units remained, once again it fell to the Italians to 'finish off' Malta. April was without doubt the toughest month for the island and it was a close-run thing. However, throughout those darkest days of March and April the hard-pressed airfields continued to handle transit aircraft, Malta being one of the air reinforcement routes to the Middle East, and in March–April some 300 aircraft landed, refuelled and got away again.

The fighter squadrons had scored 53 confirmed, 12 probables and 118 damaged in April. Axis records suggest that the actual number was far lower; despite the rigour with which a pilot's claims were investigated, it was almost impossible in the heat of air combat to get it right. The two FAA squadrons, 828 and 830, were still present but so short of aircraft that effectively they became one, the Naval Air Squadron Malta. April was also the month that brought unique recognition to Malta, when the island was awarded the George Cross. As a gallantry award, this is often called the 'civilian Victoria Cross' to show that it is awarded for the highest acts of bravery and there is some truth

The George Cross

The original warrant instituting the George Cross was dated 24 September 1940 but this was subsequently replaced by a warrant of 24 June 1941, which in turn was amended on 3 November 1942. The decoration is a silver St George's Cross with on the obverse a representation of St George and the Dragon, surrounded by the words 'For Gallantry'; each limb of the cross contains a Royal Cypher. The reverse of the medal is plain and the recipient's name and the date of the act are inscribed in this area. The cross is suspended from a ring attached to a bar ornamented with laurel leaves.

in this general description, although members of the military are also eligible for the award. The citation for Malta GC was: 'To honour her brave people I award the George Cross to the island fortress of Malta to bear witness to a heroism and devotion that will long be famous in history.'

Even if Malta's ability to strike had been drastically reduced, the campaign against Axis shipping had to continue and so the airfields in Egypt became the main focus, although all major anti–convoy operations were based on joint Malta and 201 Group strike forces.

A number of strikes were made by 39 Squadron in April and a total of 132 operational hours were flown. There was also yet another change in operational policy. Since the squadron's Beauforts were being used for long-range strikes and the range of the aircraft was insufficient for them to return to base following a mission, it was decided that in future they would fly on to Malta for refuelling and replenishment. One such strike took place on 14 April. Twelve Beauforts, including four of 22 Squadron, deployed to the advanced landing ground (ALG) at Bu Amud on 13 April on standby for a strike on a large convoy approaching Tripoli from the north. 'Owing to the blitz on Malta, several Marylands and Blenheims had to be briefed to search for the convoy from Bu Amud in Cyrenaica. One of the Marylands, piloted by Flying Officer J.B. Halbert, sighted the convoy a short distance from the east coast of Sicily. Its importance was evident from the fact that two of the four merchant vessels were of 10,000 tons each, with an escort of five warships. The Maryland shadowed the convoy until its petrol was nearly exhausted, sending from time to time clear and valuable reports of its progress. It then tried to make Malta, but was shot down four miles from the coast, all the crew being lost.' (*RAF in Middle East*, HMSO).

The following morning one of the 22 Squadron aircraft took off to locate the convoy, shadow it and pass a position report back to Bu Amud. At noon the strike force of eight aircraft took off and headed north in three formations, Flight Lieutenant Beveridge and Flying Officer Leaning leading sections of three, with a third flight consisting of Flight Lieutenant Lander and Pilot Officer Belfield of 22 Squadron. They were joined by an escort of four Beaufighters, a valuable

Presentation of George Cross to Malta, a unique use of the award.

asset during the transit past the German fighter bases on the North African coast. The strike force flew on to a position south-east of Malta and then began a creeping line ahead search for the convoy, based on the information from the reconnaissance aircraft. Unfortunately, the Beaufighters had to leave the force and return to base as they were getting perilously low on fuel. Keeping low over the water, the Beauforts continued their search and sighted the convoy at 1645. The four MVs, two of 12,000 tons and two of 10,000 tons, were escorted by six destroyers on the flanks and by no less than ninety-six aircraft (Bf 109s, Bf 110s and Ju 88s). The Beauforts moved into attack formation, hugging the waves, hoping that they would not be seen until the last moment. Their luck was out, for as they neared the release point they were spotted by the circling fighters and waves of fighters peeled off to attack the forlorn striking force. It was a race for time and although all eight Beauforts managed to drop their torps, almost immediately three aircraft were shot down as they were swamped by fighters.

Shortly afterwards, Pilot Officer Belfield's aircraft was hit and damaged; he cleared the convoy and ditched safely, all the crew took to the dinghy and were later picked up. A fifth aircraft, that of Pilot Officer Seddon, was so badly damaged that it was forced to ditch 6 miles from Malta. Their dinghy was useless so two of the crew tried to swim to Malta; Pilot Officer McGregor reached a rock ledge, collapsed exhausted after his five-hour swim, and was rescued the following morning. The rest of the crew were never seen again. Of the three aircraft to reach Malta, that of Flight Lieutenant Lander was badly shot up; most of the tail had been shot away and the hydraulics wrecked, and cannon shells had damaged the starboard aileron, smashed the windscreen and covered everything inside the aircraft with oil. Tony Leaning and Stan Gooch flew in tight formation to Malta, Gooch's aircraft having sustained hits on the fuel tanks and hydraulics, which made the job of staying with his leader very difficult. Leaning's aircraft was totally undamaged – with not even a single bullet hole! This aircraft was the only one in fit condition to fly back to base.

Stan Gooch recalled the op: 'I recall the frustration, during the sweep to find the convoy, that the leader, briefed to fly at 300 ft, was at 50 ft to keep below the radar. We failed to draw his attention to funnel smoke in the wonderful visibility and went past. We thought maybe it was a cunning move to attack from the unexpected west side. Sqn Ldr Riley, one of the four Beaufighter escort pilots, did the most beautiful shooting at long range to bring down a Ju.88. About 20 minutes later he repeated the feat, showing the first was no fluke. By now the Beaufighters were short of fuel and had to leave for Malta. A nasty sight to see them go! Eventually we came upon the convoy, and on our way in were harried by Me 109s. It seemed a good chance we would be shot down before we could get close enough to drop. Having dropped I stuck to Leaning and we were attacked four times by a most determined Ju.88 crew. Several times I nearly put a wing-tip in the sea following Leaning's evasive actions. Arriving at Malta we were saved

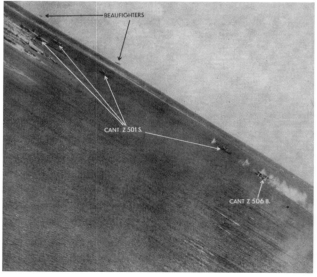

Beaufighters attacking Cant Z.501s and 506 at anchor off Bomba.

by two Hurricanes flying defensive circles around the airfield, this saved us from attack on approach and from being strafed on the ground after landing. On meeting up with Leaning and crew after landing, we knew we had lost P/O Way and crew but did not know we had lost the other five Beauforts, Leaning commented "exciting sport, but the stakes are a bit high".' (pers comm).

39 Squadron aircrew, including Tony Leaning, pose at Mariut.

It was a black day for 39 Squadron and such losses in crews and aircraft could not be sustained; fortunately it was not repeated, although losses throughout the Beaufort period were heavy. A shortage of crews and aircraft was a constant problem for 39 Squadron. Aircraft and crews of 22 Squadron had operated with 39 Squadron during April but 22 left at the end of the month for the Far East with five of its own aircraft plus three handed over by 39. This left 39 Squadron very short of serviceable aircraft and crews and although no replacement aircraft were immediately forthcoming, among the new crew arrivals at the end of the month was an experienced Beaufort pilot who was to become a legend in the Mediterranean – Squadron Leader R.P.M. (Pat) Gibbs.

March and April were somewhat quieter for the previously very successful 230 Squadron Sunderland crew of Squadron Leader Garside, he recorded two attacks on 27 March; other members of the squadron were busy in this period, six attacks and three other sightings being recorded. The attacks were made by Flight Lieutenant Milligan (27 March, 23 April and 26 April), Flight Lieutenant Squires (19 April), Flight Lieutenant Brown (22 April) and Flight Lieutenant Frame (28 April).

We make reference from time to time to the great work of the air-sea rescue teams, especially the HSLs, but a press release of 2 May noted that it was not just the ASR teams that risked their lives rescuing downed airmen. 'Three Maltese fishermen, who put to sea and rescued a Royal Air Force crew who had force-landed, have earned for their bravery a public tribute from the Air Officer Commanding. One of our torpedo-carrying aircraft was returning from a daylight attack on enemy shipping. Near the shores of Malta it was jumped by enemy fighters. After defending itself against great odds, the British aircraft was compelled to come down in the sea. A number of enemy fighters were still flying over the spot, but, disregarding them, the three Maltese fishermen at once put out in two boats from a nearby fishing village, and rescued the airmen. When they landed, the rescuers slipped away, and it was with some difficulty that they were eventually traced. Their action in rescuing the airmen in the face of heavy enemy fighter activity is another example of the gallantry, help, and fierce will to win which is daily shown by the entire Maltese population.' (AMB6860 dated 2 May). The first few days of May saw some activity over and around Malta, and mixed results, although the number of roaming German fighters made life very difficult.

This same period also the replacement of the governor, Lieutenant General Sir William Dobbie having lost the confidence of the commanders on the island and key figures back in London. Churchill had earlier said, in a speech to the House of Commons: 'That remarkable man, General

Dobbie – a Cromwellian figure at a key point, fighting with his bible in one hand and his sword in the other.' The people of Malta certainly remember him as the 'Defender of Malta'. His replacement was General Lord Gort VC, who took over (7 May) at a time when the crisis was all but over.

Around this period, Kesselring and Rommel agreed that the dual objectives should be Malta and Tobruk and that one without the other was 'not enough'. 'The protection of the sea lanes and receiving ports came within my province, and I therefore suggested to Hitler that the capture of Malta should have precedence, as a preliminary to a ground assault on Tobruk. Although Hitler agreed with this sequence, he later changed his mind. At Berchtesgaden at the end of April he endorsed Rommel's intention to launch the land operation from El Gazala first.' (Kesselring Memoirs, *ibid*).

Malta was still relying on aircraft from Egypt, especially for detachments, and was quick to comment when it thought it was being 'short-changed'. A signal of 8 May complained that 'Beaufighter V8224 of 89 Squadron arrived Luqa p.m. 6th May due 40-hour inspection when it left squadron on 3rd May flying time was 26 hours 40 mins and on arrival at Luqa was 44 hours 10 mins, feel you wish to know this as you realize how pressed we and can ill afford to do other peoples' work especially under present conditions.' (signal AOC Malta to AOC-in-C, 8 May 1942). One can image some engineering officer complaining and thus going up the chain to the extent that the most senior officers, or at least their staffs, were exchanging signals on the subject. A reply was sent the same day: 'All fully appreciate need to save you unnecessary work and Egypt Command regret dispatch Beaufighter in this condition. Original two selected had time in hand but unfortunately one had engine trouble en route and had to be replaced at once to reach you in time. Only one immediately available was V8224 and this was sent in order you should have two without delay.' (signal HQ RAF ME to AHQ Malta, 8 May 1942).

A third Spitfire reinforcement flight was arranged for 9 May, Operation Oppidan, with both *Wasp* and *Eagle* involved. This time sixty-four aircraft were flown off and upon arrival at Malta were immediately escorted to prepared blast pens for refuelling and rearming. Everything possible was done to avoid the failure of the April reinforcement, when the majority of the Spitfires were destroyed on the ground within days of arriving. Part of that plan involved experienced Malta pilots going to Gibraltar to then return with the carriers and fly off with the reinforcement groups, having also briefed and discussed with them the reality of what they were going to find on arrival.

Wing Commander Flying for Oppidan provided a brief report on 10 May: 'All pilots had reported [to Abbotsinch] by the evening of 30th April and a kit inspection was held the next morning. It was discovered that a number of them had not brought the kit laid down; 52 pilots had reported and of these the 49 with most experience were selected. It was discovered that some who had been detailed as section leaders had less experience than some of those who were not so detailed. Consequently, new section and flight leaders had to be chosen. Here it should be mentioned that one of the pilots had never flown a Spitfire before.

'On the morning of take-off, the conditions at the ship were good although the wind was lighter than ideal. The first 22 aircraft took off satisfactorily, but the 23rd failed to reach flying speed before reaching the end of the deck and crashed into the sea and the pilot (Sergeant Sherrington) was killed. The jettison tank of one aircraft failed to suck petrol and the pilot, P/O Smith, having jettisoned his tank landed aboard the carrier. This was an extremely fine performance on his part as he had never operated from a carrier before. He carried out the drill exactly as he had been ordered and obeyed all signals both over the R/T and from the deck officer landing officer with commendable coolness. It is believed this is the first time a Spitfire has ever landed aboard a carrier.'

Assuming that all went well and the Spitfires made it to Malta, the key then was speed and efficiency in the ground handling ... get down, off the runway, into a pen, refuelled and armed.

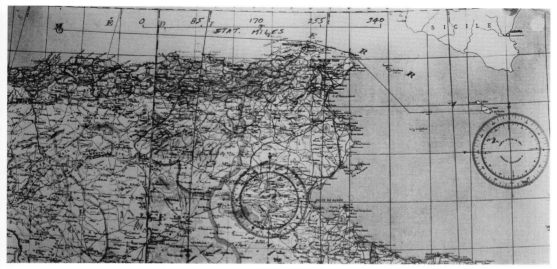

Route map for the aircraft fly-off to Malta on Operation Oppidan; the map clearly shows how close the aircraft flew to the coast trying to avoid the fighter radius of Sicily.

The process as designed was for an airman to meet each Spitfire, sit on the wing and direct it to a pen. In the pen a handling crew and the required fuel and ammunition sat ready for a quick turnaround, along with a Malta pilot who would then assume standby to scramble. It was impressive in its conception and execution. The Luftwaffe pilots, who knew that more Spitfires were due to arrive, probably thought it would be like last time, an easy way to rack up more scores. The first group of sixteen Spitfires arrived at Ta Kali around 1030, followed by a pack of 109s. The other part of the plan to protect the new arrivals was an integrated AA plan that provided arcs of fire and cover for aircraft on final approach, landing and taxying to the pens. The first Luqa batch arrived about thirty minutes later, and shortly after that, warning came of a large raid – and thirty-plus Spitfires scrambled, with 249 Squadron taking eleven of the new aircraft into the fray. Bouncing a group of 109s, they claimed one confirmed (by Pilot Officer Nash, who also got a probable) but then were themselves bounced, losing Pilot Officer Milburn. Spitfires were up again to cover the next wave of arrivals, and were scrambled again during the day as Ju 88 bombing raids appeared. Once again the defending fighters were able to disrupt the attacks so the overall tactic was successful in that, of the planned reinforcement, sixty-one aircraft made it safely to Malta. The Spitfires flew 110 sorties during the day for the loss of three aircraft – the attackers lost twenty-three aircraft, although this claim was far greater than the admitted losses. It was a brilliant success all round and a great moral boost for all on Malta. If they could prevent catastrophe for a few days, then the corner might be turned.

The heavy German raid of 10 May was indeed a turning point; it is also interesting that in his (post-war) memoirs Kesselring stated: 'On 10th May I could regard the task as accomplished. Thanks to its success, our ascendency at sea and in the air in the supply lanes from Italy to Africa was assured. It would have been easy to capture the island after the bombing assault. That this did not happen was a grave mistake on the part of the German–Italian Command which came home to roost later. With the success of this attack the OKW considered the tension so far relaxed that it transferred the greater part of our air forces to the Eastern Front. Of course sufficient forces were left in the Mediterranean to keep a watch in Malta, to curb the activity of the enemy's sea transport and to protect our own communications. As time went on, however, these forces proved too weak to neutralize the island fortress or to deprive it of supplies.'

This sounds like it was a planned end to a successful campaign, whereas in reality it was a bloody nose to what had up to that time been a successful campaign. *Welshman* had arrived in the early hours, a minelayer but on this occasion bringing high priority supplies, including a much-needed 80,000 rounds of Bofors ammunition. As always, a ship in harbour attracted the Axis bombers and most raids in the day had the ship as their primary target. A mid-morning raid of thirty or more bombers with strong fighter escort was intercepted by no less fifty fighters (thirty-seven Spitfires and thirteen Hurricanes) with one pilot recording 'terrific party over Grand Harbour. All the Ju.87s missed the target'. The twenty Ju 87s attracted particular attention from the fighters and a number of claims were made for destroyed and damaged. A second raid by a small number of Ju 88s, again with strong escort, was also intercepted convincingly, as was the last raid of the day. The evening raid was a mix of Italian and German bombers and fighters, and the defending fighters again were successful in causing losses and, more importantly, disrupting the bombing. For the defenders in the air and on the ground it was a major morale boost; for the attackers, it must have been a major shock, Malta had appeared to be finished, and the last time a Spitfire reinforcement had arrived it had simply provided targets for the Luftwaffe. The ship had been unloaded in less than five hours, under its protective umbrella of fighters. According to Lloyd: 'The Spitfires saved the *Welshman* which succeeded in leaving Malta in safety that same night.' *Welshman* was on the first of a number of such runs and this fast minelayer played a key role in running urgent supplies to Malta in 1942, her second trip being part of the June convoy.

The final scores for the day are often debated, but the overall 'Malta won and Axis lost by a big margin' was not in doubt. Some sixty to sixty-five Axis aircraft were lost or damaged, with the RAF losing only four aircraft. There is a great scene in the 1965 film *The Battle of Britain* where damaged German bombers, streaming smoke and with wounded crew, splutter over the waiting invasion barges as troops look upwards, and then a scene of empty places at the fighter squadron dinner table … the message was clear, the victorious situation of a few days before was over, the tide had turned. And so it must have seemed at bases in Sicily, with aircraft and crews missing, damaged aircraft with dead or wounded crew just making it back. And survivors saying that everywhere they looked there were Spitfires.

On 10 May the Italian Air Staff issued a 'Memorandum on the Malta Situation'. This started with a review of the invasion plans that had been under development since February and the principal aims of operations since spring:

- Neutralisation of AA defences by forcing the batteries to intensify their fire in order to exhaust their ammunition and to tire their personnel
- Elimination of enemy aircraft by concentrating first on the fighters and then on the bombers
- Close co-operation between the Luftflotte 2 and the Sicilian Air Force
- Dislocation, at all costs, of the supply routes to Malta.

The mention of depleting AA capability is interesting, and highly relevant, as the planners recognized the critical importance of reducing the AA potential of Malta ahead of any attempt at an air assault. Also interesting, and again relevant, is that the focus is not on destroying AA positions, a very difficult task, but making them less effective by depleting ammunition and wearing out the crews. This is linked to the fourth point; if AA ammunition was depleted and no new supplies could be brought in, then the guns would have to reduce rates of fire, and tired crews would be less effective. 'The intensified offensive against Malta began on the 20th March and continued with increasing intensity until the 28th April. From then on, operations had to be limited to continuous nuisance raids, aimed at keeping the Island's efficiency at a low level.

'There were two main factors which hampered the desired participation of the Italian units. The first, was the particularly adverse meteorological conditions during the season. The second, was the late transfer of the 2nd Group, which was due to unforeseen technical difficulties. In spite of this, all our units were present. Before the intensified offensive had ceased, the OBS [Oberbefehlshaber Sud] made known his intention of transferring part of Luftflotte 2 (2 Groups of Ju.88 and 2 Groups of Me.109s) to other operational sectors. As a result, the following units were to replace the: 9th Group (Mc.202), 2nd Group (Re.2001), 88th Group (Br.20) and 4th Group (S.84).'

So on paper it looked fine; Malta was on the ropes and it was simply a case of keeping her there, and with four groups (German) out and four groups (Italian) in aircraft numbers remained roughly the same. This did not, of course, take into account combat effectiveness! This, combined with the arrival of more Spitfires, set the scene for the Axis failure.

The memo also stated that in a 'summary of the situation made by the Command of Luftflotte 2 at the end of the intensified offensive, it was confirmed that:

- Malta was neutralized as a supporting base for the fleet and as a port of call for shipping
- All the serviceable ships had been destroyed or put out of action
- Enemy air activity from Malta has been severely restricted
- The supply routes to Libya were safe
- The blockade against supplies to the Island had been maintained
- The most important military installations had been destroyed.'

While some of this was true, and would have seen agreement from those on Malta, some was wishful thinking. It also gave a summary of operations:

- Bomber sorties 5,807
- Fighter sorties 5,667
- Reconnaissance sorties 345

The combined Italian and German claims were for seventy-three aircraft shot down (sixty-four confirmed and nine probable) and eighty-four on the ground (sixty-eight confirmed and fifteen probable). 'Although the results were good, they were not up to the expectations of the OBS, who issued the following directives for the last stage of operations:

1. Close co-operation must be maintained between Luftflotte 2 and the Sicilian Air Force in order to develop the process of disintegration of Malta with the aid of small formations to be employed by night and day.
2. The main objectives were to be those mentioned in the preceding plan which were not completely destroyed (equally important: airfield installations, barracks, AA batteries, stores and technical installations.
3. The enemy must be forced into combat, in order to use their inferior number of fighters.'

All sound tactics, especially using up the available fighters, but, again, the operational implementation fell short. The most accurate point made was: 'Malta was transformed from an offensive–defensive strategical base into an exclusively defensive one.' And there in lay the point. From a grand strategy point of view, Malta was an offensive base or else it was a drain on resources. If it had been negated, did it actually need to be invaded?

In its conclusions the memo stated: 'The neutralization of Malta is partial and temporary. It is necessary to continue and to increase blockade operations by using strong formations against the Eastern and Western approaches, so as to prevent the Island recovering or re-assuming the offensive, which would be extremely dangerous.' (Memorandum of the Malta Situation, 10 May 1942, Italian Air Staff, translated by AHB VII/57.

Another report by the Italians also referred to this period; considered as the fourth period of operations (20 March to 10 May 1942). 'During the first days of the second air offensive, reconnaissance over Malta revealed that there were 2 cruisers, 3 submarines, 2 merchant vessels

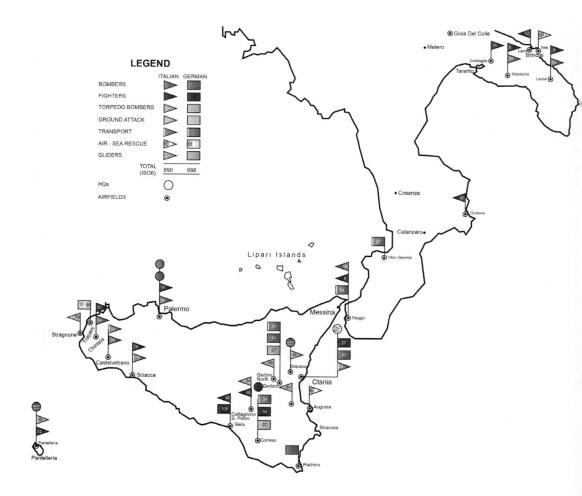

Situation map showing distribution of Axis aircraft for the planned invasion of Malta.

and about 160 aircraft, of which approximately 50 per cent were multi-engined. During the period of intensive operations, it was noted that there was an absence of submarine, and only an occasional appearance by one or two destroyers. The number of multi-engined bombers rapidly diminished until there were only 6 left. The number of single-engined aircraft was maintained at 40, by means of constant reinforcements.'

Among the indicators of success, it stated: 'Our transports bound for Italian N. Africa were carried out more frequently and regularly along the shorter route passing nearer Malta.' (Air and Naval Bases on Malta Situation Report May 1942 translated by AHB as VII/43)

Although the Italian report ends its fourth period of operations on 10 May, in reality, operations continued at pretty much the same pace throughout much of May. The 12th May brought a number of combats, and once again the defenders were able to put up a dominant force when thirty-two fighters, all but two being Spitfires, met six Ju 88s and twelve 109s that were after Hal Far. Combats were fairly inconclusive, although a Spitfire of 603 Squadron was lost, with the victor was also being quickly shot down.

The British Fighter Report of 12 May was a comprehensive document that looked at all aspects of operating fighters at Malta from a support and maintenance point of view. The following extracts focus on some of the key points. 'Fighters have never been operated from Malta to the present intensity. All available aircraft are at immediate readiness. All aircraft are widely dispersed in pens, as we cannot stand the risk of losing one by bombing. When aircraft land they must be turned around in the shortest possible time. This is about 12 minutes. Unless this is done, our fighters may easily be destroyed on the ground.'

The report goes on to praise the work of the groundcrew, who are on duty from 5.30 am to 8.30 pm, and that 'we could never reach our present standard of operating fighters except by generous assistance from the Army.' This was all about numbers, the RAF simply did not have enough ground staff. It stated that the total number of airmen – of all trades – on the island was only 1,950 and that in England 'a normal station of 32 aircraft has over 2,000 men.' The Army was also critical in supplying MT and 'if the Army MT is withdrawn the efficiency of our fighters collapses.' The author states that a Wellington bomber force is needed but 'the pens are not ready yet to give the Wellingtons adequate protection when they are on the ground. To accept them before they can be properly protected is to risk serious failure and loss of valuable aircraft.' He also stressed that to operate Wellingtons would require calling on the Army for more men.

The report then looked at the situation of the airfields, and this is worth quoting in full:

'Ta Kali. More than one all-weather aerodrome is essential. The winter is very wet. Ta Kali and Hal Far become unserviceable for days at a time. With only Luqa as all-weather we will be unable to operate fighters at the present intensity. This is very serious. Plans have been made for two all-weather strips off the aerodrome at Ta Kali. These take-off landing strips should be ready by 1st November.

'Safi: Three aerodromes on this Island is a very serious limitation. Safi can be made usable for take-off and landing for Hal Far and Luqa, should these aerodromes become unserviceable. There is much work to be done to make Safi usable. Rollers are a general limiting factor. It is important that Safi is prepared for take-off and landing at the earliest possible moment. Available rollers should be worked 24 hours out of the 24, with relief drivers.' Historians often focus on the exciting elements of air combat and neglect the maintenance, supply, infrastructure aspects of fighting a war. A lack of rollers could prevent aircraft operating, which would lead to more damage … for the want of a roller the battle was lost …

'Another long term work, and a very essential one, is perimeter tracks around all our aerodromes; it will quite impossible to operate Spitfires under the conditions obtaining last winter to our aerodromes, even at Luqa. Lorries were axle deep in mud and water. This work must be done before 1st November.

'Krendi: Work has been held up at Krendi landing strips for some considerable time owing to shortage of labour. Approaches to the aerodrome are very bad and must be cleared before we are able to use the aerodrome. There is also work for dispersal of aircraft. We should aim, if possible, in having Krendi available for operations by 1st November.'

'Hal Far: Luqa is the only aerodrome on which we can land bombers of the Wellington type. This is very serious. Work began on the Hal Far extensions some time ago, but was stopped owing to the shortage of labour. The available labour was then used on repairing aerodromes, increasing dispersal, and other far more vital and urgent work. The extension of Hal Far should be completed as soon as possible.'

The final section dealt with underground facilities, especially hangars and workshops: 'A programme is therefore necessary for building underground workshops at each aerodrome; also underground accommodation for feeding and housing the men. This is a very important item to maintain the aircraft on the island. Much work will be required at Luqa, but a ramp could easily be run down from Luqa aerodrome to the valley below and hangars cut in the rock on the same alignment as the Tal Handak petrol storage. Similar action should be taken at Hal Far in the quarry off the aerodrome. More work can be done at Kalafrana in the quarries in that area.'

This whole discussion about the number and all-weather usability of landing runs, and associated taxiways, is an important one; the success of Malta lay in its ability to keep operating its aircraft. The same is true of the complex pattern of protected dispersals and the various underground facilities, all of which made it increasingly difficult for the attackers to cause critical damage.

On 13 May the AOC expressed his thoughts on the Spitfire reinforcement flights: 'Serviceability today is 32 Spitfires. 16 more to arrive 16th May. Spitfires from Wasp and Eagle arrived 9th May and covered Welshman on 10th. When convoy arrives here would like next dose Spitfires to arrive day or two before arrival convoy. Third dose of Wasp and Eagle vital to protection of convoy when in harbour.' (Signal AOC Malta to CAS, 13 May).

The following day CAS responded: 'There is no possibility of another Wasp operation but we aim to get Spitfires into Malta by Eagle, as follows: 16 arriving about 18 May, 16 arriving about 25 May, 16 arriving about 6 June. There is no prospect of Spitfires long range tanks being available for direct flights to Malta from Gibraltar before July. In view of these limitation every effort should be made to conserve Spitfires consistent with vital operational needs of defence of Malta. Malta should avoid as far as possible accumulation of unserviceable Spitfires, firstly by concentrating on keeping serviceable those Spitfires which require least repair work, secondly by attempting to fly to Egypt those which require considerable repair but which can be made airworthy for the flight. By this means further damage to these aircraft would be avoided and a reserve of serviceable Spitfires would be built up in Egypt on which Malta could subsequently draw.' I am sure Malta would have viewed it as unlikely that they would get aircraft back from Egypt!

The scale of operations had started to reduce in by mid-May, with fewer attacks and smaller formations, increasingly by Italian formations, as the withdrawal of Luftwaffe units continued. On the 15th, for example, three SM.84s were escorted by thirty-plus MC.202s, although this was followed a short while later by a fighter sweep by forty-plus Bf 109s. Every attack was met by fighters

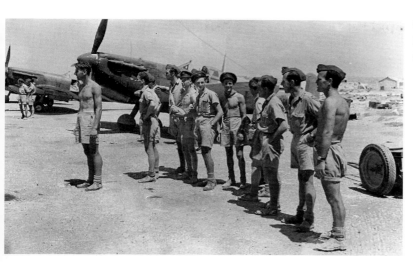

Groundcrew in 'casual hot weather 'dress'' with Spitfires in dispersal.

and every attack resulted in combats of varying intensity and result. On 18 May another batch of Spitfires arrived; the fifteen new arrivals more than making up for recent losses. With plenty of aircraft of a calibre capable of besting the Axis types, no shortage of pilots, and an effective RDF and control set-up, all Malta needed now was convoys to bring in supplies and thus truly break the siege.

20 May: 'Malta Fighter Pilot's three in an hour'. A press release stated: 'The pilot officer in the Malta night-fighter unit who shot down three Italian Breda 20 bombers on Saturday night actually accounted for them within an hour's flying. The first bomber was contacted soon after the night-fighter was airborne, and the pilot stole up to within a hundred yards before giving it a long burst. "I saw strikes on the tail unit and one engine," he said. "A large lump fell off the tail, and we saw him burning below us as he dived away. We later saw a large patch of fire on the sea, and it burned for two or three minutes."

'A quarter of an hour later the pilot sighted another bomber. He gave it a burst from very short range, and the port engine immediately started burning. That enemy aircraft was seen to crash in flames. The third bomber was contacted soon after it had dropped its bombs, which the pilot saw bursting below him. When eventually caught, the enemy aircraft was hit and an engine and the tail unit were damaged. The Italian bomber burst into flames and dived into the sea. The fighter pilot then returned to base. He has only been a little over two months on the island, but his score is four Br.20s and one Ju.88 destroyed.' (AMB 7047 dated 20 May).

The MC.202 was a much better fighter than its Italian predecessors and was a match for the Hurricanes, albeit the RAF pilots were of the opinion that the Italians were not very aggressive pilots and sought to avoid combat.

Axis shipping remained under attack in May. Following a conference attended by the squadron commander, 38 Squadron was instructed to maintain a detachment of torpedo aircraft at LG05 for the duration of the moon period. They were soon in action, a typical engagement being that of 22 May when an ASV Wellington of 221 Squadron worked with DV542 (Sergeant Youens) and AD597 (Sergeant Flanagan) of 38 Squadron: 'At 0130 hours Sergeant Youens received a revised position for convoy from ASV aircraft. He set course for estimated position, repeatedly checking by bearings on ASV aircraft. At 0215 hours Sergeant Youens sighted the convoy consisting of two destroyers and two MVs, one large of about 8–10,000 tons and the other 2–3,000 tons. The convoy was in echelon 1,200yd apart with the destroyers on the flanks. He attacked the large MV, approaching to the stern of the starboard destroyer. The destroyer opened fire with 12–14 Bofors-type guns, hitting the aircraft and causing damage. As the aircraft came round to the north-east of the convoy, Sergeant Youens saw a smoke screen beginning centering on the target ship. He could not see whether there was smoke coming from the stack or whether it was the result of a hit. The ASV aircraft reported that clouds of smoke were pouring from the ship and the next day a reconnaissance aircraft reported a large MV beached some 30 miles north of Benghazi with a gaping hole in the side. It is therefore claimed that Sergeant Youens hit the ship. The aircraft was damaged considerably, hits being registered on flaps, main surface and aileron of starboard wing, starboard side of fuselage, port engine cowling and port engine wheel covers. The aircraft succeeded in reaching LG05. Sergeant Flanagan did not sight the convoy until 0320 hours and it was effectively screened by smoke so that no favourable opportunity for attack was presented.' (38 Squadron ORB)

Torpedo strikes were also being made by the Malta detachment: 'Five aircraft torpedo strike from Malta led by Flt Lt Robinson; all aircraft were homed on to the Italian fleet successfully. The ASV aircraft dropped flares in an excellent position but great difficulty was experienced in trying to attack owing to a very thick smoke screen. Flying Officer Foulis succeeded in penetrating the smoke screen and managed to get in two attacks. He did not see any results due to the smoke screen but the ASV aircraft saw a red glow and it is thought that at least one of the torpedoes found its mark. The rest of the aircraft did not attack and brought their torpedoes back.' A similar attack was made the following night by five aircraft but, again, only one was able to drop both torpedoes.

Although the attacks on Malta were not yet over, and there was one more 'mini blitz' to come, the corner had indeed been turned and Allied commanders were now looking at putting Malta back on to the offensive.

INDIVIDUAL Scores for May 1942

S/Ldr Lawrence :   2 Ju88's Destroyed - 1 ME 109F Damaged

P/O Wigley D.F.C.:   1 Ju 87 Probably Destroyed - 2 Ju88's Damaged (posted)

P/O MacKay :   1 Ju 88 Destroyed - 1 Me 109F Damaged (posted)

P/O Broro :   1 Ju88 Destroyed - 1 Ju 87 Probably Destroyed - 1 Ju 87 Damaged - 2 Me 109f's Damaged

F/Sgt Yarra D.F.M. :   3 Me 109f's Destroyed - 2 RE1001's Destroyed - 1 Ju 88 Probably Destroyed - 1 Ju 88 Damaged - 1 Me 109F Damaged

Sgt Tweedale :   1 Ju88 Destroyed - 2 Me 109f's Destroyed - 1 Me 109F Probably Destroyed. (Deceased)

Sgt Boyd D.F.M :   2 Ju88's Probably Destroyed - 1 Ju88 Damaged. (Deceased)

Sgt Dodd :   1 Ju 87 Destroyed - 1 Me 109E Destroyed - 1 Mc 202 Probably Destroyed - 1 Me 109 Damaged

F/Sgt Farrany :   1 Mc 202 Probably Destroyed - 1 RE 1001 Damaged

P/O Lambert :   1 Me 109 Destroyed

P/O Hal Ford :   1 Ju 88 Destroyed

2.6.42.
F/Sgt Reio: 1 Cant 1003 Damaged
               1 RE 2001 Damaged

TOTAL: DESTROYED: 16
          PROBABLY DESTROYED: 8
          DAMAGED :   11

We lost 8 Pilots.

Score sheet for 185 Squadron for May 1942.

Chapter 6

Dominating the Sea Lanes: May 1942 to November 1942

T he need to protect Allied shipping was as great as the need to destroy Axis shipping, and in addition to the all-important Mediterranean convoys, this also included protecting coastal shipping along the shores of Egypt, Palestine and Syria. 'They were all liable to attack, either by bomber or submarine; and although most of them reached port unharmed, there were some losses, chiefly on the Tobruk run. A large number of Italian submarines were working in the Mediterranean at that time [early 1942]. Patrol aircraft kept watch for them 24 hours a day – the one patrol that never ends, nor will end until the hunt is ended. The results of the anti-submarine war are the most difficult of all to assess. Its successes are largely kept secret. But it can be said that of the many attacks made at this time on submarines by aircraft, mostly close inshore between Daba and Tobruk, several were successful. Nevertheless, we lost some ships to submarines on the Tobruk run.' (*RAF in Middle East, ibid*).

The hectic period for the Sunderlands in the eastern Mediterranean continued into May, four attacks and a number of other sightings being reported. Pilot Officer Howell (L5806) attacked a submarine on 1 May with bombs and DCs, the latter falling along the starboard side and causing the U-boat to 'slowly sink with no forward speed'. Flight Lieutenant Frame (W4022) was back in action on 11 May, dropping four AS bombs in an attack that appeared to damage the target. On 26 May it was Wing Commander Garside's turn again: 'At 1927 hours an ASV plot was obtained four miles on starboard beam and found on investigation to be a submarine on the surface. Attack was carried out with four 250lb AS bombs (set at one second delay) with flash bombs attached, and four 250lb depth charges set at 50ft with Mk X pistols. Bombs were observed to hit conning tower of U-boat. After smoke and spray had subsided no further trace of the submarine was seen. It is to be noticed that the flash bombs fitted to the AS bombs assisted greatly in observing result of attack. It is considered that the U-boat was destroyed. Three separate ASV plots of aircraft in close vicinity of attack were picked up immediately attack was completed. General impression being that these aircraft were circling submarine, on protective patrol, for they closed position of attack immediately after flash bombs was seen. Own aircraft continued to take evasive action.' (230 Squadron ORB, May 1942).

Although 202 Squadron operating from Gibraltar was still primarily a Catalina squadron, it did have a number of Sunderlands on strength for much of 1942, these flying ASPs in the Mediterranean and out into the Atlantic. Operational capability was increased by the detachments from other Sunderland squadrons, 10 Squadron RAAF deploying a number of aircraft to Gibraltar, and the occasional attachment of aircraft from other units. These increases were normally connected with specific operations, usually a particular convoy.

On 28 May, Flying Officer Pockley of 10 Squadron RAAF, flying W3983/R, was tasked to search for a submarine that had been attacked the previous day by a Catalina: 'Sighted oil patch with streak running ENE; saw U-boat at head of streak. Aircraft dived to attack from 1000ft up stern as U-boat turned sharply to port but was forced to take evading action owing to heavy gunfire, circled U-boat which remained surfaced. At 1415 dived to attack and raked U-boat with machine-gun fire, most of which struck conning tower. No depth charges dropped as run unsatisfactory – large quantity of light and medium flak put up by U-boat. At 1427 attacked from astern and large quantity of flak. As U-boat turned to port four depth charges released from 40ft, overshot and detonated 20–30 yards on starboard bow. Aircraft port bomb circuit unserviceable throughout so port depth charges manhandled to starboard bow racks for second attack. U-boat continually opened fire with large calibre gun when approached within 3 miles. At 1642 aircraft attacked up U-boat track as she turned to port, released four depth charges from 30ft which straddled U-boat from port to starboard across conning tower. U-boat completely lost to sight in spray, speed immediately reduced to 3–4kts and course became erratic. Subsequent observations showed large apparent dent on port side just forward of conning tower near waterline. Aircraft sustained several hits, considerable trouble experienced with aircraft machine-guns during action, three of the four tail guns being u/s. Nose gun went u/s during first attack. Great need was felt throughout entire action for forward-firing cannon as extremely heavy damage could have been inflicted on U-boat during and after above attacks. At 1825 aircraft led a Hudson to the U-boat.' The submarine made it back to port two days later.

Back at Malta, the offensive mission was back on within days of Kesselring declaring that the blitz had succeeded and Malta was finished. It seems that no one told Malta that! The next Wellington detachment arrived on the 24th, from 104 Squadron. It was in action immediately, and suffered its first loss on the night of the 28th when Z8366 (Sergeant R. Hills) had an engine failure on the way to attack Catania airfield. Dumping as much weight as possible, the Wellington headed back to Malta but crashed near Attard in the centre of the island, so close to making it back to Luqa. Four of the crew were killed. The Wellingtons of 221 Squadron scored a success on the night of 30/31 May, claiming the 6,836-ton *Gino Allegri*, a claim shared with the submarine *Proteus*.

The last week of May was the quietest of the month for the defenders, with few significant attacks, no doubt in part as the Germans and Italians shuffled units around, the former continuing to be moved to higher priority tasks and the latter seemingly unwilling to take on the role of keeping Malta 'under control'. Among the awards to Malta personnel for summer 1942 was a DFC to Squadron Leader Stanley Grant of 249 Squadron, the citation reading: 'This officer is an excellent fighter pilot. On one occasion he led a force of fighter aircraft over many miles of sea into Malta. On the same day, after his aircraft had been refuelled, he took off and destroyed a Junkers 88. For the rest of the day he remained at the head of his squadron in a series of fierce battles over the island. He has destroyed at least 4 enemy aircraft and damaged many more.' (AMB 7174 dated 5 June). He was awarded a bar to the DFC in January 1943, by which time he was a wing commander.

Spitfires and Beaufighter
at Ta Kali, summer 1942.

June started with the arrival of more fighters and more bombers. On the 3rd, Operation Tilden/Style saw HMS *Eagle* deliver twenty-seven Spitfires, while a detachment of Wellingtons arrived from 38 Squadron. There was something of a disaster though when four of the Spitfires were shot down, their formation having been bounced by 109s operating out of Pantelleria. It is possible there was an element of complacency, as recent reinforcement runs had met with few problems. Two of the Spitfires came down near Pantelleria and two near Gozo. Other than this, it was fairly quiet at Malta; there were some raids but they were now usually picked up early by radar and the fighters vectored to intercept off the coast. It was rare now for there to be more than one raid a day.

The 9th brought another thirty-two Spitfires, courtesy of the same carrier under Operation Maintop/Salient. One of the new arrivals was Sergeant George Beurling, who was posted to 249 Squadron and was to become possibly the best-known of Malta's fighter pilots. Like the other Malta 'character', Adrian Warburton, Beurling had not had a sterling career so far, as he was something of a rebel and had been marked by 'those in authority' as a difficult character. Like Warburton, this 'difficult character' was now in the right place at the right time.

The aircraft and pilot reinforcements enabled Malta to achieve its highest defensive capability to date, with its established Spitfire squadrons now manned, in the main, by experienced pilots and with the squadrons themselves having established an esprit de corps, especially the three 'Malta' squadrons, 126, 185 and 249.

In the first part of June Malta was still not part of the anti-shipping effort, this role falling to aircraft based in Egypt and North Africa, although eastern Med patrols were flown from other bases as well.

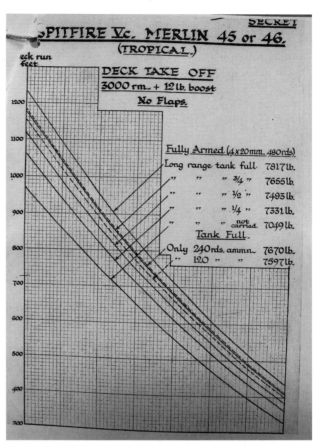

Deck take-off chart for Spitfire operations.

Sunderland of 10 Squadron RAAF, 8 May 1942. Note oil streak at top of picture.

The main anti-submarine effort remained with the Sunderlands. The 6th June saw the Australian Sunderlands in action again when Flight Lieutenant Marks dropped eight depth charges on a U-boat, probably the Italian submarine *Brin*; although no damage was inflicted to the submarine it did manage to hit the Sunderland in the starboard engine and float. The following day it was 202 Squadron's turn to find and attack a U-boat, the crew dropping a perfect straddle on their first run. Another four DCs were dropped as the U-boat submerged. The most likely victim was the *Veniero* as Italian records show that this submarine went missing at around this time.

The 13th June saw another attack by a 10 Squadron crew, Squadron Leader Burrage dropping depth charges on a surfaced submarine (both the *Bronzo* and the *Otario* claimed to have been subjected to air attack this day; most records credit the aircraft with damaging the latter). An account of this attack was included in the Coastal Command Review: 'At 0832, Sunderland O/202, from Gibraltar, flying at 4000ft sighted a submarine 9 miles ahead, making 12 kts. The aircraft dived and attacked on the beam, releasing seven Depth Charges, set to 25ft, one hung up. They straddled the submarine forward, and the explosion obscured it completely. When seen again, it appeared to be listing heavily to starboard and slightly up by the stern, but righted itself immediately. A thick stream of brown smoke poured out behind the conning tower for the next half-hour. As the aircraft circled, the submarine kept its bows always turned toward it and fired the forward gun. At 0950 the remaining Depth Charge had been changed to a serviceable rack and the aircraft was turning to make another attack when the submarine was suddenly lost to sight.'

The other concern of the planners was how to provide convoys with air cover against enemy bombers; the normal range of Malta's protective air umbrella was 60–70 miles, but the majority of the naval escort would have turned back by then, leaving the supply ships exposed. Discussions on how to extend the air cover inevitably led to the thought of long-range tanks, as used during the ferrying trips. Lloyd decided that this was a task for 601 Squadron, and as part of the plan it was to maintain a flight of four over the ships, which meant that twelve aircraft would be airborne at the same time – four on station and four on the way back to base or on the way out to take over. This would give each flight a reasonable time on station. The plan also said that if a raid was in place then any aircraft nearby (just left or just about to leave) would abandon its fuel plan and join the fight, ditching when out of fuel if that was what it took. Once ships were in normal range then other fighter units would take over. Long range fighters were best and a Beaufighter detachment of eleven aircraft of 235 Squadron arrived on the 11th.

Meanwhile, the situation in Malta was becoming critical with severe shortages of fuel and other supplies, and it was essential that a relief convoy should break the siege. To improve the chances of success, one convoy was to be despatched from Alexandria and a second from the UK via Gibraltar, with both timed to arrive at Malta within twenty-four hours of each other. Fortunately, the air assault on Malta had reduced in intensity because Rommel needed the offensive aircraft from Sicily to build up his strength for the final push on Cairo. As a consequence, the main danger to the convoys came from the Italian Battle Fleet based at Taranto, which had the capability of putting massive striking power to sea. To counter this threat, two squadrons of torpedo-armed Beauforts and six torpedo Wellingtons were put on standby. No. 217 Squadron flew its Beauforts to Malta while 39 Squadron moved a force to the ALG at Sidi Barrani. By the end of the first week of June a strike force comprising a mixed Beaufort unit, primarily 39 Squadron but joined by 217 Squadron (Wing Commander Davis) and supported by the Beaufighters of 235 Squadron, had been gathered for anti-convoy strikes. This reinforcing of units was in connection with the planned June convoys.

Loaded with vehicles, this MV was the victim of an RAF air attack – the credit being awarded to a Beaufort.

Under the overall name Operation Julius, two convoys were planned to run to Malta in mid-June to try to alleviate the growing supply problem. They were Operation Harpoon, the western convoy, and Vigorous, the eastern convoy, which comprised eleven merchant ships. Heavy enemy action was anticipated. The report on Operation Julius detailed the 'air forces employed'. The Wellingtons of 104 Squadron were moved out on 11 June to make room for other aircraft, with 235 Squadron's first eleven aircraft arriving the same day (and three others a few days later). The report stated: 'The general state of armament maintenance was very poor. We were hard pressed to make the aircraft fit for operations in the time available.'

It was also not greatly impressed with 217 Squadron's Beauforts, of which nine arrived on the 10th and a further six two days later: 'The Squadron was newly formed and did not know each other. The ASV operators were generally very inexperienced. Of the first nine aircraft to arrive none had full torpedo equipment. Although the Squadron had been at Gibraltar for a week, no action had been taken to check equipment which, on arrival, was in such confusion that all had to be removed and sorted out. By calling on the dockyard, and other local resources, nine aircraft were serviceable on the 13th June.'

It had no comment on the six Wellington of 38 Squadron that arrived on the 12th, or Malta's three PRU Spitfires, four Wellington VIIIs, five night Beaufighters (1435 Flight), or the FAA 'four torpedo and three ASV aircraft.' However: 'Six Baltimores arrived from Middle East; crews were generally inexperienced, and there was much trouble with wireless equipment and IFF.' The final comments concerned Spitfires: 'The daily average Spitfire serviceability for the operation was 95. A number were fitted with Spitfire long-range tanks to provide long range cover, but as these were limited, local adapted Hurricane tanks of 44 gallons were used for 24 aircraft – this modification worked well and tanks could easily be jettisoned.'

The report also stated that: 'It would have been impossible to have maintained all these aircraft at immediate readiness, and for very quick turn round, but for the help of the Army. All work was stopped in the Command Repair Shops, to provide a nucleus of skilled tradesmen in pens for each aircraft, where a complete maintenance crew was always at readiness.' The Army support was nearly 1,200 officers and men, plus two tanks and fourteen Bren carriers (for towing duties).

'At last light on 14th June a Spitfire on reconnaissance reported two cruisers and four destroyers leaving Palermo.' (*RAF in Middle East, ibid*). It was clear these would head towards the westbound convoy, Harpoon. 'There was a scant force of strike aircraft on the island at the time – two Beauforts with crews far from experienced, and four naval Albacores. These aircraft were assembled and sent out against the Italian warships, with a cover of 16 Spitfires to hold off the swarm of Messerschmitts. The Beauforts led the torpedo attack, hitting the leading cruiser and setting her on fire. After them came the Albacores which hit and severely damaged one of the escorting destroyers. The Italian surface force

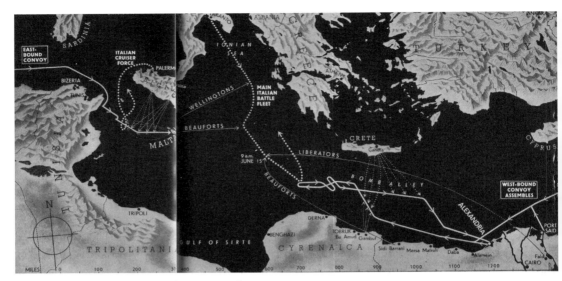

The battle of the June convoys, from east and west.

withdrew without any further attempt to sink the convoy. Albacores had another try for the warships during the afternoon. Once again they scored two hits on a cruiser and a probable on a destroyer, for the loss of one Albacore. But within an hour or so the major attack developed, this time from the air. Before dusk two large formations of escorted dive bombers had inflicted damage which slowed up the whole convoy considerably during the night. Whereas it should have been only 110 miles from Malta next morning [16th], within range of protection from Spitfires, in fact it was still 140 miles away; the Spitfires covered it nevertheless, straining petrol endurance. Under the protection of their guns the ships were damaged no more. The Spitfires and Beaufighters fought all day for the sky above, shooting down 13, probably destroying four and damaging another 13 enemy aircraft. We lost five Spitfires but saved four pilots. The warships and the convoy with some losses came into Valetta harbour, bringing at least some of the supplies which Malta needed for its existence.' (*RAF in Middle East, ibid*).

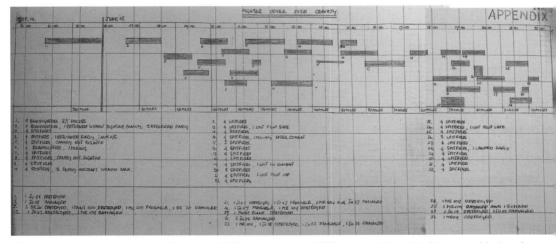

The fighter cover plan for Op Julius, from 2100 on 14 June to 2200 on the 15th, with thirty-two blocks of cover, primarily Spitfires.

The damage to the convoy was somewhat worse than this account suggests. The cruiser squadron had continued towards the convoy, which drew its limited destroyer protection away, and two destroyers were damaged by gunfire. Aircraft sank three merchant ships and also finished off the destroyer *Bedouin*. A merchant ship had also been sunk the previous day by aircraft, which left just two from the original six. The convoy then ran into a minefield, damaging one supply ship and sinking a destroyer. So the net result was that two of six supply ships reached Malta, for the cost of four supply ships sunk, two destroyers sunk, and three destroyers and a cruiser damaged.

For the eastbound convoy, Vigorous, the battle was even harder. 'Throughout the 14th, Baltimores from Malta swept back and forth over the water looking for them. One Baltimore saw two battleships, four cruisers and eight destroyers about 70 miles south of Taranto, steaming south. Just as darkness was falling, a photographic Spitfire sped across Taranto harbour and confirmed that the main enemy battle fleet had sailed.' (*RAF in Middle East, ibid*).

By this time, two of the eleven supply ships had already been lost to air attack, with another two damaged. Soon after nightfall on 14 June, three Wellingtons left Malta and four left North African bases to search for the fleet, with Malta also sending a second force of torpedo-armed Wellingtons to search the Ionian Sea. 'They found the battle fleet, nearer the coast of Greece than that of Sicily. The Wellingtons circled it, preparing to run across and launch torpedoes. The enemy destroyers wheeled swiftly round the battleships, laying a thick smoke screen through which some of the Wellingtons managed to attack, with what results they could not see.' At some point the cruiser *Trento* was disabled by air attack, and it may have been from the Wellington force.

Pat Gibbs produced an unofficial report in late 1942 dealing with Beaufort ops from Malta, which he circulated at staff level. He was the most experienced and successful torpedo leader in theatre – but his report could be read as very scathing of command and leadership, and he was ordered to withdraw it, destroy copies, and state who had seen it: 'I have seen him, pointed out the errors of his ways, and instructed him to withdraw all copies of his report and inform me when he has done so.' This from no less a person than the VCAS.

Fortunately, not all copies were destroyed; the author was surprised to find one, having failed to find it in the mid-1980s when researching for his history of 39 Squadron, with which squadron he was serving at the time. The report is comprehensive and while it is a personal view by Gibbs, and does contain a number of barbed comments, the majority of it is a solid account of the tactics and operations. It was probably lines such as 'this parochial and narrow-minded attitude I consider despicable', words that VCAS had underlined, that caused the 'upset'!

Gibbs lists four operations for the day, not all from Malta:

15th June (A)

- PRU Spitfire covered Taranto on the evening of June 14th and observed Italian fleet had sailed. ASV Wellingtons located [fleet] during night of 14th/15th June
- Italian battle fleet east of Malta, 9 Beauforts, no air escort, all aircraft dropped torpedoes and all returned, one Beaufort damaged
- No recco after attack; several hits claimed on battleship and cruisers
- It was intended to attack in sub-flights at first light, but squadron failed to join up in darkness and aircraft arrived over target at intervals individually, the majority after sunrise.

15th June (B)

- Maryland of 203 Squadron located target and homed force on to it by 'Rooster'
- Italian battle fleet east of Malta; 1 Littorio, 1 Cavour, 2 CRs, 15 D/Rs. 12 Beauforts of 39 Squadron; fighter attack en route to target; 3 aircraft missing and 4 returned damaged to base before strike

- No recco after attack; several hits claimed on Cavour
- Attack by sub-flights in succession on port bow, approach from dead ahead.

15th June (C)
- CR force seen by PRU Spitfire leaving Palermo on evening of 14th June, and sighted off Pantelleria at first light 15th by Beaufighter.
- 2 Italian CRs, 3 D/Rs; 2 Beauforts, no air escort, both aircraft dropped torpedoes, both damaged
- Hits claimed on CR
- Individual attacks.

15th June (D)
- Maryland of 203 Squadron sighted Italian battle fleet heading back to Taranto during afternoon of June 15th
- Italian battle fleet in South Ionian Sea; 9 Beauforts, no air escort, target was not located and all aircraft returned.

The official account given in the operations log is sparse and Ralph Barker's account (in *The Ship Busters*) of the strike provides a more graphic view of this operation. As well as giving a first class account of the strike, reconstructed from the memories of crews that took part, it gives an excellent insight into Beaufort operations generally.

A pair of 39 Squadron Beauforts; the squadron established a reputation from North Africa and Malta as the 'ship busters'.

'They flew at fifty feet along the coastline past Gambut, past Tobruk, past Gazala. At last they were off Derna, near the northernmost promontory of Cyrenaica. From this point they would be flying directly away from the mainland. The danger of fighters would be behind them. It was here that they met their first mischance. Some miles behind the formation, one of the tail gunners saw splashes in the water. He took them to be falling bombs. There was no shipping in sight, he could see no aircraft, and he was puzzled. He called his skipper.

"'I can see what look like bombs falling in the water about five miles behind us. Can't see anything else."

"'Keep your eyes peeled." The splashes had not been caused by bombs. A formation of Bf 109s had been on the way from an airfield near Derna to give protection to German bombers attacking the British westbound convoy. They had been carrying long-range tanks. When they saw the Beauforts, they jettisoned their auxiliary tanks and gave chase. The German fighters attacked from the southeast, diagonally behind the Beauforts. Many of the crews saw nothing until the Beaufort on the extreme left of the formation suddenly broke in half at the turret, the two parts crashing into the sea independently, the front half in flames. All the Beauforts weaved frantically, very close together, the tail gunners firing at the fighters whenever they came within range. Several of the guns in the new Mk.IIs jammed. Nevertheless, the German pilots showed great caution, picking out only the most rearward of the weaving Beauforts and diving down from the beam to a position astern. In this way the corresponding Beaufort of the extreme right was shot down. The pilot, formerly on Sunderlands, had asked for a posting which would give him more action. It was his first torpedo operation.

'Mason found himself last but one in the shattered formation. The distinction of being last now fell to a sergeant-pilot named Daffurn. His gunner called up to tell him that three fighters were on his tail. He was a long way behind the leader. His gunners opened up at the 109s, but the guns jammed almost at once. The wireless op fired a long burst from the side guns, and was immediately silenced himself by return fire, pieces of shrapnel piercing his hand, arm and legs. The three fighters were now attacking together, one from the port quarter, one from the starboard quarter, one from dead astern. Daffurn's tail gunner gave him the position of the fighters and a running commentary on the fall of the tracer. All Daffurn could do was to weave continually. Suddenly his feet shot off the rudder bars as the rudder received a direct hit. The tail gunner watched the rudder jerking brokenly from side to side. Daffurn's feet were thrust back and forth

39 Squadron Beaufort – a conversation in the cockpit.

and the aircraft swung from left to right, out of control. With a tremendous effort he forced his feet down on the rudder bars and at last held them steady. He found that the control wires had also been damaged, the rudder only operating when the pedals were completely depressed.

'All this time, as the aircraft weaved involuntarily and even more violently, the cone of fire of the fighters had been searching for them. Bursts of fire struck them from time to time, the radio was shot clean out of its housing, tracer disappeared into the engine nacelles, and the aircraft, now a flying collander, whistled shrilly as it went along. But miraculously the engines still responded and Daffurn flew on. Daffurn, with a badly damaged aircraft, no guns, no radio, and an injured gunner, decided it was hopeless to continue and turned back for Sidi Barrani. Some of the others found their petrol consumption so increased during the running fight that they now had no hope at all of striking and reaching Malta, and they too turned back. When Mason finally took stock, he found that he had only five of his twelve aircraft left.

'A Maryland had gone on ahead to reconnoitre and to home the Beauforts on to the target by radar. Mason's wireless operator identified the transmission at fifty miles range. Their track was good. Visibility was unlimited and they were some ten miles distant when they caught their first glimpse of the battle fleet. In the same moment, the Maryland appeared and fired off a star cartridge in the direction of the target. The Italian ships were almost dead ahead, slightly to port. Most of the flak was bursting above them at 200 feet. The Beauforts started taking evasive action, gently at first and then increasingly as they closed the range. Mason's original plan of attack had been to lead six aircraft himself round to the starboard side of the battleships while Gibbs took his six straight in on the port side. Mason now had two other aircraft with him, and Gibbs one. Mason intended to stick to the same plan.

'At five miles range there was a tremendous bang underneath Gibbs' aircraft, and it floundered for a moment, but Gibbs soon brought it under control. The undercarriage had been damaged and the hydraulics punctured, but the torpedo was still there. Mason had just begun to swing away to port to skirt the leading destroyers, so as to develop his attack from starboard of the battleships, and Gibbs was just turning to starboard, when the leading battleship itself began to turn. Since the battleship was bows on to them, and any turn it made must present them with a beam shot, Mason and Gibbs arrested their turns and came back on to their original course. The leading battleship was clearly turning to starboard. Soon they would be able to see the whole length of it. Mason and Gibbs both took the chance offered them and went for the leading battleship. But as Gibbs lined up on the target, his aircraft and that of the aircraft formating on him, flown by Dick Marshall, an Australian, were hit by flak from the destroyers. Oil seeped all over the floor of Gibbs' aircraft, and Marshall had his rudder control shot away, his elevator-trimmer control cut and his hydraulics punctured. Both pilots were thus forced to drop their torpedoes prematurely at some 2,000 yards distance. Mason saw the two aircraft break away across him just before he dropped.'

All five Beauforts survived the attack and reached Malta. Gibbs belly-landed his damaged Beaufort while Marshall swung as he landed and hit a damaged Beaufort of 217 Squadron on the edge of the runway. Both aircraft burst into flames and were destroyed. Marshall and his crew escaped. Had their numbers not been reduced by more than half off Derna, no doubt 39 Squadron would have registered a hit. As it was, they claimed several; but the smoke they saw rising from the *Littorio* was the result of a direct hit from a 500lb bomb dropped by the Liberators just before the torpedo attack, although some accounts credit a torpedo Wellington as causing the damage. Despite the fact that this strike had caused no critical damage to the Italian fleet, it was discovered, later in the day, that the Italians had turned around and were heading back to Taranto. It was too late to stop the Alexandrian convoy returning to port, but the strike had distracted the enemy battle fleet and given it cause to reflect on the dangers from Allied aircraft. This turn back was a major disappointment and was largely based on the lack of AA ammunition, some 80 per cent having already been used up. The western convoy managed to pass ships to Malta, but Operation Vigorous was cancelled because of the presence of the Italian fleet. Malta's fighters had been providing convoy cover from the moment it came within range, and by the time operations had finished five Spitfires had been lost.

There were Beaufighters up as escort and one 235 Squadron aircraft was shot down. Its pilot, Warrant Officer Armitage, survived but his navigator (Sergeant Hector) was killed. His debrief report, after his escape in September 1943 before the Germans took over his camp, stated: 'I took off from Malta in a Beaufighter on 15 Jun 1942 to escort aircraft attacking two Italian cruisers. I was late taking off and never saw the planes I was to escort. I saw an Allied convoy being attacked by Fiat BI.20s and I went in and engaged them. I shot down one aircraft and damaged another BI.20 and a fighter. During this engagement I was hit and crashed into the sea. Five hours later I was picked up an Italian Red Cross plane and taken to Trapani military hospital, where I remained for about six weeks.' He ended up in Campo 78 Sulmona, becoming part of a tunnel team for escape, but on 12th September 1943 he walked out of the camp and eventually met British troops on the 17th October.

The 15 June operations around the convoy was also significant in that it saw the first United States Army Air Force (USAAF) mission in the Mediterranean theatre. Among the Allied bombers attacking the Italian fleet were seven B-24 Liberators from the Halverson Project (HALPRO) operating out of Egypt alongside 205 Group. The B-24s dropped a number of 500lb bombs and claimed hits of near misses on the *Littorio*. Details of the USAAF operations in the Western Desert are covered in *The Desert Air Force in World War II: Air Power in the Western Desert 1940–1942*, Ken Delve, Pen & Sword, 2017). The main USAAF contribution to operations in the North African theatre would not be made until Operation Torch in November, but the bombers, HALPRO and later others, did contribute to the Mediterranean War prior to that. The majority of missions in this regard were against port targets; the first of these was to Benghazi on the night of 21/22, nine aircraft bombing the port under flares dropped by RAF aircraft. The main target for the USAAF for the month though was Tobruk, with ops on a number of nights in later June, one of which also saw the first combat loss, a B-24 being lost over Tobruk on the night of 29/30 (Captain F.E. Nestor and crew).

The Operation Julius report drew a number of lessons: 'A need was felt for a bombing force to neutralize enemy aerodromes, particularly Catania, where dispersal is bad, and Comiso, where the Ju.87s are based. In any repeat operation of this nature, a fast day bomber, preferably a dive-bomber should be provided. Suitable aircraft are the Boston, or a fighter bomber such as the Kittyhawk.'

It also stated that with longer nights the convoy should be under Malta air cover by dawn, thus reducing risk, but also that: 'Beaufighter cover in the Sicilian Channel in daylight is fraught with the gravest danger. The crews had a very difficult time with Me.109s and Macchi 202s. Beaufighters are admirable beyond range of the single seater fighter, but within their range, are not the aircraft for the job.'

At the routine conference between Hitler and C-in-C Navy (15 June), the Mediterranean and Malta were part of the

15.6.42

F/Lt WEST : 1 ME.09F DESTROYED
            1 JU 88 PROBABLY DESTROYED
F/SGT SIM : 1 JU 88 DESTROYED
P/O STENBORG : 2 JU 88's DAMAGED
P/O BROAD : 1 ME 109 DESTROYED

15.6.42.
        Today the boys did a protective patrol over the Welshman. This is the first sign of the convoy we have seen so far. However it is rumoured that the ships will be within range of our Spits tomorrow or the next day.

The 185 Squadron entry for a protective patrol over the *Welshman*.

Welshman enters Grand Harbour ahead of the remainder of the convoy.

agenda: 'Operation Herkules (capture of Malta). The Fuhrer recognizes how important it is to capture Malta. However, he does not believe that this can be done while the offensive on the Eastern Front is in progress, and especially not with Italian troops. Once Malta has been bled white by the continuous air raids and the total blockade, we could risk the attack.'

The cannon and machine gun armament of the Beaufighter made it a great anti-flak escort, and the anti-shipping missions were provided with Beaufighter escort whenever possible.

The reality was that Hitler, and thus German strategy, was focused on Russia and with resources stretched, priority was always for the Eastern Front, especially for aircraft. Rommel's troops took Tobruk on 21 June, a major loss to the Allies, both in terms of morale and the fact that it provided another port for the Germans to use. The only positive that day was the sinking of the 7,744-ton *Reichenfels* by Beauforts. This was listed in Gibb's report: '21st June: Convoy seen to leave Palermo p.m. 20th; searched for by ASV Wellington during night and by Baltimore on morning of 21st. Convoy of 2 MVs, 1 D/R, 1 flak ship off Lampedusa; 8 Beauforts, escort of 9 Beaufighters, enemy fighters encountered, 3 Beauforts missing, 2 returned badly damaged. Baltimore photographed after attack. 1 MV set on fire and sunk. Attack by sub-flights after approach on the beam.'

Despite the focus on the Eastern Front, on 22 June Kesselring was in the newly captured Tobruk meeting with Rommel and the dual strategy was still in their minds. Tobruk having fallen, the dual strategy was push to Egypt AND take Malta. Kesselring in his memoirs continually states that one without the other would not work, but we must take a certain degree of post-war 'told you so' in this. Rommel was certainly focused on Egypt and to him Malta was irrelevant as long as that base did not have an impact on his supplies, which of course it did.

The plans for an invasion of Malta had been in hand since February 1942 and in his memoirs Kesselring says, of his points made at the Tobruk meeting: 'The assault on the island must be the next step. The allocation of forces in the plan had been so calculated that failure was out of the question. Two parachute divisions under General Student had been brought in, including the Italian 2nd Parachute Division. Troop-transport aircraft, heavy freight-carrying aircraft and [Messerschmitt] Giants for tank transport were also available in ample quantities. In addition, there were two to three Italian assault divisions, elements of the battle fleet to shell the island fortifications and to escort the troop transports and assault aircraft, and air formations in rather greater strength than had been used for the original attack. The draft plan for the operation broadly had the following shape:

1. Attack by airborne troops to seize the southern heights as a jumping-off base for an assault to capture the airfields south of the town and the harbour of La Valetta, shortly preceded by a bombing raid on the airfields themselves and anti-aircraft positions.
2. Main attack by naval forces and landing parties against the strong-points south of La Valetta and, in conjunction with parachute troops, on the harbour itself, synchronized with bombing raids on coastal batteries.
3. Diversionary attack from the sea against the bay of Marsa Scirocco.'

(Memoirs of Field Marshal Albert Kesselring).

In 1947 the Air Historical Branch translated a study prepared by the Italian Air Ministry entitled *The Plan for the Occupation of Malta (Operation 'C3')*. This document makes fascinating reading, although it is too long to include as an annex in this book. 'The Italian Air Staff put forward to the Chief of the General Staff the view that the capture of Malta was primarily an air operation and that the ground and naval operations were necessarily of a supporting nature.' Considering the lack of amphibious assault areas – Malta is a rocky island with cliffs and few bays or beaches – air assault was certainly the only option. 'It was assumed that a total force of not less than 1,000 aircraft of all types would be needed in order to maintain strong and unceasing attacks and at the same time to carry out the following tasks, in co-operation with the naval forces:

- Blockade of the island
- Protection of transport
- Transport operation
- Protection of naval forces
- Attacks on shipping

The aircraft projection was for 578 aircraft from the Reggia (240 fighters, 140 bombers, 30 torpedo-carriers, 18 dive-bombers, 30 assault aircraft – which were defined as CR.42s with glider bombs, 120 transport aircraft) and a further 500 from Luftflotte 2. The original plan that envisaged an assault in early May had two options, the preferred one being a 'coup de main' by air assault just after twilight.

However, 'with the change in the situation on the Island, due to the transfer of fighters there and the supply of arms and ammunition by the minelayer *Manxman*, the 'coup de main' plan was scrapped, and the possibilities of an attack in force were considered. This revised operation would 'consist of a quick succession of violent attacks so as to gain a beachhead for the landing of forces, afterwards developing into an operation leading to the possession of the whole island. The number of paratroops available for the operation was considered adequate to resist for several hours so as to establish a good footing for further operations.'

It was decided that the operation should take place at full moon and in favourable weather conditions, with the main landing at Marsa Scirocco [Marsaxlokk] and the secondary landing, of light forces, on the south-west coast. There was concern over British naval interference: 'In order to combat the possible intervention of naval forces from Alexandria and Gibraltar, it was arranged that all the bomber and torpedo-bomber units, together with fighter units and assault aircraft if necessary, which were stationed in Sardinia, Libya and the Aegean as well as the torpedo-bomber units based on Sicily should attack these forces. These Italian forces were listed as:

- Sardinia: 36th T-B Stormo, 51st Bomber Gruppo, 24th Fighter Gruppo
- Aegean Rhodes: 104th T-B Gruppo, 161st Fighter Gruppo
- Aegean Gadura: 41st T-B Gruppo, 47th Bomber Stormo
- Libya K2: 131st T-B Gruppo, 133rd T-B Gruppo, 3rd Fighter Gruppo
- Libya K3: 150th Fighter Stormo
- Libya: 35th Bomber Stormo, 50th Assault Stormo, 2nd and 4th Fighter Stormo, and 12th and 160th Fighter Gruppo
- Sicily Pantelleria: 130th and 132nd T-B Gruppo.

On 30 May the Supreme Command had issued an order that in order to prepare for Operation 'C3', all air transport to Italian North Africa was to be suspended from 1 June. The Naval Supreme

Command seemed less than enthusiastic and in its study, concluded: 'The operation was, without doubt, one of great difficulty, because the defences could be considered one of the most highly concentrated in the World. It was estimated that the coastal defences of the Island consisted of 85 naval batteries, including 19 of heavy calibre; various types of defensive obstructions in the most important bays, besides those in the port of Valetta; submerged barbed wire entanglements along the beaches; all kinds of defences (both active and passive), including high tension wire entanglements and mines on the beaches. In addition, there were airfields encircling the archipelago. As the batteries were either in caves or in well-protected gun emplacements, they were not very vulnerable either from the sea or the sky.'

In the event, the need to dedicate resources to Rommel's offensive led to yet another postponement of the plan, and within a few months its total abandonment. The Axis had missed their chance; they likely could have taken Malta in 1940, 1941 or early 1942 … instead, it was Malta that would take part, in 1943, in the invasion of Sicily. The defenders did not know it yet, but Malta was safe and on the up!

The latter part of June brought significant success to Malta's strike force. In the afternoon of the 20th, a recce Baltimore on patrol over the Ionian Sea picked up a convoy of two large MVs with a destroyer escort heading to Messina. A strike force of eleven Beauforts, escorted by eight Beaufighters went on the hunt but failed to find the target. However, it was picked up again off Cape Spartivento in the evening by the PRU Spitfire. An ASV Wellington was airborne to track this but also search the western convoy route, and it was accompanied, some distance behind, by a strike force of three Albacores. Again, there was no result, but the next morning (21st) a Baltimore picked up an even better target, what appeared to be three unescorted troopship (liners) 60 miles south of Cape Bon. A strike force of five Beauforts (217 Squadron) with six Beaufighters (235 Squadron) set out, but found a convoy of two large MVs (7,000–8,000 tons), which they promptly attacked, while the Beaufighters engaged the flak ship and the three aircraft that were over the convoy, all of which they claimed as destroyed (two Ju 88s and one SM.79). The Beauforts claimed to have hit both MVs, sinking the *Reichenfels*. Two Beauforts were shot down by flak.

While in Malta, Gibbs proposed that a small detachment of 39 Squadron should operate from the island, as the bases in Egypt were proving to be at such extreme range from most targets. Back in Egypt a few days later, he continued to press his views and eventually secured agreement for a detachment of five aircraft to operate, under his command, from Malta. The first of these experimental detachments of five aircraft arrived at Luqa on 22 June and for the next few weeks operated with the twelve Beauforts of 217 Squadron. This was the first chance Gibbs had had to apply some of the hard-learned lessons from his torpedo operations over the North Sea. He was a firm believer in strikes by formations

Baltimore preparing for a reconnaissance sortie; 69 Squadron remained Malta's main recce unit.

of nine to twelve aircraft, attacking from both sides to split the defensive fire. He also believed that the air escort, usually Beaufighters, should be used for flak suppression as well as taking on enemy fighters.

A convoy had been noted by air recce in Palermo on the 22nd and 221 Squadron sent its Wellingtons on a patrol between Naples and Marettimo to bomb the ships if they tried to leave Palermo, as well as looking for targets of opportunity. At the same time, a torpedo Wellington force was sent out so as to be close at hand if targets were found; in the early hours of the 23rd an ASV Wellington picked up the convoy 35 miles east of Palermo. Over the next few hours. Wellingtons bombed these and another convoy east of Ustica Island; one Wellington attacked from 1,200ft with four 500lb bombs, claiming a hit on the stern on one ship, which was subsequently credited as damaged. The main action was to be on the 23rd and was against the original convoy. Thus, on the 23 June, twelve Beauforts of 217 and 39 Squadrons, led by Wing Commander Davies and Squadron Leader Gibbs, left Luqa to attack a convoy in the Ionian Sea. The aircraft, in four sub-flights of three aircraft, positioned to approach the convoy of two heavily laden MVs and four destroyers, and then turn in to attack both MVs from both sides simultaneously. In the attack, two Beauforts were shot down and one was so badly damaged that it crash-landed back at Malta. However, one MV was hit and was seen stern down and stationary. A reconnaissance sortie later in the day relocated the convoy in Taranto harbour and discovered that one MV was so badly damaged that its cargo was being transferred. Five days later the convoy left Taranto again, but following an attack by torpedo Wellingtons it returned to port once more.

Malta was closing down Rommel's supply line: even if a ship was not sunk, if it was damaged, delayed, rerouted or simply 'encouraged to turn back', it had a significant effect on the flow of supplies. However, Malta too was short of fuel, and on 25 June Lord Gort had signalled to the Air Ministry that current fuel stocks would only last six to seven weeks at current consumption. Lloyd added that stocks could be made to last into October if operations were limited to fighter defence and no offensive operations were flown. London did not agree; it was of the opinion that offensive

The torpedo Wellington added yet another dimension to the strike force, with longer range and the ability to carry two weapons. (*Don Tilley, SAAF*)

ops that targeted convoys were essential to the success of the land battle in North Africa, which had priority over all things, and that the Beauforts and Beaufighters must still be tasked against convoys, but were only to be called upon in 'case of vital need', which effectively meant major convoys or tankers.

Lord Gort responded that: 'The continuation of strikes and heavy transit traffic [which the ministry had ignored] entailed the very grave risk of losing Malta.' Everything really hinged on getting a convoy through, although the delivery of 11,000 gallons of fuel on 19 July by the submarine *Parthian* was appreciated.

After the quiet period of late May to late June, some on Malta thought the worst was over – but this was not quite true, although the island was now well-placed to defeat what would be the last assault. While the Italians had been moving units to Sicily, the Germans also reversed their draw down and sent reinforcements of two bomber Gruppen (KG 77) and one Fighter Gruppe (I/JG 77) to Sicily. The fighters had come from the Eastern Front and were flown by very experienced pilots, under the leadership of Hauptmann Heinz Bar.

July was thus set to be a hectic month for Malta, and it started on 2 July with a number of heavily escorted raids by the Italians, with both sides suffering losses, but the balance in favour of the defenders. More such raids followed, and on the 6th the German Ju 88s were back. The day was a busy one, with the defenders doing well; the Luftwaffe raid was the last of the day and it too was mauled by the Spitfires, KG 77 losing at least three aircraft, one crew being picked up by *HSL128*. George Beurling scored his first confirmed victories on 6 July, claiming two MC.202s, as well as damaging a bomber. On his fourth sortie of the day he claimed a 109 of JG 77 destroyed. He continued to be successful over the next couple of days, and was awarded an immediate DFM, the citation reading: 'Sergeant Beurling has displayed great skill and courage in the face of the enemy. One day in July, 1942, he engaged a number of enemy fighters which were escorting a formation of Junkers 88s and destroyed one fighter. Later during the same day he engaged 10 enemy fighters and shot two of them down into the sea, bringing his total victories to eight.' (AMB 7613. By the end of the year he had a bar to his DFM (September), had been promoted to pilot officer, and received the DSO (October).

The 7th was a bad day for the defenders, with a number of losses, although *HSL128* was able to pluck three live Spitfire pilots out of the sea (Middlemiss, Davey, de Nancrede), as well as the body of Haggas. In the two main raids on the 8th, more Spitfires were lost, but the Germans also suffered and, more importantly, the bombing was ineffective. The Italians were finding it impossible to mount sustained and effective attacks on Malta during the summer of 1942; in July the Regia Aeronautica had around 140 aircraft committed to the attacks on Malta, of which only 60 were bombers, including 15 Stukas. In terms of numbers this was not sufficient to be effective, as Malta's air defences, both fighter and gun, had become so potent that some Italian airman viewed the attacks on Malta as '*rotta della morte*' – the 'route of death'. The RAF had certainly noticed an unwillingness by the Italians to press home attacks. Just under 2,900 sorties were flown and 695 tons of bombs dropped, but there was an increased use of incendiaries (some 2,300). The main targets were once again the airfields and in fierce combat the RAF lost thirty-six Spitfires in combat, while the Germans lost thirty-seven aircraft to fighters and flak. The first attack on Ta Kali, on the 2nd, caused twenty casualties, with nine killed and eleven injured. The 'blitz' was short-lived and generally ineffective, with the most intensive day being the 6th, when some 180 sorties were flown. In the period from 1 to 18 July, the MCU launches had rescued nine Spitfire pilots (*HSL107* picking up three and *HSL128* rescuing six), along with Axis crewmen. This was both good for morale and helped keep up pilot numbers.

On the offensive side, an enlarged Axis convoy of three MVs and eight destroyers sailed on 3 July. This unusually large number of escorts reflected the importance of these supplies to Rommel. The first strike of the day failed to find the target, but it was located by a Baltimore in the afternoon and a second strike was mounted by nine Beauforts without air escort. Gibbs noted that: 'Attack was timed for last light, approach from astern, and attack by sub-flights on port side of convoy. 2 Beauforts missing, 3 failed to reach target, 2 Beauforts damaged.' A Beaufort strike force set off to search around the Greek coast for the convoy but did not make contact and returned to Malta. Later in the day, a reconnaissance aircraft located the convoy 15 miles south of Zante, and it was decided to mount a dusk strike. Gibbs planned the attack for eight Beauforts with Beaufighters as escorts, but in the event only six Beauforts got airborne, and during the outbound flight, two of these had to return to base, as did a number of Beaufighters. This left Gibbs with only four Beauforts and five Beaufighters to attack a heavily defended target at maximum range from Malta. All four dropped their torpedoes, while the Beaufighters did their best to distract the gunners on the destroyers. The largest MV was hit and forced to put into a Greek harbour for repairs. The two surviving MVs reached Benghazi on the 5th. The nominal forty-eight-hour journey had taken three attempts and sixteen days.

The main Axis offloading ports at Benghazi, Tripoli and Tobruk (since its capture in June) remained high on the list of targets for the bombers, especially from Egypt, and still including the USAAF bombers. In addition to ports, the bombers also went after supply dumps and any major concentration of equipment. The original B-24 force was joined in such attacks by B-17s of the 9th and 436th Bombardment Squadrons, the longer range of such bombers enabling them to operate from bases in Palestine. Later in July the disparate USAAF units became the 1st Provisional Heavy Bombardment Group, and continued attacks on shipping, ports and other installations, although Benghazi and Tobruk remained the most frequent targets. It was a similar picture for the bombers of 205 Group, with a concerted series of attacks on Tobruk harbour from early July, which resulted in damage to the port and shipping, but also an increase in losses:

7/8 July: 70 Sqn Wellington Z8986, Sergeant J.R. Milligan. Lost power on take-off and aircraft crashed; four killed.

7/8 July: 148 Sqn Wellington T2985. Flying Officer F. Tribe and crew killed.

8/9: 104 Sqn Wellington Z8520, Sergeant C.S. Maxfield. Suffered double-engine failure on the outbound leg and belly-landed in the desert. Crew walked 200 miles (behind enemy lines) and in an amazing rescue were saved by a Baltimore that landed and picked them up.

11/12: 108 Sqn Wellington DV674, Warrant Officer R.A. Chalmers. On return leg could not locate LG224 for landing and so pressed on to Cairo airfields, but when landing at Heliopolis collided with AD601; two killed and one injured.

11/12: 148 Sqn Wellington T2749, Pilot Officer P.W. Hoad. Hit by flak and engine caught fire; crash-landed and all PoW.

11/12: 148 Sqn Wellington DV505, Flight Sergeant H.E. Kemball. All killed.

12/13: 40 Sqn Wellington HX373, Squadron Leader F.J. Steel. Ran out of fuel on return and force-landed; all safe. The story is a bit more dramatic in that Squadron Leader Steel and Pilot Officer Adams walked off to find help and were picked up three days later by a 40 Squadron aircraft, whereas the crew that had stayed with the Wellington wreck were picked up far sooner. This whole aspect of 'walking out' is a fascinating one with many stories, some of which are recounted in *The Desert Air Force in World War II: Air Power in the Western Desert 1940–1942*, Ken Delve, Pen & Sword, 2017. Those who did make it back could become members of the 'Late Arrivals Club'.

12/13: 104 Sqn Wellington Z8588, Pilot Officer J.E. Harlton. Crash-landed near Sidi Barrani on return, which by this time was on the wrong side of the lines; one killed and rest PoW.

13/14: 10/227 Sqn Halifax W1171, Pilot Officer H.C. Drake. Operating out of Aqir and within the first few days of this 'joint' unit operating in the Middle East. Damaged over target and crashed on landing at Almaza; aircraft exploded and two crew injured.

13/14: 104 Sqn Wellington Z8650, Sergeant G.T. Cairns. Flew into ground near Wadi Natrun, one killed.

14/15: 104 Sqn Wellington Z8649, Pilot Officer G. Richards. Hit by flak and crew bailed out; 2 killed and 4 PoW.

14/15: 104 Sqn Wellington Z8657, Sergeant D.C. Davies. On return leg flew into ground near Wadi Natrun; 3 killed and 3 injured.

14/15: 104 Sqn Wellington Z8658, Pilot Officer R.C. Horton. Engine failure on return and crashed; 5 killed and one injured.

So in the space of just over a week, there was a very high loss rate – against just one target, Tobruk. However, as this was at the time the most important offload port for Rommel, it was considered worth the effort and losses. A further fifteen Wellingtons were lost against the same target in the remainder of July.

An 86 Squadron Beaufort detachment arrived on 14 July under Squadron Leader Hyde, to help replace losses and keep

Beaufort of 86 Squadron deployed to Malta to boost the torpedo-bomber force, and operated as a mixed unit with 39 and 217 squadrons.

the Malta Beaufort strike force at an operational level. Wing Commander Davies was posted back to the UK, and Gibbs was promoted to wing commander and given command of all the Beauforts in Malta. His command consisted of aircraft and crews from 39, 217 and 86 Squadrons, and it was not until 15 August that the majority of his command consisted of 39 Squadron aircraft – with the transfer of the main body of the squadron's aircraft from Egypt to Malta. Nevertheless, the unit was known as 39 Squadron Detachment in Malta.

While Malta was managing some offensive ops, the maritime war was still being fought across the eastern and western Mediterranean. The first confirmed success of the period (July to November) was made on 11 July by a Walrus of 700 Squadron FAA. The Italian submarine *Ondina* had been sighted by destroyers off Beirut, one of which made a DC attack that brought the submarine to the surface, whereupon the Walrus, running in at 40ft, placed two 250lb DC across the conning tower. Some survivors were picked up by the Navy.

Pilot Officer Egerton of 10 Squadron RAAF was engaged by a Ju 88 on 14 July, during which combat the Sunderland's gunners scored a number of hits leaving the Axis bomber diving towards the sea emitting white smoke. The following day, Pilot Officer Lawrence was on an ASP when he saw a Cant Z.501 land on the water and burst into flames, the crew of six jumping into the sea. The Sunderland landed and picked up the crew, and after returning to Gibraltar the Italians were entertained in the mess until the early evening, when they were taken to the Spanish frontier. Following Rommel's advance and the British retreat back to the El Alamein position, Axis submarines were able to shift more of their focus to the eastern Mediterranean and Levant coast, which thus became a focus of activity in the second half of the year.

Air Vice-Marshal Keith Park CB MC DFC took over as AOC on 15 July, having arrived on Malta on the 14th. His experience in the Battle of Britain led him to make some changes to the tactical use of his fighters, something he could do as he now had significant numbers of Spitfires. His basic tactic was for fighters to climb as fast as they could and gain height on the way to intercepting the enemy bombers to the north of Malta; this relied on reasonable warning time – and the climb performance of the Spitfire, but it had the effect of taking the fight to the enemy and disrupting the raids before they reached Malta.

The same day brought thirty-one Spitfires to Malta courtesy of Operation Colima/Pinpoint. While Malta was delighted with its Spitfire Vs, some were already angling for the new Spitfire IX, but these hopes were quashed in a signal to ACAS Ops on 21 July: 'I consider it would be premature to endeavour to clear the Spitfire IX for use in Malta when it is not yet cleared for operation in this country and its reliability is not yet established.' The detail went into the lack of tropicalization and the fact it could not be flown off a carrier in same way that the Spitfire V could. A further twenty-eight Spitfires arrived on the 21st, so the combined total of fifty-nine more than made up for the losses suffered. The second batch were part of Operation Knapsack/Insect.

When Malta reported on 18 July that a Beaufighter had shot down a Ju 88 near Sicily it elicited an immediate panic signal from the Air Ministry to HQ RAF ME: 'Assume you have security restrictions on operation of Malta's AI aircraft near enemy territory similar to your arrangements in Delta [Egypt]. Please state nature of present Malta restrictions. It is suggested that when Mark VII AI is used, aircraft should not fly more than half way from base to enemy coast.'

The reply stated: 'Malta restrictions at present state Beaufighters with special equipment not to go outside 40-mile radius from island, now being amended to read not to fly within 20 miles of enemy territory. Pilot in question received order to return on 40-mile line and saw target,

The AOC, Keith Park, in conversation with bomber crews. Although a 'fighter man', Park recognized that the primary role of Malta was anti-shipping.

simultaneously pilot opened fire and saw aircraft catch on fire and then followed behind till aircraft crashed within 5 miles of Sicilian coast. Vital nature of these orders has again been stressed to night fighter pilots.' (signal HQ Malta to Air Ministry, 20 July 1942).

A signal to the Air Ministry on 25 July outlined the fighter pilot situation: 'We have 135 Spitfire pilots in Malta, of these 5 are inexperienced and being returned to UK, 7 are wounded, 7 are tired and non-effective sick, 4 at Gibraltar for ferrying, one in UK. This leaves 111 operating pilots. We require 140 pilots; we therefore require a further 29 pilots. When the 64 due or some part of them arrive here, the surplus will be despatched to the UK after 1 month. Two squadron commanders and 6 Flight Commanders will be available for return to the UK, in exchange for good or experienced pilots of equivalent rank who have had experience in sweeps.' While the stats are interesting, what is more interesting is the final comment – 'experience in sweeps' – Malta was looking to increase its offensive role.

Having left reluctantly a few weeks before, the submarines of the 10th Submarine Flotilla returned, so Malta now had its subs, its bombers and its torpedo-bombers; as long as fuel and weapons could be supplied, the island was back in business. The same day, the Beaufort and Beaufighter strike force was active again, a PRU Spitfire having picked up a single supply ship with an escort of two destroyers. The nine Beauforts claimed two hits on the target ship; damage was confirmed by a recce Baltimore. A Beaufort strike force, escorted by the Beaufighters of 235, put paid to the 6,339-ton *Vettor Pisani* on the 24th. Gibbs recorded this as: 'Convoy located by PRU Spitfire on evening of July 23rd; 1 MV, 2 D/Rs. 2 E-boats off Cape Gorighambo. 6 Beauforts, escort of 6 Beaufighters, 3 Beauforts missing. Baltimore took photographs of strike and PRU photographed target later the same day. One hit MV, which caught fire and became total loss. Attack by sub-flights in succession on the port beam, after long approach from the beam.'

The next major Beaufort op was on 28 July against a large MV near Sapienza in southern Greece. Nine Beauforts took off from Luqa early on the 28th and located the convoy just before midday. As the Beauforts ran in one of their number fell victim to the intensive flak and crashed into the sea. Another aircraft was hit in the port engine as it cleared away from its attack on the MV and the pilot, Flight Lieutenant Strever, a South African, realized he would have to ditch as he had insufficient height to reach the coast. For two of his crew, two New Zealand wireless operator/air gunners, Sergeants Wilkinson and Brown, this was the second time they had been shot down within a fortnight. Strever ditched the Beaufort and Wilkinson released the dinghy from its stowage in the port wing. Soon, all four were safely in the dinghy and bobbing around some 5 miles off the coast of Sapienza. Some time later they were spotted by an Italian Macchi MC.202, which circled the dinghy and then departed. Shortly afterwards a Cant seaplane arrived overhead and landed nearby to pick them up – and take them into captivity. After a two-hour flight the Cant landed and they were taken for a very

Loading a torpedo on to a Beaufort.

mild interrogation, followed by a change of clothes and a good meal – and the news that they were to be taken to Taranto the next day. At breakfast the next day the crew had a chance to discuss their future.

'I've worked out where we are,' said Wilkinson. 'Either Levkas or Corfu. Taranto can't be more than 200 miles. If we don't do something quickly we'll be prisoners by lunchtime.'

'Not a hope here,' said the fourth crewman, Pilot Officer Dunsmere. 'We've about as much chance of eluding them here as a bunch of film stars at a world premiere. Better wait until we get to Taranto.'

'You know what they say,' said Strever, 'The best chances come immediately after capture. Once they get us to Taranto there will be no more of this being feted like transatlantic flyers. Life will start to get tough then.'

'Has anyone thought of trying to capture the aircraft and fly it to Malta? Malta's about 350 miles I reckon.'

'I've thought of it, Wilkie,' said Strever. 'I thought of it yesterday. We probably had a better chance then than we'll get today. They're bound to mount a guard on us now. Still, we'll keep our eyes open.'

At that moment they were taken to the seaplane and were airborne and on course for Taranto at 0940. The interior of the aircraft was crowded with four Italian crew, the four prisoners and an Italian guard. At the halfway point the prisoners decided it was now or never and Wilkinson leapt into action, knocking out the wireless operator and seizing the gun from the lax guard. Strever took the gun and secured the 'co-operation' of the pilot. Soon all the Italians were overpowered and while Strever took the controls and turned the aircraft towards Malta, Dunsmere and Brown tied up the new prisoners. Dunsmere tried to work out a course for Malta but had no maps and no definite idea of their position, so he drew a rough sketch map of the central Mediterranean and showed it to the Italian navigator, who made a few corrections.

With this information, they decided to make straight for Malta, but with the proviso that if they had no visual contact within thirty minutes they would turn due west and make landfall on the toe of Italy to obtain an accurate position. This they had to do, and as they neared the toe of Italy, at 1130, the Italian engineer changed to the secondary petrol tanks and indicated that there was only enough fuel for another hour. They turned again for Malta and flew on, not wanting to consider what would happen if they missed Malta. With the fuel gauges on empty they spotted the island of Gozo and, a few minutes later, the coast of Malta. As they neared the coast of Malta, they were intercepted by ten Spitfires, the first of which sprayed the wing of the Cant to 'persuade' it to land. They landed on the water and climbed out on to the wing, waving white garments to show the Spitfires that they were non–hostile. The Spitfires circled for a while and then departed. An air–sea rescue launch from Malta picked them up one and a half hours later.

They were given a jubilant welcome when they arrived back at the squadron, just in time to recover their personal kit, which had been divided up among the other members. For their combat exploits, but not mentioning the Cant incident, Strever and Dunsmere were awarded the DFC and Wilkinson and Brown the DFM. The citation read: 'Lieutenant Strever, Pilot Officer Dunsmere and Sergeants Brown and Wilkinson were the crew of an aircraft which operated from Malta in June and July, 1942. During this period, they performed excellent work in attacking enemy merchant vessels and naval forces, and all displayed initiative, courage and devotion to duty of a high order.' (AMB 7956).

By August 1942 Malta had a notional strength of 163 Spitfires, of which 120 were serviceable, and this enabled the island not only to defend itself but also to go on to the offensive once more.

The improved situation, and it has to be said, the offensive mindset of Park and some of his leaders, led to the adoption in August of a new Fighter Interception Plan for Malta. This was summarized in a report issued by Air Ministry Air Tactics: 'Our fighter forces in Malta are now approximately equal, if not superior, to those of the enemy. The time has, therefore arrived for the RAF to put a stop to the enemy daylight attacks on our aerodromes, or other military objectives in Malta. A simple fighter plan has now been introduced with the object of intercepting enemy raids North of Malta before they can cross the coast and bomb our aerodromes.

'Our fighter forces in Malta are now approximately equal, if not superior, to those of the enemy. The time has, therefore arrived for the RAF to put a stop to the enemy daylight attacks on our aerodromes, or other military objectives in Malta.'

In effect the squadrons are controlled by the Fighter Sector Controller in such a way that they can get their operating height up sun, and are then vectored forward to positions to enable the first squadron to intercept enemy high fighter cover. The second squadron is manoeuvred into the best position to intercept the close escort to enemy bombers. The third squadron, having got its height up sun, is then vectored to intercept the enemy bomber formation about ten miles before it reaches the coast, and carry out a head-on attack followed by a quarter attack, with the object of forcing the enemy to jettison his bombs in the sea.'

The summary highlighted that 'the execution of the plan demands the following:

1. RDF warning and information must be good and reliable.
2. Take-off of squadrons to be: squadron at stand-by to be off within 2 minutes; squadron at immediate readiness off in 3 minutes; squadron at readiness off within 5 minutes.
3. Fighter Sector Controlling must be of the highest quality, and squadrons must implicitly obey the orders of the Controller.
4. Sea Rescue – an efficient sea rescue service having sufficient high-speed launches
5. Good shooting by pilots, who must not open fire at long range, thus giving away the element of surprise and wasting valuable ammunition.
6. Wireless discipline must be good.

The success of the new interception plan was outlined in Park's 'Fighter Interception – Malta; Instruction No. 2': 'The following results have been achieved by our Spitfire squadrons during the first two weeks of the forward plan of interception:

a. Total number of day raids against Malta – 40
b. Number of bombing raids that reached the coast – 10
c. Number of raids intercepted before crossing the coast – 9
d. RAF aircraft destroyed and damaged on the ground by bombing – 4
e. Enemy aircraft casualties – 34 destroyed, 9 probables, 18 damaged
f. Own losses – 13 Spitfires destroyed, 5 pilots lost

'The above results reflect great credit on the Spitfire squadrons and Fighter Sector Controllers, because they effected a great reduction in the wastage of aircraft on the ground (34 were destroyed or damaged in the first two weeks of July). The interception of the majority of bombing raids before they crossed the coast saved many lives of personnel on aerodromes, also prevented the wastage in labour and materials required for aircraft pens, runways, roads, etc.'

Park then went on to describe what he called the change in enemy tactics to a 'Fighter v Fighter' battle, the daylight bombers having been withdrawn. 'Enemy introduced fighter sweeps over Malta, usually at very high altitudes, between 20,000 and 30,000ft. It was thought that the enemy's object was mainly to regain his air superiority over Malta in order to enable to reintroduce bombing raids. Due to short warning of raids and the absence of heights from the RDF system, the enemy fighter formations frequently arrived over Malta with a height advantage over our fighter patrols.'

Initially the Spitfires tried to climb to engage, but with inadequate time they were usually attacked while still in the climb. The solution adopted was to 'restrict our defensive patrols to a height limit of 20,000ft. This had the advantage of forcing the enemy to come down to a height that suited our Spitfires instead of fighting at extreme altitude where the enemy fighters appeared to possess better performance than we possessed.'

During the first week of August, two more Beaufighter squadrons arrived in Malta, 248 Squadron from the UK and 252 Squadron from Egypt, both being primarily assigned to the strike force for anti-air and anti-flak duties. Coastal Command had been advised on 22 July that 248 Squadron was to be released for Malta, and by the end of that week the first five aircraft had been delivered to 44 Group, which was responsible for the transfer to Malta. The first four Beaufighters arrived in Malta on 3 August, joined by four more over the next two days, and a plan that all sixteen should be in place by the 10th. Additional Beauforts arrived from the 39 Squadron parent unit in Egypt. In part their role was also to provide an offensive capability against any attempt by the Axis to disrupt a major supply effort for Malta, the Italian 'fleet in being' still being a threat, while the Beaufighters also provided an offensive capability to attack airfields. However, it was not until late August that this enhanced force was called into action – but that second half of August was to prove critical in the 'fuel war'.

In the meantime, things in Malta were desperate, with shortages of fuel, spare parts and munitions. Torpedoes were always in short supply as they had to be brought to Malta by submarine and crews were instructed to bring their torpedoes back if the first three aircraft scored hits on the target ship. Furthermore, an aircraft on a rover patrol was only to drop if a suitably large target presented itself.

The lack of supplies also affected living conditions, and during the worst stages of the siege of Malta life was grim and uncomfortable. 'Accommodation was in single-storey stone buildings, often damaged, and somewhat cell like with their spartan furniture. Likewise, meals were frugal and uninviting – no wonder Strever and his crew appreciated the excellent meals given them by the Italians! Maltese wine was fairly plentiful but not really popular and the local brewery was out of action. Social life was very limited as the nearby town of Valetta offered very few attractions.'

Although the fighter squadrons had a club on the sea front and sea bathing could have been exploited, the squadron was very much base-bound. Add to this the constant threat of air attack, and the 'outdoor' life of the desert of a few months earlier began to appear attractive to 39 Squadron crews.

A key convoy was scheduled for August and despite only five of the fourteen merchant vessels making it to Malta, one of those was the all-important 10,000-ton tanker *Ohio*, damaged and 'floating at deck level'. This one vessel provided Malta's aircraft with enough fuel for two to three months. This was Operation Pedestal and was also the last convoy to Malta that faced heavy opposition; it truly was a make or break convoy for both sides. On 10 August the convoy cleared the Straits of Gibraltar. The same day, the Beaufighters of 248 Squadron swept over airfields in Sicily in an attempt to disrupt air effort, claiming six aircraft destroyed. The force initially included no fewer than four carriers: *Victorious* with thirty-eight aircraft (eighteen Fulmars, fourteen Albacores, six Hurricanes), *Indomitable* with forty-four aircraft (twenty-two Hurricanes, twelve Albacores, ten Martlets), *Eagle* with eighteen aircraft (sixteen Hurricanes and two Fulmars), and *Furious* with the thirty-eight Spitfires for Malta. The composition of the forces was:

Force W:
• Battleships 2: *Nelson* and *Rodney*
• Carriers 3: *Eagle*, *Indomitable*, *Victorious*
• Cruisers 3: *Charybdis*, *Phoebe*, *Sirius*
• Destroyers 12: *Antelope*, *Eskimo*, *Ithuriel*, *Laforey*, *Lightning*, *Lookout*, *Quentin*, *Somali*, *Tartar*, *Vansittart*, *Wishart*, *Zetland*

Force X:
• Cruisers 4: *Cairo*, *Kenya*, *Manchester*, *Nigeria*
• Destroyers 12: *Ashanti*, *Bicester*, *Bramham*, *Derwent*, *Foresight*, *Fury*, *Icarus*, *Intrepid*, *Ledbury*, *Pathfinder*, *Penn*, *Wilton*
• Tug 1: *Jaunty*

Force R:
• Oilers 2: *Brown Ranger*, *Dingledale*
• Corvettes 4: *Coltsfoot*, *Geranium*, *Jonquil*, *Spiraea*

Operation Bellows:
• Carrier 1: *Furious*
• Destroyers 8 (Force H): *Amazon*, *Keppel*, *Malcolm*, *Venomous*, *Vidette*, *Westcott*, *Wrestler*, *Wolverine*

Minesweeping Force:
• Minesweepers 4: *Hebe*, *Hythe*, *Rye*, *Speedy*
• MLs *121*, *126*, *134*, *135*, *168*, *459* and *462*

At 0715 on the 11th the escorting Sunderland reported enemy aircraft, and from 0830 onwards Ju 88s started shadowing the convoy. One was shot down and one damaged. The launch of the thirty-eight Spitfires from *Furious* started at 1230 (Operation Bellows); less than an hour later *Eagle* was torpedoed by *U-73*, being hit by four torpedoes and sinking, with the loss of 160 of her crew. The U-boat captain transmitted: 'Convoy – 15 destroyers and escort ships, 2 cruisers, 9 to 10 freighters, one aircraft carrier, probably one battleship. Fan shot at aircraft carrier. 4 hits from 500m distance. Loud sinking noises. Everything ok'. This U-boat had a successful career between September 1940 and its eventual loss in December 1943, claiming eight MVs and four warships sunk, and three ships damaged. (Note: For all 'things' U-boat one of the best sources of reliable information is http:// uboat.net) The remaining carrier and escorts turned back to Gibraltar at 1830, with Ju 88s making unsuccessful dusk attacks. It was too dark for the fleet fighters to engage, so the ships' defence relied on the anti-aircraft fire.

The next day started well for Force H when *Wolverine* rammed and sank the Italian submarine *Dagabur* north of Algiers. The convoy was still being shadowed and the aerial defence capability of the convoy after the loss of *Eagle* comprised thirty-four Hurricane, ten Martlet and sixteen Fulmar fighters, which were tasked to maintain a constant air patrol of twelve fighters, reinforced as needed. Just after 0900 the bombers were back, with thirty Ju 88s attacking, losing two aircraft for no result. Attacks by aircraft and U-boats continued, with another submarine sunk; the Italian *Cobalto* being rammed by *Ithuriel*.

Fleet fighters were heavily engaged, especially in the evening, with large numbers of enemy fighters and then a heavy and co-ordinated attack by dive-bomber and torpedo-bombers between 1800 and 1850. *Indomitable*, *Foresight* and *Rodney* were all hit or damaged, although only *Foresight* was sunk (by the Navy as it had suffered severe damage). At 1855 Force Z, the main fleet, turned back west, while Force X, the convoy escort, pressed on – with only limited air cover provided by a few Beaufighters. The whole of the Axis air and submarine attack was now focused on Force X. At 2000 on the 12th *Nigeria* and *Cairo* were torpedoed by U-boats, the latter having to be sunk, and the former being escorted back to Gibraltar. In the hour between 2000 and 2100 heavy attacks were made. During this attack *Empire Hope* was bombed and abandoned, and *Clan Ferguson* was torpedoed and blew up, the latter loaded with 2,000 tons of aviation petrol and 1,500 tons of explosives among other items. However, ninety-six survivors reached the Tunisian coast to be interned by the French. The *Brisbane Star* was torpedoed and fell out from the convoy.

Map showing the Pedestal convoy shipping losses in 'bomb alley'.

At midnight, MTBs lying in wait off Cape Bon commenced their attacks and just after 0100 on 13th two Italian boats torpedoed the cruiser *Manchester*. Stopped, it was subsequently decided that she should be scuttled, which was done at 0500, most of her survivors reaching the Tunisian coast and internment. Within an hour, the scattered merchant ships of the convoy were picked off by the small, fast MTBs, with *Almeria Lykes*, *Glenorchy*, *Santa Elisa* and *Wairangi* being sunk.

Meanwhile, the surface threat from Italian cruisers had greatly diminished; the lack of fighter cover resulted in their withdrawal eastward and being harassed by reconnaissance aircraft from Malta. The final blow for the cruisers came when submarine *Unbroken* damaged the *Bolzano* and *Muzio Attendolo*. No further threat was posed by Italian surface warships. At 0700 on the 13th the remainder of Force X, with the three remaining MVs, was 120 miles west of Malta, but still faced attack. Just after 0800 a bomb hit *Waimarama*, causing such an explosion that it destroyed not only the ship but the bomber responsible; *Ledbury* rescued forty-five men. This was followed ninety minutes later by a most determined dive-bombing attack by Stukas directed principally at the tanker *Ohio*. She was near-missed several times and actually struck by a Ju 87, which she shot down, her steering gear being disabled. An hour later more attacks further damaged and stopped her. *Port Chalmers* was set on fire, though she continued with the convoy.

The final air attack came at 1130, with no further effect on the convoy; at 1230 the convoy came under short-range air protection and proceeded without further problems. It arrived at Malta at 1600. There was good news when *Brisbane Star* arrived at 1430 on the 14th 'after a cruise around the Gulf of Hammamet and successful interview with local French authorities'. The French had tried to persuade the captain to enter port and surrender, an option supported by some on board as the ship had a number of wounded, but the captain refused and made a night dash to Malta. Even more crucially, the tanker *Ohio* arrived at 0755 on the 15th, having been towed the last 100 miles. The ships that arrived in Malta landed 32,000 tons of cargo and 15,000 tons of fuel. This was only about 40 per cent of the total that had been sent; the table below shows the full extent of the losses.

	MV Name	Tonnage	Fate
1	Glenorchy	9,000	Sunk
2	Empire Hope	12,700	Sunk
3	Waimpama	12,850	Sunk
4	Santa Elisa (USA)	8,400	Missing
5	Clan Ferguson	7,350	Sunk
6	Deucalion	7,500	Sunk
7	Dorset	10,600	Sunk
8	Almeria Lykes (USA)	7,800	Sunk
9	Rochester Castle	7,800	Damaged, arrived Malta, one month repairs
10	Brisbane Star	12,800	Damaged, arrived Malta, one month repairs
11	Port Chalmers	8.500	Undamaged, arrived Malta
12	Melbourne Star	12,800	Undamaged, arrived Malta
13	Ohio (tanker)	9,500	Damaged, arrived Malta, extensive repairs

Despite the comment above about fleet fighters being too slow and weak, they still put in claims for thirty-nine confirmed and five probables. As soon as the ships were in range of Malta they were given cover and 'aircraft from Malta worked ceaselessly and answered every call that was made to the utmost limit of their ability.' (VA Malta to C-in-C).

The vice admiral's signal focused on *Ohio* and he rightly praised the various ships that assisted in towing the prized tanker to safety: 'Towage was outstanding feat of courage, determination and good seamanship on part of all concerned.' He also recorded that: 'Enemy air attacks ceased once short range Spitfire cover was reached.'

The SO of Force H added he was: '... loud in his praises for both Beaufighters and Spitfires from Malta who seemed to do everything possible under circumstances of being bereft of their fighter direction ships HMS Cairo and HMS Nigeria. Long-range Spitfires were out as early as possible on D4 and Force X had a number of Spitfires overhead for the remainder of journey. They shot down a number of enemy aircraft and undoubtedly reduced scale of attack.'

The all-important tanker *Ohio* was heavily damaged but limped into harbour 'held up' by escorting ships.

The impressive Pedestal carrier force.

The Pedestal report included comments on the effectiveness of the air attacks:

- Considering the weight of the air attacks, they were singularly ineffective. Although the various forms of attack were often co-ordinated, it is noteworthy that the T/B aircraft seldom pressed home their attack.
- Fleet fighters intercepted all bombing attacks on Force F, but except for Martlets, were too slow and weakly armed to break them up effectively.
- The enemy aircraft were more effective against the ships of the convoy when carriers had parted company and it is probable that four ships were directly sunk as the result of air attack.

HQ Malta signalled to Air Ministry: 'Very grateful for reinforcement 37 Spitfires sent by carrier, only two crashed on arrival due to bad landings, and many of the pilots are more experienced than pilots of last two reinforcements.' This was indeed a welcome addition, as according to a survey of aircraft on 10 August, they were down to seventy-seven serviceable Spitfires. The same statement also listed serviceability of other types: Spitfire PRU (3), Beaufighter Coastal (24), Beaufighter Fighter (8), Wellington (4), Beaufort (22), Baltimore (8), miscellaneous FAA (4), for a total of 151.

Spitfire in protective pen and being refuelled from fuel cans.

With fuel and weapon stocks replenished, and with no significant attacks on their airfields, the RAF squadrons at Malta renewed the anti-shipping attacks with vigour. The first victim was the 8,236-ton *Rosalino Pilo*, damaged by Beauforts on the 17th and finished off by a submarine. Gibbs recorded this as: 'PRU Spitfire located convoy off Pantalleria, 1 MV and 2 D/Rs off Lampedusa; 6 Beauforts, escort of 6 Beaufighters, 3 Beau-bombers, with 8 long-range Spitfires. 2 Beauforts were damaged. MV hit, set on fire and stopped, ship was abandoned and afterwards sunk. Attack by sub-flights on either bow after approach from dead astern, with a synchronized attack by Beaufighters.'

The Spitfire escort was unusual, but this first reference to Beau-bombers indicated what became a standard tactic with the force mix. The idea of the Beaus was to distract gunners so that the vulnerable Beauforts could make their torpedo runs. In his (unpopular) report, Gibbs described the tactic: 'On sub-flights reaching a distance of 4–5 miles from the target, the sub-flight leader deployed his aircraft into line astern, led them into the dropping sector, weaving and making small changes in height, and turned into attack at 2000/1500 yards from the target in the standard manner. Tactics of the diversion were for the torpedo leader, on sighting the target, to signal the escort to climb. The Beau-bombers climbed ahead to 4000 feet and shallow dive-bombed the target, while the Beaufighters climbed to 2500 feet and raked the escort with cannon fire. The timing of the diversion relative to the torpedo attack was therefore achieved automatically by the difference in speed of Beauforts and Beaufighters.'

The attacks on shipping combined with attacks on dock facilities in Italy and North Africa was certainly having an impact; Lieutenant General Lewis H. Brereton, in command of United States Army Middle East Air Force (USAMEAF), claimed on 10 August that the USAAF bombing campaign against Axis ports had reduced supply intake at the three ports of Benghazi, Tobruk and Matruh by an estimated 40 per cent. This was based on destruction or disruption of the port facilities, as well as shipping in harbour. The USAAF contribution to the overall bomber force increased again in mid-August with the arrival of the 12th Bombardment Group and its B–24s. However, as autumn approached many of the bombers in Egypt switched their attention to the direct support of the land operations.

In August Air Vice-Marshal Park told his fighter leaders: 'Because our Spitfires, using the forward plan of interception, have recently stopped daylight raids it does not mean that only fighter sweeps are likely to be encountered over or near Malta in the future. Any sign of defensive tactics by our fighters will encourage the enemy to reintroduce bombers or fighter-bombers. Therefore, the more aggressively our fighters are employed the better will Malta be defended against daylight bombing.'

The same day another twenty-nine Spitfire VBs arrived with Operation Headlong/Baritone. HMS *Furious* had flown off the first eight aircraft at 0730 on 17 August; by 0940 all thirty-two had been flown off; one crashed on take-off (pilot drowned) and two had technical problems and the pilots bailed out but were rescued by escorting destroyers. The report by Wing Commander Flying on board *Furious* gave the details of the operation, and on the 17th he recorded: 'At 1430 hours all pilots were issued with the necessary maps and information cards and thoroughly briefed by me on the operation in hand. At 1700 hours all pilots reported to the hangar where their R/T helmets were tested and their flying kit and small kit checked and stowed in their own aircraft. The Ward Room bar was closed to RAF officers at 2130 hours, when all paid their mess bills and were then despatched to bed.'

Another little pen picture of reality … close the bar, pay your bill, go to bed. He then described the fly-off: 'A white line, one-foot wide and running the length of the flight deck, was painted on in such a position as to appear under the pilot's port cannon during a straight take off. A wind speed over the deck of 40–44 kts was obtained. Four pilots from Malta, embarked at Gibraltar, led the first four formations.' He noted the three mishaps: Sergeant W.J. Fleming (EP194) swung on take-off and 'stalled his aircraft opposite the island and crashed over the port side. He was drowned.' Sergeant McDougall (EP606) 'was unable to retract his undercarriage. He flew ahead of the destroyer detailed to watch him and bailed out. He was immediately rescued unhurt.' Sgt T.G. Sullivan (EP152) flew with the formation for twenty minutes but then had to return with engine trouble and bail out, being 'immediately rescued unhurt'.

The Italians, true to their word, were mounting another convoy to relieve Rommel. This was the 7,800-ton tanker *Pozarica* escorted by destroyers, a flak ship and seven aircraft. On 20 August, Wing Commander Gibbs led a twelve Beaufort strike against the tanker. Unfortunately, the tanker was not as low in the water as was anticipated and so the depth setting on the torpedoes was too great, and all torpedoes ran under the ship. The attackers lost a Beaufighter and two Beauforts, although both Beaufort crews were picked up by the destroyer escort. Back at Malta thoughts were turned to a second strike, and plans were laid for a sortie the next day when up to date reconnaissance information would

Log book extract August 1942 for I. Footit, a 39 Squadron navigator, showing the shipping strikes on 20 and 24 August.

be available. This second strike consisted of nine Beauforts and nine anti-flak Beaufighters, plus six dive-bomber Beaufighters. By this time, the convoy was nearing the Greek coast and it was here that the strike aircraft caught up with it. Gibbs scored a good hit, as did one, possibly two, other aircraft. One aircraft of the last sub flight was shot down, the crew being picked up by an escort destroyer. Post-strike PR showed the tanker

Spitfires of 229 Squadron.

stationary and leaking oil; later she was seen again, beached and abandoned.

On 20 August, 229 Squadron had sent an offensive sweep of eighteen Spitfires over Sicily, a move reminiscent of the fighter sweeps flown over Europe from the UK – and a great morale boost to the pilots in that they were now hunting the enemy on their turf. They were led by Group Captain Walter Churchill, an experienced fighter pilot with the DSO and DFC, both awarded in May 1940 for operations in France, and who had arrived with one of the recent Spitfire reinforcements. This first op proved quiet with no ground or air reaction from the Italians. On the third mission (27 August) Churchill elected to strafe some of the enemy airfields and was shot down when attacking Biscari.

In the letter that Air Vice-Marshal Park sent to Mrs Churchill he said: 'I am writing because I feel that it may be some comfort to you in your great loss to know that your husband met his end leading a fighter formation in a most successful attack on the enemy. Although Walter Churchill has passed on, his fine example and inspired leadership will live on in Malta to the end of the war. He arrived in Malta leading a formation of reinforcing Spitfires to protect the last vitally important convoy. During his all too short stay in Malta Walter Churchill was an inspiration to the fighter squadron in the air and on the ground. If it was ordained that Walter Churchill was to give his life for his country I feel sure he would have chosen to end it as he did, leading a fighter formation on a daring and most successful fighter sweep over enemy territory.' He is commemorated by a Commonwealth Graves Commission stone in the Syracuse War Cemetery on Sicily.

A German navy report of late August no longer trumpeted that the Mediterranean situation was favourable. It maintained its stance on capturing Malta: 'The opinion of the Naval Staff regarding the importance of the capture of Malta remains unaltered. The capture of Gibraltar remains a most desirable object for the future. It is particularly important to seal off the Mediterranean completely in case of a long drawn-out war. We now have 15 submarines in the area. Heavy damage was again caused by enemy bombers.' (Fuhrer Conference 26 August 1942).

On 26 August a mixed force attacked a convoy at the very mouth of Tobruk harbour – a 6,000-ton tanker, 6,000-ton MV and 900-ton freighter. The tanker was sunk, and later in the day the MV went the same way. The tanker and its escort had originally been picked up on the 24th by a PRU Spitfire. A strike force of nine Beauforts with nine Beaufighters as escort went out from Malta and found the target but no confirmed hits were made, One Beaufort was lost and one damaged. Such was the importance of destroying tankers that it was hunted down on the 26th. The following day, the Beauforts and their escort were out again after a supply ship was spotted south-east of Cape Matapan, with a Baltimore confirming the location. The attackers claimed three torpedo hits and one bomb hit (by a 227 Squadron Beaufighter), leaving the ship burning and sinking. The victim was the *Istria* (5,400 tons). The Beaufighters also claimed an escorting Cant and Ju 88.

One point of note for all these attacks is that the convoy was located by a PRU aircraft, Spitfire or Baltimore, and Gibbs acknowledged the role of Malta's PRU: 'Reconnaissance consisted normally of a PRU sighting giving course, speed, composition and disposition of the convoy; the original report was followed up if necessary by further PRU sorties. If it was thought that there would be difficulty in the strike force locating, a Baltimore was sent off in advance of the strike to send out a W/T sighting report if the target was not found in the position anticipated from the last PRU sighting. If the target's progress was normal, the Baltimore maintained

'The capture of Gibraltar remains a most desirable object for the future' – Fuhrer Conference 26 August 1942. Gibraltar actually continued to improve its facilities and support, as evidenced in this early 1943 shot.

W/T silence and remained to photograph the strike. The passage of ships at night has been checked by ASV Wellington.

'This comprehensive reconnaissance has been very valuable to the leader of the strike, since he has always been in possession before take-off of very full information concerning the disposition of escort vessels and the position of targets relative to the coastline. This information has enabled him to navigate the force so as to achieve the best bearing of approach to the attack without unnecessary manoeuvring within visibility of the target.'

The final Beaufort success of the month was yet another tanker on the 30th. The Beauforts had twelve Beaufighters as escort and the co-ordinated attack went well, with at least two torpedo hits (of four dropped) on the 5,077-ton *San Andrea*. The tanker caught fire and sank, and yet another valuable load of fuel was lost to Rommel. The Beaufighter escort had opened the attack by dropping six 250lb bombs on the tanker and using cannon and machine-gun fire on it and the escorting destroyer. For good measure, it also claimed a number of the escorting aircraft.

The latter part of August was a poor one for 202 Squadron with the loss of a number of aircraft; W6003 capsized and sank after landing at Gibraltar on 12 August, all the crew escaping without injury. On 28 August, Sunderland W4029 landed after an escort sortie and burst into flames; two of the depth charges exploded and only one of the pilots survived the incident. Two days later, all four engines cut-out on 'R' due to an air lock in the fuel; however, the aircraft landed safely and was taken in tow. Another U-boat was attacked by Flying Officer Walshe (W6002) on 14 September and two of the five depth charges exploded against the port bow and two by the conning tower,

The 39 Squadron detachment at Malta. (*Don Tilley, SAAF*)

lifting the submarine out of the water. While the Sunderland circled the scene, the submarine crew abandoned the stricken vessel, the *Alabastro*. This was 202 Squadron's one and only U-boat victory with the type, the squadron bade farewell to its Sunderland element in October.

September remained quiet on Malta, with fewer than sixty air raid warnings and so very little for the pilots to do, other than when sweeps were organized. For the recce and offensive aircraft, it was busier, especially as the war in the desert was in another crisis period for the Allies, Rommel having pushed the Eighth Army back to Egypt. His offensive had stalled for two reasons – resilient defence at the very last line, El Alamein, and lack of supplies, as

An Italian convoy, the picture is captioned as being taken from the *Manara*, one of the ships that was hit on the 6th.

he had not captured as much Allied stores, especially fuel, as he had hoped. And with Malta back in action, his convoy route was precarious. The anti-shipping successes continued in the first week of September, with a joint force of Wellingtons, Albacores and Swordfish severely damaging the 4,300-ton *Monti* on the 3rd, with the ship finally having to be beached. Three days later, the 6th, it was the turn of 39 Squadron's Beauforts again, with the 7,000-ton *Manara* being torpedoed and having to be beached. Additional submarines arrived in Malta on the 12th with the 1st Submarine Flotilla moving across from Alexandria.

Two more ships were claimed in September, the *Carbonia* on the 17th, sunk by Beaufighters of 227 Squadron, the first such success – although from 1943 onwards it would be 'Torbeaus' that would become the scourge of Axis shipping in the Med. On the night of 28th/29th the Wellingtons of 69 Squadron claimed the *Ravenna*, damaged and then beached. When 39 Squadron returned to Malta in November after its sojourn at Shallufa, the situation was very different. Conditions, both operational and social, had improved greatly, to such an extent that this period has been recalled by many as the most comfortable of the whole Beaufort era. The problems of food stocks, however, continued to be discussed at the highest level. Field Marshal Alanbrooke noted in his diary for 28 September: 'Long COS attended by Cater of Colonial Office and by Mr Rowntree, catering advisor to the Governor of Malta. He had sad tales about food situation on Malta. Somewhat of

Routine matters continued as usual despite operations … Mess Bill for Lieutenant Don Tilley, September 1942.

an alarmist. I do not think that he was examining the problem from a war point of view. Slaughtering cattle and horses had certainly not been taken fully into account in his calculations. In any case he must have a definite estimate of the situation from the Governor himself.'

A few days later (2 October) the subject was covered again: 'Our COS meeting was again mainly taken up with discussing plans for the future feeding of Malta. The present supplies finish about the middle of October. Future supplies will depend on success of Middle East offensive and North African adventure. If neither succeeds God knows how we shall keep Malta alive, and even so the timing of both these alternatives will inevitably run Malta very low before relief can come.'

Group Captain J.A. Tester (Signals 6 RDF) visited Malta in late October and produced a report for AHQ Malta, primarily on the radar and control capability, but the initial paragraphs actually discussed food: 'The chief topic of conversation in Malta is the food. Why this should be is not quite understood, as the food in more varied than rations in the Western Desert and in general seems of good quality.' Against this comment someone has made a pencil note in the margin 'Little Bograt!' – so clearly one reader of the document was not impressed.

The report continued: 'On the whole the food appeared to me adequate in quantity and quality, but the fact remains that people seem to lose weight in Malta and there is considerable sickness, particularly of the stomach trouble variety. There are many mosquitoes and sand fly, which are undoubtedly responsible for quite a lot of sickness.

'Civilian morale at present is comparatively high owing to the recent air successes and the fact that bombers, in the day time at least, have practically disappeared in attacks on the Island, which are carried out almost exclusively by fighter bombers. Seeing the attacks are nearly always directed at the aerodromes and the bombs are small, there is little tendency to cease work on the sounding of the alarm. Regarding Service morale, in general all people connected with fighters have their tails well up. I even heard fighter pilots say they would rather be in Malta than anywhere else in the world.'

The bulk of the report concerned the performance of the ground and air radar, including problems of enemy jamming, and the functioning of the filter room and operations room. In general, Tester found the situation reasonable. He was very impressed with the searchlights: 'I believe that the searchlights in Malta are better than in any other area. Over a period of ten days with the assistance of SLC equipment, 36.5 per cent of the raids crossing the coast were illuminated. Brigadier Woolley, OC 7th AA Brigade, is very keen and watches the statistics of his units very closely.'

Flight Lieutenant 'Moose' Marshall DFC, 39 Squadron – one of the squadron's characters and considered a great torpedo-bomber pilot during this period. He was listed as FTR (Failed to Return) from a sortie in November 1942.

He was less complimentary about night interception: 'Night interception by AI Beaufighters is not good in Malta. Over one period there were 68 night fighter sorties to 75 enemy night sorties, which only resulted in 5 contacts.' He was unable to determine the exact nature of the problem, but believed it was lack of experience with the controllers, and especially with height readings. His report concluded: 'The state of Malta's defences from an RDF and ground control point of view can be considered satisfactory, although a number of points still need attention.'

The Italians viewed the period that ended on 10 October as the fifth period in operations against Malta, which had started on 10 May with the ending of the previous intensive campaign. It was stated that: 'Operations in Egypt stopped the offensive against Malta. As the pressure of air attacks was relaxed, Malta regained her offensive capacities with extraordinary rapidity, especially in the air. In the middle of Sept 1942, reconnaissance over the Island revealed 3 corvettes, 5 steamers (4 of which were oil vessels), 5 submarines and 185 aircraft. There was much more submarine activity during this period, although there was very little air activity in relation to the number of aircraft on Malta, but this may have been due to a shortage of fuel. Following the resumed offensive air activities, naval traffic bound for Italian N. Africa had to make use of the longer coastal routes and to be escorted by aircraft thus placing a great burden on the Air Force.' ('Air and Naval Bases on Malta Situation Report' May 1942 translated by AHB as VII/43).

Once again the loss of shipping stung the Germans into the 'final destruction' of Malta. The new air campaign opened on 10 October 1942. However, they now faced an effective air defence and the waves of bombers were disrupted north of Malta, despite having fighter escort. The 'October Blitz' involved some 2,400 sorties and from the Axis point of view was a total failure. German losses were around fifty aircraft in a ten-day period, enough to persuade Kesselring that he did not have the strength to achieve the task. The RAF lost thirty Spitfires, but more than 50 per cent of the pilots were safe – a marked improvement in

Comiso was one of the main Axis airfields on Sicily and housed a variety of units and types.

survivability over some previous periods. Furthermore, no significant damage was done, none of the target airfields were closed, and Malta's offensive operations were not curtailed.

Air Ministry Middle East News Service   Air Ministry Bulletin No. 8273

MALTA'S BIG DAY

The Luftwaffe and the Regia Aeronautica have taken one of their biggest threshings over the island fortress of Malta since the war began.

During Sunday and Monday, a total of 39 enemy aircraft, 19 bombers and 20 fighters, have been destroyed, and many more damaged.

In addition our night fighters shot down a Heinkel 111 on Sunday night.

It is possible that when all the claims have been investigated the score may be even higher.

This two days' impressive success has been achieved at a cost of six of our fighter aircraft, of which the pilots of two are safe.

At the same time the enemy has inflicted practically no military damage to offset his staggering losses.

Despite the warning administered on Sunday, when our fighters shot down 15 enemy aircraft, seven Junkers 88s and eight of the escorting fighters out of five waves of raiders, there was another down attack on Monday morning.

Our pilots began the day by destroying five Junkers 88s and a fighter, severely damaging many more than that number.

From then onwards, the air defenders of Malta went from strength to strength and a raid at mid-day produced what may be termed "classic" interception.

An enemy bomber force, powerfully protected by fighters, left Sicily to attack the island. Spitfires pounced out of the blue on the incoming raiders. They dived down on the enemy some 30 miles out to sea and massacred them.

Extract of press release for 'Malta' Big Day', 13 October 1942.

A series of heavy raids started on 11 October, primarily by Ju 88s with 109s of JG 77 and JG 53 providing escort. Some 257 sorties were flown against Malta and the Germans lost nine aircraft. Malta had enough Spitfires for some squadrons to be on standby and some on reserve, which enabled a much more effective use of aircraft and pilots. The attackers did, however, manage to reach at least some of their targets, although damage was limited. The following day the Luftwaffe attacked airfields with no real success, but losing fifteen aircraft. The Air Ministry Middle East New Service issued a press release on 13 October entitled 'Malta's Big Day'. It opened with 'The Luftwaffe and the Regia Aeronautica have taken one their biggest thrashings over the island fortress of Malta since the war began. During Sunday and Monday [11th and 12th], a total of 39 enemy aircraft, 19 bombers and 20 fighters, have been destroyed, and many more damaged. In addition our night fighters shot down a Heinkel 111 on Sunday night. This two days' impressive success has been achieved at a cost of six of our fighter aircraft, of which the pilots of two are safe.'

The point of a press release is to boost morale for one's own side, while causing the enemy concern, hence the nature of the wording of such statements. This one continued: 'The main point, however, was that not one single enemy aircraft in this strong formation was allowed to get anywhere near the coast of Malta ... How long the enemy can stand losses on this scale remains to be seen.' (AMB 8273 dated 13 October).

Clearly they could continue for a few more days, and on the 13th the focus was Luqa, and 219 sorties were flown with little real effect. The press team stated that: 'Soon after dawn on Tuesday [13th], the enemy lost his one thousandth aircraft over or near Malta since the war began in the Mediterranean.' This 1,000th victory was credited to Pilot Officer G.F. Beurling DFM* 'who destroyed two other hostile aircraft in the same fight – a performance which is becoming quite a habit with him. Beurling is a 22-year old Canadian who had gained all his decorations and his commission since coming to Malta in June. His sense of positioning is instinctive and he must be one of the best marksmen in the RAF. He has now destroyed 24 hostile aircraft in Malta, and had two to his credit before he arrived.'

The statement also payed tribute to the anti-aircraft defences: '... and Malta's magnificent gunners, whose sustained effort over a period of nearly two and a half years has put up a record which of its kind may never be beaten. They have been murderously bombed and machine-gunned for months on end, and for long periods when fighters were scarce they had almost the sole responsibility for defending the island. Yet never once did they falter or let anyone down, and when, in April this year they shot down 138 enemy aircraft during the month, the garrison and people realized even more clearly than ever their debt of gratitude to the Royal Artillery.' (AMB 8278 dated 14 October).

George Beurling was shot down on the 14th, being injured, and narrowly escaping his damaged and burning aircraft. By this time, he had scored twenty-seven confirmed while operating

There appears to be some confusion over the 1,000th victory, with some crediting it to Beurling and others to Squadron Leader Lynch of 249 Squadron, seen here in his Spitfire with groundcrew chalking up the 1,000th.

with 249 Squadron over Malta. The citation for his DSO read: 'Since being awarded a Bar to the Distinguished Flying Medal, this officer has shot down a further 3 hostile aircraft, bringing his total victories to 20. One day in September, 1942, he and another pilot engaged 4 enemy fighters. In the ensuing combat, Pilot Officer Beurling destroyed 2 of them. As a relentless fighter, whose determination and will to win has won the admiration of his colleagues, this officer has set an example in keeping with the highest traditions of the Royal Air Force.' (AMB 8416). A similar number of sorties was flown on the 14th, the main target being Ta Kali, where some damage was caused to the operating surfaces, at a cost of five attackers lost. The Air Ministry press release noted four main raids during the day:

1. 6 a.m.: twelve Ju.88s in two formations, escorted by 50 German and Italian fighters. 'The enemy were intercepted by Spitfires north of Malta and the first formation turned back. The second formation kept on its course and was heavily engaged, one Ju.88 and two Me.109s being destroyed. One Spitfire was lost, but the pilot was saved.
2. 9 a.m.: ten Ju.88s, escorted by 50 German and Italian fighters. 'They were intercepted by Spitfires 20 miles north of the island. Three Ju.88s and two Me.109s were destroyed, and all the remaining bombers and several more fighters were damaged. From this engagement, three Spitfires were missing, but one pilot was saved.'
3. 12 o'clock: Eight Ju.88s, escorted by some 40 fighters 'were intercepted 15 miles NE of Malta. One Ju.88, four Me.109s and two Italian fighters were destroyed, and as many more damaged. Most of the raiders jettisoned their bombs in the sea. One Spitfire was lost, the pilot, though wounded, was saved.'
4. 3.30 p.m.: ten Ju.88s, escorted by 40 fighters, were 'intercepted north of the island. No less than seven out of the ten bombers and one fighter were destroyed. The Spitfires suffered no losses in this engagement.' (AMB 8295 dated 15 October)

Of particular note is the fact that all interceptions took place some distance from Malta. Two Spitfire pilots were recused by the MCU on the 14th (Nash and Beurling) and two more on the 15th (Farquarson and Bryden).

Although the Luftwaffe flew 250 sorties on the 15th, many were intercepted before they reached Malta, a 'forward interception' tactic that had been introduced some time before but was not increasingly effective as more fighters were available and the RDF and Sector Control were more experienced. By September 1942 the RDF organization comprised eight eight AMES units at seven locations: Dingli still had two (242 and 504), while the other had one each – Ghar Lapsi (241), Gozo (521), Kaura (314), Madliena (502), Ta Silch (501), and Wardia (841). Interestingly, despite the number of sorties, and the RAF flew 110 or so, each side only lost four aircraft. The following day was slightly busier, with 260 Axis

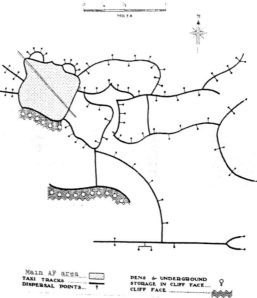

A 1942 plan of the extensive dispersals at Ta Kali, including use of the cliff face for pens and underground storage.

and 125 RAF sorties. Of those Axis sorties, the majority were fighters, the ratio of fighters to bombers having been increased to try to win air superiority (shoot down Spitfires) and protect the bombers. Damage was again light, but the overall campaign was having an effect on the availability of Spitfires, not through losses but through serviceability. The RAF press release claimed 'Malta bags 100th Raider'; and reported that: 'During the four main raids by the enemy on Malta on Thursday [15th] our Spitfire pilots destroyed five bombers and nine fighters. Our losses were four Spitfires, but three of the pilots are safe. On this day, half way through the month, Malta's fighter pilots destroyed their 100th enemy aircraft in October.'

The following day a press release claimed that in the intensive period from 11 to 15 October '98 aircraft have been destroyed in the defence of the island; 93 by our Spitfires. During the same period our losses have been 18 fighters with ten of the pilots safe.' Of more interest is the next statement: 'Italian and German war communiques present a travesty of the facts.' It said that the Italian communiques claimed seventy-four RAF aircraft destroyed (by German and Italian aircraft) and admitted a loss of seven, whereas German communiques claimed fifty-eight RAF aircraft destroyed for the loss of thirteen. So a fairly large discrepancy between the RAF claims and the Axis claims, which is not unusual. Regardless of the claims, the end result was the same – interceptions were being made some distance from Malta, bombing was ineffective, and the RAF was in the ascendancy.

The 17th saw 245 enemy sorties met by 103 Spitfire sorties, from a serviceable force down to around 40 aircraft. The

The Allies were by now dominating the eastern Med, with additional squadrons operating from various airfields. 52 Squadron was operating over this area and on 2 September, Pilot Officer Carpenter shot down this Fiat RS.14. (*52 Squadron*)

Beaufighter of 255 Squadron at Gibraltar. Aircraft continued to stage through Gib, and from October Spitfires with 170-gallon ferry tanks were flying Gib to Malta direct.

following day the Germans attempted two raids, but neither made it to Malta, being intercepted offshore and driven back. There is perhaps an indication here of a weakening of morale, with the formations turning back once engaged.

Wellingtons of 69 Squadron scored another success on the night of 18th/19th, damaging the 8,000-ton tanker *Panuco* such that it had to be beached. The tanker had been found off Cape Spartivento during the afternoon of the 18th by the submarine HMS *Una*, and although the escort prevented an attack, the submarine was able to give an accurate position update of this valuable target.

The 19th was the final day of the Axis offensive and 210 sorties were mounted, although most were intercepted and turned back, the bombers frequently just jettisoning their bombs. The RAF pilots reported a reluctance to engage on the part of the enemy. Whereas in the previous blitz the Luftwaffe had been able to assert dominance, it was now clear that Malta was able to protect itself more effectively, in the air with Spitfire Vs and on the ground with extensive hardened facilities and an ability for rapid repair. Such was the need to get new fighters to Malta that October saw the start of direct ferry flights from Gibraltar, the Spitfires carrying a 170-gallon ferry fuel tank.

Sergeant Park: October: 'We were patrolling at 21,000 feet, 20 miles north-east of Grand Harbour, when we sighted nine Junkers 88 with a swarm of fighters heading south. We turned into the attack, Red 1 and myself going into the bombers. I got on one bomber's tail, but my guns

Excellent cartoon dated 26 October 1942 showing the German commander and his Italian colleague (and note caricature of them both) as RAF aircraft destroy their precious supplies, with a Beaufort taking pride of place. (*Don Tilley, SAAF*)

had frozen so I broke away, and after shaking off two attacking Messerschmitt 109s, I dived away down to 10,000 feet. On hearing the Ground Controller broadcast the height and position of the bombers, I went east to Kalafrana Bay, where the bombers were seen heading back to the north-east. I tried to intercept them, but was jumped by two M.E. 109s. I turned quickly to avoid, and after a complete turn got on a Messerschmitt's tail. I closed in without opening fire to about 100 yards, when he changed his turn and I gave him a three-second burst from dead astern. He went into a steep dive straight into the sea.' Sergeant Park arrived in mid-July and had been gradually adding to his score, including two Ju 88s shot down on 12 October. He was killed in another air battle on the 25th.

The renewed air offensive had turned out to be short-lived and ineffective. The Italian summary recorded this as the sixth period of operations, between 10 and 20 October: 'The aims of the third air offensive were:

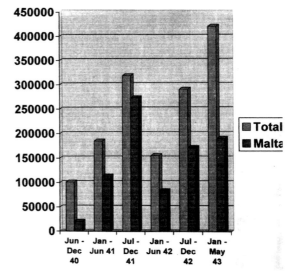

AXIS CENTRAL MED SHIPPING LOSSES [Tons] 1940-43

Graph of axis shipping losses in the central Med; although this covers the period from June 1940 to May 1943, the key strategic periods coincide with operations in North Africa, and the size of the Malta bar increases when the Island was not under intense air attack.

1. Eliminate the enemy fighters during the first phase by engaging them in combat
2. Remove the offensive capability of the Island as much as possible during the second phase by bombing.

'The intended results, however, were not achieved, due to the comparatively small number of aircraft employed.' ('Air and Naval Bases on Malta Situation Report' May 1942 translated by AHB as VII/43). Twenty-nine more Spitfires arrived from the carrier *Furious* under Operation Train on 29 October.

Beaufighters of 227 Squadron made an anti-shipping attack on 14 October, when three aircraft attacked an MV and destroyer off the coast of Tripoli. They attacked at mast height, but two were shot down almost immediately, while the third dropped two 500lb bombs and strafed the MV, but with no observed result. One Beaufighter crew was subsequently picked up a destroyer that was guided to the spot by a PRU Spitfire. During October, night anti-shipping attacks were made by Wellingtons, now the major type involved in this type of attack, and using torpedoes and bombs, as well as Albacores and Swordfish. During the month, claims were made for nine ships hit, with four of those sunk. The most successful night attack on shipping was late in October; a Baltimore picked up a convoy off the coast of Greece and later a torpedo Wellington of 69 Squadron found the convoy of one tanker (*Luisiano* of 2,550 tons) and an MV, along with two destroyers. The Wellington dropped against the MV, claiming a hit, and with the ship being assessed as 'severely damaged'. A second Wellington attacked and sank the tanker.

The failure of the supply route to Rommel, especially the near total destruction of all fuel supplies, meant that the planned Allied offensive stood more chance of success, especially as its commander, Montgomery, had built up overwhelming superiority and the Desert Air Force and other RAF units had achieved air supremacy. Montgomery launched his offensive on 23 October, and from that point on it was an Allied drive – albeit hard fought at times – across North Africa. The most significant event in the western Mediterranean in late 1942 was, of course, Operation Torch, the Allied landings in Tunisia in November. The advance in North Africa helped Malta, just as Malta helped the campaigns in North Africa, as airfields in Cyrenaica could be used to provide air cover for convoys from Alexandria to Malta, which now became a safer route than that from Gibraltar to Malta. The last intensive air attacks on Malta had ended within weeks of starting, the defenders having taken a high toll of the attackers, although sporadic attacks continued into mid-November. 'During this period little damage was done to the airfields or the construction work taking place. Progress naturally decreased during this increased attack but it is to the credit of the Maltese that in spite of their hardships they put in a remarkably high percentage of working hours. On the fall of Benghazi, Malta's siege was raised and convoys from the east arrived safely. Immediately following the first arrivals of essential supplies of food, petrol and oil, etc. convoys arrived with the long awaited engineer stores and plant for airfield construction work. The next and greatest phase of airfield development on the island was due to begin.' (AP 3236).

The 16 November convoy from Egypt was given air cover for its entire route, at first from North Africa and then from Malta and, despite a number of attacks by enemy aircraft, all its ships arrived safely. The harbour was full and protected by Spitfire air patrols. It was a turning point in that Malta now had a reasonable level of supplies with which to increase its offensive.

The final book in this series covering the Desert and Mediterranean War will include the North African campaign (El Alamein and Operation Torch), and the invasion of Sicily and Italy, from November 1942 to May 1945, including Allied domination of the Mediterranean.

Appendix A

Greece and Crete

The Allied operations in Greece and Crete from late 1940 to May 1941 were seen by many as a distraction from the main campaign in the desert, and to others as an essential part of the overall campaign, not least as it was keeping a promise to an ally. I had intended to provide more details in this book, but we ran out of space, and so this campaign has been moved to this appendix and cut down in size.

On 28 October 1940 Italian forces invaded Greece from Albania. In response to Greek requests, British air forces were sent from Egypt, followed some time later by ground troops. The diversion of resources to Greece at a time when the British forces in the Western Desert were in a position to oust the Italians from Africa has been seen as one turning point in the fortunes of the Desert War – and has caused much detailed and often bitter argument. However, many German scholars have seen Hitler's insistence on sending troops to the Balkan/Greek theatre as a significant factor in the failure of the invasion of Russia. This appendix takes only a brief look at Greece and Crete, through selected events and operations of the RAF squadrons. The initial RAF effort comprised three squadrons of Blenheims (30, 84 and 211) plus the Gladiators of 80 Squadron; all were soon engaged on successful operations against the Italians as the latter found their 'simple' conquest turning into defeat. Air Vice-Marshal Sir John D'Albiac was given additional squadrons, in part to make up for a reduction in the combat strength of the Hellenic Air Force (HAF).

The Blenheims of 84 Squadron moved into Menidi in early November, the officers taking over a summer residence and the airmen putting up a tented camp in the pine woods to the north of the airfield. Over the next few days this initial detachment ('A Flight') attacked Valona and Durazzo. On the 13th, three crews were tasked against bridges and troop concentrations near Koritza, claiming destruction of the bridge. Two aircraft failed to return (L3189 Flight Lieutenant Mudie and L3178 Sergeant Sidaway) with the loss of all crew; the third aircraft (Sergeant Nuttall) returned to base but his aircraft was heavily damaged. By the end of the month the rest of the squadron had arrived, as had part of 211 Squadron and the Gladiators of 80 Squadron. The latter started to fly escort missions for the Blenheims, which was most appreciated, as on the occasions when the Italian fighters intercepted the bombers, damage and losses were high.

The Gladiators of 80 Squadron had moved to Greece in mid-November, based at Eleusis but with forward operations from Yannena. Initial tasking included offensive patrols as well as bomber escort. On 12 December, 230 Squadron sent an advanced party to Scaramanga as this provided an ideal location from which to

84 Squadron Blenheim at Menidi, December 1940.

mount searches for Italian naval vessels. 'This was an almost ideal flying boat alighting area. The site of the moorings is off a Greek naval base at the east end of the lake. There is a slipway capable of taking one Sunderland, though designed for launching ships the Greek Navy had installed an electric winch for hauling out. The new centrally-heated Drawing Office was used to accommodate officers and men.' (*230 Sqn ORB*)

No. 80 Squadron was operating from Trikala but on 4 December it was reported: 'Owing to the very poor conditions under which the Squadron is accommodated, the remainder of the Squadron at Trikala moved by road to Larissa.' Yannena had been used as the forward operating base but in the first week of December virtually everyone was at Larissa. The squadron was having problems with unserviceable aircraft, but by 11 December: 'After nearly 5 days of hard work the U/S aircraft were more or less ready for immediate operations.' (80 Sqn ORB).

The lack of good roads made it more difficult for units to move around and for them to be supplied; it was also to cause a problem in the retreat and evacuation. Additional squadrons arrived in January and the situation appeared quite promising. One of those units was 112 Squadron, which had already built a fine reputation as a Gladiator fighter squadron in the Western Desert. The squadron had also, in December, flown a number of Gladiators to Greece for the HAF. On the 3rd, four aircraft (Flying Officer Cochrane, Flight Lieutenant Fry, and Pilot Officer Smith from B Flight, and Second Lieutenant Geraty) flew to Larissa to be attached to 80 Squadron for ops.

The squadron flew its first mission, as 112 Squadron, on 1 February when two aircraft patrolled over Athens, but the real task did not start until the 9th when a detachment moved to Yannena to join 80 Squadron in operations over the front line. That same day, Pilot Officer Vale of 80 Squadron was involved in a combat that again seemed to confirm the Italian reluctance to engage: 'At 1040 hours, 14 Gladiators took off on an offensive patrol over Klissoura area, led by S/Ldr Jones. Just after reaching the patrol area "tally ho" was given on sighting three enemy bombers, which turned back before an interception could be made. Two Gladiators had to leave the formation with engine trouble. The patrol was carried on until about 1155 hours "tally ho" was given for a formation of five CR42s, which apparently did not observe our formation until very late and then three broke away and went down to the North. I was slightly behind the main formation and headed the two CR42s off until they both broke away downwards, followed by two Gladiators.

80 Squadron personnel at Yannina.

80 Squadron – from the desert to the snow of Greece!

'I then observed about six more formations of 5 CR42s above us and so I gave "tally ho" and I immediately climbed. A dog fight started and from my position the policy of the EA seemed to be diving attacks and gaining height straight away. One CR42 dived on me from above but I managed to evade his fire by pulling round and up towards him. I fired a short burst which seemed to scare him away. I then saw a CR42 diving down on to a Gladiator and so carried out a diving quarter attack and he pulled away which left me in an astern position close in. I carried on firing until the EA turned over on its back and the pilot left the machine. I saw his parachute open and so gained height and fired a long burst at a CR42 which dived down on me from above. I then broke away from the combat and owing to shortage of ammunition and fuel returned to base with Flying Officer Cullen who came up and formated with me.'

The Hurricanes of 33 Squadron arrived in Greece in late February, the first op, an escort of Blenheims, taking place on the 25th. The target for 11 and 211 Squadron was Buzat. The first success came on the 28th when the squadron contributed four Hurricanes in a fighter force that also included six Hurricanes and seven Gladiators of 80 Squadron and eleven Gladiators of 112 Squadron. The formation intercepted fifty bombers and fighters in the Tepelenë area and a major fight ensued. According to the 33 Squadron ORB, the claims were:

- 80 Sqn: 7 CR.42, 5 Cant Z.1007, 2 SM.79 destroyed + 3 CR.42 and 2 G.50 probable
- 112 Sqn: 4 CR.42 destroyed + 6 G.50 probable + one BR.20 damaged
- 33 Sqn: 2 Cant Z.1007 damaged

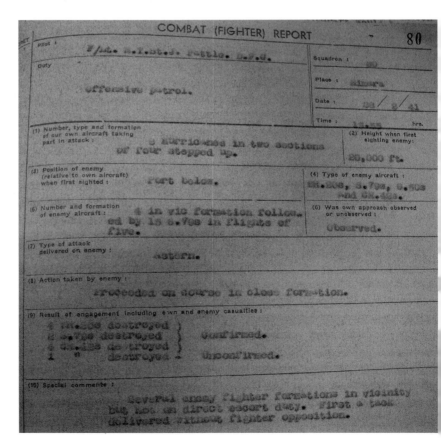

Combat report, 28 February 1941, Pat Pattle.

The 112 Squadron history for 28 February states: 'This was a record day in the Squadron's history. Eleven pilots joined in a general offensive over Sarandë–Argyrokraston–Valona–Tepelenë with the result that five G.50s and five CR.42s were shot down and two CR.42s and one BR.20 damaged. The formation, which consisted of 19 Gladiators echeloned in vics of three, plus ten Hurricanes in vics flying at 14,000ft saw the enemy aircraft below them. In the resulting fight, Flight Lieutenant Fraser and Flight Lieutenant Fry got two each, Sergeant Donaldson got one and a probable; Squadron Leader Brown one G.50, on which he made an

Pat Pattle (left), the most successful fighter pilot in the Greek campaign.

unobserved stern attack. The enemy aircraft turned steeply to starboard, with the Gladiator easily able to turn inside it and deliver full deflection shots. Flight Lieutenant Abrahams got one G.50 and was himself shot down while attacking the starboard aircraft of another flight of five G.50s. Flight Lieutenant Abrahams, who was the only casualty, reappeared at Yannena on 1st March, having landed by parachute on our side of the lines. Thus every pilot (of 112) in the formation inflicted some damage ion the enemy in a fight in which 27 enemy aircraft were destroyed, for the loss of one. The whole battle, which was fought about 20 miles NE of Argyrokastron, took place over the front line, in full view of both armies, a fact which greatly encouraged the Greeks.'

In March 1941 'the British had to decide whether they ought to drive the Italians from their last strong points on Tripolitania and this definitely liquidate the Italian colonial empire in North Africa or whether they ought to keep their promise to Greece. After German troops entered Bulgaria on 2 March, they decided to give assistance to threatened Greece.' This comment in a post-war German summary of Luftwaffe operations in the Mediterranean, was very perceptive and its premise has been much debated. The stark choice was military reality vs. political benefit/policy; there can be few at the time that truly believed the British intervention would lead to victory. The Greek commander had asked for nine British divisions plus appropriate air power, and initially been offered two – and very limited air cover. During March the Allied forces disembarked in Greece; the 2nd New Zealand and 6th Australian Divisions, and the 1st Brigade of the 2nd Armoured Division, by which time the air elements were already in action.

No. 112 Squadron continued intensive ops in early March against, what the diary referred to as 'Mussolini's bedraggled Eagles' and continued to add to their score, albeit not without loss. The third 'big fight' took place on 13 March when fourteen Gladiators, led by the CO (Squadron Leader Brown) were patrolling near Tepelenë when they engaged a large group of CR.42s and G.50s. 'Squadron Leader Brown attacked the leader of a vic, but it successfully avoided him. He got on the tail of another who turned and dived but it eventually crashed. Flight Lieutenant Fraser attacked three aircraft and shot them all down. First he attacked a CR.42, which had not seen him and the aircraft burst into flames and crashed near Buzi. He attacked another CR.42 which flick–rolled and dived. He followed him down and got in two long bursts, after which the aircraft levelled out and slowed down, with the pilot slumped forward in the cockpit. The aircraft dived vertically into the ground north of Corvode. Climbing back again to 8,000ft he got onto the tail of another CR.42 and continued firing until it burst into flames and was destroyed. The final scores for the day were: Flight Lieutenant Fraser (3), Flying Officer Cochrane (3), Pilot Officer Groves (2).' (*112 Sqn ORB*)

Of more significance for the Mediterranean War, perhaps, was the German decision to 'co-operate' with their Italian allies in the theatre. Hitler communicated with Mussolini in December his concern over the psychological and military consequences that would arise from the Italian intervention in the Balkans and Greece, his concern being that this would provide an excuse for the British to send forces to Greece – and that British aircraft would then, using Greek bases, be in range of such strategic assets as the Romanian oil fields. The letter suggested for the first time that the Italian and German air forces should collaborate in the Mediterranean. At this stage he was thinking in terms of German aircraft supporting Italian operations towards Egypt, and also that the Mediterranean would become the 'tomb of the British Navy within 3-4 months'. This was the first time that Hitler had taken the Mediterranean theatre (and Western Desert) into consideration as part of his overall strategy, albeit with tight timings and force constraints, as he was already firming up his plans for the invasion of the Soviet Union. A few more months were to pass before the Germans joined the battle in the Balkans and Greece.

The Germans declared war on Greece and Yugoslavia on 5 April, and their offensive opened the following day, driving the Allies away from the Metaxa Line and into headlong retreat. An Me 110 was seen on the 10 and the pilots of 112 Squadron had no illusions that their Gladiators were no match of the Luftwaffe. The squadron diary commented: 'If any Gladiators are left their next appearance no doubt will be in the British Museum.'

The German plan was for 12th Army to assault Yugoslavia and then Greece, supported by VIIIth Air Corps initially and, with the Greek campaign, 4th Air Fleet/VIII Air Corps and X Air Corps (Sicily) weighing in as well. The air attack on Belgrade, which effectively opened the German campaign, took place on 6 April. The (German estimated) 357 'combat-efficient' aircraft of the Yugoslav Air Force, which included some German types such as the 109, were soon neutralized. This campaign sits outside of the coverage of this book but it overlaps with the Greek campaign, X Air Corps attacking the Greek port at Piraeus (Athens) as early as 7 April.

The 33 Sqn ORB records: 'On April 6th Germany declared war against Greece. On April 7th, 12 Hurricanes led by S/Ldr Pattle carried out a fighter sweep over the Rupel Pass area of Bulgaria during the later afternoon. During this patrol S/Ldr Pattle surprised and shot down two ME109s confirmed, whilst F/O Wickham, further North was engaging three more ME109s and shot down one of them confirmed. F/Sergeant Cottingham, still further North in the Rupel Valley, shot down one more ME109, the pilot bailing out. While the parachute was falling, another 109 circled round to give protection, and this aircraft was also shot down by F/Sergeant Collingham.'

This was an excellent start, but within a few days the tables would turn and the Allied aircraft would lose their air advantage. On 19 April Pat Pattle recorded his most successful single day, downing six, which took his score to between forty-five and fifty, some even suggest as high as sixty, as he was well known for being particularly reluctant to claim anything that was not definite. Sadly, he took off the following day against advice, as he appeared to have a fever, and was shot down and killed.

Most of the Blenheims were destroyed on the ground by Luftwaffe attacks, against which the few RAF fighters could make no impact. The RAF was running out of airfields and by the 19th was confined to airfields in the Athens area – not that Air Commodore D'Albiac had many aircraft left. When the Germans attacked the Athens airfields on the 20th, the raid was opposed by fifteen Hurricanes, with five shot down and others damaged, at a cost to the Germans of maybe eight aircraft. With total air superiority, the Luftwaffe turned its attention to shipping, destroying a number of Greek ships over the next few days, while the Allied ground forces tried to move to the Isthmus of Corinth and the Greek equivalent of Dunkirk.

The collapse continued and the Athens area was bombed and strafed every day between 19 and 22, although for some strange reason the airfield at Hassani was untouched – but, equally strangely, the RAF aircraft were ordered to stay on the ground. 'By late on 22nd April the last of the road party struggled in, many having walked a great part of the journey or having been picked up by the Army. On 22nd they received final orders to burn all papers, the aircraft to leave for Crete and the ground personnel to get to Argos, leaving at nightfall. By the time they got to Argos the Squadron was hopelessly spread out. By now about 11,000 Army and Air Force personnel had reached the place and the Germans were not far behind. Two of the ships standing by to take the troops off were dive-bombed and left burning, one, loaded with high explosive blew up with a terrific crash.'

The evacuation was still confused and by 23 April some 17,000 RAF personnel were at the coast waiting for ships. The 112 Squadron party moved to Nafplion, 5 miles from Argos: 'The entire party marched in good order and arrived at the water's edge without incident. As the harbour was too shallow for large ships to put in, an invasion barge was brought alongside and the airmen were put safely on board. After 70 hours without sleep the men just dropped where they were put, and allowed the Navy to carry them to Crete. The ship was the *Glen Earn*, an auxiliary cruiser, and late in the afternoon of 25th April they arrived at Suda Bay. There were no tents or blankets and so the airmen lay down under the trees in what they arrived in. What remained of 112 Squadron was at Heraklion and flying defensive sorties. On 29th it was decided that one Flight would remain in Crete and the other should move to Egypt; on the toss of a coin, "A Flight" left and "B Flight" stayed behind.' (*112 Squadron history*)

Meanwhile the evacuation had become increasingly difficult. In a daring and risky evacuation, a large proportion of the British (and New Zealand) troops were evacuated to Crete, part of this work being undertaken by Sunderlands which would appear at remote bays to lift key personnel to safety. Between 24th April and 1st May, the Navy evacuated over 50,000 men, but virtually no equipment. Most went only as far as Crete, although the lucky ones were taken all the way to Alexandria.

Kalamata was one of the small harbours that Allied forces used for evacuation.

Crete

It was obvious that Crete would be next as the Germans could not allow the Allies to keep possession of the island, not least because it had a number of good airfields (Maleme, Canea, Retimo, Heraklion) that could be used by bomber forces to threaten German strategic assets, such as the oil facilities at Ploesti. The assault would be supported by General Loehr's 4th Air Fleet, with elements of XI Air Corps (Student) and VIII Air Corps (Richthofen). The former was important as it was the air assault corps of 7th Air Division (three parachute regiments and one glider assault regiment, plus various support units to a total of some 25,000 men). The airlift was provided by some 500 Ju 52s and 100 gliders. It was to be both the high point and low point of German airborne operations. In the offensive role, VIIIth Corps had some 650 aircraft. The RAF aircraft strength for the defence of Crete amounted to a small number of Hurricanes and Gladiators, a mixed bag from 33, 80 and 112 squadrons, and twenty-three Blenheims of 30 and 203 squadrons. The initial task was to provide air cover for ships arriving from Greece and those departing from Suda Bay for Egypt. The Hurricanes of 80 Squadron had moved into Maleme on 24 April. Pilot Officer W. Vale:

29th Apr: Raid alarm. Took off in Hurricane and intercepted Do17 heading out to sea. Got within 400 yards of enemy aircraft and fired all my ammunition. Enemy aircraft last seen losing height with black smoke pouring from port engine. Own aircraft slightly damaged.

29th Apr: Raid alarm. Took off in Hurricane, intercepted 9 Ju88 dive bombers. Attacked formation of two at 6,000ft and after firing a short burst at starboard engine, enemy aircraft went down in flames and crashed into sea just North of Maleme aerodrome. I then chased two more which were escaping out to sea, and after about 5 minutes got near enough to open fire and after a long burst the enemy aircraft nosed into the sea. I observed two survivors which I reported by R/T. While returning to base I carried out a head on attack on a single machine, but after one short burst I ran out of ammunition.

William Vale received a DFC and a bar to the DFC for his operations in Greece and Crete. The DFC was awarded in February (AMB 3405) and the bar to the DFC in July (AMB 4420). The DFC had no specific citation. The bar to the DFC citation read: 'Following the evacuation operations from Greece, this office remained at Maleme aerodrome with some members of his unit. In the course of preliminary enemy air attacks on objectives in Crete, Pilot Officer Vale proved himself to be a staunch pilot. Frequently against odds, he continued his attacks against the enemy and destroyed four or their aircraft during an attack on the anchorage at Suda Bay. He displayed great courage and determination.'

The 33 Squadron ORB recorded for 13 May: 'three enemy aircraft dropped bombs in close vicinity of the aerodrome and Maleme village and machine gunned the aerodrome surrounding, but no damage was done.' And the following day: '0600 hours; one enemy aircraft dropped six bombs on West side of aerodrome, damaging Blenheims of 30 Squadron which were already unserviceable. 0900 hours; a few hours after the bombing a large number of Me109s strafed the aerodrome for half an hour. Three Hurricanes took off to intercept, Sergeant Ripsher and Sergeant Reynish getting off before the strafing had developed. In the third machine, Squadron Leader Howell took off as the aerodrome was being strafed. He passed 20 yards to the rear of one enemy aircraft and across the path of another, and keeping very low until he reached the hills, he was then able to climb safely. A few minutes later he shot down one Me109 confirmed. Meanwhile Sergeant Reynish was in combat with three E/A, one of which was seen to dive steeply into the hills after the Hurricane made an astern attack. Sergeant Reynish was then attacked by nine more Me109s and all disappeared behind the hills. At the same time Sergeant Ripsher sighted six E/A out to sea and attacked. One E/A was seen to dive steeply towards the sea. Sergeant Ripsher was also attacked and apparently damaged, and was killed whilst making his approach to the aerodrome. Sergeant Reynolds was shot down and bailed out over the sea, and succeeded in swimming a distance of two miles to safety. In the first raid one Hurricane was burnt out on the ground, while in the evening raid a second was also destroyed,

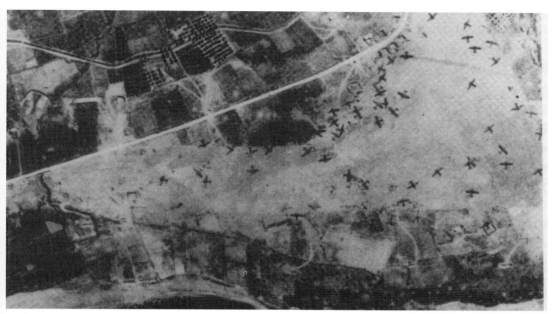

Maleme airfield with Ju 52 scattered over the field.

beside aircraft of other units on the aerodrome. Squadron Leader Howell returned after an absence of 3½ hours, having landed at Retimo to refuel and rearm.' (33 Sqn ORB).

The Blenheims soon left and by mid–May the British garrison of around 28,000 troops had maybe twenty to twenty-five fighters as their air cover, and it is recorded that only 50 per cent were serviceable. Overall command rested with General Freyberg, with Group Captain Beamish as the air commander. The assault on Crete was delayed through lack of supplies, most crucially building up the aviation fuel supplies (an estimated 800,000 gallons for XI Corps alone – an indication of the scale of the logistics 'back end' ... never mind bombs, bullets, and the host of other things needed to keep a technological force operational).

The German air assault began on 20 May, with paratroop and glider assaults meeting mixed results – and heavy casualties. The 33 Squadron ORB recorded: 'On the morning of the 20th began the long-awaited airborne invasion of Crete, heavy bombing and strafing by large formations of enemy aircraft heralding the arrival of hundreds of parachute troops as they dropped from Ju52s flying at only a few hundred feet above the ground, some of them towing gliders which were released over the dry river bed which ran alongside one side of the aerodrome.' However, the assault on Maleme proved successful and became a bridgehead for German reinforcements. The heavy losses, especially to the air-landing troops (and their Ju 52s), and the fierce resistance of the Allied troops against the lightly armed paratroops, caused far higher casualties than expected, and it was clear that seaborne troops and heavy equipment would be needed. And for that to happen, the Germans would need to dominate the sea lanes around Crete. On the evening of the 21st, the 33 Squadron ORB recorded: 'At nightfall the Squadron was nearly surrounded again, but the Maoris managed to clear the road to Canea, leaving the Squadron in a safer position.'

Meanwhile, Admiral Cunningham had deployed the Mediterranean fleet to guard the sea lanes, and a task force of battleships, cruisers, destroyers – and the carrier HMS *Formidable*. It was a risk but one that had been taken. The air-sea battle began on the 21st when an Italian supply convoy was

Sunderlands played a major role in the evacuation of key personnel from Greece and Crete; here a 230 Squadron aircraft awaits passengers off Crete.

destroyed by the British fleet – but Richthofen's pilots joined the battle and sank the destroyer *Juno* and damaged the cruiser *Ajax*. It was an indication of what was to come the following day.

The 22 May brought the first major air-sea battle around Crete. In the early morning the cruisers *Fiji* and *Gloucester* dodged bombs dropped by Stukas; the cruisers *Naiad* and *Carlisle* were damaged in an attack by Ju 88s and Do 17s, but both survived, albeit *Naiad* was badly damaged and had to leave the area. A few hours later the battleship *Warspite* was badly damaged and the destroyer *Greyhound* sunk. An attempt to rescue survivors led to the positioning of the *Fiji* and *Gloucester* to provide flak cover with their rapid-firing guns, but both were low on such ammunition after their early morning battle. Essentially they became targets that were not able to protect themselves, and *Gloucester* was sunk. Admiral King forbade any more rescue attempts and withdrew his forces, but *Fiji* was caught and sunk (one of the few successes to bomb-carrying 109s).

An attempt to reinforce and resupply on 26 May led to the carrier *Formidable* being damaged, its small number of aircraft making no impact on the German air superiority. Resupply turned to evacuation, and as usual the Navy was heroic in its efforts, but at some loss in sunk and damaged ships. By 30 May the Navy had lost three cruisers sunk (*Gloucester*, *Fiji*, *Calcutta*) and six destroyers (*Kelly*, *Kashmir*, *Juno*, *Imperial*, *Hereward*, *Greyhound*), with a further fifteen ships damaged (one carrier, three battleships, seven cruisers, four destroyers). According to the 'Luftwaffe War Diaries ',[author to add book details on proof] the Navy had also suffered fourteen ships damaged – severe damage to a battleship (*Warspite*) and three cruisers (*Naiad*, *Orion*, *Perth*) and slight damage to two battleships (*Valiant*, *Barham*), one aircraft carrier (*Formidable*), three cruisers (*Ajax*, *Carlisle*, *Dido*), and four destroyers (*Nubian*, *Decoy*, *Kelvin*, *Napier*).

The German build-up continued and in essence the Battle of Crete was over by the 23rd, although action on land, air and sea continued for a few more weeks, the final surrender taking place on 1 June. Crete now became an Axis air base and played a role on the convoy battles. As such it was also frequently on the target list for RAF bombers from the Middle East.

Appendix B

Chronology 1940–42

Note: this is a selective chronology covering Malta and the Mediterranean, and noting other strategic dates. Sinking of enemy ships are generally excluded (*see* Shipping appendix), major convoys are listed, but also see Convoy appendix.

1940
April
19   Sea Gladiators form Hal Far Fighter Flight (ready 4 May)
26   Establishment of 3 AACU with Swordfish

June
10   Italy declares war
11/12   First attack on Italy (by Bomber Command; Genoa and Turin)
11   First Italian air raid on Malta
?   First Hurricane reinforcements to Malta
11   Start of East African campaign
20   Establishment of Middle East reinforcement route via Takoradi (West Africa)
21   Surrender of France
28   First Hurricane sorties from Malta
28   Sunderland of 230 Sqn claims first aircraft sinking of an Italian U-boat (*Argonauta*)
29   Sunderland of 230 Sqn sinks Italian U-boat (*Rubino*)
30   Swordfish of 830 Sqn make first attack on Italian target, Augusta harbour
        Force H formed at Gibraltar

August
2   Hurricanes arrive Malta – Operation Hurry
4   Formation of 261 Sqn
12   No. 200 Group at Gibraltar placed under Coastal Command

September
13   Italians cross border of Egypt
16   Italians occupy Sidi Barrani (high point of Italian offensive)
17   First air attack on Benghazi (by FAA)
19   Formation of 431 Flight (Marylands) and disbandment of 3 AACU
23   Sunderland detachment from 228 Sqn
24/25   French aircraft bomb Gibraltar

October
28   Italy invades Greece

November

5	Start of RAF detachment to Greece
11	Battle of Taranto; FAA attacks
11	First RAF offensive mission in Greece (attack on Valona airfield)
17	Hurricanes from Operation White (only four of twelve arrive)

December

1	148 Sqn formed with Wellingtons; Malta's first bomber squadron
9	Start of first British offensive in Western Desert
10	Hitler announces intention to assist Italians and base Fliegerkorps X in the Mediterranean
16	Italians driven out of Egypt

1941

January

3	Luftwaffe units transferred to Mediterranean and North Africa theatre
10	431 Flight becomes 69 Sqn
10	Start of first Malta 'blitz'
16	First heavy German attack; the '*Illustrious* blitz' (16–23)
22	Allies capture Tobruk
27	First combined strike by Malta: recce and strike, *Ingo* sunk by Swordfish

February

	'Sink on Sight' powers extended in central Mediterranean
6	Allies capture Benghazi
12	Bf 109s first appear over Malta
26	Heavy raid destroys six Wellingtons and damages nine aircraft

March

	Expeditionary Force to Greece
9	Wellingtons depart Malta
23	Convoy MW6 arrives with supplies
23	228 Sqn departs Malta
28–29	Battle of Cape Matapan
30	German offensive in Western Desert

April

	'Sink on Sight' powers extended in eastern Mediterranean
3	Operation Winch, twelve Hurricanes arrive, Malta
3	Germans capture Benghazi
6	German advance into Greece and Yugoslavia
12	Start of Siege of Tobruk
21	Greece requests withdrawal of Allied forces
22	Operation Demon (evacuation of Greece) commences
24	Operation Dunlop, twenty-three Hurricanes arrive in Malta
27	Germans capture Athens
27	21 Sqn Blenheim detachment arrives Malta (to 11 May)

27	Axis forces cross into Egypt, Halfaya Pass
29	Completion of evacuation of Greece

May

1	252 Sqn Beaufighter detachment arrives Malta
	First attacks (by Blenheims) on Axis convoys to North Africa
6–12	First successful two-way convoy (Alexandria to Malta; Gibraltar to Malta)
14	First attacks on airfields on Crete
16	139 Sqn Blenheims arrive Malta
17	Surrender of Italian forces in East Africa
19	RAF aircraft evacuate Crete
20	German air assault on Crete
21	Operation Splice, forty-six Hurricanes arrive in Malta (only four stay)
21	82 Sqn Blenheim detachment arrives Malta
25	Air Vice-Marshal H.P. Lloyd arrives to take over as AOC Malta (takes over on 1 June)
28–31	Evacuation from Crete
31	Armistice with Iraq

Air Vice-Marshal Hugh P. Lloyd

Having served in the First World War in the Royal Engineers, Lloyd enlisted in the RFC and joined 52 Squadron. He remained in the RAF post-war and by early 1939 he was CO of a bomber unit – 9 Squadron, although he was soon promoted to group captain and by early the following year he was senior staff officer (SASO) with 2 Group. His appointment to Malta was likely connected to the fact that this group was to provide Blenheims for anti-shipping, which many saw as a key role for Malta. However, the increased air threat to Malta was considered by many to need a 'fighter man' and so in 1942 he moved to the Middle East as SASO, and remained a key commander in the Mediterranean war.

June

6	46 Sqn detachment arrives in Malta
8	Allied forces enter Syria
18	Forty-three Hurricanes arrive in Malta from Operation Tracer (thirty-four go on to Middle East)
22	German invasion of Russia. Move of Luftwaffe forces
27	Twenty-one Hurricanes arrive in Malta from Operation Railway I
30	Thirty-five Hurricanes arrive in Malta from Operation Railway II

July

11	End of hostilities in Syria
18	Start of Allied reinforcements to Cyprus
25	Operation Substance supply convoy arrives in Malta
26	Italian E-boat attack on Grand Harbour

August

Bombing offensive against Tripoli

2   Operation Style arrives in Malta

2   Malta Night Fighter Flight formed (1435 Flight)

5   First success for 1435 Flight

6   38 Squadron Wellingtons arrive (to 25 Oct)

30 Wellingtons attack Tripoli and sink four ships

September

Bombs-racks fitted to Hurricanes in Malta for attacks on Sicily

20   First fighter-bomber attacks by Malta Hurricanes

25–28 Operation Halberd, convoy from Gibraltar

October

9   Formation of Western Desert Air Force

14 Italians order Operation C3 (invasion of Malta) study

16 Operation Callboy, Albacores to Malta

17 104 Sqn detachment to Malta

21 Naval Force K arrives in Malta

21 Wellington attack on Naples, use of 4,000lb bombs

29 Hitler orders Luftflotte 2 to the Mediterranean

ASV Wellingtons start operating from Malta

November

9   Force K destroys convoy of seven ships (40,000 tons)

12 Operation Perpetual Hurricanes of 242, 258, 605 squadrons to Malta

14 *Ark Royal* sinks (torpedoed on 13th)

18 Start of Operation Crusader offensive in Western Desert

Extension work on Gibraltar runway

December

10 Siege of Tobruk ends

22 Start of German air assault on Malta

24 Allies capture Benghazi

AHQ Gibraltar formed (200 Group disbanded)

1942

January

Personnel of 242 and 605 squadrons arrive

11 Air Vice-Marshal K.R. Park takes post as AOC Malta

19 Convoy MF3 arrives in Malta with 24,000 tons of supplies

21 Rommel counter-attacks as Crusader stalls

29 Axis captures Benghazi

February

4   Rommel halted at Gazala line

20–22 Operation Onset, convoy Alexandria to Tobruk

March

2/3	Wellingtons of 37 Sqn sink three ships in Palermo harbour
5	Luftwaffe starts intensive attacks on Malta
7	Operation Spotter, first Spitfires (fifteen) to Malta
10	Malta's first Spitfire squadron (249) declared operational
13/14	Last op by 37 Sqn before leaving Malta
14/15	Operation MF8; air-sea operation against Rhodes
21	Operation Picket, Spitfires to Malta
23	Operation Fullsize, three of four MVs reach Malta
24	185 Sqn re-equip with Hurricane IIs
27	229 Sqn arrives in Malta from Middle East

April

3	Gibraltar runway extension to 1,150 yards complete (extension to 1,550 yards started)
7/8	Peak of the first Malta blitz
16	Malta awarded the George Cross
20	Operation Calendar, forty-six Spitfires reach Malta, with 601 and 603 squadron pilots
21	148 Sqn Wellington detachment arrives Luqa
26	10th Submarine Flotilla departs Malta

May

7	Lord Gort takes over as governor of Malta
9	Operation Oppidan, sixty Spitfires to Malta
10	*Welshman* arrives in Malta with critical ammunition supplies
10	Kesselring announces 'mission complete' for the Luftwaffe
11–12	First USAAF attack on Ploesti, first op in Middle East/Med theatre
24	104 Sqn Wellington detachment to Luqa
26	German offensive at Gazala, Operation Theseus – the Battle for Egypt

June

3	Operation Style/Tilden, twenty-seven Spitfires to Malta
3	38 Sqn Wellington detachment to Malta
9	Operation Maintop/Salient, thirty-two Spitfires to Malta
10	217 Sqn Beauforts to Malta
11	235 Sqn Beaufighters arrive in Malta
14–17	Operations Harpoon and Vigorous resupply convoys
18–26	White House conference; decision to invade North Africa in 1942
21	Axis captures Tobruk

July

1	German offensive in Egypt halted at El Alamein
4	Third German air assault on Malta starts
15	Air Vice-Marshal K.R. Park takes post as AOC Malta
15	Operation Colima/Pinpoint, thirty-one Spitfires to Malta
21	Operation Knapsack/Insect, twenty-eight Spitfires to Malta
22	10th Submarine Flotilla returns to Malta

August

11   Operations Bellows, thirty-seven Spitfires to Malta; loss of HMS *Eagle*

13   First MVs from Pedestal convoy arrive in Malta

16   Operation Baritone

17   Malta restarts anti-shipping strikes

31   Battle of Alam El Halfa (to 6 Oct)

September

12   1st Submarine Flotilla to Malta

October

11–19   Last phase of blitz on Malta

23   Allies launch El Alamein offensive

29   Operation Train, twenty-nine Spitfires to Malta

November

6   227 Sqn and 272 Sqn Beaufighters arrive in Malta

8   Start of Operation Torch, landings in North Africa

11   French (Vichy) ceasefire in North Africa

13   Allies capture Tobruk

14   Allies enter Tunisia

20   Operation Stoneage, supply convoy MW13 reaches Malta

20   Allies capture Benghazi

Appendix C

Battle Honours and Awards

RAF squadrons were entitled to place appropriate 'Battle Honours' upon their Standards. Before we look at these in detail it is necessary to say a few words about the Standards themselves. The system was instituted on 1 April 1943 by King George VI to mark the 25th anniversary of the Royal Air Force. The basic requirement for a squadron to receive a Standard is completion of twenty-five years of service; however, a Standard might also be granted to a squadron that 'earned the Sovereign's appreciation for especially outstanding operations.'

Once the squadron has completed the qualifying requirements it receives a list, from the Air Ministry/MoD, of the battle honours to which it is entitled, with a note of those that may be placed upon the Standard. The squadron then selects the honours it wishes to display, to a maximum of eight, and this, along with the formal request for a Standard, is forwarded to the Sovereign for approval. The original limit of eight has since been raised.

The list below shows only those Battle Honours related to the campaign area and periods covered by this book; for a complete list of Battle Honours, visit the RAF Heraldry Trust website (www.rafht.co.uk).

Malta 1940–42: Squadrons participating in defensive, offensive, and reconnaissance operations from Malta during the period of enemy action against the island (10 June 1940 to 31 December 1942).

39 Squadron Battle Honours include Greece 1941, Mediterranean 1941–1943 and Malta 1942. (RAF Heraldry Trust, www.rafht.co.uk)

Mediterranean 1940–43: Operations over Italy, Sicily and the Mediterranean and Aegean Seas by aircraft based in the Mediterranean area (including reconnaissance, convoy protection, mining, and attacks on enemy ports and shipping) between the entry of Italy into the war and the initiation of air action preparatory to the Sicilian campaign (10 June 1940 to 30 June 1943).

Greece 1940–41: Operations over Albania and Greece during the Italian and German invasion, whether carried out by squadrons based in Greece or operating from external bases (28 October 1940 to 30 April 1941).

Egypt and Libya 1940–43: Operations in the defence of Egypt and the conquest of Libya, from the outbreak of war against Italy to the retreat of the Axis forces into Tunisia (10 June 1940 to 6 February 1943).

Campaign Medals

Campaign medals have been (indeed, still are) a matter of great debate, with many veterans of the opinion that 'their' campaign should have been recognized with a specific medal or bar. For the operations covered in this book, with the exception of some Gibraltar operations, the main campaign medal was the Africa Star.

The Africa Star

The Africa Star was awarded for one or more days' service in North Africa between 10 June 1940 and 12 May 1943. The ribbon is pale buff with a central red stripe and two narrow stripes, one of dark blue and the other light blue, representing the desert, the Navy, the Army and the RAF. The qualification was to have landed in, or flown over, any of the areas that qualified for the award, or territory occupied by the enemy. Areas that qualified were North Africa, Abyssinia, the Somalilands, Eritrea, Sudan and Malta. Three bars were issued with the Africa Star; One for First Army, one for Eighth Army, while the third was one for which RAF personnel were eligible 'North Africa 1942–1943', for those who served under the command of AOC Western Desert, AOC NW African Air Forces, AOC Malta, or any others who operated against the Germans or Italians between 23 October 1942 and 12 May 1943.

Gallantry Awards

All the standard gallantry awards were, of course, available to those fighting in this theatre of war. Aircrew of the Allied squadrons received a significant number of awards; the only award not made in the theatre (for an air action) was the Victoria Cross (VC). The following list of gallantry awards highlights only a few typical (if one can say such a thing about a gallantry award) examples awarded in the theatre. I have an ongoing database project with the Aviation History Research Centre (AHRC) to create a searchable database of every British gallantry award for RAF and Allied air force personnel.

Joint Awards: Some awards were joint – the same mission but with a DFSO, DFC, DFM, or other medal to different members of the crew. Also notable in the one below is that there is no specific citation; this is frequently the case, and it does at times seem somewhat arbitrary as to if an award came with or without a citation.

Joint award to Flight Lieutenant Riley (DFC) and Sergeant D. Bowie (DFM): Like a number of those awarded to Malta aircrew at this period, there was no specific citation, just the general 'citation': 'The King has been graciously pleased to approve the following awards and appointments in recognition of gallantry and devotion to duty in the execution of air operations.'

DSO/DFC group to Tony Spooner; the Africa Star campaign medal is fifth from left.

DSO/DFC Group to Tony Spooner

The group of medals for Tony Spooner includes two gallantry awards, the DFC being for service from Malta with the Special Flight. Medals are mounted in the approved sequence, so Order (DSO), gallantry (DFC) and then campaign, which in this case includes three campaign medals, the centre of which is the Africa Star.

DFC: AMB 5933 dated 24 December 1941; Flight Lieutenant A.H. Spooner, Special Flight, Luqa: 'One night in November, 1941, this officer was the captain of an aircraft co-operating with our naval forces in the Ionian Sea. Extremely unfavourable weather conditions prevailed, clouds being down almost to sea level but, in spite of this, Flight Lieutenant Spooner carried out a search extending for some 300 miles of open sea. Flight Lieutenant Spooner succeeded in locating 2 convoys, each consisting of a merchant vessel and a destroyer, and it was entirely due to his skill and persistence in the face of great odds that a naval force was directed to the target and thus able to destroy the convoys. In October, 1941, Flight Lieutenant Spooner attacked an 8,000–ton enemy merchant vessel, setting it on fire. Two nights later, he shadowed a convoy which was

Tony Spooner DSO DFC was one of leading exponents of air attacks on shipping.

subsequently attacked by our naval aircraft and 3 merchant vessels were seriously damaged. During October and November, 1941, this officer was successful in locating 3 enemy convoys and, as a result of attacks by our aircraft, several enemy ships were set on fire and others were damaged. In the latest attack, which was on 4 ships, only 1 was to be seen the next day. Throughout, this officer has displayed exceptional skill and determination.'

DSO: Squadron Leader A.H. Spooner, Apr 1944, 53 Sqn: 'This officer has participated in a large number of sorties and has invariably displayed a high degree of skill and courage. One night recently he piloted an aircraft which attacked two U-boats. The vessels were surfaced and in close proximity arid Squadron Leader Spooner released several depth charges over both of them in the same attacking run. Some nights later, Squadron Leader Spooner attacked two more U-boats. In all his encounters with the enemy, this officer has displayed great determination and has pressed home his attacks in the face of heavy opposition. He has set a very fine example to all.'

Distinguished Service Order (DSO)

The DSO was established in 1886 for rewarding individual instances of meritorious or distinguished service in war. Within the RAF in the Second World War only commissioned officers were eligible for the award; any recipient who subsequently performed another suitably approved act of gallantry was awarded a bar, attached to the ribbon, with a further bar for each additional qualifying act. The award consists of a gold cross, enamelled white, edged gold, having on the obverse, within a wreath of laurel enamelled green, the Imperial Crown in gold, and on the reverse, within a smaller wreath, the Royal cypher. It hangs from its ribbon by a gold clasp ornamented with laurel, while another similar clasp is worn at the top of the ribbon. The 1in wide ribbon has narrow blue borders. Any bars awarded are worn on the ribbon or if the ribbon alone is worn, on undress uniform, then they are depicted by one or more small silver roses – depending on the number of bars to which the wearer is entitled.

Wing Commander A.H. Donaldson: 'During the period 11th to 14th October, 1942, this officer participated in engagements against enemy aircraft attempting to attack Malta. Brilliantly leading his formation in attacks on bombers, regardless of the fighters which escorted them, Wing Commander Donaldson played a large part in the success achieved. Attacks on the islands were frustrated and several enemy bombers and fighters were shot down. On the I4th October he received, wounds in the feet and head and two of his fingers were shot away. Despite this, he flew to base and skilfully landed his aircraft. Wing Commander Donaldson displayed leadership, courage and fighting qualities in keeping with the highest traditions of the Royal Air Force. He destroyed three enemy aircraft, bringing his victories to five.'

Distinguished Flying Cross (DFC)

The Distinguished Flying Cross was established on 3 June 1918 to be awarded to officers and warrant officers for 'an act or acts of valour, courage or devotion to duty performed whilst flying on active operations against the enemy.' The cross is silver and consists of a cross flory terminated in the horizontal and base bars with flaming bombs and in the upper bar with a Tudor rose. This is surmounted by another cross of aeroplane propellers, with a roundel within a wreath of laurels and the letters 'RAF' on a rose-winged ensign by an Imperial Crown. On the reverse is the Royal Cypher above the date 1918. The cross is suspended from a straight silver bar, ornamented with sprigs of laurel, and connected by a silver link. The ribbon is 1.25in wide and was originally of violet and white alternate horizontal stripes, although as with the AFC this was changed to a diagonal format in July 1919. Likewise, awards made during and since the Second World War carry the date of the award on the reverse lower limb. The cross is issued unnamed but recipients or family often have them engraved. Bars are awarded in the usual way and, as is common to most awards, are depicted by a rosette worn on the ribbon if the medal is not worn.

Wing Commander Robert Yaxley, 252 Squadron: 'This officer commanded a detachment of fighter aircraft which recently carried out a series of sorties with the object of assisting in the safe passage of our convoys in the Mediterranean. Attacks were made on certain aerodromes and seaplane bases which resulted in a loss to the enemy of at least 49 aircraft and a further 42 damaged. The successes achieved undoubtedly contributed largely to the fact that the convoys were able to proceed without loss; only 1 ship was damaged but it succeeded in reaching port. The courageous leadership and determination of this officer is worthy of the highest praise and throughout he set an example which proved an inspiration to his fellow pilots.'

Distinguished Flying Medal (DFM)
The Distinguished Flying Medal was instituted on June 3, 1918, and is awarded to non-commissioned officers and other ranks for 'an act or acts of valour, courage, or devotion to duty performed whilst flying in active operations against the enemy'. It is oval shaped and in silver. On the obverse is the Sovereign's effigy and on the reverse is Athena Nike seated on an aeroplane with a hawk rising from her right hand above the words 'FOR COURAGE'. The medal is surmounted by a bomb attached to the clasp and ribbon by two wings. The ribbon was originally thin violet and white alternate horizontal stripes. From July 1919, the stripes were similar but running at an angle of 45 degrees from left to right. Bars are awarded for subsequent acts and since 1939 the year of award engraved on the reverse.

Flight Sergeant Louis G.C. De Lara, 249 Squadron: 'One day in October, 1942, this airman was the pilot of one of a section of aircraft engaged on a sortie over Malta. Within a short time, 2 large formations of enemy bombers were intercepted. Despite heavy odds. Flight Sergeant De Lara so skilfully led his section in attack that they caused the enemy to jettison their bombs into the sea on each occasion. Throughout, this airman displayed brilliant leadership and high courage. He has destroyed 5 enemy aircraft.'

George Cross
George Cross (GC) to LAC Albert Osborne (AMB 7461 dated 10 July 1942)
'During a period of fierce enemy air attacks on Malta, Leading Aircraftman Osborne has displayed unsurpassed courage and devotion to duty. In circumstances of the greatest danger he was always first at hand to deal with emergencies, whether in fire fighting operations or in rescue work. The following are examples of his promptitude and gallantry: Rendered safe the torpedo of a burning torpedo aircraft, working 3 feet from the main petrol tank for ten minutes. Extinguished a burning aircraft during a heavy bombing attack. Attempted to save a burning aircraft and subsequently removed torpedoes from the vicinity. Assisted in saving the pilot of a burning aircraft and extinguishing the fire. Saved an aircraft from destruction by fire. Attempted for six hours to extricate airmen from a bombed shelter, despite continued heavy bombing and danger, from falling stone-work. Fought fires in two aircraft, his efforts resulting in the saving of one. Freed the parachute of a burning flare caught in an aircraft, enabling the pilot to taxy clear. Checked the fire in a burning aircraft, the greater part of which was undamaged. The last three incidents occurred on the same day. Leading Aircraftman Osborne was unfortunately killed on 2nd April, 1942. During an intense air attack he led a party to extinguish the flames of a burning aircraft. A petrol tank exploded and he was injured

and affected by the fumes. On recovery, he returned to fight the fire and was killed by the explosion of an air vessel while attempting to pour water over torpedoes which were in danger of exploding. This airman's fearless courage and great leadership on all occasions have been beyond praise. The Air Officer Commanding, Royal Air Force Mediterranean, has stated that he was "one of the bravest airmen it has been my privilege to meet."'

British Empire Medal
BEM to F/Sgt Herbert Cagby (AMB 7583 dated 28 July 1942)
'An aircraft was set on fire during an enemy air attack on an aerodrome in Malta. Whilst a second wave of bombers were diving to attack Flight Sergeant Cagby, displaying complete disregard for his own safety, removed about fifty 40lb bombs from the vicinity of the aircraft. His courageous and prompt action prevented an explosion and thereby saved valuable property. He has, on many other occasions, displayed courage and devotion to duty which has set a fine example."

BEM to Lac Hale and LAC Stepton (AMB 8822 dated 29 December 1942)
Joint citation LAC Hale, LAC Stepto: 'Leading Aircraftmen Hale and Stepto have been employed in an airfield clearance party at Malta for several months. They have both performed their duties with the greatest zeal, often displaying complete disregard for their personal safety when clearing runways while heavy raids on the airfield have been in progress. They have set a magnificent example.'

Order of Battle

Airfields and Units

The Gladiators started life with the Fighter Flight at Ta Kali.

There are often differences in the records, or published works, concerning squadrons operating out of Malta. The primary sources, such as squadron operational record books (ORBs) are sometimes not very good at recording dates of detachments, and Malta had plenty of those. In some cases, records have been lost. In other cases, the official or planned detachment or date, such as might be listed in the secret organizational memoranda (SOM) are at variance with other official sources. Thus it is likely that the table below contains errors, especially if compared with some published works.

Maryland recce from Malta and the western desert was the 'eyes of the fleet'.

Airfield	Squadron	Year	Dates	Main aircraft	Notes
Hal Far	38	1941–43	Dec 1940–Feb 1943	Wellington	
Hal Far	46	1941	Jun	Hurricane	became 126 Sqn
Hal Far	185	1941–43	12 May 1941–5 Jun 1943	Hurricane, Spitfire	formed from 261 Sqn and 1430 Flt
Hal Far	229	1942	28 Mar 1942–29 Apr 1942	Hurricane	
Hal Far	242	1941–42	Nov 1941–17 Mar 1942	Hurricane	absorbed into 126 Sqn
Hal Far	249	1941–42	21 May 1941–23 Nov 1942	Hurricane, Spitfire	
Hal Far	605	1942	Nov 1941–17 Mar 1942	Hurricane	absorbed into 185 Sqn
Hal Far	806	1941	Jan–Mar	Fulmar	
Hal Far	828	1941	Oct 1941–	Albacore	
Hal Far	830	1940	Jun 1940–	Swordfish	
Kalafrana	228	1940–41	summer 1940–Mar 1941	Sunderland	
Kalafrana	230	1940–41	summer 1940–Mar 1941	Sunderland	
Luqa	18	1941	Oct–Nov 1941	Blenheim	detachment
Luqa	21	1940–42	25 Dec 1941–14 Mar 1942	Blenheim	det. 1940–41; disbanded 1941
Luqa	22	1942	Feb 1942–Apr 1942	Beaufort	
Luqa	23	1942–43	27 Dec 1942–7 Dec 1943	Mosquito	
Luqa	37	1940–42	13 Nov 1940–1 Dec 1940	Wellington	detachments 1941–42
Luqa	38	1940–43	Dec 1940–Feb 1943	Wellington	detachments
Luqa	39	1941–43	Dec 1941–Jun 1943	Beaufort	detachments and main base periods
Luqa	40	1941–42	31 Oct 1941–14 Feb 1942	Wellington	Disbanded
Luqa	40	1942–43	Nov 1942–Jan 1943	Wellington	detachments
Luqa	46	1942–44	May 1942–44	Beaufighter, Mosquito	detachments
Luqa	69	1941–44	10 Jan 1941–9 Feb 1944	Maryland, Hurricane, Beaufort, Baltimore, Wellington	
Luqa	78	1940–41	Jul 1940–Apr 1941	Whitley	detachment

Airfield	Squadron	Year	Dates	Main aircraft	Notes
Luqa	82	1939–42	Aug 1939–Mar 1942	Blenheim	detachment
Luqa	86	1942	Jul-42	Beaufort	joined 39 Sqn
Luqa	89	1941–42	Dec 1941–Dec 1942	Beaufighter	detachment
Luqa	104	1941–43	14 Oct 1941–Feb 1943	Wellington	detachment
Luqa	105	1940–41	Oct 1940–Dec 1941	Blenheim	detachment
Luqa	107	1941	May 1941–Aug 1942	Blenheim	detachment
Luqa	110	1939–41	Jun 1939–1941	Blenheim	detachment
Luqa	113	1941	Sep	Blenheim	detachment
Luqa	126	1942–43	6 Apr 1942–10 Jun 1943	Spitfire	
Luqa	138	1941	Aug 41	Whitley	detachment
Luqa	139	1940–41	Jun 1940–Oct 1941	Blenheim	
Luqa	148	1943	1–14 Feb 1943	Spitfire	formed and disbanded, as 1435 Sqn
Luqa	148	1940 –42	1 Dec 1940–Dec 1942	Wellington	formed, and detachments
Luqa	162	1942–43	Apr 1942–Aug 1943	Blenheim	detachment
Luqa	185	1941–43	12 May 1941–5 Jun 1943	Hurricane, Spitfire	formed from 261 and 1435
Luqa	217	1942	Mar 42	Beaufort	joined 39 Sqn
Luqa	221	1942	Jan 1942–Aug 1942	Wellington	detachment
Luqa	227	1942	20 Aug 1942–26 Nov 1942	Beaufighter	formed from 248 Sqn
Luqa	242	1942	Jan–Mar 1942	Hurricane	detachment
Luqa	252	1941	Dec	Beaufighter	detachment
Luqa	252	1942	Sep 1942–Jan 1943	Beaufighter	detachment
Luqa	261	1940	2 Aug 1940–20 Nov 1940	Sea Gladiator, Hurricane	formed from 418 and Malta Fighter Flt
Luqa	272	1941–43	Jun 1941–Nov 1942	Beaufighter	detachment
Luqa	458	1942–44	Oct 1942–Jan 1944	Wellington	detachment
Luqa	605	1942	Jan 1942–Mar 1942	Hurricane	detachment
Luqa	1435	1942–43	23 Jul 1942–1 Feb 1943	Spitfire	Renumbered as 148 Sqn
Qrendi	229	1942–43	10 Dec 1942–25 Sep 1943	Spitfire	

Airfield	Squadron	Year	Dates	Main aircraft	Notes
Qrendi	249	1942–43	23 Nov 1942–24 Sep 1943	Spitfire	
Ta Kali	69	1941	31 Oct 1941–29 Nov 1941	Maryland, Hurricane	
Ta Kali	89	1941–42	Dec 1941–late 1942	Beaufighter	
Ta Kali	126	1941–42	28 Jun 1941–6 Apr 1942	Hurricane	formed from 46 Sqn
Ta Kali	185	1941–43	May 1941–June 1943	Hurricane	detachment
Ta Kali	227	1942–43	26 Nov 1942–1 Mar 1943	Beaufighter	
Ta Kali	229	1942	3 Aug 1942–10 Dec 1943	Spitfire	renumbering of 603 Sqn echelon
Ta Kali	238	1941	summer 1941	Hurricane	detachment
Ta Kali	242	1942	Jan–Mar 1942	Hurricane	absorbed into 126 Sqn
Ta Kali	248	1942	summer 1942	Beaufighter	aircraft to 227 Sqn
Ta Kali	261	1940–41	20 Nov 1940–12 May 1941	Hurricane	absorbed into 185 Sqn
Ta Kali	272	1942	6 Nov 1942–4 Jun 1943	Beaufighter	
Ta Kali	603	1942	summer 1942	Spitfire	air echelon became 229 Sqn
Ta Kali	605	1941–42	summer 1942	Hurricane	into 185 Sqn
Ta Kali	MNFU	1941	Aug–Dec	Hurricane	Became 1435 Flt
	1435 Flt	1942	4 Dec 1941–2 Aug 1942	Hurricane, Spitfire	Became 1435 Sqn
	1435 Sqn	1941–45	2 Aug 1942–May 1945	Hurricane, Spitfire	Db 9 May 1945
	418 Flt	1940	Jun–Aug	Hurricane	
	Ftr Flt	1940	Apr–Aug	Sea Gladiator, Hurricane	

RAF Order of Battle: Malta

The following Order of Battle lists are based on the SD161 documents; this does not always reflect the actual position of units! However, they are useful on the grounds that they are an official source and they do list all units and not just flying squadrons. I have excluded units such as SHQ (Station Headquarters) and admin units.

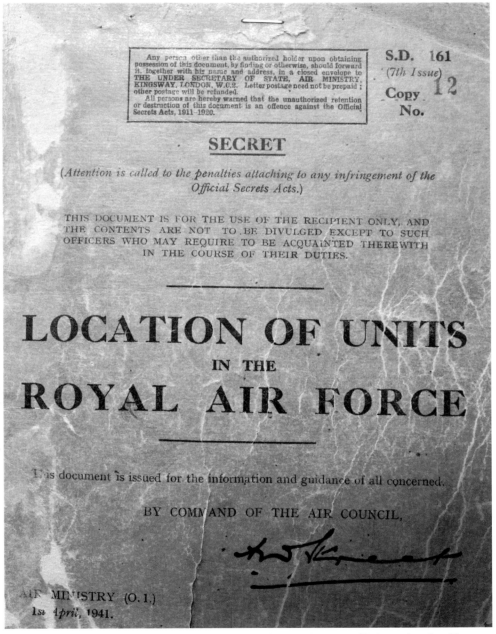

The SD161 Location of Units in the Royal Air Force is a good source of information, but like most official records does not always reflect the actual situation on the ground.

Mediterranean Command: August 1940			
Location	Unit	Aircraft	Remarks
Valetta	AHQ		
	Met Station		
Kalafrana	Inter-Command W/T Station		
Hal Far	Station Flight	various	
Luqa	261 (F) Sqn	Hurricane	
	431 (GR) Flt	Maryland	
Ta Salvatur	DF Station, 241 TRU, 242 TRU,		

Malta Command: April 1941			
Location	Unit	Aircraft	Remarks
Valetta	AHQ		
	Met Station		
Kalafrana	Inter-Command W/T Station		
Hal Far	Station Flight	Magister (3), Swordfish (1), Seal (1), Gauntlet (1)	= IE
Luqa	148 (B) Sqn	Wellington (16)	
	69 (GR) Sqn	Maryland (7+5), Beaufort (7+3)	(7+5) = IE + IR; forming
Ta Salvatur	DF Station, 241 TRU, 242 TRU, 3 AME Stations		
Ta Kali	261 (F) Sqn	Hurricane (16)	

Malta Command: November 1941			
Location	**Unit**	**Aircraft**	**Remarks**
Dingli	241, 242, 504 AMES		
Valetta	HQ Mediterranean		
	Met Station		
Kalafrana	Inter-Command W/T Station		
Hal Far	Station Flight	Magister, Swordfish, Seal, Gauntlet	
	185 (F) Sqn	Hurricane	
Luqa	104 Sqn	Wellington	detachment
	40 Sqn	Wellington	detachment

Malta Command: November 1941			
Location	**Unit**	**Aircraft**	**Remarks**
	69 (GR) Sqn	Maryland	
Madliena	502 AMES		
Ta Silch	501 AMES		
Ta Kali	126 (F) Sqn	Hurricane	
	261 (F) Sqn	Hurricane	

AHQ Malta: March 1942			
Location	**Unit**	**Aircraft**	**Remarks**
Dingli	241, 242, 504 AMES		
Valetta	AHQ Malta		
	Met Station; 841 AMES		
Kalafrana	Inter-Command W/T Station		
Hal Far	Station Flight	Magister, Swordfish, Seal, Gauntlet	
	185 (F) Sqn	Hurricane	
Luqa	40 (B) Sqn	Wellington	
	69 (GR) Sqn	Maryland	
	21 (B) Sqn	Blenheim	
	107 (B) Sqn	Blenheim	
Madliena	502 AMES		
Ta Silch	501 AMES		
Ta Kali	126 (F) Sqn	Hurricane	
	249 (Gold Coast) Sqn	Hurricane	

AHQ Malta: June 1942			
Location	Unit	Aircraft	Remarks
Dingli	242, 504 AMES		
Ghar Lapsi	241 AMES		
Gozo	521 AMES		
Gudja	841 AMES		
Valetta	AHQ Malta		
	Met Station		

AHQ Malta: June 1942			
Location	Unit	Aircraft	Remarks
Kalafrana	Inter-Command W/T Station		
Kaura	314 AMES		
Hal Far	Station Flight	Magister, Swordfish, Seal, Gauntlet	
	185 (F) Sqn	Hurricane	
Luqa	69 (GR) Sqn	Maryland, Spitfire	
	126 (F) Sqn	Hurricane	
	221 (GR) Sqn	Wellington	detachment
Madliena	502 AMES		
Ta Silch	501 AMES		
Ta Kali	1435 (NF) Flt	Beaufighter	
	249 (Gold Coast) Sqn	Spitfire	
	601 (F) Sqn	Spitfire	
	603 (F) Sqn	Spitfire	

Hal Far area with location of the drogue target range – the observation post at Wardia Tower, for example. The SDS161 is particularly useful in listing the 'other' units, flying and non-flying, that are often ignored in histories. Aircraft of the Station Flight at Hal Far would have been towing targets for use in this range.

Appendix E

Anti Shipping Scores

Year	Month	Day	Ship Name	tonnage	Scored by other	Aircraft Type	Unit	Fate	Pilot
1940	Jun	28th	Argonauta		aircraft	Sunderland	230 Sqn	sunk	Flt Lt W.W. Campbell
1940	Jun	29th	Rubino		aircraft	Sunderland	230 Sqn	sunk	Flt Lt W.W. Campbell
1940	Sep	30th	Gondar		aircraft	Sunderland	230 Sqn	sunk	Flt Lt P.H. Alington
1940	Oct	18th	Durbo		aircraft	London	202 Sqn	sunk	Flt Lt N.G. Eagleton
1941	Jan	5th	Vulcano		mine			sunk	
1941	Jan	9th	Giovanni Mari		mine			sunk	
1941	Jan	18th	Lelio		mine			sunk	
1941	Jan	27th	Francesco Stocco		mine			damaged	
1941	Jan	22nd	Liguria		scuttled			sunk	
1941	Jan	22nd	San Giorgio		scuttled			sunk	
1941	Jan	9th	Carlo Martinolinch		Ship		HMS Parthian	sunk	
1941	Jan	9th	Palma		Ship		HMS Pandora	sunk	
1941	Jan	9th	Valdivagna		Ship		HMS Pandora	sunk	
1941	Jan	10th	Vega		Ship		HMS Bonaventure; HMS Southampton	sunk	
1941	Jan	15th	Cita di Messina		Ship		HMS Regent	sunk	N3259 E1411
1941	Jan	19th	Neghelli		Ship		HMS Greyhound	sunk	
1941	Jan	22nd	Diego		Ship		HMAS Vampire	sunk	
1941	Jan		Sardinia		ship/sub?		Proteus (Greek)		
1941	Jan	27th	Ingo		aircraft	Swordfish	830 Sqn	sunk	N3427 E1411
1941	Feb	15th	Juventus	3950	aircraft		FAA		
1941	Feb	20th	Guidonia	64	aircraft				
1941	Apr	16/17th	Romagna	149	aircraft		FAA/RAF		
1941	Apr	20/21st	Marocchino	1524	aircraft + ship				
1941	May	22nd	Perseo	4857	aircraft + sub				
1941	May	26th	Marco Foscarino	6342	aircraft	Blenheim	139 Sqn	sunk	
1941	May	30/31st	Florida II	3414	aircraft	Blenheim	82 Sqn + 139 Sqn	sunk	
1941	May				aircraft	Blenheim		sunk	

Year	Month	Date	Name	Tonnage		Aircraft	Squadron	Status
1941	Jun	3rd	Montello	6117	aircraft	Blenheim	82 Sqn + 139 Sqn	sunk
1941	Jun	3rd	Beatrice C	6132	aircraft	Blenheim	82 Sqn + 139 Sqn	sunk
1941	Jun	10/11th	Nadia	247	aircraft			
1941	Jun	10/11th	Mario Bianco	258	aircraft			
1941	Jun	10/11th	Giorgina	253	aircraft			
1941	Jul	1st	Eritrea	2517	aircraft	Wellington	148 Sqn	sunk
1941	Jul	2nd	Sparta	1724	aircraft	Wellington + Swordfish		sunk
1941	Jul	2nd	Annunziatina	20	aircraft			
1941	Jul	15th	Barbarigo	5293	aircraft			
1941	Jul	22nd	Preussen	8230	aircraft	Blenheim	110 Sqn	sunk
1941	Jul	22nd	Brarena	6996	aircraft	Blenheim + Swordfish	x	sunk
1941	Aug	5th or 6th	Nita	6813	aircraft	Blenheim + Swordfish	x	sunk
1941	Aug	10th/11th	California	13060	aircraft	Swordfish		sunk
1941	Aug	17th	Maddalena Odero	5479	aircraft	Swordfish		sunk
1941	Aug	23rd	Costanza	582	aircraft			
1941	Aug	30th	Cilicia	2747	aircraft			
1941	Aug	30th	Egadi	861	aircraft			
1941	Aug	30th	Riv	6630	aircraft	Wellington		sunk
1941	Aug	30th	Neptune	395	aircraft	Wellington		
1941	Aug	30th	Fiammetta	393	aircraft	Wellington		
1941	Aug	30th	Giuseppina V	367	aircraft	Wellington		
1941	Sep	3rd	Adrea Gritti	6338	aircraft	Swordfish		sunk
1941	Sep	3rd	Pietro Barbaro	6330	aircraft	Swordfish		sunk
1941	Sep	11th	Alfredo Oriani	3059	aircraft	Blenheim		sunk
1941	Sep	12th	Caffaro	6476	aircraft	Blenheim + Swordfish + Wellington	x	sunk

Year	Month	Day	Ship Name	tonnage	Scored by other	Aircraft Type	Unit	Fate	Pilot
1941	Sep	12th	Nicolo Odero	6003	aircraft	Wellington	38 Sqn	sunk	
1941	Sep	17th	Filuccio	248	aircraft				
1941	Sep	17/18th	Col de Lana	5891	aircraft				
1941	Sep	20th	Monselet	3371	aircraft	Blenheim	107 Sqn	sunk	
1941	Sep	22/23rd	Marigola	5996	aircraft + sub	Swordfish		sunk	
1941	Oct	5th	Rialto	6099	aircraft	Swordfish	830 Sqn FAA	sunk	
1941	Oct	8th	Paolo Z Podesta	863	aircraft				
1941	Oct	11th	Casaregis	6485	aircraft	Swordfish	830 Sqn FAA	sunk	
1941	Oct	13th	Rosa	246	aircraft				
1941	Oct	13th	Luciana	37	aircraft				
1941	Oct	13th	Tommaso	29	aircraft				
1941	Oct	13th	Antoniotto Usodimare	24	aircraft				
1941	Oct	14th	Bainsizza	7993	aircraft	Swordfish	830 Sqn FAA	sunk	
1941	Oct	18th	Caterina	4786	aircraft	Swordfish + sub	830 Sqn FAA	sunk	
1941	Oct	20th	Nereo	216	aircraft				
1941	Oct	23rd	Achille	2415	aircraft	Blenheim	107 Sqn	sunk	
1941	Oct	25th	Galileo Ferraris		aircraft	Catalina	202 Sqn	sunk	Sqn Ldr N.F. Eagleton
1941	Oct	30th	Orsolina	344	aircraft				
1941	Nov	5th	Anna Zippitelli	1019	aircraft	Blenheim		sunk	
1941	Nov	5th	Maria Bruna	246	aircraft				
1941	Nov	8th	San Antonio	249	aircraft				
1941	Nov	28th	Speranza	445	aircraft				
1941	Nov	28th	Berbera	2093	aircraft	Blenheim	18 Sqn + 107 Sqn	sunk	
1941	Nov	28th	Priaruggia	1196	aircraft	Wellington			
1941	Nov	30th	Cape Faro	3476	aircraft	Blenheim	18 Sqn	sunk	
1941	Nov	30th	Nuovo Ciccillio	43	aircraft				

Year	Month	Day	Ship	Tonnage	Cause	Aircraft	Squadron	Result	Pilot
1941	Nov	30th	Generala Gerbi	143	aircraft				
1941	Dec	1st	Iridio Mantovani	10,540	aircraft + shipBlenheim			sunk	
1941	Dec	6th	U-332		aircraft	Catalina	202 Sqn	damaged	Flt Lt H. Garnell
1941	Dec	12th	Barbiano		ship			sunk	
1941	Dec	12th	Giussano		ship			sunk	
1941	Dec	14th	Gallatea					sunk	
1941	Dec	17th	Lina	1235	aircraft		FAA	sunk	in port
1941	Dec	24th	Pietrino	667	aircraft				
1941	Dec	24th	Bagnoli	245	aircraft				
1941	Jan	6/7th			aircraft	Swordfish	830 Sqn	damaged	
1942	Jan	6/7th	Perla	5741	aircraft	Albacore	828 FAA	sunk	
1942	Jan	23rd	Victoria	13098	aircraft	Beaufort + Albacore	39 Sqn + 826 Sqn	sunk	
1942	Feb	2nd	Napoli	6142	aircraft + sub	Albacore	828 Sqn	sunk	
1942	Feb	13th	Ariosto	4115	aircraft	Albacore	828 Sqn	sunk	
1942	Mar	2/3rd	Cuma	6652	aircraft	Wellington	37 Sqn	sunk	
1942	Mar	2/3rd	Securitas	5366	aircraft	Wellington	37 Sqn	sunk	
1942	Mar	2/3rd	Le Tre Maria	1086	aircraft	Wellington	37 Sqn	sunk	
1942	Mar	17/18th	Achaia	1778	aircraft	Swordfish	830 Sqn	sunk	
1942	Mar	22nd	U-731		aircraft	Blenheim	203 Sqn	damaged	Plt Off Beresford-Peirse
1942	May	1st	U-573		aircraft	Hudson	233 Sqn	damaged	Sgt Brent
1942	May	2nd	U-74		aircraft	Catalina	202 Sqn	sunk	Flt Lt R.Y. Powell
1942	May	30/31st	Gino Allegri	6836	aircraft + sub	Wellington	221 Sqn	sunk	
1942	Jun	2nd	U-652		aircraft	Swordfish	815 FAA	sunk	Lt G.H. Bates
1942	Jun	7th	Veniero		aircraft	Catalina	202 Sqn	sunk	Fg off R.M. Corrie
1942	Jun	9th	Zaffiro		aircraft	Catalina	240 Sqn	sunk	Flt Lt D.E. Hawkins
1942	Jun	13th	Otario		aircraft	Sunderland	202 Sqn	damaged	Sqn Ldr R.B. Burrage

Year	Month	Day	Ship Name	tonnage	Scored by other	Aircraft Type	Unit	Fate	Pilot
1942	Jun	21st	Reichenfels		aircraft	Beaufort	217 Sqn	sunk	
1942	Jun	21st	Vettor Pisani		aircraft	Beaufort	86 Sqn + 217 Sqn	sunk	
1942	Jul	11th	Ondina		aircraft	Walrus	700 Sqn FAA	sunk	
1942	Aug	4th	U-372		aircraft	Wellington	221 Sqn	sunk	F/Sgt Gay
1942	Aug	4th			aircraft	Swordfish	815 Sqn FAA	damaged	
1942	Aug	12th	Cobalto		sub	sub	Ithuriel	sunk	
1942	Aug	13th	Bolzano		sub	sub	P42	damaged	
1942	Aug	13th	Muzio Attendolo		sub	sub	P42	damaged	
1942	Aug	17th	Rosalino Pilo	8326	aircraft	Swordfish	815 Sqn FAA	damaged	xx damaged vy Beauforts 86 Sqn and sunk by sub?
1942	Aug	18th			aircraft				
1942	Aug	21st	Pozarica	7800	aircraft	Beaufort	39 Sqn	sunk	
1942	Aug	22nd			aircraft	Wellington	221 Sqn	damaged	
1942	Aug	25th			aircraft	Bisley	15 SAAF	damaged	
1942	Aug	26th			aircraft	Wellesley	47 Sqn	probaby sunk	
1942	Aug	27th	Dielpi	1527	aircraft	Beaufort	39 Sqn	sunk	
1942	Aug	27th	Istria	5400	aircraft	Beaufort + Beaufighter	39 Sqn + 229 Sqn	sunk	
1942	Aug	30th	San Andrea	5077	aircraft	Beaufort	39 Sqn	sunk	
1942	Sep	3rd	Monti	4301	aircraft	Wellington + Swordfish + Albacore	x	sunk	damaged and beached
1942	Sep	6th	Manara	7000	aircraft	Beaufort	39 Sqn	sunk	damaged and beached
1942	Sep	14th	Alabastro		aircraft	Sunderland	202 Sqn	sunk	Fg Off E.P. Walshe
1942	Sep	17th	Carbonia	1237	aircraft	Beaufighter	227 sqn	sunk	
1942	Sep	28/29th	Ravenna	1148	aircraft + sub	Wellington	69 Sqn	beached	
1942	Oct	7th/8th	Titania	5397	aircraft/sub	Sub + FAA		sunk	
1942	Oct	14th			aircraft	Blenheim	13 Hellenic	damaged	

Year	Month	Date	Name	Tonnage	Cause	Aircraft	Squadron	Status	Notes
1942	Oct	16th	Amsterdam	8676	aircraft	Albacore	828 FAA	sunk	damaged and beached
1942	Oct	19/20th	Titania	5397	aircraft + sub			beached	
1942	Oct	18/19	Panuco	8000	aircraft	Wellington	69 Sqn	sunk	
1942	Oct	29th	Luisiano	2552	aircraft	Wellington	69 Sqn	sunk	Sqn Ldr Ensor
1942	Nov	13th	U-411		aircraft	Hudson	500 Sqn	sunk	Sqn Ldr Ensor
1942	Nov	13th	U-458		aircraft	Hudson	500 Sqn	damaged	Sqn Ldr Ensor
1942	Nov	14th	U-595		aircraft	Hudson	500 Sqn / 608 Sqn	sunk	
1942	Nov	14th	U-605		aircraft	Hudson	233 Sqn	sunk	Plt Off J.W. Barling
1942	Nov	15th	U-259		aircraft	Hudson	500 Sqn	sunk	Fg Off M.A. Ensor
1942	Nov	17th	U-331		aircraft	Hudson	500 Sqn	sunk	3 ac; Sqn Ldr I.C. Patterson, Flt Lt A.W. Barwood. Sgt Young
1942	Nov	17th	U-566		aircraft	Hudson	233 Sqn	damaged	Sgt E.H. Smith
1942	Nov	17/18th	Giulio Girodami	10534	aircraft	Albacore	FAA	sunk	
1942	Nov	18th	U-613		aircraft	Hudson	608 Sqn	damaged	Fg Off J.B. Petrie
1942	Nov	19th	U-413		aircraft	Hudson	608 Sqn	damaged	Fg Off A.F. Wilcox
1942	Nov	20th	Lago Tana	783	aircraft				
1942	Nov	24th	U-263		aircraft	Hudson	233 Sqn	sunk	Sgt E.H. Smith
1942	Nov	25th	Algerine	1371	aircraft	Beaufighter		sunk	
1942	Nov	24/25th	Favorita	3576	aircraft	Wellington + sub	69 Sqn	sunk	damaged by aircraft sunk by Splendid
1942	Nov	24/25th	Luigi	4283	aircraft	Wellington	69 Sqn	sunk	
1942	Dec	1st	Audace	1459	aircraft	Beaufighter	227 Sqn	sunk	
1942	Dec	2nd	Puccini	2422	aircraft	Albacore	FAA	sunk	
1942	Dec	2nd	Velocce	5464	aircraft	Albacore	FAA	sunk	
1942	Dec	3rd	Palmaiola	1800	aircraft	Albacore	FAA	sunk	
1942	Dec	3rd	Minerva	1905	aircraft	Albacore	FAA	sunk	
1942	Dec	13th	Foscolo	4500	aircraft	Albacore	FAA	sunk	
1942	Dec	13th	Macedonia	2875	aircraft + sub	Albacore	FAA	sunk	aircraft + Umbra

Year	Month	Day	Ship Name	tonnage	Scored by other	Aircraft Type	Unit	Fate	Pilot
1942	Dec	13/14th	Ste Bernadette	1596	aircraft	Wellington	40 + 104 Sqn	sunk	
1942	Dec	13/14th	St Gerando	4310	aircraft	Wellington	40 + 104 Sqn	sunk	
1942	Dec	21st	Etruria	2633	aircraft	Albacore	FAA	sunk	
1942	Dec	28/29th	Isco or Iseo	2366	aircraft	Albacore	821 + 828 Sqn	sunk	
1943	Jan	14th	Narvalo	810	aircraft	Beaufort	39 Sqn	captured	Fg Off J.N. Cartwright
1943	Jan	15/16th	Agostino Bertani	8329	aircraft	Wellington	40 + 104 Sqn	on fire	
1943	Jan	19th	Edda	6107	aircraft + sub	Albacore	821 Sqn	sunk	damaged by Albacore, sunk by Unbroken
1943	Jan	22nd	Ruhr	5954	aircraft	Beaufort + Albacore	39 Sqn + 821 Sqn	sunk	
1943	Jan	23/24th	Verona	4459	aircraft	Beaufort + Wellington	39 Sqn + 221 Sqn	sunk	
1943	Jan	23/24th	Pistola	2448	aircraft				
1943	Feb	1st	Pozzuli	5345	aircraft	Wellington	221 Sqn	sunk	
1943	Feb	10th	U-108		aircraft	Catalina	202 Sqn	damaged	Sqn Ldr W.E. Ogle-Skan
1943	Feb	12th	U-442		aircraft	Hudson	48 Sqn	sunk	Fg Off G.R. Mayhew
1943	Feb	13/14th	U-620		aircraft	Catalina	202 Sqn	sunk	Flt Lt H.R. Sheardown
1943	Feb	13/14th	U-381		aircraft	Catalina	202 Sqn	damaged	Flt Lt H.R. Sheardown
1943	Feb	15/16th	Capo Orso	3149	aircraft	Wellington	221 Sqn	sunk	
1943	Feb	17/18th	Col di Lana	5891	aircraft	Wellington	221 Sqn	sunk	
1943	Feb	19th	U-562		aircraft	Wellington	38 Sqn	sunk	Fg Off I.B. Butler
1943	Feb	21st	Thorsheimer	9955	aircraft	Beaufort	39 Sqn	sunk	
1943	Feb	24/25th	Alcamo	6987	aircraft	Beaufort	39 Sqn	sunk	
1943	Mar	4th	U-83		aircraft	Hudson	500 Sqn	sunk	Sgt G. Jackimov
1943	Mar	12th/13th	Sterope	10495	aircraft	Beaufort + Albacore	39 Sqn + 828 Sqn	damaged	
1943	Mar	13th/14th	Caraibe	4048	aircraft	Albacore	828 Sqn	sunk	
1943	Mar	21st/22nd	Manzoni	4550	aircraft	Wellington	221 Sqn	sunk	

Year	Month	Day	Name	No.	Aircraft	Means	Result	Squadron	Crew/Notes
1943	Mar	28th	U-77		Hudson	aircraft	sunk	48 Sqn + 233 Sqn	2 ac: Fg Off I.B. Harrop; Fg Off E.F. Castell
1943	Apr	5th	U-167		Hudson	aircraft	sunk	233 Sqn	2 ac: F/Sgt K.R. Dalton, Flt Lt W.E. Willets
1943	Apr	11/12th	Fabiano	2943	Wellington	aircraft	sunk	458 sqn	
1943	Apr	16/17th	Monginevro	5324	Albacore	aircraft	sunk	821 Sqn	with MTB
1943	Apr	18/19th	Mostaganem	1942	Wellington	aircraft + sub	sunk	221 Sqn	
1943	Apr	23/24th	Aquino	5079		aircraft			
1943	May	7th	U-447		Hudson	aircraft	sunk	233 Sqn	2 ac: Sgt J.V. Holland, Sgt J.W. McQueen
1943	May	28th	U-755		Hudson	aircraft	sunk	608 Sqn	Fg Off A.K. Ogilvie
1943	Jun	4th	U-594		Hudson	aircraft	sunk	48 Sqn	Fg Off H.C. Bailey
1943	Jun	16th	U-97		Hudson	aircraft	sunk	459 sqn	F/Sgt D.T. Barnard
1943	Jul	8th	U-603		Catalina	aircraft	damaged	202 Sqn	Flt Lt G. Powell
1943	Jul	9th	U-435		Wellington	aircraft	sunk	179 Sqn	Fg Off E.J. Fisher
1943	Jul	18th	Romolo		Wellington	aircraft	sunk	221 Sqn	2 ac: Fg Off E. Austin, Fg Off W. Lewis
1943	Aug	24th	U-134		Wellington	aircraft	sunk	179 Sqn	Fg Off D.F. McRae
1943	Sep	6th	U-760		Wellington	aircraft	damaged	179 Sqn	Fg Off D.F. McRae
1943	Sep	11th	U-617		Wellington	aircraft	sunk	179 Sqn	2 ac: Sqn Ldr D.B. Hodgkinson, Plt Off W.H. Brunini
1943	Sep	12th	Topazio		Blenheim	aircraft	sunk	13 Sqn	Fg Off G H Finch
1943	Sep	24-26th	U-667		Wellington + Hudson	aircraft	damaged	179 Sqn + 233 Sqn + 48 Sqn	5 ac: 179: Fg Off A. Chiltern, F/Sgt D.J. McMahon, Fg Off S.H. Nicholson: 233 Fg Off A.G. Frandson; 48 Fg Off E.L. Ashbury
1943	Oct	21st	U-431		Wellington	aircraft	sunk	179 Sqn	Sgt D.M. Cornish
1943	Oct	24th	U-566		Wellington	aircraft	sunk	179 Sqn	Sgt D.M. Cornish
1943	Nov	1st	U-340		Wellington	aircraft	sunk	179 Sqn	Fg Off A.H. Ellis

Year	Month	Day	Ship Name	tonnage	Scored by other	Aircraft Type	Unit	Fate	Pilot
1944	Jan	8th	U-343		aircraft	Wellington	179 Sqn	damaged	2 ac: Fg Off W F Davidson, Flt Lt J Finch
1944	Feb	24th	U-761		aircraft	Catalina	202 Sqn + VP63	sunk	3 ac: 202 Flt Lt J. Finch; VP63 Lt T.R. Woolley, Lt H.J. Baker
1944	Mar	16th	U-392		aircraft	Catalina	VP63	sunk	3 ac: Lt R.C. Spears, Lt V.A. Lingle, Lt M.J. Vopacek
1944	May	15th	U-731		aircraft	Catalina	VP63	sunk	2 ac: Lt M.J. Vopacek, Lt H.T. Worrell
1944	May	17th	U-616		aircraft	Wellington	36 Sqn	sunk	2 ac: W/O J.M. Cooke, Plt Off H.R. Swain
1944	May	19th	U-960		aircraft	Wellington + Ventura	36 Sqn + 500 Sqn	sunk	2 ac: 36 Plt Off K.H. Bulmer; 500 W/O E.A. Munday
1944	Jun	19th/20th	Velino	1339	aircraft	Albacore	828 Sqn	sunk	
1944	Jul	17th/18th	Romolo		aircraft	Wellington	221 Sqn	sunk	

Convoys and Reinforcement Flights

Op Name	Year	Month	Day	Carrier	Carrier	Aircraft to Malta	Number	Lost
HURRY	1940	Sep	2nd	Argus		Hurricane	12	0
WHITE	1940	Nov	17th	Argus		Hurricane	12	8
						Total for 1940	**24**	**8**
WINCH	1941	Apr	3rd	Ark Royal		Hurricane	12	0
DUNLOP	1941	Apr	27th	Ark Royal		Hurricane	24	1
SPLICE	1941	May	21st	Ark Royal	Furious	Hurricane	48	2
ROCKET	1941	Jun	6th	Ark Royal	Furious	Hurricane	48	1
TRACER	1941	Jun	14th	Ark Royal	Furious	Hurricane	48	3
RAILWAY I	1941	Jun	27th	Ark Royal	Furious	Hurricane	22	1
RAILWAY II	1941	Jun	30th	Ark Royal	Furious	Hurricane	42	8
SUBSTANCE	1941	Jul	24th	Ark Royal		Swordfish	7	0
STATUS I	1941	Sep	9th	Ark Royal		Hurricane	14	0
STATUS II	1941	Sep	13th	Ark Royal	Furious	Hurricane	46	1
CALLBOY	1941	Oct	18th	Ark Royal	Furious	Albacore	11	0
PERPETUAL	1941	Nov	12th	Ark Royal	Argus	Hurricane	37	3
						Total for 1941	**359**	**20**
SPOTTER	1942	Mar	7th	Eagle	Argus	Spitfire	15	0
PICKET I	1942	Mar	21st	Eagle		Spitfire	7	0
CALENDAR	1942	Apr	20th		Wasp	Spitfire	47	1
BOWERY	1942	May	9th	Eagle	Wasp	Spitfire	64	4
LB	1942	May	19th	Eagle	Argus	Spitfire	17	0
STYLE	1942	Jun	3rd	Eagle		Spitfire	31	4
SALIENT	1942	Jun	9th	Eagle		Spitfire	32	0
PINPOINT	1942	Jul	15th	Eagle		Spitfire	32	1
INSECT	1942	Jul	21st	Eagle		Spitfire	30	2
BELLOWS	1942	Sep	11th	Furious		Spitfire	38	1
BARITONE	1942	Sep	17th	Furious		Spitfire	38	1
TRAIN	1942	Oct	29th	Furious		Spitfire	31	2
						Total for 1942	**382**	**16**
						Total 1940–42	**765**	**44**